SOCIAL FERMENT IN INDIA

SOCIAL FERMENT IN INDIA

Alexandra George

with a foreword by
Christoph von Fürer-Haimendorf,
*Professor Emeritus of Asian Anthropology
in the University of London*

THE ATHLONE PRESS
London and Atlantic Highlands, NJ

First published 1986 by The Athlone Press Ltd
44 Bedford Row, London WC1R 4LY
and 171 First Avenue, Atlantic Highlands, NJ 07716

© Alexandra George 1986

British Library Cataloguing in Publication Data

George, Alexandra
Social ferment in India
1. India—Social conditions
I. Title
954.05′2   HN683

ISBN 0–485–11287–6

Library of Congress Cataloging-in-Publication Data

George, Alexandra, 1952
Social ferment in India
Bibliography; p.
Includes index
1. India—social conditions—1977
2. Caste—India.   I. Title
HN683.5.G43   1986   306′.0954   86-17257

ISBN 0-485-11287-6

Typeset by Inforum Ltd, Portsmouth
Printed in Great Britain
by Biddles Ltd, Guildford

For my mother

Contents

Foreword

The present nostalgic interest in the India of the British Raj is finding expression in a multitude of films, television programmes and works of fiction. Yet there exists only a handful of academic publications which deal in a comprehensive way with the problems facing contemporary India and at the same time succeed in tracing the causes of the recent outbreaks of violence to their historical roots.

The author of this analysis of the social ferment in India, who has attempted just such a course, combines a literary study of ancient Hindu traditions with personal investigations of current events in a variety of areas, both urban and rural. Adopting the approach and methods of a trained journalist she has invested her descriptions with a vividness uncommon among political scientists and has produced a survey of the present condition of India which is likely to be appreciated by readers intent on gaining an informed picture of the South Asian subcontinent without having to delve into the maze of historical writings.

This picture is of a complexity not paralleled in any other part of the world. The reason for the coexistence of a unique variety of ethnic groups, culture patterns and styles of living is fairly obvious. While in most other regions rising civilizations replaced those that had preceded them, and conquering populations either eliminated or absorbed earlier inhabitants of the land, in South Asia the arrival of new immigrants and the spread of their way of life did not necessarily cause the disappearance of earlier and materially less advanced communities. The old and the new persisted side by side, and the phenomenon of cultural and ethnic heterogeneity was only partly due to the size of the subcontinent and the dearth of communications. More important was an attitude basic to Indian ideology which accepted the variety of cultural forms as natural and immutable, and did not consider their assimilation to one single pattern in any way desirable. This accounts for the fact that only a few decades ago primitive tribes, maintaining their traditional culture, could be found at no great distance from historic centres of advanced civilizations. In the chapters on the mechanism of the present change in this situation and the resultant confrontations between tribal and non-tribal populations the author discusses the chances of the survival of tribal ways of life with clarity and compassionate insight.

The differences between backward tribes and progressive Hindu communities are not the only divisive factors in the country's national life. Though India has no 'racial problem' in the modern sense, it must not be forgotten that three of the major racial sections of mankind overlap and dovetail in South Asia. The population of the North and of large parts of Peninsular India constitute the easternmost branch of the Caucasoid race; in the Himalayan regions and all along India's eastern borders dwell people of Mongoloid race; and among the tribal populations of South India persists a very dark-skinned racial element. Such racial distinctions are irreducible and clearly recognizable, and it is hence inevitable that people of mongoloid racial type from the North-East feel like aliens when they visit such places as Delhi and Bombay.

Though linguistic differences can be overcome more easily by the adoption of the locally dominant tongues, there still remains the fact that four major language families are represented on Indian soil, namely the Indo-Aryan, the Dravidian, The Tibeto-Burman and the Austroasiatic, each of which is divided into numerous mutually unintelligible languages and dialects. This built-in diversity is one of the greatest threats to the political unity of the country, for language is the main focal point of regional patriotism. After the end of British rule, which imposed on the subcontinent a political unity such as had never before existed, there arose a strong popular demand for the reorganization of administrative units according to the languages spoken by the majority of the population. In answer to this demand 'linguistic states' were created, and language thus assumed the role of a determinant of political structure, and the multi-lingual, multi-cultural and multi-racial Republic of India is now divided into largely autonomous units which ideally are mono-lingual and mono-cultural.

In addition to the traditional divisions based on language, race and culture, there is in present-day India the equally important contrast between the indigenous social order and a political system derived from western sources. The development of a system of government modelled on foreign examples was made possible by the acceptance of the ideal of parliamentary democracy on the part of the politically conscious middle class, whose leading members had been educated in European schools and universities. These men associated the ideals of freedom and national independence *not* with a return to the indigenous forms of government, which colonial rule had superseded, but with the establishment of those institutions which they considered essential features of a modern democracy. Yet side by side with the intellectual preference for a basically foreign system of political organization appeared an emotional craving for the re-establishment of traditional cultural values, expressed in the emphasis on indigenous forms of dress and the use of the vernacular as the medium of education. In these conflicting attitudes there is no doubt an element of 'split personality', for as the Indian intellectual had become used to move in his professional life within the realms of western values, while conforming in his family life to values rooted in Hindu or Muslim tradition, so political leaders professed acceptance of western ideals of democracy and parliamentary rule without being conscious of their inevitable inconsistency with some of the basic principles of the traditional social system.

As it is against all historical experience that such an inconsistency can persist, it must be assumed that some kind of compromise will ultimately take place. This may be achieved either by an adjustment of the system of government to the traditional social order, or by the social order changing to such an extent that it will fit the prevailing type of government.

The legislation passed since Independence by the Indian parliament suggests that the Union government has made every effort to reform the social order in such a way as to bring it into line with the ideals of democracy as understood in the West. The introduction of universal franchise, abolition of untouchability, legalization of inter-caste and inter-communal marriages, and the removal of legal discrimination against women, are all measures inspired by ideals rooted in western values. Yet, anyone familiar with the reality of the Indian social scene knows that much of this legislation is difficult to enforce, and from this we can conclude that government policy and popular social consciousness are still widely out of step. Yet there can be no doubt that legislation has some effect on the direction in which Indian society is developing, however slow such development may be. It is much more difficult to discern to what an extent values and principles inherent in the traditional social order are modifying the system of government. For the time being any influence they may be exerting is expressed in the manipulation of the prevailing system of government rather than in a demand for a change in the system.

Parliamentary democracy and the system of political parties competing for the support of the electorate developed in a society where the individual was not born into a tightly organized group which demands his loyalty and affords him support in his dealing with the rest of the community. In India, on the other hand, such groups – the castes and sub-castes – dominate social life, and inevitably influence their members' attitude to other groupings of a social or political character. The very fact that a caste is capable of functioning as an effective pressure group, and that its members cannot leave it and join another group at will, places it into a position of a political power which can be used by political parties to manipulate the conduct of voters.

One of the merits of Alexandra George's book is the lucid way in which the gap between theory and practice is being demonstrated by numerous concrete examples, derived largely from the author's imaginative interviews with personalities in public life. As an introduction to the Indian contemporary scene the volume will be invaluable to westerners working in India, be they diplomats, members of international development agencies or sociologists seeking an understanding of the complex and often confusing process of the transition from an oriental, hierarchically structured society to a modern social system capable of coping with growing industrialization and technological sophistication. Rajiv Gandhi, the present head of the Union government, symbolizes in his career and personality the determination of India's élite to lead the second largest Asian nation from a backward-looking traditionalism to a new era of highly developed technology and an ideology conforming to the principles enshrined in the charter of the United Nations.

London, October 1985   CHRISTOPHER VON FÜRER-HAIMENDORF

Preface

This book was written after two and a half years of cultural contact with India. My first encounters as a journalist led me to become more and more interested in the ramifications of the Indian scene. This led in turn to reading and travel with a purpose. I tested the opinions of writers against my travel experiences and my own experiences against their theses. I soon veered to the view that there cannot be any single approach to the understanding of India. Even amongst the foreign community in Delhi, which one might expect to be well informed, information was derived mainly from the Indian press and limited contacts with the political leadership.

A second source of assessments about India would be the very detailed studies made by both foreign and Indian social scientists, such as Srinivas' famous monograph on the Coorgs, Bailey's studies in Orissa, Béteille's work in Tanjore, and, more recently, Harriss's book based on fieldwork in North Arcot, Tamil Nadu. These provide certain deep insights. But even those which try to interpret the patterns of social evolution necessarily depend on micro studies of a particular area. Such studies focus on the economic scene, with a small but important segment of them also discussing social factors such as caste. A few studies have also focused on individual tribal areas, but the literature on tribes, although extensive, has largely been semi-anthropological and describes interesting customs which are considered unusual or which contribute to various theses on the interrelationship between customs of so-called primitive societies.

There is now an almost grudging acceptance that Indian culture and customs derive to some extent from such primitive societies within India. However, once again there is an assumption that such derivations are relatively minor and are relics of what is somewhat patronzingly described as the 'Little Traditions' and have to be absorbed within the so-called 'Great Tradition'. At a time when the rest of the world is finding racial theories about Aryan cultural supremacy and master races totally outdated or obnoxious, there is if anything a revival, at least subconsciously, of such assumptions in the Indian cultural scene. A challenge certainly arose from the Dravidian movement in the South, but even the Dravidian movement seems to be taking on attitudes of a countervailing traditional Dravidian cultural aristocracy with little attempt at understanding the contribution of the original tribal or lower-caste aboriginal inhabitants – the Avi-Dravidas – to this culture.

A third school of writers is becoming increasingly fascinated by ancient Indian cultural roots. It is delving into the evolution of concepts surrounding major deities and cultural practices. Such writers rarely venture, however, beyond the confines of their self-imposed scholastic disciplines to consider the continuity of Indian thought into the modern world or to interpret current trends according to these thought patterns as they may have been modified or intensified by historical cultural contacts.

Throughout my travels, interviews and reading I could not help noticing the persistence of such a relationship between the economic, political, social and cultural scenes. Richard Lannoy in *The Speaking Tree* had broken new ground with a similar approach. Some Indian writers are also delving deeply into various aspects of the origins of Indian culture. Again, however, their studies, because of the necessary preoccupation with detail, do not impinge on a wider audience.

I have attempted in this book to bridge some of the gaps in understandings. The difficulties in depicting the scene on such a large canvas are forbidding but there seems a need in the modern world to draw back from time to time and attempt a wider view of the immense specialized knowledge which is increasingly emerging. It is for this reason that I have presumed to lead off with a view from the vantage point of one of India's oldest legends regarding the 'Churning of the Ocean', and to proceed from there to other viewpoints which I have had the opportunity of glimpsing from first-hand experience, right through to an assessment of current Marxist land reforms in a modern Indian state. The variegations of the Indian scene are so wide, and their interlinking so complex, that even an acute and sensitive observer could spend a lifetime without being able to reach a comprehensive assessment of the continuous change. Yet for an understanding of one of the world's largest populations, an attempt must be made. I hope that this book will be a contribution towards that attempt.

New Delhi
2 September 1983

At the time of writing this book the Punjab issue had not acquired the political dimensions it was to assume in 1984 and 1985. For this reason I have dealt with the Sikh problem in the Postscript following visits to India in May and November 1985.

New Delhi
10 December 1985

Acknowledgments

This book has used an interdisciplinary approach to interpret the current Indian scene and people in many fields have been generous with their time. Advocates, civil servants, economists, journalists, psychologists, scholars and writers of Indian culture and history, sociologists and politicians spared me time for interviews. Their names appear in the notes wherever acknowledgment is due.

The ferment that is taking place in Indian society is exemplified by the pioneering role being assumed by the Supreme Court which is establishing a tradition of intervention on behalf of the underprivileged. Chief Justice of India, P.N. Bhagwati, and Supreme Court Justice D.A. Desai have been at the forefront of this new trend. Both of them spared time to brief me. I am also grateful to A.R. Bandyopadhyay, Central Land Reforms Commissioner, for several discussions on the implications of agrarian policies and to D. Bandyopadhyaya, former West Bengal Land Reforms Commissioner, who was also helpful in my study of the West Bengal land reforms. P.S. Krishnan and Dr Bhopinder Singh, who were handling programmes for Scheduled Castes and Scheduled Tribes respectively, clarified many details of their programmes. Many other administrators provided perceptive insights into various political, social and economic issues.

I could not help noticing during my reading that some of the perceptive new analyses of Indian culture were by women, both foreign and Indian. Amongst non-Indian writers the names of Stella Kramisch, Anncharlott Eschmann, Wendy O'Flaherty and Anne-Marie Blondeau stand out. From Indian itself Iravati Karve and Malati Shengde broke entirely new ground in their theses. In the same mould is Pupul Jayakar who gave me some profound insights. In his discussion of his work *The Speaking Tree* with me, Richard Lannoy attributed his own particular insights to the female component of his personality. Intuition can be no substitute for scholarship but without its illumination scholarship might never find its way forward.

During my two and a half years of field work in several Indian states I have received assistance from numerous local and state administrations. I wish to thank especially the Dungarpur and Banswara district administrations, Rajasthan, and the Tribal Development Commissioner, Udaipur, for extending facilities during my field work amongst the Bhils. Kind assistance was also rendered to me by the following: the administration of Jhargram, Midnapore district, West Bengal, during my work on land reforms; the administration of Bastar, Madhya Pradesh, during my extended visit there; the administration of Koraput district, Orissa, during my trip to the Bondo Hill tribes; the Collector of Keonjhar district, Orissa, for helping arrange a brief trip to the Juang; and last, but not least, to the Lahul administration in the remote Himalayan frontier region of Himachal Pradesh and to Nawang Norbu, the local Bhotia language teacher, for showing me around this Buddhist valley.

Several organizations and institutions have been most generous and helpful during my field tours and research work. I wish to thank the St Xavier's School for Social Work, Ranchi, Bihar, for allowing me to participate in a field trip; Bunker Roy and his team at the Social Work Research Centre, Tilonia, Rajasthan; Dr N.N. Vyas, Principal, and the Tribal Research Institute, Udaipur; Mrs Savitri Suri and the Centre for Women's Development Studies, New Delhi, who allowed me to accompany their research team to Chapta village, Etawah district, Uttar Pradesh; the sisters of the Ursuline Convent, Banari, Ranchi district, were particularly hospitable and especially helpful in showing me around the villages in the area; P.R. Dubhashi, Director, Indian Institute of Public Administration, for allowing me to use the Institute's library. Finally thanks are due to Jawaharlal Nehru University for arranging an opportunity to address a seminar.

During my field work many people were generous with their time. In particular Father Père Ponètte, Jesuit Convent, Ranchi, shared with me some valuable insights into the Chotanagpur tribes, gathered over more than five decades of work and study amongst them. Edmund Kiro, Museum Assistant of the Anthropological Survey of India Museum at Jagdalpur, Bastar, was an excellent guide around Bastar. Lalu Singh, a Gandhian, who is presently living in a cave in the Jamuna ravines while acting as go-between for surrendering dacoits and the Uttar Pradesh police, present a colourful picture of the region while giving a tour of the ravines reclamation project and neighbouring villages. Satish and Pradalini Hembron took time to show me their native Santhal village.

Most of all I wish to thank all the villagers and tribals for giving me so much of their time and hospitality during my stay in their villages. Many parts of the countryside have witnessed substantial changes for the better since Independence in terms of improved farming technology, development facilities, electrification, etc., even if only upper or 'dominant' castes have been the main beneficiaries. One such village is Chapta in western Uttar Pradesh, an area which, in addition, has been one of the main regions for the launching of the Green Revolution in the mid-sixties. The social changes occurring there were exemplified by the Scheduled Caste Community Health Worker, Balak Ram, who was a great help in making contacts with the Scheduled Caste hamlet. Balak Ram represents a new assertive generation of Scheduled Caste individual, and the kind of harassment he is presently facing from the upper-caste Thakurs in the village represents a future trend of increased conflict that is bound to spread as modernization grows apace. Even in the remotest areas of the Himalayas like the secluded village of Malana, Scheduled Caste children are forging ahead in the village primary school. Sangat Ram, a Scheduled Caste artisan, was the most go-ahead person in Malana and was helpful in establishing contacts with the clan members of this semi-tribal society. He provided a striking contrast to the latter's innate conservatism.

The compact tribal village with its atmosphere of cheerfulness and unity provided a pleasant contrast from the undercurrents of caste tension in the mixed village. Even where a tribal village was unable to take to agriculture because its members were too poor to own a plough and animals as at Chingri and Akri villages in eastern Ranchi, an atmosphere of peace and happiness prevailed. This is because eastern Ranchi, with its gentle rolling hills and forests, is still untouched by the forces of modernization, unlike the area around Ranchi where thousands of acres of tribal land have been expropriated for the construction of industries.

This may be the last decade when one can see the tribes with their own structures of society and thought uneroded. For with the growing stress on industrialization the tribal homelands, which contain the bulk of the country's mineral wealth, are slowly being 'colonized', while government programmes supposed to up-lift them are actually disrupting tribal societies. The well-known

anthropologist, Christoph von Fürer-Haimendorf, in his
book, *Tribes of India*, seemed to think that Bastar, the largest
tribal district in India, was one of the more successful stories of
tribal administration. My impression from a long tour was that
much the same kind of process is going on there. The only
exceptions were the villages in the hilly forest tracts of Abujmar in
Bastar which have been declared a reserved area for the 15,000
Hill Marias. During my tour of the area the headman Boronga
and the Hill Marias of Gummia Beda village were especially
hospitable.

Even the homeland of the Bhils, India's largest tribe numbering 5.2 million at the 1971 Census, is being swamped with
outsiders. One area of their concentration is South Rajasthan.
Even though special development programmes are supposed to
be under way, most of the beneficiaries have been upper-caste
Hindu farmers like the Patels in the mixed villages. In compact
Bhil villages like Jalu Kuwa, Dungarpur, government programmes are nowhere in evidence. Yet a stay there made it evident that
the Bhil culture is being eroded by enforced contact with the local
administration. It is sad, as Haimendorf has pointed out regarding the North-East, that India's development work in these
remote border pockets remains largely unrecognized and is
obviously far more successful than in the main heartland.

The first six months of putting pen to paper were spent in the
Himalayas amongst the Tibetan community in Mcleodganj. The
happy attitude of the Tibetans and the beauty of the natural
scenery with the backdrop of mountains enclosing this village
provided an ideal setting. The staff at the Bhagsu Hotel also
contributed to the environment by the cheerfulness and easy-
going manner so typical of the hill people of India.

The second stage of the book involving interviews and the final
draft were done in Delhi. I am particularly grateful to T.S. Murty
and Dr Roma Standefer Murty for their hospitality on numerous
occasions. My stay in Delhi was made particularly agreeable by
my hosts Prabha and Chingi Suri and the Suri family.

A very special debt of thanks is due to R. Yusuf Ali for various
discussions and criticisms. I should like to thank Mrs Fiona
Smith for help in compiling the index.

All views expressed in this book are entirely my own and do not
in any way reflect those of the people mentioned above.

SOCIAL FERMENT IN INDIA

Introduction

There was a time according to Hindu tradition when the Heaven-born and the Impious foresook their feuding. They joined hands to churn the cream of life from the primeval milky ocean. Their churning stick was a mighty mountain, the axis of the universe. The chieftain of the serpent people lent them his coils to twist the churning stick. Many significant gifts to mankind came out of the ocean during the churning; among them the Magic Tree that grants fulfilment of wishes; the miraculous cow, bestower of bounty; then, a spate of virulent poison. Shiva, the primeval 'Great God' took it upon himself to swallow the poison. Only then did the nectar finally emerge. Both the Devas, the Heaven-born, and the Asuras, the Impious, wanted it for themselves. After some tension, Vishnu appears on the scene in the shape of a beautiful temptress whose 'mediation' the Asuras accept under her blandishments. She serves the precious nectar to the Heaven-born until there is none left for the 'Impious' Asuras. These naturally feel cheated and create an uproar which renews the ancient feud.

So ran the story of the time 'in Hindu tradition when the Heaven-born and the Impious foresook their feuding to seek the cream of life together'. The very first sentence raises issues of fundamental importance to the understanding of the Indian scene. Was there ever such a time in the shadowy hours before the dawn of history? Were the two groups of people merely symbols of good and evil or did the story reflect an actual conflict? What do we mean by the term Hindu in its tradition? Above all, is there any relevance of this or other Indian myths to the present scene?

In a brilliant study by a Maharashtrian scholar, Malati Shengde, entitled *The Civilized Demons of the Rig-Veda*,[1] a new interpretation is put forward on the symbolism and imagery of the *Rig-Veda*. Malati Shengde maintains that the mythical accounts represented a very real conflict which was later blotted out from human memory by transforming it into a myth. Her thesis needs to be related to that of O.K. Ghosh in his work, *The Changing Indian Civilization*.[2] He maintains that the priestly caste in the pre-Aryan 'Asura' civilization, over a gradual period of time, may have switched to the winning Aryan side. This premise finds support in the fact that the very detailed analytical concepts and inward thinking found in the later parts of the Vedanta coincide more with the highly evolved Sumerian and West Asian riverine civilizations than with the ethos of the more primitive, nomadic herdsmen who were the Aryans.

One interpretation might be that Vishnu represents elements, at least, of a pre-Aryan deity who was adopted by the Aryans, the Devas. During their period of symbiosis with the pre-Aryan Asuras, Vishnu, because of his intimate association with the Asuras, enabled the Aryans to achieve ascendancy when his powers were transferred to their cause. The mediation of the temptress was supposed to be acceptable to both sides. She was, however, really working for the Devas who used her knowledge of the Asuras, whose propensity for women was well known to Vishnu, to trick them out of the nectar.

Malati Shengde limits her exposition of such a transference of deities to Varuna (the lord of the Ocean) and to the sage Usanas, but other scholars also see in the very word *Vishnu* linguistic affiliations to the early Dravidian (non-Aryan) root *vin* which means 'blue/sky'.

Whenever there has been a churning or social ferment in Indian society, the poisonous fumes of such ferment have been only too evident. So they are even today. To an Indian mind the question is who will swallow the poison. The emitting of the poison from the ocean causes a great deal of turmoil as no one knows what to do. One of the oldest deities, Lord Shiva, who seems to be a pre-Aryan God and whose prototype has been found on seals of the Indus Valley civilization, comes to help and swallows the poison. Even this powerful deity is overwhelmed by the poison which leaves an indelible blue imprint in his throat. Shiva seems to have been an old aboriginal great god of India and in the earliest legends was looked down upon as a barbarous character unfit to be the husband of Sati, the daughter of Daksha, an early sage.

Whereas one view of the myth of 'The Churning of the Ocean' might interpret it as a mythological rendering of the moral concept of battles between good and evil, more imaginative and resourceful scholars place great importance in such accounts as representing not merely the confrontation but an interaction between two cultural groups whose personality traits have been depicted in fairly consistent detail. The Devas seem to stand for the still semi-nomadic Aryan groups, strongly oriented towards male supremacy with male deities of the sky and air. The Asuras, on the other hand, seem to be linked with an old cultural complex that spread from the Mediterranean at least to the Indus Valley civilization, with possible influences on what later came to be known as the Dravidian South. Settled cultivation, a reverence for the earth and water and homage to a great female goddess would be the main characteristics of this group.

There are references in tradition to a period when the relatively uncivilized Devas of the Aryan groups were somehow subordinate to the Asuras. A good deal of mixing, cultural, religious and linguistic, and perhaps even racial, probably took place before the so-called Aryan ascendancy. This ascendancy, mounting to later cultural domination, was probably achieved less by any 'pure' Deva/Aryan cultural elements than by a mixed group who were even more fanatic in denying any Asura heritage, in condemning it as evil and in shaming its practitioners into an inferior status.

There are remarkable parallels in the evolution of this Indian mythological tradition with those of Greece where a similar process seems to have taken place. In India perhaps the mental make-up and outlook of the emerging new society would have been conditioned by the survival problems of a small dominant élite, buttressed by a religious sanction from a priestly class in whom some scholars see the continuance of an older Asura priesthood which compromised with the new Deva leadership to maintain its spiritual ascendancy and privileges. Such scholars would trace the subtlety and depths of the philosophy evident in the later Upanishads to something much more than a mere evolution in a straight line from the early hymns of the *Rig-Veda*. In other words, this process would be interpreted as the permeation of Indian thought by a fundamentally Asura priesthood which had placed intellectual and spiritual powers at the disposal of the Aryan-orientated Deva power-structure. Thus there had begun the process of Brahminical intellectual and spiritual guidance to the ruling power structure (the Rajanya (later Kshatriya, or Warrior Caste)) which the priesthood legitimized in return for protection and privileges.

Thus a power balance was struck between the priest and warrior. Yet whenever the Kshatriyas became too powerful and threatened the Brahmin ascendancy, new groups were co-opted to destroy them. The legend of Parasu Ram recounts how in early times the Kshatriyas were exterminated by the latter after they were considered too grasping. After Parasu Ram committed this act he seems to have earned merit by this deed and to have been regarded as one of the incarnations of Vishnu. Since this act is his only claim to fame one must conclude that he must have fulfilled the wishes of the priestly class.

An interesting sidelight to the tale is that Parasu Ram's father, Jamadagni Rishi, was identified in a remote village called Malana, in the Himalayan state of Himachal Pradesh, with an original folk hero, Jamlu, who also destroyed the old leadership of the village polity. In the 1980s Jamlu is still revered as the main village deity to the extent that all property belongs to this animistic god. No visitor to the village can ever touch one of the village houses, let alone the shrine. This particular legend may be the first example of connivance by Brahmins for the destruction of the existing ruling class and is to be viewed in this context with other legends regarding the origin of such dominant classes. Parasu Ram, in another part of the legend, hunted down at his father's behest his own mother, Renuka, who sought shelter among outcastes. He decapitated her, but later sought her restoration to life. In the granting of his boon, his mother's head got mixed up with that of an outcaste woman. The restored half-Brahmin/half-outcaste form was identified with Elamma, primeval goddess of the South.

Throughout Indian history new Kshatriyas have been created. In particular during the first millennium AD, before the Muslim invasions, the Rajputs, who are not an ethnic group, came into dominance. Their rise is chronicled in stories about their emerging out of the firepits and their purification through fire at Mount Abu. It seems very clear that the Rajput clans originate partly from tribal ancestry, such as the Bhils, and partly from barbarian invaders. Thus the local robber baron was elevated by the Brahmins to become the defender of the faith in the real sense. As in most countries most new converts to the faith, as in this case, the Rajputs, became even more fanatical defenders of the faith than the old establishment.

The period when the Rajputs were given all kinds of ancestries to legitimize their newly won status seems to have been a period of anarchy. The Mauryan Empire had collapsed and warriors from the North-West were invading India. Above all there was the feeling in the Brahmin mind that Buddhism had led to a new kind of ascendancy. Although Buddha never said anything that clashes head on with the Brahmins, he definitely made it clear that human beings are all equal. This struck at the very roots of the whole caste system and the Brahmin ascendancy. Subsequently the Brahmins tried to ban the Buddha as a false prophet. In yet another example of the Hindu tendency of resolution of a problem through assimilation, the Buddha was ultimately deified and made into an incarnation of Vishnu. There is of course the other interesting speculation that the Buddha was of semi-Mongoloid tribal stock, a view put forward by Richard Lannoy in *The Speaking Tree.*[3]

This brings us to the problem of assessing at least the relative antiquity of the legend in time. It does not feature in the earliest extant Indian tradition of the *Rig-Veda* which, in the opinion of the most plausible present scholarship, depicts events in society about the turn of the first millennium BC. In the *Rig-Veda* there is certainly a story regarding the theft of ambrosia akin to that in Greek mythology. It involves retrieval of the Divine Gift by the swallowing of the opponent who took it. The imagery of the myth regarding 'The Churning of the Ocean' is fundamentally different.

For its clear exposition, one has to wait till the much later *Mahabharata*, although there seem to be references in the post-Rig-Vedic Brahmanas. The recension of the many traditions of the epic are dated by most scholars to a period between 400 BC and AD 400. In other words after the Buddhist teachings and probably contemporary with the new bid for Brahminical supremacy after the collapse of the Mauryan empire and during the period of 'barbarian invasions', both physical and cultural.

The very details in 'The Churning of the Ocean' legend fit the period perfectly, especially in their symbolism. Apart from the identity of the Heaven-born and the Impious already discussed, one finds a conscious attempt at synthesis of all earlier disparate elements in the Indian scene. Vasuki, the Lord of the Serpent people, is roped in both figuratively, as well as physically, into twisting the Churning Stick. He has always been regarded as the symbol and ancestor of the 'Naga' groups and dynasties to whom, although they represented a different Indian tradition, the Brahmins of the day turned for protection of their order against the forces of anarchy. Many Naga dynasties stretched from the border of Rajasthan through Mathura to the Central Indian tribal areas. Even the symbolism of the churning relates well to this period when Krishna, the foster child of humble wandering groups of milkmen, was being elevated from a localized folk hero and leader to an incarnation of the divine Vishnu and the spokesman of the subtle discourses found in the *Gita*, one of the later interpolations in the *Mahabharata*. Even the precious gifts that emerged from the churning each possesses its own symbolism. There was the Magic Tree that fulfils all wishes. It appears as a seal in the Indus Valley civilization with, beneath it, a figure generally supposed to be a prototype of Shiva wearing a magnificent horned headdress like the Bison-Horn Maria tribals of Bastar in Central India today.

As regards the Magic Tree, the Greeks who followed Alexander mentioned this miraculous tree and the modern sociologist Lannoy took it for the title of his book. Then there was the miraculous cow which dispensed ever-flowing bounty, perhaps again a symbol of its special place in the society of Krishna's foster parents who surged north-eastwards from the borders of Gujarat and took over Mathura from the demons who had hitherto held it. (Even today the Delhi State Lottery is named Kamadhenu after this cow.)

These are mere illustrations from the catalogue of gifts. The great embodiment of woman power Sri (Shakti) was also ascribed in origin to emergence (like Aphrodite of Greece) from the churning of the ocean. Could this be a condescending Brahminical acknowledgement of her power which had in earlier times been dominant in the older civilization to which in reality the Brahmins belonged? There was Airavarta, the White Elephant. This is a very old symbol which was perhaps, to use Shengde's inelegant but telling description, 'mythopoeised' as the mount of the conquering Aryan folk-hero, Indra. Yet surely the elephant would originally have been in reality a powerful symbol of indigenous India. Indeed the earliest references to the animal in the West link ancient Indian tradition to the time of Solomon and Hiram, King of Tyre. The word transmitted by the Phoenician traders into Hebrew is a clear reflection of a non-Aryan root which persists till this day, along with similar names like that of the peacock (the national bird of India) in Dravidian languages. Finally, the White Elephant would have to be accommodated because of its later associations in Buddhist tradition.

The meaning and origin of the word *Hindu* and what is meant by Hindu tradition again finds no place whatsoever in the Vedas to which modern advocates of a Hindu revival or renaissance would return for inspiration. Its first recorded evidence is in early Greek writings linking it to the river Sindhu which, however, does appear in the Vedas purely as the name of the river. However, it is not a Greek word and was probably obtained by the Greeks from the Persians of the day who were of course pre-Islamic and who, after the churning of the ocean in their own society, retained the word *Asura*, not as a defeated enemy, but as their God of Light, Ahuramazda. The later Greek writer Plutarch recorded an interesting legendary account of the river. He had collected from somewhere the story that the river had been originally named Mausolos after a son of the sun; that it was renamed after a young man called Indos who was drowned in the river when he plunged into it to escape the pursuit of an angry king whose daughter he had ravished while she was 'celebrating the feast of Bacchus' – the usual Greek rendering of Shiva. Whether this in any way reflected some garbled version of a local folk tradition of the Punjab is difficult to tell. An erudite German scholar, Gustav Oppert, dug out a coincidence in the Indian tradition of a child of the Sun-God, Kalinda, who later gave her name to the other sacred river, Jamuna. Again one finds the unbroken tradition to this day with a Kalindi colony rising in affluent south Delhi.

From the Greeks and Persians the word *Sindhu* entered the Arab world during its heyday and since then has been used by Muslims of West Asia to describe an inhabitant of the geographical area of India. Even today the politician Subramanian Swamy recorded confusion during his travels in West Asia. When asked his religion he replied, 'Hindu'. His Islamic questioners pressed him again saying that they knew he was an Indian national which was what they understood by Hindu but wanted to know his exact religion. This brings one to the controversy in modern India posed by certain Hindu revival movements which will be discussed later.

To the Hindu mind the term Hindu is really synonymous with a territorial area. This is based on a certain amount of fact as non-Indian countries also equate the term Hindu with territoriality. This point has always been stressed by the Rashtriya Swyam Sevak Sangh (RSS), an organization for a Hindu renaissance, and the Bharatiya Janata Party (BJP), a leading Opposition Party, to the present day – 'Hindu rashtra' or the 'Hindu State'. However, this ignores the fact that the original term derived from the river Sindhu which, in those days, referred to a very small area which is now a part of Pakistan.

Credit for the creation or extension of a unified cultural identity throughout the subcontinent is usually ascribed to the Brahmin élite. Three main trends are discernible in their thinking, much of which may have been formulated out of subconscious reactions to their environment. First came the period of genuine spiritual and intellectual introspection. Old traditions speak continuously of such sages meditating in forest retreats and being disturbed in their meditations and rituals by surrounding 'barbarians'. The latter, no doubt, resented the intrusion of unfamiliar elements into their own territory, accompanied by alien rites and observances which sought to denigrate their own beliefs. The stage was thus set for the second ingredient of Brahminical policy – the evolution of a defensive strategy to safeguard their beleaguered outposts. Friendly local power structures had to be created to protect them. In return the Brahmins would extend spiritual patronage to such rulers and demand in return special social privileges and land grants. Finally, they sought to build up an impregnable all-India network of caste monopoly as spiritual preceptors, advisers on state policy and sole arbiters of truth and conduct. A generation after Independence, despite professions of socialistic and egalitarian patterns of society, this monopoly in the inner circles of policy-framing is still very much in evidence.

From early times they envisaged India's territory as extending from the Himalayas to both the Western and Eastern Seas. In the early ninth century AD the Brahmin preceptor, Sankara, is credited with the vision of elevating four pre-eminent religious centres, to stake out and symbolize this geographical dominance: Dwarka, on the west coast in Gujarat, associated with Krishna and the Yadavs and perhaps an even earlier mystical sanctity; Puri, on the east coast in Orissa, the seat of Jagannath, originally an aboriginal tribal deity; Sringeri, in the deep South, Sankara's own home; and Badrinath, near the snowline of the Himalayas, where South Indian priests have officiated from Sankara's time to this day.

To achieve their territorial aim they had to cope with the very large multilingual populations who were originally outside their fold. To some extent they enlarged their fraternity, although again in theory this was totally impossible since one cannot create a Brahmin. In practice, however, reality differed: for example, from the very holy lake of Pushkar in Rajasthan, the Bhopat Brahmins, who still very jealously guard their rights, seem to have been Beldars, or 'labourers who wield a spade'. This pattern extended to many areas in India. One can see it even today right in the east, in Manipur, where Manipuri Brahmins are so obviously of Mongoloid descent that they cannot possibly be considered Aryans by birth. Indeed according to the *Rajasthan District Gazetteer* for Ajmer: 'History records innumerable instances of people in India who became Brahmins from Kshatriyas and Vaishyas; some even from aboriginal tribes.'[4]

This is an early illustration of conflict between theory and practice within the Hindu fold. At the same time ideas probably spread among the Brahmin preceptors out of the experience of the Mauryan Empire and in particular Ashoka who ruled in the third century BC. The latter himself owed a debt in his concept of 'universal ruler', named in India the Chakravartin, to the old Persian Empire. This experiment with the polity of a universal emperor who also had some sort of divine sanction seems to have caught on with the thinkers of the day. They envisaged a sort of dream of a universal ruler of all India, guided by the Brahmin fraternity. In evolving a common tradition acceptable to the peoples of each region they obviously had to accommodate an enormous amount of local traditions, deities and rituals. Possibly these original local traditions and deities were not as mutually disparate as they were made out to be – a very large question on which so far there has been totally inadequate research. The technique seems to have been to identify a new local tradition or deity with a similar one which had already been assimilated earlier during the creation of the Puranic legends. So as this process spread out to the remoter regions one found a transplantation of such legends.

This accounts, for example, for the name 'Manipur'. All its associations in detail with the legend of Chitrangada are found and claimed specifically as a local legend in a specific place in Karnataka, in a specific place in Orissa and ultimately in Manipur where the latest transplantation finally blossomed in its well-known form. This process was probably followed right up to the ultimate recension of the two main epics, the *Mahabharata* and the *Ramayana*. Both seem to have had a kernel of very old folk tradition and to have been expanded to bring within their orbit personalities and happenings of later centuries as they became known.

The noted archaeologists B.B. Lal and Sankalia have been undertaking projects on the same lines as Schliemann who dug up Troy. The latter had used clues from the study of Homer to locate and excavate the city of Troy which was earlier considered mythical. Lal and Sankalia are already inclined to the view that the *Ramayana* story and Lanka itself probably originated in eastern Central India, perhaps Bastar or Orissa, with the tradition only being transferred to Ceylon (Sri Lanka) at a later date. Similarly the *Mahabharata* mentions the king of Pragjyotisa fighting at the head of his troops along with his allies, the Cinas and Kiratas. The mythological connection was apparently extended to Assam early in the first millennium AD from the western Himalayas, in the north of Himachal Pradesh where the Pragjyotisa kingdoms and the Cinas seem originally to have been located.

It is significant that in remote valleys of the Kinnaur district of Himachal Pradesh one finds highly localized traditions both of the battles of Bana Raja, an area called Kamrup, and indeed the temple of Kamakhya Devi, all of which were to achieve later pre-eminent fame in their ultimate place of transplant – Assam. Names are also transplanted in the West. Boston may conjure up memories of its tea-party – even perhaps of its own Brahmins. Its origin in the sleepy shire town of East Anglia is almost forgotten. Similarly the story of the abduction of Rukmini and the fight between Krishna and Shishupal got transferred from their Central Indian location to the extreme frontier. Any study of local traditions in India will multiply such illustrations.

An interesting feature in the absorption of local traditions has been the way in which local people have been made to become ashamed of their own original heritage or, if their own original folk hero was too strong to be ignored, to accept his incorporation in what later came to be known somewhat arrogantly as the 'Great Tradition'. However, such folk heroes were generally assigned, at least on one side of the family, some Asura ancestry. Sometimes this was disguised by mythical accounts such as those of the seduction of a Brahmin's daughter by the Moon-God; or birth from the seed of an ancient sage which was scattered on the earth, or in an earthen pitcher, both obvious symbols of a 'daughter of the soil'. Often such a sage or Brahmin had non-Aryan affiliations.

Some scholars even see in the whole epic *Mahabharata* a clever priestly manipulation of an earlier folk theme to rationalize and legitimize the seizure of power by an upstart group, the Pandavas, from the more legitimate traditional rulers, the Kauravas. Schaeffer has developed this theme and brought to light an interesting analysis to show that the peripheral tribes beyond the heartland around Delhi tended to be allies of the losing side, the Kauravas. A similar theory has been advanced regarding the *Ramayana*. This sees the hero Rama, manipulated by an ambitious class of priests, as being manoeuvred into exile so as to come under their tutelage, and then used for the destruction of the older and possibly more legitimate leader of thought of the day, Ravana. The latter, who was very much recognized to be a 'Brahmin and a scholar' but who possibly symbolized the resistance of genuine native Indian tradition to the beginnings of Sanskritization and Aryanization, was ultimately depicted as the embodiment of evil by the same process described in Shengde.

Sita, wife of the deified folk hero Rama, herself came from the eastern frontiers of the then Sanskritized part of India. Her origin was as a foundling in a furrow (*Sita*), itself an Austric, non-Aryan root word. Certain *Ramayana* traditions, still alive today in South-East Asia and in Rajasthan, even ascribe to her some original relationship with the family of Ravana himself. Perhaps such traditions were not, as the orthodox would have one believe, corruptions of the real story but harked back to genuine older folk traditions.

Accounts of local or regional dynasties in the first millennium AD are often preserved piecemeal in obscure local documents or in district gazetteers, and the various legends noted in them normally would be dismissed as mere semi-literate 'Little Traditions'. The significance of their symbolism upon the wider canvas of Indian history has hardly yet been studied. However, there are welcomed stirrings of new interest. Pupul Jayakar's book, *The Earthen Drum*[5] is an outstanding contribution in this field. Even the beginnings of such a study, however, would shed new light on the origins and impact of the Muslim invasions.

This period of Muslim dominance is normally dated from the Fall of Delhi in the late 12th century. India's late Prime Minister, Mrs Gandhi, stressed, however, the very relevant point that the

earliest Islamic influences came not through such wars of conquest but through the traders loosely described as Arabs (totally
unlike the Central Asian conquerors who followed them). These
Arabs came from the shores of the Red Sea and Persian Gulf and
must be regarded merely as the descendants of traders who had
been linked with South India and Gujarat from the most ancient
times and had only become Muslim in the seventh or eighth
centuries AD. The earlier picture of forcible conversions by
relatively small armies of marauders from Islamic Central Asia of
almost one-quarter of undivided India's population is now giving
place to a more balanced view.

The religious fanaticism of the invaders against so-called
idolaters is, of course, a matter of fact. Even here, however, they
seem to have held in especial horror, perhaps rooted in their own
history, the temples and images especially linked with reverence
for the lingam. The especial singling out and destruction of
Somnath on the Gujarat coast by Mahmud of Ghazni and the
transportation of a piece of the broken lingam to Mecca indicates
some special bitter feeling comparable to that which made the
Romans plough salt in the fields after the destruction of Carth-
age.[6] Both the vanquished were devotees of a much older animistic rite which, on the advent of the Semitic religions, be they
Judaism, Christianity or Islam, became especially feared and
hated. The Ka'aba at Mecca was indeed founded on the destroyed remnants of an older animistic shrine.[7] The very area of
Yemen from which the earliest trade with the Indian ocean
originated and from where, according to a legend quoted by
Herodotus, the Phoenicians sprang, was also a stronghold of the
old faith. By a strange quirk in history this attitude of Mahmud of
Ghazni can be likened to that of the early Vedic Aryan followers of
India in the *Rig-Veda* and their horror for the phallus-worship-
pers (Sisna-Devas).

It is also far too simplistic to view the rapid spread of Islamic
power from the end of the twelfth century merely as an alien
victory by a superior fighting force. One aspect, inadequately
studied by all except an occasional Muslim scholar who elicits
violent reactions from his Hindu counterparts, is the part played
by the more oppressed Sudra, or outcaste elements, in welcoming
Islam as a way out from their servitude towards a life of greater
self-respect. Some Hindu thinkers by implication lend tacit
acquiescence to such thought by pointing out that two areas of

India (the North-West and the East), present-day Pakistan and Bangladesh, were the most prone to Islamic conversion because they had been weakened in their social resistance through the earlier ascendancy of Buddhism and its egalitarian preachings.

There are also two other aspects of the spread of Muslim ascendancy which have also been inadequately evaluated. It is a commonplace that dissension within the ranks of Hindu rulers of the day played a considerable part. The origins of such dissensions, however, go deeper than mere minor feuds over territory or women. The key figure usually projected as the hero of Hindu resistance is the Chauhan ruler of Delhi. The Chauhans were the last of the four great Rajput groups who somehow acquired Kshatriya status earlier in the first millenium AD. Even later accounts glorifying them separate them as if on a slightly different footing from the three other really blue-blooded Rajput clans who are invariably ascribed an origin from the firepit at Mount Abu to the 'Solar' dynasty. In the earliest traditions the Chauhans were even bracketed with the Lunar dynasty which somehow was usually associated, especially further east, with more tribal origins. This therefore to some extent tarnished the ancestry.

The Chauhans rose to power just before a clash with Islamic forces in present-day Afghanistan, where a confederation of Rajput princes from what is now present-day India had rallied to the support of a local Hindu Afghan chieftain. The Chauhan rise to power was marked by the overthrow of the earlier legitimate power in Delhi, the Tomars. The latter were linked with a long-established power centre further east in Uttar Pradesh, Kanauj. Kanauj in turn had as its allies the Chandelas of Central India who were first regarded as subordinate, then equal in status. The Chandelas were very much of the Lunar dynasty and closely linked with the tribals. The great folk heros of Central India, Alha and Udal, fought for the Chandelas and in alliance with Kanauj against the Chauhans of Delhi who had abducted a princess from the Kanauj court.

Again the whole picture emerging from the folk poetry of Bundelkhand, the centre of Chandela power, paints a picture entirely different from that current among the dominant Indian élites. Jaichand of Kanauj is not in their eyes the venal traitor to the Hindu cause who held aloof when India was being attacked by the Muslim invaders. For them, Prithiv Raj Chauhan is just another ambitious and arrogant Rajput ruler. Although by then the Chauhans had perhaps lived down the earlier slight taint of status inferiority *vis-à-vis* the other three Rajput clans of the west, they themselves quoted it very much against the Chandelas of Bundelkhand. Part of the feud between the Chauhans and Chandelas in fact centred around the championing of folk heros of dynasties or princesses who were somehow thus slighted in status. Alha and Udal also had a trusted comrade-in-arms, a Muslim, who rode with them fighting indiscrimately against feudal Rajputs or Muslims alike.

Yet the projection of the Chauhans by the literate élite was such that it is still a name to conjure with. An encounter in the narrow byways of the old walled city of Delhi brings history up to date. A vivacious dark woman of decidedly Gond tribal features is trading musk. She comes from a district deep in the heartland of Central India. Yet she claims to be a Chauhan – a symbol of her rise in caste status. In the erstwhile princely Rajasthan the exponents of Hindu revival claim to be reconverting Muslims and attracting them back to Hinduism by renaming them as 'Chauhans'.

Another inadequately explored aspect of the so-called Muslim period of Indian history relates again to folk culture, and especially to the spread of Islam in villages through the less orthodox Muslim religious divines. Some of these were viewed with suspicion and disfavour by orthodox Muslims themselves, but it was they and their practices, perhaps deriving from Sufi trends in Islam, which struck a chord of response from the village folk of India. One may even speculate regarding the rise of Sufi cults out of West Asian cultural centres where the older 'Asura' matrifocal traditions had been the strongest.

In India, at any rate, such religious groups like the Chistis and Aulias struck an immediate equation even with their antagonists. They would sit in rural areas and, by performing miracles and exorcizing spirits, 'conquer' the powerful local deities of the soil. At Mehrauli, the centre of the first Muslim city of Delhi, the antagonist with whom yet an equation was struck in an almost drawn confrontation, was Jogmaya, the goddess who is adored widely by village folk at centres of worship like Pushkar in Rajasthan. At Mahoba, the Chandela capital, local traditions talk less about battles between feudal rulers and their armies than about the places where a particular Muslim divine sat almost like a Hindu ascetic achieving *samadhi*, and exorcized the earlier goddesses, emblems of power, Guraiya-Devi and Maniya-Devi.

Maniya-Devi was the patron goddess of the Chandelas and it was before her shrine that Alha in bardic tradition had even cut off his own head as an offering for success in battle. In 1982 in Ayyanagar, a village very much under the Delhi administration, the women light lamps at Diwali not merely, according to the 'Great Tradition' of the dominant élite, for the successful return of Rama from Lanka. Indeed he forms no part of the evening ritual. Instead they go around the outskirts of the village lighting lamps at the traditional animistic places of reverence: the place where ancestral spirits gather; the place where an old Hindu saint achieved samadhi; and the place where a Muslim saint underwent a similar religious experience. The strength and tenacity of such local traditions have been immensely underestimated in an assessment of the ancestral roots of Indian tradition.

So much for the village scene. Even at the top of the power structure such cultural fusion as did take place was less on the basis of concepts framed by modern theoreticians. One feels somehow that Akbar would have been totally baffled if he had been ascribed a 'secular outlook' or an 'ecumenical approach'. Occasionally a ruthlessly realistic modern Indian writer, like Nirad Chaudhuri, will point out that there is after all a fundamental and total divergence between Hindu ways of thought and those of the 'revealed religions'. Neither Islam nor Christianity, unless they lose their identities, can ever be expected to regard Christ or Mohammed as incarnations of Vishnu, or even perhaps as one of the many manifestations of a cosmic divinity to which there are many roads. Yet it is a fact that somewhere along the line there were periods and trends in the history of Islam in India when a great growing togetherness did in fact take place.

Among the early pre-Mughal rulers, Feroze Shah Tughlak stands out. He gives the impression of being the first Muslim ruler of North India who was more than an alien despot. He no longer looked back over his shoulder towards Central Asia but became an essentially Indian ruler concerned about irrigation projects and the betterment of his subjects. Even the architecture from his period at Haus Khaz shows a grace and sensitivity contrasting with the more starkly aggressive monuments of his predecessors. One finds cloisters for scholars beside a great lake. He took immense trouble to bring to his new capital an ancient Ashoka pillar from far away and erected it on a mound with almost religious reverence, although in his day the inscription remained undeciphered and uncomprehended. Even today in the cells underneath this mound, one can hear devotees, both Muslim and Hindu, praying ecstatically in an older tradition whether Bhakti, Sufi or Shamanistic. One cannot help wondering whether the site itself was not chosen because of some earlier ritual significance or tradition.

Then one comes to Akbar. There seems to have been within him something more than mere intellectual curiosity or the pragmatic tactical instincts of a ruler trying to synthesize a new religion for his subjects. No doubt he absorbed some non-Muslim thought from his Rajput and Christian wives whom he seems to have treated with honour and understanding and not merely as a despot's concubines. However, the accounts of his sojourns at Fatehpur Sikri and attempts to understand Hindu tradition are intriguing in their implications. The site itself was in the wilderness on the very verges of the rural folk tradition of Central India. There was a certain mysticism about the whole proceedings which the orthodox Muslim divines feared and hated. Even in his unchallenged temporal power he drew the bitterest condemnations from them. Later in the Moghul dynasty, when the blood in the rulers' veins was predominantly Hindu-Rajput, a similar prince, Dara Shikoh, also displayed the same tendencies and India's history might have been totally different if he had succeeded in the battle of succession against his brother, Auranzgeb, in whose reign there was a totally orthodox swing back to Islamic fundamentalism. Even Aurangzeb, although portrayed as the arch enemy and arch destroyer of Hindu tradition, seems occasionally to have been influenced by the Indianness of certain traditions. At Pushkar he is supposed to have endowed some temples and to have come under the spell of its traditions. The Sikh guru, Teg Bahadur, before his martyrdom, accompanied Aurangzeb's Rajput general in his campaign against the Assamese partly it is said, to defeat the spells of the tribal enemy.

India still lives with the fundamental problem of a relationship with a Muslim minority of over 10 per cent largely unresolved. If anything, after a certain period of euphoria that things were settling down after the traumatic experiences of the Partition killings, the communities seem once again to be growing apart. However, the problem is no longer merely one which can be blamed on Islamic fundamentalism, conversions due to OPEC money and so forth. It is part of the larger and more fundamental problem of adjustments between reviving Hindu tradition and, in greater or lesser extent, all other religious groups or cultural minorities. Again no single reason usually advanced, least of all that of an economic backwardness, sounds satisfying. Under no circumstances, for example, could the Sikhs as a community be considered economically backward, socially oppressed or denied access to positions of power. Yet somehow, even among them, there is a drawing away arising from the feeling that they must either accept total identification as Hindus or be in some way regarded as outside the pale of the inner circle of the Indian polity.

This leads one to the last fundamental issue, the relevance of Indian traditions to the present day. Every country has its legends and traditions. Yet it would be obviously ludicrous to relate a British understanding of the nuclear zero option to stories about King Arthur, Merlin or Morgan the Fay. India presents a somewhat different picture. The Chief Minister of Andhra Pradesh, N.T. Rama Rao, who was swept to power in one of India's most important states in January 1983, owed much of his charisma to having played similar characters from Indian mythology in the cinema. As the ancient folk hero, Rama, the masses who elected him hoped that he would restore the 'Ram Rajya', as India still describes his 'Polity of Excellence'. In the same film he played the dual role of Rama's adversary, Ravana, who passionately accused Rama's conquering followers of having stolen the very cream or essence of life from Ravana's people, the Asuras. Even today open-air dramas portray Ravana and his Asura warriors in the traditional costumes of the South.

Despite the fact that India is the world's tenth industrial power and has some of its leading scientists, such traditions continue to permeate Indian thought and symbolism. The modern exponents of Hindu Renaissance theory like Dr Karan Singh talk about going back to the source of Hinduism, the Vedanta, for inspiration. He believes the Vedanta expresses an essentially dynamic view of the world and its philosophy calls for a proper synthesis of spiritualism and materialism in the modern world. Dr Karan Singh assesses the fundamental core of Hindu belief as fourfold. Firstly, he considers the fundamental Vedantic teaching postulating that whatever exists is a manifestation of the Divine; secondly, the whole world is one family; thirdly, the Divine dwells in every being; and, fourthly, Truth is one, though its manifestations may be many.

The implications of these doctrines need serious thought for their application to modern Indian society. If all beings are divine, this means that the lowest Scheduled Castes, or Untouchables, must also be included. Yet in the Laws of Manu, the ancient classical Hindu Law book, the Untouchables are considered to be outside the pale of Hinduism. To this day, because of this concept, they have been totally oppressed. The modern Hindu reformist is ambivalent about Manu. He does not denounce him categorically, yet would view some of his more draconian provisions as outdated.

Politically such theories as those expounded by Dr Karan Singh lead to an obsession with oneness and, by implication, assume the superiority of the Hindu way of life. Truth, says Dr Karan Singh, has many faces but it is essentially one. Therefore a liberal Hindu would claim that Christ and Mohammed expressed one kind of truth which was essentially identified with the basic tenets of Hinduism. The followers of these revealed religions, however, would deny this and proclaim their faith in their own one God. Dr Karan Singh's conclusion thus means that any Indian is equated with a Hindu and that, although no Hindu would object to anyone practising any kind of ritual, there is the feeling that all citizens are Hindus and should recognise this fact.

To some extent this claim is valid. Even early twentieth-century Western scientists were drawn to Indian thought because the ancient Hindu notion of non-dualism seemed to match their own empirical research. It is of interest, for example, as regards the interrelationship of matter and energy that the imagery evoked in the scientists responsible for the first nuclear explosion at Los Alamos, USA, in 1945 was derived consciously from the Vedas: 'A power brighter than a thousand suns'. It was not an imagery evoked from some Apocalyptic vision in the Book of Revelation as one might have expected from their cultural background.

In India itself there has been a perceptible shift amongst intellectuals and scientists, educated in Western thought and seemingly outwardly modernized, away from westernized concepts of modernization towards traditional Indian concepts. For example, Ardhendy Chakravarty, a Bengali nuclear scientist from the Saha Institute of Nuclear Physics relates nuclear theory

to the ancient Indian concept of the immanence of energy even in
seemingly inert matter. The source of his inspiration also derives
from the Vedanta as it did for the nineteenth-century Indian
thinkers who were most exposed to Western thought, like Aurobindo and Swami Vivekananda.

In fact one of the most important issues which is surfacing
today is the whole question of the fundamental difference between so-called Western thought and Eastern thought as exemplified by the Vedantic philosophy of 'A-Dvaita', or non-dualism.
In analysing the basis of the difference between these two systems
one has to tackle very fundamental moral precepts such as good
and evil. In Hindu thought there is no God Creator in the
Western sense. In the East good and evil are regarded as different
sides of the same conceptual coin. Hence there is no such thing as
the Western concept of sin. To quote V.C. Channa, Lecturer
in Social Anthropology at Delhi University: 'Our religion is
monism. We combine good and evil in the same figures in our
religion. We are more relativistic in our morals. But if you imply
that because there is a relativist element it will be disordered,
chaotic, that there will be anarchy, this is erroneous; because
along with relativism there is always cause and effect, the doctrine
of karma.'[8]

In the Judaeo-Christian religion the idea seems to be of an
all-powerful God who gives justice and metes out punishment
accordingly. Good and evil are two separate categories and the
concept of right and wrong, and hence of sin, arises. According to
Hindu thought the Divine resides in every human being; thus the
soul-force being revered has somehow communicated itself to
other generations. This contrasts with the Western view of
Divinity which resides in God alone.

Once the Deva–Asura conflict was resolved in favour of the
temporal supremacy of the Devas and the establishment of Aryan
ascendancy and native tribal elements such as the Dasyus, the
new priesthood, which developed into the Brahmin caste and, as
has been discussed earlier, derived largely from Asura or other
autochthonous elements, evolved subtle changes to circumscribe
the concept of universal divinity to benefit élite groups. On the
one hand, the Brahmins recognized the depths of feeling regarding the unity of all creation – human, spirit, animal and even
inanimate – which permeated tribal thinking. On the other hand,
they had chosen to ally themselves to a minority ruling élite,

already perhaps racially and culturally mixed, but claiming Aryan provenance. To bolster their dominance they evolved a subtle system of different qualities of life-style (*dharmas*) to be enjoined on different categories of people. This led to the development of a factual hierarchy which could be disguised under the concept of universal harmony.

Even today, Channa deprecates Western preoccupation, deriving from Dumont's classic work, with the Indian 'Homo hierarchicus'.[9] He recalls the ancient Hindu ritual of the death ceremony where the priest intones that 'authority is meant to bring harmony in society'. He deduces therefore that harmony and not hierarchy is the end value of the system. The implication is that the authority of hierarchy is thus merely a means to that end. Perhaps the modern Hindu sociologist, in the ferment of modern Indian society, feels himself as part of a similar beleaguered élite, like the ancient sages surrounded by sceptical, if not actively hostile barbarians.

At any rate, any contradiction, however subtle, had to be resolved. Man, animals and universe are one and, if good deeds are performed, this right action results in a rebirth into a higher status. Bad acts, however, result in a regression. It is interesting to note that while an Untouchable, or Harijan, may become a pig for insulting a Brahmin, one never hears specific instances of a Brahmin going down the scale for any misdeeds.

The notion of hierarchy thus seems in fact to be central to the entire caste system. Therefore the Constitutional guarantee espousing the equality of all is basically antithetical to the Indian ethos. As V.S. Naipaul points out in his book, *A Wounded Civilization*:

> The freedom that came to Independent India with the institutions it gave itself were alien freedoms, better suited to another civilization; in India they remained separate from the internal organization of the country, its beliefs and antique restrictions.[10]

The modern Indian intellectual élite does not hide its antagonism to writers such as Naipaul whom they accuse of having lost touch with India and rushing into superficial judgments. Sometimes, however, such judgments seem to accord more closely with realities than their intellectual critics will admit.

The gulf in which modern Indian society finds itself today can indeed be related philosophically to the concept of 'maya', or illusion and its relation to reality. In connection with this Malati Shengde mentions the concept of 'maya', or illusion, in passing. The word is generally translated as 'illusion' or 'unreality'. The root word in the Indo-European languages is 'ma' and this, quite contrary to being an 'illusion', is a very active word associated with creative construction. If one grafts on to Shengde's line of thought the transfer of allegiance to the conquering Aryans by an old pre-Aryan priestly caste, one is faced with the overturning of a positive psychological frame of reference into an illusion. To cite the case in a different way, the old priests could never face the fact that their own great civilization had been put down and that they had made a deal with the opposition. When the psyche cannot face up to a reality the latter becomes transformed into an illusion. It is interesting to note that one finds the same phenomenon in the Indo-Aryan language, English, with regard to the very same idea: an invention is a very positive thing but can also connote a lie or an 'invention'. The same applies through 'artefact' to 'artifice'. Another synonym for a lie is a 'fabrication'.

A dichotomy therefore exists in the Hindu mind. For example, since ancient times the same leaders of thought give the impression of having fawned on power, yet at the same time have kept alive a genuine spiritual tradition since the time of the Upanishads composed between 1750 BC and the third century BC. The anthropologist M.N. Srinivas has noted this dichotomy in modern times: 'The way people fawn on the powerful and the next minute discourse on the hoary tradition of Indian spirituality is too common to deserve comment.'[11]

The dichotomy which many scholars have attributed to the Muslim conquests thus has far more ancient roots. The historian D.D. Kosambi thinks that the mixture of the pre-Aryan religion with the Aryan-made Indian religious thought is such that: 'The element of consistency and logic is unfortunately all too rare in such 'thinking'; which never faces reality or gives a clear record of single facts.'[12] Kosambi's terminology and his exasperation at what he calls the incapacity to face reality or keep a clear-cut record of single facts are perhaps coloured by the training of his own mind in the Western mould of thought. A more understanding interpretation might be that, out of the very early cultural confrontation necessitating for sheer survival some form of synthetic *modus vivendi*, there arose a perception of two separate cultural realities which could be transposed almost at will between myth and current fact.

The theoretical problem of the meagreness of early Hindu historical tradition seems allied to this issue. There is a common complaint of an absence of historical sense in terms of consecutive records of events. Apart from the Kashmir chronicles, there are few examples of coherent Indian historical tradition apart from the *Puranas* which are themselves semi-mythological accounts. Even the date of the Mauryan Empire could only be fixed finally because of Greek and Persian records. The Muslims had a strong historical sense as did the tribal Ahoms of Assam. The conclusion one draws is that a sort of 'collective amnesia' pervades the Hindu élite when it wishes to blot out or obfuscate unpalatable 'other realities'.

Sudhir Kakar, one of India's leading psychologists, trained in the Freudian school, looks at the problem more sympathetically. When questioned in his house in Delhi's élite garden suburb of Vasant Vihar, he argues that the Indian ego is underdeveloped in relation to outside reality although 'the same ego does very well with the whole realm of states of fantasy and other streams of consciousness which are underdeveloped in the Western ego. Therefore the Indian personality will always transform outside reality into an inner one. So history would be converted into myths, that is to the inner reality. It is one way of dealing with the world.'[13]

Again, when Westerners talk about the inconsistency of the Indian personality, to an Indian this appears meaningless and irrelevant. Witness Gandhi's gentle raillery against obsessions with consistency. Sudhir Kakar has some further interesting comments: 'The problem is simple in the sense that for a Westerner the consistency or inconsistency relates to some immutably absolute values; for example, justice. Something is either just or unjust. To an Indian mind values are contextual. In different situations a particular thing may or may not be right. Bravery is not always a virtue. It may be for a Kshatriya, or the Warrior Class, but not perhaps for a Banya, or Trader. Such contextual value-judgments would attract the charge of inconsistency. Yet it is merely the emphasis in a culture which stresses the context of what is to be done, in what situation, with what people. The line of action is not the same as would be needed in another situation. It is the judgment of a context which determines the action rather than the absolute nature of the action itself.'

All these illustrations of differences in perception lead to a single basic conclusion. One can never lose sight of the past in understanding a culture. If one could assume that in India myths and legends found in the ancient classical texts were irrelevant to the present, then the recounting of the imagery of 'The Churning of the Ocean' legend becomes futile. It is the central premise of this book that this is not the case. At present all Indian analysis of the contemporary scene has failed to construct a coherent account. Richard Lannoy's *The Speaking Tree* shows a very clear understanding of the problem by its very title. The author also makes the statement that India's future would derive from its ancient roots.

As a generalization this cannot be faulted. But the question arises as to what constitute, for the modern Indian, the roots of Indian culture. It is precisely on this point that no Indian can agree. In European culture one can argue about Judaeo-Greek influences. The main sources of the tradition are universally recognized; the main point of contention is the degree of influence of one or the other sources. In Indian culture most of the so-called Indian tradition is based on the almost deliberate blanking out from the mind of the elements which hitherto constituted the deepest strata of Indian culture. As Richard Lannoy has pointed out in *The Speaking Tree* this submerged tradition is tremendously tenacious and keeps reappearing and reasserting itself.

Richard Lannoy, who has achieved his scholarship not merely by direct study but through a quiet osmosis of Indian culture over the last 30 years, expounds lucidly on this point while a guest of an ancient aristocratic family: 'This submerged tradition goes back to that original encounter between two kinds of people or two kinds of cultures which came into a very extraordinary kind of interaction and symbiosis. It has been viewed as one of the great racial encounters of the world, the most dramatic encounter betwen black and white. If you want characterization of it, it is like the difference between earth and air. The Aryans worshipped sky gods while the indigenous population were people who were sedentary, deeply rooted as it were, earthbound in the best positive sense of the word.'[14]

Another aspect of the problem under discussion was the effect of the repeated incursions into India over the centuries. The nature of the Muslim impact has already been discussed. Much earlier there was the so-called invasion of Alexander the Great. Today historians place little importance on its military aspect. They stress rather the cultural trends it set loose. A whole cultural ferment linking Greece, Persia and India took place. One of the Hellenistic generals became a Hindu while mercenaries settled down in India. In this way new trends of thought were being disseminated. This was the period, for example, when carving in stone made its appearance in India.

Such incursions into India were less physical conquests than challenges to the mind and culture. On the one hand, there was a rush to ape certain cultural patterns of the new dominant society. On the other, there was a conscious or subconscious trend of reaction stimulated by an inferiority complex. However, it was not merely later conquerors who ingrained such a complex into the Hindus. The same process had been initiated right from the beginning by the Aryans against the 'dasyus', or darker-complexioned peoples of the subcontinent whom they had originally subjugated and dispossessed. As an educated tribal Oraon Catholic priest of Chotanagpur, a tribal area of South Bihar, admitted frankly: 'An inferiority complex runs in the tribals' blood.' The influx of outsiders to man the huge industries set up on expropriated tribal land in Chotanagpur is only a continuation of what has been happening for thousands of years to other groups in India. One of the by-products of this cultural domination is the sense of superiority and inferiority, mixed with certain racial overtones and colour complexes, that permeates Indian society. Even an official of the Marxist Government of West Bengal has failed to overcome such prejudices. During a visit to the tribal girls' hostel in Jhargram subdivision in Midnapore district, a predominantly Santhal tribal region, the caste-Hindu Tribal Welfare Officer commented: 'Some of these Santhal girls are not so bad looking. They have fair skins.'

Thus the Muslim and British conquests were merely contributory factors which aggravated a particular trend of mind. It has now become so ingrained that the Hindu can live in two worlds without being aware of the dichotomy. A perceptive westerner, Lannoy, sees some inconsistency in a plant geneticist at a famous scientific institute in Bangalore, trained in the Darwinist school, who has firmly retained his belief in reincarnation. The sociologist Srinivas has also drawn attention to the inconsistency of many factory workers who 'carry over religio-magical attitudes to the tools they work with'[15] and who at the traditional festival of Dussehra worship the tools of their trade. However, all this theorizing can perhaps be overdone. No doubt in the bylanes around Lourdes, an important pilgrimage spot for Roman Catholics, commemorating an apparition of the Virgin Mary, one could find highly sophisticated agricultural machinery, some of whose operators might simultaneously be staunch Catholics and reverence the miracle in their home town.

The interaction of successive waves of cultural assault may also have contributed to a related aspect of the Hindu personality which baffles every Westerner, including the educated Indian totally brought up on Western thought: the lack of clarity and the ambivalence in every attitude. This is reflected in the divergence between theory and practice whether in development programmes or any other policies. Many Indian sociologists like M.N. Srinivas, as well as historians, would admit a good deal of this schizophrenia. Nirad Chaudhuri in *The Continent of Circe*[16] talks about it, although this particular writer attributes it to the Muslim conquest and British colonialism. Even Supreme Court Justice D.A. Desai, one of the most liberal judges on India's highest legal bench, admits he is a prisoner of his own tradition: 'I was brought up as a Brahmin, I performed my daily rituals, I donned the sacred thread and then I would come and say I had a secular outlook.'[17]

A classic example of the way in which the British colonial era aggravated this attitude of mind can be seen from Macaulay's famous minutes recorded after a prolonged discussion on whether education should be conducted in Sanskrit, Hindi, regional languages or English. He finally persuaded the British Government, especially in the aftermath of the 1857 Mutiny, to opt for the total dominance of the English language and, through it, English thought: 'There shall thus arise to our interest a large class of people, Indian by birth but English in taste, in opinion, in morals and in intellect.'

A modern Indian may justifiably blame on to this policy much of the admitted cultural schizophrenia which subsequently beset its governing administrative élite. Less widely realized, however, were other ramifications of Macaulay's policy. Part of the new class rose against the imperial interest precisely because Western liberal precepts of egalitarianism were found to be totally at variance with the actual behaviour of the Imperial administrators. Indeed, it may be argued that, for better or worse, the real success of Macaulay's policy lay in its brainwashing of the opposition, the Congress Movement. At the time of Independence most politicians, especially ex-Congressmen and women and many Opposition party leaders, were steeped in this educational tradition.

Gandhi himself was a classic example. His success lay precisely in his reinterpretation of Western liberal concepts through traditional Hindu symbols. Simultaneously he bewildered the British by tweaking their conscience and playing upon their moral precepts which he had understood so well. His sincerity seemed that of a good Methodist missionary. His campaign against Untouchability perceived of this evil essentially in Christian terms: he regarded the practice as a sin and he communicated that sense of guilt to his followers. But Gandhi also realized that he would create a major uproar if he called for the total abolition of the caste system. Thus in order to unite the peoples of India, including the Untouchables, into the freedom movement he chose to tread the Middle Path. Even though Gandhi himself was serious in his demand, his followers merely went along with him because they saw it as a tactical ploy to draw the people of India together against Imperial rule. In his writings Gandhi's own attitude to caste remains one of ambivalence, although there can be no doubt regarding his own sincerity. But he was a realist and realized deep down the impossibility of totally abolishing the caste system for a long period. For the Indian side of his thinking would also favour the reform of traditional Hindu society into a new harmony without destroying any of its fundamentals.

He spread the term 'Harijan' (the people of God) to designate the communities known as Untouchables. Later the word became loosely synonymous with the statutory term 'Scheduled Castes' defined under the Constitution. With the spread of education among these groups and disillusionment among them about any real change of attitude in the dominant castes, a more militant leadership among them rejected the term as being piously condescending and intended to divert attention from practical amelioration of their status. Such groups now prefer the term 'Dalit' (the oppressed). This background has to be borne in mind during the usage of such loosely synonymous terms for the more precise but cumbersome official designation of 'Scheduled Caste'.

The problems of these communities will be discussed in greater depth in subsequent chapters on caste and on the Scheduled Caste groups in particular. They remain, despite constitutional commitments and massive government programmes, a major unresolved ingredient in the ferment of Indian society. They are linked with problems facing other minorities and groups who feel growingly restless over the impression that they continue to be manipulated into subordination by a dominant social minority which continues to control all the levers of power. An understanding of these perceptions in Indian terms in the Indian historical background is necessary for any adequate assessment of either the current scene or of India's immediate future.

CHAPTER ONE

India on the threshold of the eighties

One of the greatest dilemmas facing modern India is the problem of how to make the normative order coincide with the existential order. The Constitution proclaims a new kind of equality, that of individual mobility, a very different proposition from traditional caste mobility, and thus stands in direct contravention of the traditional collectivism of Indian society. Secondly, while the Constitution proclaims equality of rights and opportunity for all, the caste system which regulates society is based on a strict hierarchy. Caste is more than a system, it is a 'state of mind': 'The psychology of the vast majority of Hindus is still fundamentally a caste psychology.'[1] The difficulties faced by India's leaders in bringing about an egalitarian system are rendered even more difficult because of the cumulative nature of inequality, especially at the bottom of the hierarchy.

Today there is a widening gap between the aspirations of the people and the accomplishments of the polity because the modern state was adopted from the Western world where it had evolved gradually over the centuries. In the Indian context certain social factors have to be taken into consideration in conjunction with certain historical developments. The most important of these is the very sweeping commitment to total equality in all spheres made after Independence by the Founding Fathers of the Constitution. In contrast, the process of reducing inequalities in Western society was relatively gradual. Reforms were achieved step by step after the French Revolution and under the impact of industrialization. It was only in the 1940s that women achieved the vote in France.

The very historical process of India's Independence movement, especially under the influence of Gandhi and Nehru, dictated the sudden and all-embracing commitment to equality, both social and economic, as formulated at one fell swoop in the Constitution. In India the leadership of the movement had been fundamentally in the hands of an upper-class educated élite whose main quarrel with the imperial concept was again the divergence between liberal constitutional theory in the home country and its practice in the imperial possession. The upper-class Indian leadership was also conditioned by the practical necessity of egalitarian commitments to achieve support and unite the masses to make the Independence struggle into a mass movement. The dichotomy between legislation and practice, between planning and implementation, and, therefore, between the normative and existential order, must therefore be viewed against the background of the very sudden and sweeping commitments which in other countries took generations to formulate. Even today André Béteille, one of India's leading sociologists, wonders if this dichotomy is a uniquely Indian phenomenon: 'It may be unique in some respects, it may be unique in some forms of expression but I'm very struck by the same thing in the American context in relation to both Blacks and women.'[2]

Sudhir Kakar belives that the ambivalence one can observe amongst educated Indians today towards India's modern institutions may not stem *ipso facto* from an inherent dichotomy in the Indian personality. Says Sudhir Kakar: 'It may be that the theories that have been superimposed in practice have not really been taken into account, which means that the commitment to that theory will be much less.'[3]

One problematic aspect in India's quest for modernization is the traditionalism which impedes its practice and implementation. The Constitution, together with the ideology of every party, is committed to a social order in which equal rights and opportunities are in principle guaranteed to all. The adoption of a new political system based on adult franchise, the spread of agitational politics and general elections should not be overlooked as vehicles in the transformation of the social perceptions of the masses. The problem is how to make the normative order coincide with the existential order. For the anthropologist Dumont has pointed out in his brilliant but controversial study of caste that: 'On the ideological plane, the major fact is the insertion of an egalitarian subset at the juridical and political level without a corresponding voluntary modification of the overall framework.'[4]

India may be characterized by what Béteille has called a disharmonic system 'in which the normative order is inconsistent with the order of existence, inequalities exist in fact but are no longer accepted as legitimate.'[5] Furthermore, real influence is more narrowly held than in Western countries on account of the rigid and inegalitarian social stratification, and social monopolies of property and education result in inequalities of power, whatever the Constitution prescribes.

Another factor which has emerged in recent years is the rejection by intellectuals of the interpretation of the term 'modernization' in its meaning of catching up with the rest of the world. Today one hears talk about the Indian road to modernization. Earlier the intellectual élite had given outright support to modernization but had been somewhat afraid of pushing things to their logical conclusion. They were thus forced to adopt a gradualist approach because of the traditionalists. Even sociologist Gunnar Myrdal had noted the ambivalence towards modernization amongst the élite:

South Asian Planners remain in the paradoxical position: on a general and non-committal level they freely and almost passionately proclaim the need for radical social and economic change whereas in their planning policies they tread most warily in order not to disrupt the traditional social order.[6]

Today, however, modernization ideals have gained such acceptance that the country can never return to the traditional order based on the earlier rigid hierarchy. Yet Béteille has recently remarked that the modernization process may not be effacing the old inequalities: 'The overall impression is that India has not only inherited great inequalities from the past but that it is creating new inequalities without fully effacing the old.'[7] Today a totally new trend in social, economic and political thinking is questioning the basis of the Western pattern. Dr Karan Singh, the leader of the Virat Hindu Samaj, the Hindu Renaissance movement, says: 'We have to develop our own pattern of modernization. We have got to solve the problem of poverty, deprivation, ill health and illiteracy in our own way.'[8] Few would disagree with him. However, the problem remains one of defining in clear terms what such advocates of the Indian way to modernization mean by it. Basic problems like deprivation, poverty and illiteracy stem basically from an inegalitarian society. When questioned about the reconciliation of egalitarianism with Hindu tradition and its ancient texts, such reformers find it difficult to trace back such a concept to a clear and unambiguous source. Dr Karan

Singh will talk about the universality of Hinduism, the presence of divinity in every part of creation and universal benefit for all. This concept of *sarvodaya*, or the 'good of all', was also the plank of the socialist leader Jayaprakash Narayan, but there is little evidence of its having been spelt out in concrete terms or getting off the ground. The only other text usually cited is from the *Gita* wherein any form of worship is acceptable and whoever devotes himself to the divinity of Krishna achieves salvation. The uncompromisingly Hindu Revival Organization, the Rashtriya Swyam-Sevak Sangh (RSS), claims to work for the abolition of caste distinctions but its programme seems conditioned less by genuine altruism than by an attempt to mobilize the lower castes in defence of Hindu unity against various threats which it perceives might fragment it.

Indeed the difficulty of implementing the constitutional commitments to an egalitarian society are very largely rooted in the caste system characterized by the dominance of the religious order over the secular. One may state without exaggeration that hierarchy and caste form part of the unconscious psychological element of the Hindu. To ask a Hindu to carry out his social and political duties and relationships in a spirit of secularism and egalitarianism, which are structurally and fundamentally opposed to hierarchy, is perhaps asking too much. Historical antecedents point to this unconscious response of the Hindu to his spiritual traditions which are rooted in inequality, despite the interpretations of reformers.

Another problem impeding the implementation of the constitutional principle of equality of opportunity is the scarcity factor. In a country with deep community affiliations and centuries of hierarchical tradition, it becomes inevitable that the community factor will prevail under conditions of scarcity. As Béteille points out: 'You can have a more generous attitude towards equality under conditions of abundance.'[9] A.B. Vajpayee. leader of one of India's main Opposition parties, the Bharatiya Janata Party (BJP), himself admits: 'Jobs are few. Candidates are many and so I would like to appoint the person who belongs to my caste because I can only appoint one person. I can only have one peon so I would like to have a peon who will work not only in my office but also in my kitchen. So I appoint a person belonging to my own caste. This will continue for some time.'[10] Béteille has himself noted the system of patronage which operates in politics and which he describes as a network of 'interpersonal relations which branch out in every direction.'[11] This is confirmed by Syed Shahabuddin, a Muslim MP until the December 1984 elections, who adds the other dimension that it operates against minorities. He comments: 'Apparently you have a system in which all are equal, but actually underneath it operates under an insidious system of patronage.'[12]

This brings one up immediately against another problem of egalitarianism – the secular state as envisaged in the Constitution. A considerable controversy arose at the end of 1982 when a group of 45 Muslim MPs sought an interview with Prime Minister Indira Gandhi and presented a memorandum questioning whether communal forces were not gaining ascendancy over secularism. Over a decade earlier Lannoy had described his own perception of this factor:

> The difficulty India faces in forming a contemporary national self image may be more clearly appreciated when it is realized that while India is now building a modern secular state, its traditions are permeated by a sophisticated religious sensibility.[13]

A lot of rethinking is, however, presently going on about the meaning of the term 'secular state' since Lannoy wrote this in the sixties, for a certain generation of dominant political leadership after Independence seems to have proceeded on the assumption, influenced by Western values, that one must eschew any form not only of religious teaching but even of religious expressions of thought. Dr Karan Singh, the Hindu Revivalist leader, has questioned the policy of banning the teaching of spiritual thought and of ancient traditions like the *Ramayana* in schools.

Dr Karan Singh, son of the former Maharaja of Kashmir and erstwhile Health Minister during Mrs Gandhi's Emergency, speaks at length on this subject in his mansion in Delhi's diplomatic enclave where he has maintained his lifestyle of princely elegance. Dr Karan Singh maintains that 'because of what I consider to be a wrong interpretation of secularism our educational system has become totally devoid of any values. This is where a value system based essentially on Hindu values can help strengthen the moral fibre of the people.'[14] Syed Shahabuddin agrees: 'The greatest failure of Independent India has been the failure to instill in our children a new Indian mind which is truly secular.'[15]

Dr Karan Singh asks why India does not opt for the pattern of education followed in Singapore whereby each community possesses its own religious institutions. Today in India schools are supposed to keep away from imparting religious instruction. This policy has led to the backlash of Hindu revivalism among the Hindus and to the demand among minorities for their own religious institutions – the *madrassa* among Muslims and convent schools among Christians.

There is undoubtedly a movement away from secular ideals in India today. This can be measured by the response to Dr Karan Singh's Virat Hindu Samaj meetings which are even being attended by Congress (I) party members. Mrs Gandhi was perturbed by the infiltration of its appeal into her own ranks. She asked her party members not to have any truck with the movement, following reports that many Congress (I) members had participated, for fear of eroding her secular image. Indeed today there is a growing suspicion among minorities, both religious and cultural, that the original secular ideals enshrined in the Constitution are in practice being eroded to such an extent that it no longer reflects the real feelings of the majority community. Some even doubt that it ever did so, although there is almost unanimous agreement on the genuineness of Gandhi and Nehru in this regard. Dr Karan Singh on this issue is illuminating: 'It is only in the Hindu majority India that you have both democracy and secularism. This is a fact for which I feel the Hindus have not received enough credit. After all, theoretically, if the Muslim areas could opt to be Islamic republics, there was no theoretical reason why the Hindu majority area could not have become a Hindu state.'[16]

Syed Shahabuddin, an earnest advocate of the minorities, uses his barrister's skill to marshal a telling case for his community. He defines secularism not in terms of a denial of religion but in terms of the 'equidistance of the state *vis-à-vis* all religions. Therefore there must be equal treatment of all religions by the state and, above all, the right of the individual to practise and propagate a faith of his own choice. In actual practice the Muslims feel this is not quite the reality of the situation.'[17]

He admits that under pressure of the passions of Partition it would have been understandable if India had tried to declare herself a Hindu state, but he admires the deeper practical wisdom of Gandhi and Nehru in understanding that this would be fatal for India's future. He asserts: 'If all the Muslims were to disappear from India overnight, can India do without a secular order? Every sect of Hinduism would become a religion and the Hindu society would start clashing within itself. Secularism is necessary for a country like India because there is so much cultural plurality, so much regional diversity and so much religious variety. So in order to keep peace in society you must have the state power exercised in the manner that every citizen, irrespective of the gods he worships, irrespective of the language he speaks, irrespective of the area in which he lives, feels that he is equal in the eyes of the state.'[18]

Syed Shahabuddin has failed to draw a distinction between his rather dubious prognostication of quarrels between Hindu sects and the very genuine problem of cultural, linguistic and regional pluralities. Hinduism has always been catholic in regard to rituals and patterns of belief but he has a point if he is thinking of the seeming condition for this catholicity – the recognition of the universality of the Hindu family. The emerging problem of Hindu–Sikh attitudes in the eighties is an illustration of this. It has begun to involve an alienation of Sikh feelings by insistence on the theory that they are really part of Hindu society, an alienation quite separate from, but perhaps contributing to, a small extremist demand for a political Sikh homeland of Khalistan.

Everywhere there is the growing suspicion that the ideology of the RSS is gaining influence far beyond the organization's actual membership. It was stated with brutal forthrightness by the then RSS chief, M.S. Golwakar in 1947:

The non-Hindu people of Hindustan must either adopt Hindu culture and language, must learn and respect and hold in reverence the Hindu religion, must entertain no idea but those of glorification of the Hindu race and culture, i.e., they must not only give up their attitude of intolerance and ungratefulness towards this land and its age-long traditions but must also cultivate the positive attitude of love and devotion instead – in a word they must cease to be foreigners, or may stay in the country, wholly subordinated to the Hindu nation, claiming nothing, deserving no privileges, far less any preferential treatment – not even citizen's rights.[19]

It may be argued that this was an extreme and understandable outburst in the wake of the Partition massacres. However, even in the 1980s similar vitriolic writings have appeared in the mouthpiece of the RSS, *The Organizer*. These do not exclude even vicious communal attacks on a recent Muslim President of the Indian Unions. It is significant that, while laws exist making actionable speeches or writings liable to wound the feelings of particular communities or arouse communal passions, no action seems to be instituted in practice.

Even within government, in another sphere, an experienced and sensitive tribal administrator has published some revealing assessments regarding what he calls the tribal defence mechanism against its apprehension of Hindu cultural dominance. From his administrative experience he was constrained to write:

> The policy of promoting and focusing attention on the tribal traditional institutions and arts was not, however, unreservedly endorsed, and there was apprehension in the highest echelons of government that this emphasizing of the tribals' cultural identity was an indirect, if not direct, incitement to the forces of separatism. There was a school of thought that considered it preferable, in the interests of the unity of India, to focus attention rather on the broad mainstream of Indian culture – to promote the study of Sanskrit and inculcate the patterns of behaviour, dress and belief prevalent in the main body of the country . . . There was thus a wide divorce between policy as enunciated and its implementation in the field. Nehru had explicitly declared that: 'There was no point in trying to make of the tribals a second-rate copy of ourselves'. But that was precisely what was happening.[20]

Apart from the dichotomy between theory and practice, between professed democratic, constitutional principles and the oppression of the masses, India faces another kind of problem which is thwarting her development. The nature of the crisis is an institutional one. The parliamentary system, the bureaucracy, the judiciary and 'mixed' economy have been suffering an erosion of their declared values since Independence. The main reason for this state of affairs is that the institutions framed under the impact of Western thought are antithetical to the Indian value system. When formulating the Constitution and provisions for the formation of the Constituent Assembly, the educated élite more or less drew inspiration from other Western models and opted for a direct system of election without pondering on its suitability to Indian traditions and institutions. As a result some of India's leading politicians are today questioning the suitability of the present political system. A.B. Vajpayee, BJP leader, has voiced reservations about the present electoral system: 'Under the present system we have got government on a minority vote. This distorts the whole process. For on account of the division of votes a candidate who secures even a minority vote gets elected.'[21] A.B. Vajpayee favours a mixed system of representation: 'Some members should be elected from geographical constituencies and others from the list put forward by the respective parties. It will have to be a mixture of both territorial and proportional representation.'[22]

The parliamentary system has not resulted in the exercise of a true democratic franchise based on the free choice of every citizen to elect as his representative the person best able to speak for his territorial constituency. In practice, the constituency is not territorial and people vote in the interests of their community, often on the basis of caste.

This problem of choosing an elected representative is of course not unique to India. Even in England, the home of the 'Mother of Parliaments', a sober Labour MP, Brian Mathieson, questioned the validity of the system as it exists today. In his book, *The Masters of Power*, Brian Mathieson pointed out that the days were now gone when a miner's son like Keir Hardie could get elected because he was a 'good man'. Nowadays it is the party who chooses a candidate mainly for his capacity to achieve victory for the party. It is the party that finances the electoral campaign. The candidate having been elected, it is the party that dictates, through the Party Whip, the way the candidate will vote on any issue. This is a far cry from genuine representation for the electorate of a constituency.[23]

However, in India the problem becomes even more acute because, cutting across party lines, dominant castes or caste community groups have developed, at the regional level, patron–client networks based on traditional loyalties. In each state several castes are constantly fighting for power and people are mobilized by using the caste idiom. Modern party politics has resulted in the emergence of large agglomerations of caste groups like Jats,

Okkaligas, Ahirs and Rajputs which play a vital role in state politics and, through politics, in the allocation of resources and distribution of benefits to followers. The coming together of such cognate *jatis*, or subcastes, has been termed 'horizontal stretch' by the anthropologist M.N. Srinivas. He compares this process of fusion with the trend in pre-British India when small groups of kin broke off from parent groups to enhance their economic opportunities in a process called fission. Therefore one feature of social change in India in the modern context has been the change in caste referent. As political and social relations have expanded, groups of castes across a wide region have tended to unite instead of identifying with the subcaste as in the old days.

The second President of India, Dr S. Radhakrishnan, remarked: 'Caste has ceased to be a social evil but has become a political evil and an administrative evil. We want to get out votes and we set up candidates suited to the people who have to vote.' This phenomenon began to develop especially in the early sixties. For example, in 1950 the Congress party in Gujarat gave more weight to party commitment and party work in the distribution of party tickets. If other things were equal, the party then gave preference to a candidate's caste. However, in the sixties and thereafter the party has given more weight to the caste of a candidate.[24]

Such defectors are often paid heavily but this is not the only reason for the phenomenon. There is much cynical comment in the press and among the vocal élite about their activities. Yet the fact remains that they continue to flourish. Their brazen changes of allegiance do not seem to excite the revulsion that might have been expected from the electorate because after all there is the tacit understanding that their main aim must be to achieve or maintain the power and influence needed to further their community's interests. The same factor operates in the case of dissident groups within the same party which seek to topple the existing leadership from time to time.

The anthropologist G. Bailey makes a telling point when he points out that Hindu ethics has its public face, *dharma*, or normative rules, and its private wisdom, or pragmatic rules, to distinguish between the principles they espouse and the tactics they adopt. Even the political ideology of parties which is general and abstract are given different interpretations in the contexts of different local conditions.

In Indian politics the parliamentary system has failed to bring social and economic justice because at the local level the dominant castes have the power and influence. Local politics are generally controlled by one or more dominant castes which have to be taken into account when any state cabinet is being constituted which therefore leads to the district dominance of castes:

> A concomitant of this trend is the disjunction of talent from politics; professional vote collecting élites are formed through the maintenance of power by mutually adjusting positions and privileges rather than through recruitment on the principles of achievement and personal competence and integrity.[25]

The dominant castes who possess economic power or numerical support are able to rally not only their own caste, but often sharecroppers and agricultural labourers who are dependent on them for employment and financial borrowing in times of distress. According to Béteille: 'The role of caste in elections, as with a large part of political life in general, carries with it an aspect of skilful manipulation of new conditions for the traditional ends of clientele and patronage.[26]

In many areas the lower castes vote for the dominant caste nominee either through a mixture of fear, traditional subservience or ignorance. Ganesh, a landless labourer from Harua village, Chhatharpur district, Madhya Pradesh, is an oil presser, a low caste. He admits: 'I don't know anything about politics or parties. The village headman tells us who to vote for.' According to Nawab Ahmed Khan, a Muslim from Chapta village, Etawah district, Uttar Pradesh, and former head constable, the landlords tell agricultural labourers who to vote for: 'This sort of thing is commonplace.' The agricultural labourers in Chapta village, who are largely Harijans, agree: 'If the landlords or upper castes ever hear we voted for a person they didn't want, there would be all kinds of problems regarding land.' Balak Ram, the Community Health Worker of Chapta village, who is himself a Harijan, says: 'Sometimes at polling time the police come to make sure no harassment takes place.'

If the lower castes appear to want to exercise their own choice of candidate, in many instances the dominant castes do not hesitate to use violent coercion. In the most backward states, like Uttar Pradesh and Bihar, where casteism is rampant, political booth capturing, either to prevent Harijans from casting their votes, or to manipulate the votes, is a common occurrence during general and local elections. In his work *Caste, Class and Power*, a study of Sripuram village in Tanjore district, South India, Béteille had also noted the role of organized violence at the village level in maintaining power. Another important aspect of the new political system is the appearance of networks of interpersonal relations which branch out in every direction. In the same work he notes that 'the creation of new political opportunities and new bases of power have provided congenial conditions for the development of elaborate networks of patronage . . .'[27]

It seems inevitable that given the whole background of groupism and caste in India that the splintering that occurs within the political party system is inevitable. As Srinivas has pointed out, adult franchise provided 'a new area of activity for caste.' The proclivity to using caste for political ends is not confined to one party but is used by parties across the line. As a result the party system seems to be slowly crumbling. People do not cast their votes because they want a free enterprise system or socialism. The concept is to vote for a person or group who can help your own person or group to achieve higher status or power. Therefore the only possible hope for any intelligent Scheduled Caste or Scheduled Tribe who are not dominant in a particular constituency is to somehow bargain with various political parties to obtain a deal for his group.

The Scheduled Castes and Tribes are constitutionally defined categories constituting approximately 100 million and 45 million respectively. They come from communities which are listed by government notification. The Scheduled Castes are made up largely of the former 'Untouchable' castes, while the Scheduled Tribes constitute diverse aboriginal groups which retained their tribal community structures. When there is a large defined percentage of either group in a constituency it becomes reserved so that these 'backward' groups may achieve a reasonable representation in the State and Central legislatures. For a detailed discussion of these groups see chapters 7, 8 and 9.

The result of casteism in politics has not had a totally negative impact for these underprivileged groups. The one hundred million Harijans constitute a significant vote bank, hitherto tapped largely by the Congress (I), which has come to rely on this particular caste vote. This may be one of the reasons why the

Congress (I) continues to give the greatest importance to reservations in education and in public and government employment to the Scheduled Castes and Tribes, despite the active anti-reservation protests in many parts of the subcontinent.

The political parties depend on vote banks and the vote banks need them to further their own community interests, although there may be complete cynicism and disillusionment with the party system created by vested interests. Therefore, unless a state of complete lawlessness and anarchy prevails, everyone will still want elections. For the electoral system will still provide them with the hope of obtaining higher status of power through some sort of bargaining.

This would appear to be one of the by-products of modernization which has been grafted on to the Indian ethos. The mixture has been quite lethal. A further ingredient is nostalgia for the past. People are talking about the Rule of Rama and of other traditional Hindu concepts of rulership. This must not be interpreted as a longing for authoritarianism. Mrs Gandhi called such Hindu revivalism 'Fascist', but this is using Western terminology. To the extent that hero worship was based on the Indian concept of 'Raja and Praja', there was always a feeling not only of moral responsibility towards the people but of non-dualism. That is to say, the Raja must look after his people because everyone is part of a great family. The question which the revivalists have not resolved is the manner of translating such a dogma into the modern state with its police apparatus, communications systems, etc. The feeling of balance between the ruler and the people is very much there as with Mrs Gandhi.

Lannoy believes that the challenge India faces in the eighties is that of positive pluralism. He points out: 'India will have to find new ways of positive pluralism. If there is any vitality in India, which I think there is, it will evolve in an Indian way. It will be a different kind of political pluralism, a differently structured pluralism, a socially differently articulated pluralism and a culturally differently articulated pluralism.'[28]

Unless India solves this problem of pluralism in its own peaceful way, by synthesis and accommodation as it has done historically, any attempt to force a central government on the states, as witness Auranzgeb, the last powerful Moghul emperor who ruled in the seventeenth century, leads ultimately to the break-up of the country.

From the 'united India' angle of the Hindus, there was great glee when Pakistan was split up in 1971. The basic issue at the time was that Pakistan split up because the Punjabi element of Pakistan treated the Bengalis as an inferior race, in the same way as the North Indians treat anyone beyond the Hindi heartland as being of a lower hierarchical level.

Even the Congress (I) party, which is committed at least to cultural pluralism, interprets any move by regional parties to form wider links of understanding among themselves as a first step towards secession. The Prime Minister came out strongly against an initiative in March 1983 by the Chief Ministers of the four southern states, Andhra Pradesh, Tamil Nadu, Kerala and Karnataka, to form a council of their own to discuss common problems. Yet there was no suggestion whatsoever that these chief ministers or their parties entertained the remotest idea of secession.

While many states are demanding more powers, especially financial ones, from the Centre, it must be remembered that the states themselves are by and large based on linguistic boundaries. These often coincide with distinct cultural areas and, occasionally, as in the case of Kashmir, Nagaland and Punjab, with different minority religions. Greater strength or power to the states tends therefore to be viewed sometimes as an expression of sub-nationalism, raising once again the ancient problem of defining nationality/national minorities and their place within a single nation-state. One of the most important minorities, the Muslims, which constituted 25 per cent of the population of undivided India, did in fact break away at the time of Independence to found a separate unfriendly state of Pakistan. The geographical dispersion of Muslims resulted, however, in India still having a 12-per-cent Muslim population, including a Muslim majority area of 70 per cent in the state of Kashmir and one or two Muslim majority districts in other states.

Today even this community upon which the Congress (I) has traditionally been able to rely upon as a vote bank is losing faith. Syed Shahabuddin, who contrasts its present leadership with that of Gandhi and Nehru, points out that the fundamental rights granted to minorities in the Constitution are 'slowly whittling down'. He notes: 'There is an overall tendency to cast everyone in the same mould. Notwithstanding Mrs Gandhi's assertions of respect for the cultural identity of the minorities, in actual practice there is a process of Hinduization of tribals, just as there is a process of assimilation which is eroding the cultural identity of the Muslim community.'[29] Syed Shahabuddin believes there is 'an insidious effort, a subterranean move' slowly to assimilate the Muslim community.

He explains the problem: 'This has been the tendency in Indian history. Call it synthesis, assimilation, whatever you like. So many new movements were born in the course of 5,000 years of our history. Today they are no longer there. They have all been absorbed in the broad framework of Hinduism. Buddhism has become another form of Hinduism. Today Sikhism is considered another cult of Hinduism. So the cultural identity of the minorities is getting diffused.'[30]

Syed Shahabuddin agrees with Lannoy that a genuine plurality of cultures, quite apart from the question of religion, is necessary for India: 'In order to keep peace in society you must have a state power exercised in the manner that every citizen, irrespective of the gods he worships, irrespective of the language he speaks, irrespective of the area in which he lives, feels that he is equal in the eyes of the state.'[31]

Dr Karan Singh, the leader of the Hindu Renaissance, wants to bring about a sense of 'unity and solidarity' with the whole of Indian society and sees his movement as 'part of the great churning process of human consciousness all over the world.' If translated politically this would be very dangerous. When he talks about the whole world being a family the minorities suspect that they will have to conform with increasing rigidity to the cultural pattern laid down by the head of the family who will claim to be the sole authoritative arbiter of its definition. To quote Syed Shahabuddin: 'In a given context when you emphasize the all-embracing and comprehensive character of Hinduism then everyone feels apprehensive that all you wish to do is to assimilate all other religions and to absorb them. This sets up tensions in society.'[32] Shahabuddin's main criticism, however, is against the RSS which the minorities consider to be an extremist Hindu movement and which Shahabuddin believes has greatly contributed to the communal tension in the country. He sees Dr Karan Singh's movement, the Virat Hindu Samaj, with its 'broad catholicity', as being more representative of true Hinduism than the 'xenophobic preachings' of the RSS. Yet any government which tried to ban the RSS today would probably fall because the movement represents a broad spectrum to the extent that it is felt to be the defender of Hinduism. As Syed Shahabuddin has pointed out, 'The RSS is a "state of mind" which says: "The Muslims got their share. Why don't they all go away?" This feeling is at the back of the minds of many people. That is why I said that some low level of tension communal tension is always present in our society.'[33]

Shahabuddin, when talking about communal tension, is mainly concerned with the Hindu–Muslim problem. This tends for historical reasons to be a particularly acute symptom which diverts attention from a much deeper malaise in the body politic. Shahabuddin himself occasionally glimpses the wider perspective. He views as incorrect the common historical interpretation of a confrontation between Hindu cultural resistance and the Islamic bigotry of the Muslim ruler, Auranzgeb. Instead he sees this as a distortion of India's age-old problem of reconciling the needs of Central authority and regional pluralism.

The 1980s are witnessing an extremely frothy re-emergence of this problem in the churning of the political ocean. Some (Mrs Gandhi belonged to this group) see the new trend in regional pluralism as positively poisonous. Up to the time of her death Mrs Gandhi's speeches consistently decried regionalism, equating it with 'fissiparous tendencies' and 'incipient secession'. Unfortunately the positive aspects of this political pluralism anticipated by Lannoy over a decade ago have escaped attention. The resounding defeat of the Congress (I) in Andhra Pradesh in January 1983, a traditional stronghold of the Congress (I) party which had remained unshaken even in the post-Emergency days, was almost entirely due to regional revulsion against the affairs of the state being directed in the minutest detail from Delhi. In the recent elections there, although caste appears to have played some part, the situation brought together, to a greater degree, a much wider emotional grouping on a territorial and linguistic basis of the Andhra people as a whole. In fact, their attempt to establish their cultural self-respect cut across earlier divisions of caste and community.

Oddly enough the Congress (I), as the premier political party claiming total commitment to national integration and unity in diversity, tends to counter such regional movements by trying to split them by invoking appeals to old caste or community disparities. Or, as in the case of the Punjab (for a discussion of the

Punjab crisis see pp. 294–6 and 301–15), which has become the most serious challenge to Indian democracy, by playing far more dangerous games, including the instigation and encouragement of violence to weaken the regional religious Sikh Akali Dal party whose calls for decentralization came to be interpreted by Mrs Gandhi as 'secessionist'. Here one sees a reversion to the old tactics of Kautilya, the political theorist of the Mauryan empire in the third century BC, whose prescription for strengthening central imperial unity was the sowing of dissent among the democratic tribal republics of the time. It is perhaps understandable that a country like India, with its enormous diversities, and with the experience of Partition still within living memory, should feel beleaguered by what it feels are potential forces of secession. There may even be the feeling of a drift towards anarchy. It was Indian symbolism and imagery which coloured Yeats' famous poem: 'Things fall apart. The Centre cannot hold.'

Yet despite this understandable fear there are signs that the path to positive regional pluralism is being painfully constructed. A genuine reconciliation between the needs of the Central authority and regional decentralization may now, for the first time, be emerging. This is perhaps the most important issue before India in the eighties. The slogan 'unity in diversity' is no longer acceptable as a mere catch-phrase.

An allied political development which is having fundamental repercussions upon the body politic is the Assam imbroglio. For the first time in 1983 a major mass movement in a whole state, Assam, engulfed the political system with resistance to the political process itself. The tragic trail of violence which resulted has somewhat obscured the true significance of this episode which in fact again derives from the dichotomy between constitutional theory and the reality of practice. The constitution and its derivative laws clearly define citizenship and the means for its acquisition. In practice, however, Assam was flooded by immense numbers of immigrants from Bangladesh who merely settled down without acquiring Indian nationality as prescribed by law. Occasional government measures to oust them invariably foundered because, although in theory the Hindu element of these immigrants were Bangladeshi nationals requiring formal grant of Indian citizenship, the Indian mind could hardly regard such Hindus as foreigners. Although many probably migrated purely for economic betterment, they tended to be regarded, without verification, as refugees returning to the Motherland. On the other hand, serious attempts to oust the Muslim elements of the immigrants foundered because of lobbying by the Muslim vote banks that in eviction programmes they were being discriminated against in favour of Hindu immigrants who were equally and constitutionally foreigners.

Years of inaction in confronting the problem squarely due to this dichotomy, resulted in a serious threat of the Assamese being reduced to a numerical and cultural minority in their own homeland. The ultimate ordering of elections, based on admittedly totally defective electoral rolls and against the resistance of a major section of the people, was justified by Government on the grounds of a single article of the Constitution necessitating such elections within the prescribed period, while at the same time ignoring other aspects of mandatory constitutional provisions defining nationality, citizenship and the preparation of electoral rolls involving these. The reality therefore was a constitutional breakdown which has still not been resolved and which is based on this fundamental dichotomy. The real significance of the Assam movement was that it forced the unpleasant reality of this dichotomy upon the Central Government.

Despite these fundamental contradictions within the political system, it is difficult, however, to envisage what better system could emerge more in line with the true Indian tradition. After Independence the intellectual élite had assumed that the Indian village was some sort of ideal entity through which all development plans could be canalized. This led to catchphrases like 'democratic decentralization' and a plethora of legislation seeking to establish the *panchayat raj*, or village councils. In fact, however, in most parts of India the village polity was itself a stronghold of exploitative and oppressive practices by dominant castes or of other less favoured groups.

Gandhi himself favoured some form of democracy at the grass roots. The last document framed by Gandhi indicated a feeling that the Indian National Congress Party, a heterogeneous organization which had united disparate elements of Indian society with fundamentally conflicting interests for the overriding priority of obtaining Independence, had outlived its usefulness. He wanted to keep India out of the 'unhealthy competition with political parties and communal bodies',[34] and called for the party's disbandment and its reconstitution as a dedicated cadre-based organization based on indirect elections from the grass roots for the next task of rural transformation. When other Gandhian leaders like Jayaprakash Narayan talked about party-less democracy at the village level, they also recognized the need for decentralization. However, J.P. Narayan failed to spell out clearly his ideas on the subject.

BJP leader, A.B. Vajpayee, also favours decentralization and thinks that the panchayat system can be translated into the modern context: 'People should learn to manage their own affairs at the grass roots. How can you run the affairs of such a huge country from New Delhi?'[35]

Talk about decentralization leads one to the question of reviving traditional caste panchayats. This old system, which is now virtually defunct, would seem to lead one in the direction of proportional representation or even to separate electorates. One then comes up against the counterproblem of the fear that separate electorates would lead to a break-up of the country. Yet if separate electorates are not created, the person elected, even from a reserved constituency, would probably have to depend on votes largely from other elements and not from the nominee's own group; therefore he will not really be representing his own group. This is beginning to be a problem in Nagaland, a state in North-East India with a predominantly Mongoloid tribal population.

In most states the creation of a separate district with all its development paraphernalia is a welcome populist measure. Recently, however, a Congress (I) government in Nagaland tried to create a separate district in a plains area around the railhead where a considerable non-Naga business community had grown up. There were major demonstrations and traffic stoppages because of this and the state government was forced to defer, if not abandon, the decision. The Naga fear was that a separate district would entail a non-Naga majority in its area leading to non-Nagas being elected as spokesmen for a portion of their tribal state. Such a situation had already arisen in another nearby tribal state of Meghalya. All over India there are indications from successive censuses that predominantly tribal areas are becoming progressively diluted with non-tribals who ultimately come to form a majority. In 1980 the tensions due to this process exploded in Tripura into mass killings of Bengali settlers.

Apart from the incipient crisis in the political system, the state of the administrative apparatus is one of the main instruments that diverts the channels of social change from their declared courses because its delivery system is plagued by a diffusion of responsibility and lack of coordination. Post-Independence India has taken over from the British pattern the theoretical relationship between elected representatives and the permanent official. Problems associated with this system of dual responsibility arose to a lesser extent under the British, and only in the last stages of imperial rule. Sardar Patel, the first Home Minister, understood this whole theoretical relationship between the elected representative and the official well. In fact he is on record as having insisted that the official examine every issue and express frankly his own view, although the ultimate decision of the elected representative must be carried out.

This convention has been rapidly eroded although lip service continues to be paid to it. Its validity is assumed in all training courses and discussions on the role of the bureaucracy. In practice a totally opposite reality prevails and a nexus has been established at all levels between political groups in power, or likely to achieve power, and the cadres of the bureaucracy. It would be unfair to assume that all blame goes to the political leadership for corrupting the theoretical conventions or for browbeating the bureaucrats. Nowadays such cases have indeed occurred, but many bureaucrats have also gone out of the way to court politicians for the sake of their own advancement to the detriment of a sound examination of issues, decision-making and a sincere implementation of programmes. Whatever the apportionment of blame for this state of affairs should be, there is now in most states, and even in parts of the Central administration, a total dichotomy between declared conventions of relationship between the political leadership and the civil servant and the actual deep involvement of both in manipulations aimed at political advancement and power.

In addition, the attitude of the bureaucracy has changed very subtly since British days, although the feeling of confrontation between the bureaucracy and the public is still there. Today different reasons exist for the alienation which persists between the public and bureaucracy. Earlier the bureaucracy remained aloof from the people by virtue of its administrative functions. Today, however, a much more sinister element has been grafted on to the basis of the British inheritance: that of the old Hindu value of superiority. The bureaucrat today sees himself less as even an employee of government than as a repository of status and power which he can increase by manipulations of his position. The communication gap which exists today is illustrated by an account given by Lannoy. He recalls the expression of blankness verging on idiocy on the hill villagers' faces during a lecture being delivered by an official during a meeting held by the leader of the Chipko Movement, Sunderlal Bahuguna. (The Chipko Movement was started to stop commercial exploitation of forest produce by outside contractors in the Garhwal region of the Himalayas.) Lannoy contrasts it with the sudden look of animation and intelligence on their faces when Sunderlal Bahuguna began to talk to them. The official himself had been talking perfectly reasonably and, to an outside observer, convincingly. Yet he could not bridge the perception gap between himself and the audience.

Thus the bureaucracy continues to be estranged from the masses even today. While the British administrative system was able to achieve a blend between paternalism and the rule of law, modern India has possibly had no alternative but to opt for an impersonal system based on rules, regulations and directives in view of the complexities of modern development programmes. Béteille has noted that the nature of this rule is in direct contravention of the personal and paternalistic nature of contacts in traditional Indian society.

Such areas of success as are evident to a traveller can usually be traced to a local atmosphere where this traditional form of contact has been blended into the programme. The obvious rural progress in far-flung villages of the Himalayan state of Himachal Pradesh owes a lot to the personal and paternalistic influence of a former Chief Minister, Dr Y.S. Parmar. He had the gift of not merely securing official obedience but of leading a willing and interested administrative team. Even in the chaotic administrative system of Delhi, and despite the controversy over expenditure on functions such as the Asian Games, it was all too evident that, once a clear personal lead was given to the programme, a miracle of coordination and efficiency was suddenly achieved. At the other end of the spectrum is the depressing experience of travelling in a jeep-load of officials in such states as Bihar, Uttar Pradesh, Rajasthan and Madhya Pradesh. Throughout the day the entire chatter seems to revolve either around arrangements for the reception and feeding of some VIP whose forthcoming visit is incidentally the only reason for a tour into the interior, or about the latest gossip in the corridors of power regarding which minister or senior official is manoeuvring into a position of advantage.

There is another perhaps equally serious perception gap. It is doubtful whether the top leadership in Delhi has grasped the extent of degeneration of the delivery system in the field. There is a growing awareness of inefficiency, red tapism and procedural bottlenecks, but these are probably regarded as inevitable tribulations to be borne in common with those posed by bureaucracies the world over. The virtually total lack of commitment on the part of official agencies to the real aims of development programmes goes largely unperceived. Too often also, when an occasional idealistic local official naively tries to implement a declared government programme, he usually gets promptly transferred.

An area of fruitful study later in the eighties, if a genuinely impartial body of researchers can be found, will be the relative field performances in states governed by fairly stable regional leadership. Travellers from Andhra Pradesh have already noticed a marked improvement at least in punctuality and office efficiency under the new regime of N.T. Rama Rao, leader of the Telugu Desam regional party which swept the state polls in January 1983. The rise of such regional parties like those of N.T. Rama Rao may be the beginning of a new trend towards a delivery system more rooted in the value systems of local societies while at the same time refusing to be obsessed by obscurantist reversions to the past.

The same problem of values faces the judiciary and its system which is at present facing a crisis because there is a growing dichotomy between law and justice. This state of affairs has arisen largely because the system has failed to give redress to the masses at large. The main reasons being the prohibitive costs of litigation, the inaccessibility of the courts to the rural masses and the fact that the courts are concerned more with evidence than with truth. This means that any group of influential people who need witnesses to give evidence will always win against a downtrodden litigant who cannot muster more witnesses. In a recent Supreme Court judgment delivered on 18 September 1982 on a writ petition filed by the civil rights group, the People's Union for Democratic Rights (PUDR), to insure observance of labour laws, the then Supreme Court Justice (now Chief Justice of India) P.N. Bhagwati, who sees himself in the role of an activist, commented:

> The time has come when the courts must become the courts of the poor and struggling masses of this country. They must shed their character as upholders of the established order and the status quo. They must be sensitized to the need of doing justice to the large mass of people to whom justice has been denied by a cruel and heartless society for generations.[36]

Justice Bhagwati has introduced the concept of writ petitions for public interest litigation regarding Fundamental Rights of the Constitution in an attempt to make the legal system more accessible to the poor. Any letter written by a member of the public is to be treated as a writ petition. The main idea behind this innovation is to enable the courts to take speedy cognizance of the violation of fundamental rights affecting the poor. In particular violation of the Minimum Wages Act, the Untouchability Offences Act, and other acts of oppression by influential groups or by the state machinery. According to Bhagwati:

> Public interest litigation ... is essentially a cooperative or collaborative effort on the part of the petitioner, the State or public authority and the Court to secure observance of the constitution or legal rights, benefits and privileges conferred upon the weaker sections of the community and the reach of social justice to them.[37]

Many lawyers have criticized Justice Bhagwati's public interest litigation stating that it is adding to the staggering number of arrears. The Justice's liberal views are well known and he accused lawyers of adopting 'a totally perverse view smacking of an élitist and status-quoist approach.'[38] In his judgment on the PUDR writ petition it was stated:

> It is true that there are a large number of arrears pending in the courts. But that cannot be any reason for denying access of justice to the poor. No state has the right to tell its citizens that because a large number of cases of the rich and the well-to-do are pending in our courts, we will not help the poor to come to the courts.

Supreme Court Justice D.A. Desai believes that writ petitions are working on three fronts: with regard to the Minimum Wages Act, bonded labour and under-trial prisoners. However, Justice Bhagwati admits that implementation of court decisions is a problem and wants to form social action groups to help resolve this problem.

The poor are not only denied justice at the grass-roots level, the judiciary, time and again, at the state levels, has demonstrated its class/caste bias in judgments. This proclivity has in fact been pointed out by the CPI(M) leadership in West Bengal. D. Bandyopadhyaya, former West Bengal Land Reforms Commissioner, maintains the land reforms of this Marxist state government have been consistently thwarted by state High Court rulings in favour of the status quo. In cases involving killings and arson by upper or middle castes perpetrated against Harijans, the High Courts have often acquitted the culprits.

In May 1971 the Madras High Court acquitted on appeal eight landlords already sentenced to ten years' rigorous imprisonment for the burning to death of 42 Harijans, including 22 children, in January 1969 in Kilvenmani, East Tanjore district, Tamil Nadu. The class bias of the court was evident in its ruling: 'Most of them were rich men owning vast extents of land . . . it is difficult to believe that they themselves walked bodily to the scene and set fire to the houses.' In contrast, the murder of a single landlord's agent resulted in confirmation by the High Court of sentences against eight Harijans, one of them for life imprisonment and the others for various terms of rigorous imprisonment. A significant feature of the incident was the testimony by the American anthropologist Joan P. Menscher that she was told in the village well before the final outcome of the trial that none of the wealthy landowners would actually be sentenced but that the Harijans would be cruelly punished.[39]

Both Supreme Court Justices D.A. Desai and P.N. Bhagwati agree that literacy and education are the most important factors in changing people's age-old attitudes. Both agree that legislation alone cannot bring about social transformation. A perfect illustration of this problem is the Untouchability Offences Act, 1955, which makes it a criminal offence to bar Harijans from access to temples, wells, roads, teashops and restaurants. This law has proved to have a limited effectiveness when faced 'with the resistance of coherent social groups whose own internal sanctions are both stronger and more certain of application than those threatened by the law.'[40] Gobinda Mukhoty, Supreme Court advocate and head of the civil rights group, the People's Union for Democratic Rights (PUDR) comments: 'As long as the stranglehold on the thinking of the citizens is not removed, nothing will be achieved by the passing of laws like the Untouchability Offences Act. Such laws will remain ineffective as long as the master–slave attitude of our people is not changed.'[41]

Furthermore, not only have the High Courts often upheld the claims of the higher castes but there is an indication that at the lower levels of the legal system there is often active government support of their claims. Up to 1971 the High Courts, in appeals concerning temple entry and anti-disabilities legislation pertaining to the Untouchability Offences Act, 1955, had nine rulings against Untouchables' rights and two in their favour. One of the reasons for this reception by the High Courts is linked to the act itself which requires that a forbidden act be committed on the 'grounds of untouchability'.

In contrast and in keeping with the present trend the Supreme Court has been enlightened and liberal with regard to the question of Untouchability. In 1966 the Supreme Court suggested that a religious sect's apprehension about pollution of their temple by Untouchables 'is founded on superstition, ignorance and complete misunderstanding of the true teachings of the Hindu religion.'[42]

The divergence between the law and its practice persists on many levels and has even led to judges on the Supreme Court openly advocating the need for the judicial system to be overturned from within. For many laws are based on assumptions that are not valid. The British themselves came up against this problem many times. In the *Gazetteer of the Bombay Presidency* for Poona for 1885 it is clear, for example, that the British had assumed that a careful survey of land records and the introduction of the judicial system would in themselves provide justice and equality for all. In fact it intensified oppression and exploitation. After the British introduced laws to curb the powers of moneylenders, it was found that the laws were being twisted in favour of the money-lenders. The Limitation Act of 1859 had been passed with the object of helping the borrowers by making it impossible for the lender to bring forward old claims which the borrower could not disprove. Yet the exact opposite happened:

The lender wrested the provisions of the Act to his own advantage by forcing the debtor, under threat of proceedings, to pass a fresh bond for a sum equal to the amount of the original bond together with the interest and often a premium. His inability to pay on account of the uncertainty of the seasons made this practice of passing new bonds at the end of every two or three years press specially hard on the Poona husbandmen.[43]

It was when dealing with extreme acts like *sati*, or self-immolation by widows, that after much debating and after obtaining support from Hindu reform movements, the British decided to outlaw and suppress it. As late as the 1980s, after many decades during which it was assumed that the custom was completely dead, it revived in isolated cases in Rajasthan. One such case in 1982 even achieved advance publicity and was attended by a large village concourse including officials and was photographed for the press. The widow actually immolated herself on the funeral pyre amid scenes of ecstatic devotion from the crowd. Beyond some occasional press comment and a passing reference in Parliament, nothing seems to have been done about the incident and there was no public outcry against it even to the extent that there is regarding liquidation of extremists by the police in alleged armed encounters with 'Naxalites', or extreme Leftists.

Justice Desai comments: 'The Supreme Court should have gone into the matter. It should have issued notice to all the people who were responsible, who participated, who encouraged the widow to immolate herself, and sent them in for abetted murder.'[44] When asked why the Supreme Court failed to take action in the matter, Justice Desai retorted: 'Some Supreme Court judges want to go much further in cases of economic injustice, but in social cases we are not yet ready to do so.'[45]

In fact certain aspects of the Indian Penal Code show that many notions in the Hindu ethos completely escaped the British drafters. It is of interest to note, for example, that the British found the need to introduce an Indian Penal Code, given that English law is based entirely on precedents. It was as if Hindu thought so perplexed the Western mind that it was found necessary to define all offences in an attempt to come to grips with Hindu thought. It is also possible that, on account of the variety of customary laws prevailing in different parts of India, the British needed to bring some uniformity into the law and the only way of achieving this was to define all offences.

Many aspects of Hindu thought are in themselves completely alien to modern Western ethics. The concept of *samadhi*, an active term signifying a renunciation of one's existing life in order to achieve unity with the absolute, is a case in point. Technically, according to Western law, samadhi can be classified as suicide which the Indian Penal Code treats as a cognizable criminal offence. The Code makes no mention of the concept of samadhi, showing again how the legal system was in many ways alien to Hindu thought and concepts. On the other hand, certain modern concepts like murder had to be codified and, interestingly enough, suicide is considered an 'extreme sin' in Hindu customary law. When the Gandhian leader Acharya Vinoba Bhave decided to achieve samadhi in his ashram in 1982 and announced to the world that he would starve himself to death, his decision was based on the feeling that his time had come and that he had nothing more to contribute to the world. After his death the newspapers failed to make any comment that technically Vinoba Bhave had committed a crime under the Indian Penal Code. If such an inference had been drawn, a huge public outcry would have ensued. For even in pre-Independence days the British had never generally interfered in religious customs. This is probably why this contradiction has never been resolved under the Code. For even Justice Desai disagrees that Acharya Vinoba Bhave committed suicide: 'No system of law can be understood if divorced from its cultural heritage as ours is. We believe right from five thousand years of our history that a person may inflict torture on themselves to convert the other side to their point of view. We have a British legal system which is totally divorced from our heritage. It is a hybrid law.'[46]

Despite the divergence that exists between the legal system inherited from the British and Indian tradition, even Hindu revivalists like Dr Karan Singh remain committed to the Western legal system. However, Dr Karan Singh does favour introducing certain Hindu concepts into the legal and administrative system. Similarly Justice Desai has pointed out that the present generation of Supreme Court judges are not products of foreign training but are fully aware of their Indian heritage and thus able to bring about a synthesis in law. Dr Karan Singh also feels that, while there is no need to change the legal system, there should be a return to the traditional panchayat system and points out that the traditional way of settling a dispute by consensus has a certain legal backing. However, such people never spell out how settlement by consensus can coexist with the imported system based on rules of evidence and appeals to distant courts.

In some parts of India a system known as *Lok Adalat*, or 'People's Judiciary', has been reintroduced at the grass-roots level. Justice Desai claims that the system has created a revolution in Gujarat: 'Hundreds of thousands of cases have been resolved through this body which is based on participatory justice.'[47] Though somewhat limited in scope to compoundable offences and to social problems, it is undoubtedly a step in the right direction, especially if locally acceptable decisions can be reached to minimize litigation over land. Even Justice Bhagwati notes that: 'At lower levels, reform of the legal system is necessary because the adversary system of justice cannot work very effectively. Our system is such that a litigant has first to file an action in a court of law located sometimes 20 or 30 miles away. Then he has to pay for lawyers and for court fees. Witnesses have to be presented by both sides and the court has to decide the case on the basis of the evidence given. All this could be avoided if the judge goes to decide the case on the spot. Then the case can be decided in half an hour.'[8]

The same divergence between theory and practice can be observed in the economy. On paper, planning carried out by those in the top echelons of the Planning Commission is excellent, yet programmes never get off the ground because fundamental power structures and interests are ignored. It is not just a question of the dilution of efficiency but something much deeper. People talk about the need for political will to execute programmes. There can, however, be no political will under the present democratic structure of constitutional power which flows from a majority of votes. Under Indian conditions groups tend to vote or have their votes garnered by local political manipulators with the strength to understand and exploit local group interests. Therefore any programme, however well conceived in theory to improve the lot of the weaker sections, comes up against the basic stumbling block of the impossibility of antagonizing dominant local interests who deliver votes. As Srinivas has pointed out in his address to the Tenth International Congress of Anthropological and Ethnological Sciences entitled 'The Future of Indian Caste':

'In modern India cognate castes have to fuse together to achieve power. If fission characterized traditional caste, fusion characterizes modern caste. Cognate castes come together . . . as a matter of political convenience.'[49] There is, however, no sign as yet of the lowest caste groups fusing into a conglomeration strong enough to challenge local power structures.

This is the fundamental reason why none of the major programmes targeted at the 'weaker sections' have ever really got off the ground. Mrs Gandhi's earlier 'Garibi Hatao' ('Banish Poverty') degenerated into a mere slogan. The Janata 'Antyodaya' Programme made little impact. Innumerable schemes like the Integrated Rural Development Programme (IRDP) seeking to benefit the 600 poorest families in every development block has similarly foundered, as has the TRYSEM scheme to train rural youth for self-employment. The one programme that showed signs of reducing exploitation was the Food For Work Programme. This was deftly transformed into a rural employment programme, substituting cash payments for food and opening the doors to a revival of contract systems and wage exploitation.

The same dichotomy applies when dealing with the powerful and the rich on the one hand, and the poor and dispossessed on the other. The tax system is full of loopholes enabling the wealthy to evade the laws, while the system of indirect taxation means that the poor become the main contributors to the public exchequer. This is not to say that, from time to time, genuine attempts are not made to plug the loopholes in the tax laws in the declared aim of bringing about a more egalitarian society, but somehow new loopholes are always discovered and there is a lack of will in actually penalizing the rich and powerful.

Tax evasion, in fact, is one of the main sources for the black economy which some economists now estimate to be equivalent to 30 per cent of the national economy. Enforcement agencies and political parties can threaten selectively the wider circle of defaulters in order to generate further protection money for themselves. Indeed if the tax laws were implemented, it would be impossible for the wealthy in Delhi to build lavish mansions and even to run one or more family cars. In fact most of the opulent homes that have sprung up in Delhi's posh colonies like Vasant Vihar and Greater Kailash have been largely built from black money. For concealment of black income in the form of investment in real estate has become a common practice. A more detailed analysis of this can await discussion in a later chapter on corruption.

The main factor in assessing social change in India in the eighties is whether the gap between theory and practice is widening or narrowing. One may ask whether the framers of the Constitution had recognized that, if India was to break out of her past, high and sweeping declarations of rights had to be made, far in advance of social realities, so that some sort of change could come about. Similarly, one may ask whether today the country's thinkers and planners are moving ahead with the declared intent that the society will catch them up. Or is the gap too wide to breach? If this is the case, the growing ferment that India has been witnessing may continue to mount. As Muslim leader Shahabuddin has said regarding the gap between the precepts in the Constitution and their practice in actual life: 'The wider the gap, the greater the grievances, the narrower the gap, the lesser the grievances.'[50] Notwithstanding the hiatus between declared principles and policies and their application and implementation, Béteille thinks there has been a 'tremendous advance in legal equality but by no means a proportionate advance in economic equality. I think that's where we stand today.'[51] Taken together, these two comments add up to a revolution in rising expectations.

CHAPTER TWO

The countryside

India is largely an agrarian society where over half a billion people derive their livelihood from the land. A fair proportion of those living in country towns and classified as urban also maintain rural roots and even family landholdings in their original villages. In the context of a rural society land is the major form of wealth and accounts for two-thirds the value of all assets.[1] Therefore any government espousing a socialist ideology will be expected to effect a transformation in property relations in order to create a more equitable society.

It would be difficult to match elsewhere in the world the intellectual awareness of the need for land reforms or the pains-taking thought and studies undertaken by India's planners in the field of rural development. Yet perhaps in no other sphere of India's programmes since Independence has there been more dichotomy between theory and practice than in the realms of agrarian reform and rural development. It provides a striking example of 'maya': if not a total illusion, a manifestation of a totally different reality from the originally creative thought, legislation and planning that have been directed at the rural scene. Even many sociological studies seem to reflect the same dichotomy in thinking.

Officially every party's goal is the abolition of rural poverty. For all but three years since Independence the Congress has been in power at the Centre, yet every programme to uplift the poor has been nullified by vested interests. Every major political party is dominated by or is unable to antagonize these same rural interests. Secondly, the administration at the Centre, state and district levels is dominated by social groups whose interests and upbringing tally with those of the same vested interests. It seems unable to strike an equation with the really poor groups, the majority of whom belong to the lower castes. Thirdly, the Congress (I), although supported still, to a considerable extent, by the 'weaker sections' of society, is also increasingly dependent in its organizational structure on the traditionally dominant castes and classes. Therefore, unless the nature of the political system, itself enmeshed in the traditional social structure, succeeds in evolving some genuinely egalitarian change there is little hope of even the existing well-conceived programmes being translated into effective practice.

The reason for the dominance of upper peasant castes in politics resides in the fact that these strata became politicized in the early part of the twentieth century. They became directly linked to political parties which were formed at the district, provincial and even national levels. For example, from 1880 to 1930 a devolution of power took place in the Madras Presidency which meant that local factional leaders needed control over their own areas if they wanted to keep their positions. District-wise patron–client networks were thus organized throughout the Madras Presidency and these were to become the basis for later political parties. This further ensured the continuing dominance of the upper castes over the lower castes and the latter's inability to voice their own demands. The patron-client relationship was really an extention of the jajmani system into the political arena; an extension of caste-governed traditional relations whereby the lower castes followed the upper castes by virtue of their status and power.

In his study of a South Indian village Béteille maintains that the district dominance of castes can be demonstrated by making a study of the caste composition of candidates who have sought elections from different constituencies. He finds that in all the constituencies of North and South Arcot in Tamil Nadu power was held by dominant castes'.[2]

Even in constituencies which are reserved for Scheduled Caste groups, the Scheduled Caste candidates, whatever their party, cannot achieve election unless they obtain the backing of upper-caste groups who are otherwise dominant, whether numerically or by influence, in the power structure of the constituency.

The caste factor is directly related to rural poverty for wealth and power can largely be correlated with caste. In turn, in an agrarian society where land is the major asset and closely associated with power and status, the land pattern holdings are highly skewed in favour of the higher and 'dominant' castes.

Gunnar Myrdal in *Asian Drama* rightly points out that in South Asia land is the key to status and power. Conversely, since the material basis of inequalities is the inequitable distribution of land, it follows that a landless labourer or sharecropper at the bottom of the social ladder is deprived of all economic and social power.

In India the bulk of the labourers and sharecroppers come from Scheduled Caste, Scheduled Tribe and lower caste groups. It must be remembered that when one talks of such labourers at the bottom of the social scale, one is not, as in other countries, dealing with individuals who might with difficulty better their prospects at least in the next generation. In India there is the added burden of caste by birth and the concept enshrined in religious tradition that the fourth Estate of the Sudras and, still more, of the Scheduled Castes below them were only meant to serve the will of their master castes.

A close look at statistics shows that despite all the government development and welfare programmes specifically targeted for the uplift of the 'weaker sections', patterns of wealth remain highly skewed. While 22 per cent of rural families own no land and 47 per cent own less than 1 acre, 3 to 4 per cent appropriate all resources put at the disposal of farmers by the government.[3] A survey conducted by the Reserve Bank of India in rural areas revealed that the top 10 per cent of the population accounted for more than half the rural assets and the share of the bottom 10 per cent was only 2 per cent.[4] Furthermore, every year 5 million people are joining the 317 million people estimated to be living below the poverty line. It has been estimated that out of a total rural population of 510 million, as many as 374 million are absolutely poor because they do not even get Rs 70 a month per person.[5]

Since most of these people have insufficient land or no land at all, they are unable to benefit from various government schemes. The National Sample Survey estimate of the percentage of households below the poverty line increased in rural areas from 38.11 per cent in 1960/61 to 45.12 per cent in 1973/74 and close to 48 per cent in 1977/78. The Rural Labour Enquiry itself estimated that the total real earnings of rural workers (defined as those who get the majority of their income from rural wage labour and who constituted 31 per cent of the population in 1974/75) decreased by 10.18 per cent over the period 1964/65 to 1974/75.[6]

After Independence the national leaders had assumed that

institutional change could be brought about by concentrating on the village as a unit. In the early fifties the Community Development Programme (CDP) was launched. Its basic aim was to awaken the people to participate and determine their own development and to improve the economic lot of the stagnant and neglected countryside. The basic approach was to concentrate on all social and economic problems, including credit, health and basic education, and to create a modern infrastructure for agriculture.

The concept was based on community consciousness and it largely failed on this count. For the national leadership had idealized the old village system based on the village *panchayat*, or council, and has made the fundamental mistake of thinking it could be revived without splitting it by the inevitable extension of party rivalries. More important, the leadership wrongly assumed that the traditional panchayat was based on participatory democracy with all castes participating in decision-making. In actual fact decision-making was confined to the dominant castes of a village. For example, in a recent study of village Randam in eastern North Arcot, Tamil Nadu, the author notes that the new panchayat is dominated by the upper castes in the same way as the old panchayats had been.[7] This meant in effect that the flow of benefits would accrue to the dominant castes. A typical case in point is agriculture. It was these groups who benefited from the agricultural extension services and liberal aid being offered for the modernization of agriculture.

In fact the government's Fourth Evaluation Report in 1957 had noted that the basic weakness of the CDP was that it had created a wide disparity in the distribution of its benefits. Within blocks disparities had been created between accessible and remote villages; within villages between cultivators and other classes; and among cultivators the greater benefits had accrued to those bigger holdings which had the largest financial resources. Francine Frankel notes that by the early sixties the CDP had produced social effects contrary to those intended: 'By the early sixties disparities in income status and power between the larger landowners and the majority of subsistence cultivators and landless labourers began perceptibly to widen.'[8]

A similar fundamental misconception marked the approach to the cooperative movement. In the early 1950s both Nehru and his prominent economic adviser, Mahanalobis, were impressed by the Chinese success story in the early years after the Communist takeover. Emphasis was then given in India to the formation of cooperatives. It was soon realized that these must be multi-purpose providing inputs as well as marketing, rural credit and the minimum needs of consumer goods. Elaborate organizational structures were created. In very few cases, however, did they meet with the slightest success.

The fundamental aspect of social realities had been ignored. It was perhaps inevitable that in a traditionally hierarchical and even exploitative social system, combined with an electoral party system and an unclear economic philosophy which assumed the possibility of cooperation between a 'socialistic pattern' and free-enterprise capitalism, the weaker sections of society some-how did not benefit. In practice, of course, there was a total lack of will at all levels to take the hard options that would ensure success for cooperatives. The whole cooperative administration and its policies became subservient to the economic interests of domi-nant groups.

Later delegation of far-reaching powers to registrars of coop-eratives and the mushrooming of local staff merely drew them into the vortex of these dominant local vested interests. In the same way as the CDP, after its genuinely idealistic beginning, began to rely more and more on 'progressive farmers' (represent-ing again the dominant groups) to boost the physical achieve-ments of the programme in their quarterly progress reports, the cooperative movement also involved itself in conservative banking principles demanding all sorts of securities for credit and sub-serving the interests of the richer middle peasantry whose mem-bership also coincided with the dominant castes.

Occasional local success stories inspired by dedicated social workers or officials were merely exceptions which proved the rule. Again, whenever such a cooperative was heading for a success which might harm the economic interests of the domi-nant local élite, it was quickly killed by a variety of tactics ranging from the transfer of the official, the sowing of dissension, or a smear campaign against the social worker; or the subtle mobiliza-tion of all manner of rules and regulations to be applied strictly against the cooperative, while private economic enterprise con-tinued to evade them with impunity.

The clearest commentary of cooperative activities lies in early evaluation reports. The All-India Rural Credit Survey (1951/

52), carried out by the Reserve Bank of India, showed that the major part of loans from cooperatives went to the bigger agriculturalists. It estimated that half the borrowed funds were utilized for unproductive family expenditure and a little less than one-third was spent in farm improvement. The Reserve Bank of India Rural Credit Review Committee found in 1961/62 that only 2.6 per cent of cultivator households in the poorest asset groups had reported any cooperative borrowing, while the proportion rose to 19 per cent for the highest asset group.

Like the rest of India's institutions the Community Development and Cooperative Programmes thus underwent a quiet but radical shift, and even reversal in emphasis, from the original objectives envisaged after Independence. From the prime aim of achieving people's participation, leading to genuine people's control over planning, these programmes shifted completely to the achieval of physical targets predetermined from the top of the planning hierarchy. The stage was thus set for the much publicized Green Revolution to make India self-sufficient in food.

This overriding target coincided with a significant structural change in the earlier Community Development machinery at block and district levels. This had envisaged all local development programmes to be coordinated and supervised by the Block Development Officer (BDO), or, at district level, by the Collector. This was always resisted by the hierarchical structure of the technical departments as their own vested interests were linked with those of the minister in charge of the department concerned. In practice and, sometimes even by administrative directives, the local extension workers and their programmes within the block were restored to the departmental hierarchy.

Such government departmental institutions achieved greater importance as funds for financing individual investments in land improvement increased. Between 1966 and 1969 minor irrigation loans to individual cultivators amounted to Rs 2.99 billion as against Rs 1 billion during the entire five years of the earlier Third Plan. The strengthening of the panchayat system also suffered comparatively in allocations and attention as all efforts were concentrated on the Green Revolution. This may be said to have been launched in the mid-sixties when India suffered vagaries of the weather, price spirals and food shortages leading to invocation of the 'scarcity manuals', a euphemism for the old British Famine Code. Starvation deaths were reported in several states along with food riots in West Bengal and Kerala.

The compulsion of such events determined the main thrust of the Green Revolution strategy which was to achieve the quickest increase in food production from the areas and sections of farmers who could deliver the goods most effectively. Francine Frankel points out that the small peasant farmers and landless labourers were thus the main losers because the earlier emphasis on people's participation and panchayat raj might eventually have brought them into the political and economic mainstream through their involvement in rural development.

With its exclusive emphasis on food production rather than social goals success depended on suitable incentives to selected farmers in selected regions to adopt a new technology. Price policies were modified. Emphasis on government subsidies for food grains to the poor was shifted to remunerative incentive prices for farmers to whom government often supplied inputs like fertilizers at subsidized rates. The net result was economic deterioration for the poor as inflation in food costs also raised consumer prices. Finally, the large outlays required for the Green Revolution strategy and its effective supervision led government to concentrate its energy on a few immediately promising areas like the Punjab, Haryana and western Uttar Pradesh. This meant proportionately lesser shares to remoter more difficult and more needy districts.

The expectation of sustained agricultural transformation was realized only in the wheat-growing regions which accounted for approximately 13 per cent of acreage and output of food grains. Seven states – Bihar, Gujarat, Haryana, Madhya Pradesh, Andhra Pradesh, Rajasthan and Uttar Pradesh – constituting 88 per cent of the area under wheat and 95 per cent of the irrigated area contributed 93 per cent of production. Punjab, Haryana and western Uttar Pradesh alone accounted for 69 per cent of the irrigated area.[9] The success of the programme can be gauged from the fact that between 1966 and 1969 total output increased two-thirds over 1964/65 levels.

Wheat was the simplest crop to introduce because the areas of Punjab, haryana and western Uttar Pradesh had initial advantages and a fairly equitable pattern of landholdings. Wheat itself is a less risky crop in terms of its susceptibility to disease relative to the initial strains of rice that were introduced in eastern India. The High Yielding Varieties (HYV) made little progress in the rice-growing areas for it was found that local varieties were better adapted to the monsoon pattern. Rice is India's largest foodgrain crop accounting for approximately 31 per cent of the total area under foodgrains and over 40 per cent of the country's total output.

Another constraint in the eastern paddy-growing regions was the more unequal distribution in landholdings which were highly skewed with a small percentage of large holdings and a high number of small holdings. This meant government credit would be less accessible to a larger number of people.

A certain dynamisim also gets built into a situation such as prevails in the eastern belt. In this region the existence of larger holdings means that the advantages of tenanting out land are much greater than the gains accruing to the landlord who cultivates land through the latest technology. For under existing tenurial arrangements, farmers are able to lease out scattered plots to sharecroppers who are willing to pay 60 or 70 per cent of the gross product as rent.

Except in areas where consolidation had taken place – Punjab, Haryana and western Uttar Pradesh – all classes of landowners, from large to marginal holders, found it uneconomic to invest in modern agricultural techniques. For great inequalities in landholdings, such as those that prevail in the rice-growing belt of Andhra Pradesh and Tamil Nadu, acted as important constraints on two levels.

Firstly, they acted as a constraint in terms of the smaller farmer adopting the technology because his access to inputs, credits and all the factors that could give him the ability to invest in the new technology would be much more limited.

Secondly, the relative profitability regarding the production of land relative to other sources of incomes is another constraint. A large farmer may be making more profit by leasing out his land and by moneylending. Therefore the traditional landlord may have diverse sources of income of which cultivation will be only one aspect. This would affect the actual motivation of the larger farmer to invest in the new technology.

In the Punjab itself, although there are a large number of landless, the relatively greater equal distribution of landholdings meant that institutional credit has been accessible to a wider range of farmers. Furthermore, in the case of Haryana, methods for the more equitable distribution of irrigation waters have been developed over a period of several decades for farmers with land along a canal. This contrasts with South India or regions where canals were recently introduced and where the farmers situated at the tail end lose out while those at the head end benefit disproportionately.

Thus the structural limitations of the land distribution and land tenure system limited the area in which the Green Revolution could be launched since a ten-acre plot was considered the minimum size for the application of the technology according to economies of scale.

The new technology made capital accumulation in land profitable. This led to increased inequalities in agriculture because capital accumulation is a cumulative process. Large landholders began to increase their farm size by acquiring more land. This was especially the case in view of the scale economies associated with mechanization. According to T.J. Byres, as far as assets other than land are concerned, between the mid-sixties and early seventies, there was a marked shift in distribution in favour of large holdings while the difference between the poor and middle peasants probably declined.[10]

The vast differences between the new technology increased the inequalities between the irrigated and non-irrigated areas. In a well-known study by V.M. Dandekar and Nilakantha Rath the economists in fact argued that: 'the new inequalities thus created are more glaring than the previous ones stemming entirely from the unequal distribution of landholdings.'[11] For example, Harriss found that the rates of profit in HYV for the big farmers in Randam village, North Arcot, were twice those of the older varieties. He notes, however, that 'The rate of profit in paddy output has not increased very much by the introdution of HYVs on smaller farms.'[12] He concludes that the HYVs have increased disparities between households in Randam.

At the outset the Green Revolution increased the need for labour because there were two crops a year and fertilizers and pesticides had to be spread. But as more operations became mechanized, labour became displaced and the bargaining power of unskilled labour was reduced. Furthermore, the management and supervision of hired labour had acted as a constraint on the expansion of holdings; mechanization was an important factor in allowing farmers to resume their land for personal cultivation, thus leading to the eviction of tenants. It therefore allowed the farmer to bring in much greater portions of land under cultivation.

This was not the case everywhere. It would appear that conditions varied tremendously in different parts of the country. In Tamil Nadu Harriss found that in eastern North Arcot the larger farmer who had made all possible modern investments in land by the mid-seventies was not in a position to expand his holding as the market for land was so limited. Harriss's findings seem to accord with those of the economist Utsa Patnaik who in 1976 had noted that productivity of the HYV would taper off and even decline after a time.

As regards North India a sample study made of Haryana in 1976 found that many of the former tenants who lost land had been transformed into landless agricultural labourers. Sheilla Bhalla, an economist at Jawaharlal Nehru University, found that the agricultural labour force had grown two and a half times in the decade since the onset of the Green Revolution. Although the new technology had benefited this labour force because the shift in demand from casual to permanent labour meant a greater security in employment, she found that no collective bargaining had developed among them.[13]

Bina Agarwal, Reader of Economics at the Institute of Economic Growth, New Delhi, also believes there is consistent evidence to show that the proportion of the agricultural labour force in Green Revolution areas has increased. In the case of Punjab which she has studied, she does not believe this is due only to the entry of migrant labour, largely from Rajasthan, eastern Uttar Pradesh and Bihar, into the Punjab and Haryana. Rather her own studies have led her to conclude that several factors are responsible for this. Firstly, previous tenants have been thrown off the land. Secondly, there has been a decline in the ability of the artisan to survive using his traditional skills because of competition from factories. This means this group has been moving into the agricultural labour force. Thirdly, there has been a rise in population.

A study of mechanization in the Punjab[14] by Bina Agarwal shows that different levels of mechanization have varied impacts on employment. The study looks at the problem of employment in terms of the use of the machine by operations. The author found that other studies which had shown a negative or positive increase in employment had simply compared farms with and without tractors without allowing for other differences. They did not allow for the fact that there might be tubewells on the tractor farms which might be neutralizing the labour displacement effect of tractors. Nor did the previous studies allow for the fact that tractors may not be used for all operations. If the tractor was used for all operations, it was found that the labour displacement was much greater; whereas it was found to be much less if tractors were used only for ploughing, as was the case in the early seventies. Ploughing generally tends to be done by either family or permanent labour rather than by hired labour, whether the operation is carried out by tractors or bullocks. Bina Agarwal found that, although the labour time put in by families was reduced, no one was thrown off the land since the land was family-owned.

In North Arcot, Tamil Nadu, Harriss found that the replacement of traditional water lifts by pumpsets had reduced the number of attached labourers.[15] He cites another study for Chingleput district, Tamil Nadu, showing the labour-displacing effects of the introduction of pumpsets. In this area irrigation by hand for paddy cultivation had been required before these were introduced. In 1973 the study found that many landlords, who used to lease out land to Harijans who supplied the labour for irrigation, had begun using electric pumpsets. The labourers who had previously been sharing the yield on a fifty/fifty basis now found themselves unemployed.[16]

Similarly in Kerala the landless and marginal farmers have lost many days of work because of the introduction of tractors. The use of motorized vehicles in the same state has led to loss of employment for head-load workers.[17] Even the *World Development Report, 1982* reports that: 'Where neither agriculture nor other parts of the economy are growing rapidly, the effects of premature mechanization can be disastrous for those who lose their jobs.'[18]

These findings seem to accord with an all-India pattern. According to the Rural Labour Enquiry Reports agricultural labourers have been increasing in numbers between 1964/65 and 1974/75. While the number of rural households increased by 16.6 per cent, agricultural-labour households increased by over 35 per cent, indicating that marginal peasants are losing land. According to the All-India Debt and Investment Survey, the poorest 30 per cent of the rural population accounted for barely 2.5 per cent of the asset holdings in 1961 and this was reduced further in 1971.

Apart from the increase in the agricultural labour force Dandekar and Rath had argued as early as 1971 that the new technology would reduce the employment potential in agriculture:

> Underemployment of farm labour will be reduced and wages employment will be rationalised and better paid but a large number of landless workers will be thrown out of agriculture. The fact which is concealed in 1971 will become evident, namely that there is not enough room in agriculture for so many people.[19]

Government studies and economists of different ideological schools present conflicting views of the impact of the Green Revolution on wages. According to the Rural Labour Enquiry Reports between 1964/65 and 1974/75, the rise in wages has not kept up with inflation. In real terms in Tamil Nadu, Andhra Pradesh and West Bengal there has been a decline in daily wage earnings. According to the government's Directorate of Economics and Statistics regarding farm wages for 1970/71 to 1973/74, when the Green Revolution was supposed to be making a major impact, in western Uttar Pradesh real wages declined by 18 per cent. A sociological study of the impact of the Green Revolution has shown that, whereas the landowner's income per unit of land increased between 50 and 100 per cent, the income of labour increased between 25 and 30 per cent.[20] Studies relating to the effects of the Green Revolution on the economic conditions of agricultural labour show that the share of labour in increased output due to the new technology was not more than 5 to 15 per cent. National Sample Surveys indicate that there has been a deterioration in the nutrition situation in recent years which supports studies showing the decline in real wages.

On the other hand, a World Bank monograph claims that real wages have risen significantly in the Green Revolution areas while elsewhere where per capita agricultural output has remained stagnant real wages have also remained constant.[21] The monograph claims that not only have the smaller farmers benefited directly as a result of the new technology but that rural labourers have also benefited indirectly through an increase in the demand for labour. According to the monograph this is attested to by the significant increase in real wages in areas like the Punjab, Haryana and western Uttar Pradesh in spite of the coniderable amount of mechanization and in-migration.

Another study by T.J. Byres claims that in many years the rise in money wages lagged behind price changes:

> leading to reduced real wage rates for most operations between 1965 and 1968 and again in 1974, 1975 and 1977 and that, although male labourers have gained the increase in the real value of their wages, it is much smaller than the growth rate of output alone would suggest.[22]

In Tamil Nadu, which is a more traditional society and where the Green Revolution has made partial headway, Harriss has noted that wages in 1973/74 were as little as Rs 2.50 for male labourers ploughing with their own team, while for the more arduous tasks of transplanting, performed by women, the wage rate was Rs 1 a day. The author concludes that wages do not operate according to supply and demand but are rather linked to the prices of foodgrains and 'represent in effect subsistence wages.'[23]

According to a study by B.N. Chinnapa on paddy incomes it was found that although the agricultural labourers benefited from the introduction of HYVs in North Arcot nonetheless: 'The 33 per cent increase in wages earned from HYV cultivation by agricultural labourers compares poorly with the nearly 76 per cent increase in the national income earned by cultivators.'[24]

In fact the scope for hired employment in agriculture is very limited owing to the growing pressure of population on land, fragmentation of holdings and employment of family labour. The number of agricultural labourers increased from 28 million in 1951 to 48 million in 1971 and finally to 55 million in 1981 and today comprise 30 per cent of the total agricultural workforce. Marginal households with holdings under 1 hectare account for another one-third of rural households. The latter also frequently work as agricultural labourers to supplement their meagre earnings from the land.

The bulk of the agricultural labour force relies on casual employment and is often migratory in character. The majority are comprised of lower-caste groups, Scheduled Castes and

Scheduled Tribes. Most micro-level studies have in fact found that caste, to a great extent, correlates with class in the sense that the landholding patterns in most villages show the majority of land in the hands of dominant castes. Studies from all over the country confirm this. For example, in Kerala anthropologist Joan Menscher notes that few if any households belonging to Harijans own more than 10 to 20 cents (100 cents: 1 acre) around their households while the majority own 5 cents or less.[25] Harriss notes that in Randam village, North Arcot, Tamil Nadu, the dominant caste households own 61.7 per cent of the land. Out of 85 Harijan households, 63 are landless, while the rest own 6.1 per cent of the land. P.S. Krishnan, former Joint Secretary for Scheduled Castes and Scheduled Tribes, Home Ministry, points out that most Harijans are landless agricultural labourers. A few may be marginal and small landowners, but they are rarely to be found in any larger category according to his own prolonged studies.

Approximately 85 per cent of the agricultural labourers in the country are employed as casual labourers. This means they only obtain employment for six months of the year or less, with the result that unemployment and underemployment are assuming alarming proportions. The Social Work Research Centre (SWRC), a voluntary organization based in the middle of the Rajasthan desert at Tilonia, has found that employment is the poor villagers' first priority. SWRC director, Bunker Roy, says: 'They are only employed for 3 months at harvest time. For six months they are underemployed. For the other three months they are unemployed. While some get two crops on their land, others only obtain one crop a year from their holdings.'[26]

The bulk of the sharecroppers and agricultural labourers belong to the lower castes, Scheduled Castes and Scheduled Tribes. For them life is a constant struggle. Param Lal is a gardener, a low caste, from Kuswahai village. Chhatarpur district, Madhya Pradesh. He became landless a few years back when he lost his 3 bighas of land to the moneylender over a Rs 1,000 loan. In the summer of 1982 he was working as a road labourer far from his native place in the Himalayan village of Dharamsala. Kamlata is an oil presser, a low caste, from Bahuri village in the same district. He is landless and rarely has the opportunity to return to his village to visit relatives as he can only find casual work outside. In any case he finds his village too oppressive: 'The landlords beat us up if we do not work properly.'

Bajwhali Sooran Lodhi, a low-caste landless labourer from Etawah district, Uttar Pradesh, now has a semi-permanent job working as a labourer on a reclamation project in the Chambal ravines in his own district. Before he found this job he had no security: 'Some days we went hungry. Some days we had only one meal. Other days were alright.'

A Home Ministry study dated February 1982 on rural conditions in Tamil Nadu points out that rural inequalities in the country as a whole are increasing.[27] According to the study rural inequality is at its worst in Tamil Nadu. The percentage of agricultural labourers to the total agricultural workforce in the state is one of the highest in India. According to the 1971 census 40 per cent of the total male population working in agriculture were landless. Similarly in Bihar in 1976 the percentage of agricultural labourers to the total agricultural workforce was 42.26 per cent.[28] Joan Menscher notes with reference to Tamil Nadu that the increase in the landless labour force can in part be attributed to the land reform legislation: 'It is certain that the ranks of the landless increased after 1951, as more and more landlords decided it was not safe to give land to the tenants.'[29]

The Home Ministry study notes with reference to the whole country that there are growing pressures on small farmers to leave their lands to become landless agricultural labourers, a decline in the real wages of agricultural labourers and a tendency for mass poverty to continue and increase. Despite the introduction of various laws, the bargaining position of agricultural workers has not improved. This is reflected in the fact that, except in Bihar, Kerala, Punjab and Uttar Pradesh, where some marginal improvements were recorded by the National Commission on Agriculture, real wage rates were lower in 1980/81 than in 1960/61. If money wage rates are properly deflated it can be shown that the real incomes of agricultural workers were actually lower in 1963/64 compared to 1950/51. The 27th Round of the National Sample Survey, which covered the period October 1972 to September 1973, showed that the annual household income of agricultural workers in different states declined between 1963/64 and 1970/71.

In Andhra Pradesh, for example, in the early seventies, which was marked by a steep rise in prices, there was a fall in real wages in relation to the consumer price index for agricultural labourers, although real wages began to rise in 1974/75.[30] The long-term trend in real wages in the state is one of stagflation despite the fact that there has been a considerable increase in agricultural production over the period.

There are important regional variations in the actual position of agricultural labourers. Some areas have a larger percentage of permanent labourers; in others agricultural labourers work mostly on a casual basis. In some areas wages are paid in kind; in others wages are almost always in cash. The position of permanent labourers varies greatly from that of being almost hereditary family servants bound by debt from generation to generation or for a number of years, to that of being relatively free contractual labourers. The latter are in a more privileged position compared to daily labourers because they have security of employment. An element of compulsion is, however, very high in many forms of contract labour, especially where the contractor has links with police, government officials and local landowners.

A classic case was that of an old man, Kairia, of village Ailha, in Manikpur subdivision of Banda district, Uttar Pradesh. In his youth his father was unable to repay a loan of Rs 20. The family, through extortionate manipulation of alleged interest rates, became bonded labour and the old man had been freed only a year earlier in 1979. The old man belonged to the Kol community which used to be a virile tribe. In Uttar Pradesh they are now notified as a Scheduled Caste and have been reduced to total subservience in the local village economy dominated by the Thakur landlords.

The decline of the traditional village economy, or *jajmani* patron–client system, based on personal ties, has introduced an element of insecurity into the lives of the landless labourers and sharecroppers. Under the old system every member of the village was guaranteed a share of the harvest from the landlord's field for services performed during the year, and during festivals and marriages labourers received gifts of food from their masters. The increasing monetization of the economy means that the landlord no longer feels any obligation to help his workers in times of distress or illness.

In a study of Kamarpur village, Jalpaiguri district, West Bengal, in the fifties, the jajmani system meant that landlords gave loans, agricultural implements, seeds, ploughs and pairs of bullocks to their labourers. Sometimes the landlords provided them with a small plot of homestead land, 'offering offspring of cows and goats to tenants on a sharing basis.'[31] In Nagar Khas village in Basti district, eastern Uttar Pradesh, one of the poorest and most backward areas of the country, the labourers recall that the jajmani system used to guarantee them more security. They claimed that in the old days they were guaranteed a fixed share of the produce, while under the new system the landlords never paid them the statutory minimum wages.[32] Lannoy warns that: 'Unless greater attention is paid to the landless agricultural labour force, enhanced economic activity in the agrarian sector cannot be effective in bringing about a unified institutional system in the rural areas.'[33]

In recent years there have been growing reports of clashes, especially in Bihar and Uttar Pradesh, between agricultural labourers and landowners over payment of prescribed minimum wages and other land-related issues. These clashes are closely interrelated with the caste factor. The violence has followed a consistent pattern. Upper and dominant castes in a village regard any claims by agricultural labourers, the bulk of whom are Scheduled Castes, as an outright violation of caste rules. In the traditional system, the lot of the lowest castes is to serve the "Twice-Born" castes. The increasing level of caste violence in the countryside, which will be discussed in the chapter on the Scheduled Castes, is evidence of a major social change.

As long as the Harijans continued to fulfil their traditional tasks as menials in the village economy, the dominant castes had no reason to resort to violence 'to put them in their place'. Increasing reports of violent confrontation from Bihar shows that some sort of awakening is taking place. The main reason for the growing consciousness is rooted in the principles of equality embodied in the Constitution which politicians never fail to espouse during election periods. Secondly, the ideology of every political party is also committed to a social order in which equal rights and opportunities are in principle guaranteed to all.

Jagjivan Ram, the foremost Harijan politician in the country who served as Agricultural Minister during the Emergency and as Defence Minister under the Janata regime, comments: 'The social structure in India has not changed but the weaker sections, that is the Scheduled Castes and Scheduled Tribes, have started fighting the dominant castes and raising their voice against the payment of low wages. The fight is still unequal as the stronger castes have much better resources at their disposal.'[34]

The dependence of the agricultural labourer on the landlord makes his position especially precarious. Moreover, the Harijans are always in a minority in a village and all the economic resources are controlled by the caste Hindus. In instances where agricultural labourers have gone on strike to demand higher wages, economic circumstances have frequently compelled them to succumb to pressure. To quote Jagjivan Ram again: 'If the Harijan asserts himself, his cattle will be stopped from going to the field for grazing, he will be stopped from taking grass from the field, he will be prevented from taking fuel and other things from the common village lands and ultimately no one will engage him on wages. That is the whole lot of the Scheduled Castes.'[35]

The only way an agricultural labourer can win his demands for better wages is by becoming economically independent of the landlord. Recent press reports of May 1983 regarding increasing clashes in parts of Bihar seem to indicate that government schemes for the Scheduled Castes are actually having some effect. In May 1983 a battle was going on between landlords and agricultural labourers supported by Naxalites, an extremist pro-Maoist organization (see pp. 81–2). The *Indian Express* of 25 May 1983 reports that: 'The landless are continuing their fight only because some of them have found alternative means of livelihood in the rearing of goats, pigs and poultry.'

Although the report does not say where the animals came from, the only possible source would be special government schemes for the 'weaker sections' which will be discussed below.

The problem of exploitation applies to all categories of rural labour, especially with regard to payment of Minimum Wages. While the Minimum Wages Acts are flagrantly violated in most parts of India, sharecroppers and labourers have succeeded in gaining some modest improvement in wages in some cases. The importance of the voluntary organization in the struggle for their rights should not be underestimated for it can provide them with leadership and self-confidence.

In a state like Bihar, where caste oppression is at its worst, many voluntary organizations of all ideological orientations from Gandhians to extreme Leftists have sprung up in the last two decades and some are beginning to have an impact. For example, in May 1980 the Jan Kalyan Kendra (Organization for the People's Awakening) working in Bhojpur, Bihar, incited the agricultural labourers in Patarihan village to go on strike for legal prescribed minimum wages. They refused to plough the fields until their demands were met. The organization persuaded the labourers to hold out even though famine broke out in July. The agricultural labourers were forced to resort for loans to the landlords who refused to render them assistance. The voluntary organization had succeeded in instilling some sense of unity among the lower castes as the latter, including the barber and washermen, joined in the boycott of the landlords.[36] In this case the report does not say whether the JKK was successful. But demonstrations of resistance by the lower castes are significant because such incidents were unheard of 20 years ago.

The Social Work Research Centre at Tilonia, Rajasthan, has also succeeded in gaining higher wages for Harijan female road-construction labourers. After attending a number of social education classes a new sense of confidence had been instilled into them and in August 1980 they finally went on strike in Harmara village, Silora block, to demand that road contractors pay them Rs 7, the statutory minimum wage for Rajasthan, instead of Rs 4.

In some cases the landlords raise wages voluntarily if they realize that it is in their better interest to do so. In Chapta village, Ajitmal block, Etawah district, Uttar Pradesh, most of the agricultural labourers in the village are low castes and Harijans. The daily wage has now been raised from Rs 5 to Rs 6 by some landlords. This is a modest improvement although it is not equal to the statutory minimum wage of Rs 8 for the state. However, even in Marxist-ruled West Bengal, labourers in Midnapore district reported in December 1981 that they only received Rs 4, half the statutory minimum wage of the state. Even the Labour Department has been unable to implement legal wages. The power structure in villages has ensured in many cases that agricultural labourers are maintained at their subsistence level. D. Bandyopadhyaya, former West Bengal Land Reforms Commissioner, believes that wages set by each state should be regarded as normative: 'It legitimizes the movement to reach the norm.'[37] But Supreme Court Justice Desai disagrees: 'The Minimum Wages legislation binds everyone whether it is the state, a private employer or an individual. After all what is the concept of the minimum wages? That this is just the minimum enough to keep body and soul together.'[38]

One of the most pernicious aspects of traditional peasant

societies is the stranglehold of the money-lender on the peasantry. Most peasant households require consumption loans during the lean seasons when money-lenders offer inferior-quality paddy at higher rates of interest. Different types of money-lending practices prevail in the countryside. Usufractory mortgage is generally more remunerative since to obtain loans the borrower has to pawn land documents, bicycles, ornaments and other personal household effects. During the mortgage period the land is cultivated by the borrower but the money-lender takes the produce from the land as interest. Since it is virtually impossible for the borrower to repay the original amount on account of the high interest rates, in many cases the money-lender eventually takes over the land.

Param Lal, is a gardener, a low caste, from Harua village, Chhatarpur district, Madhya Pradesh. Some years ago he lost 3 bighas of land to a landlord-money-lender over a Rs 1,000 loan as he was unable to return the amount over a five-year period. This is not surprising as according to Param Lal: 'If we borrow Rs 100 we have to pay back Rs 10 interest a month. Sometimes we have to pay Rs 1 a day as interest. The money-lenders lynch us.'

Rates charged by money-lenders are inordinately high. According to Bunker Roy, director of SWRC at Tilonia, money-lenders in the area charge Rs 3 interest on Rs 7 for a temporary consumption loan. Two- to ten-per-cent interest per month, compounded every six months, is charged on a short-term, or *khatta*, loan. The interest on long-term loans where land is mortgaged or items are pawned is less. Pani, a Harijan from Falodia village, Silora block, Ajmer district, Rajasthan, admits that she often borrows consumption loans from the money-lender, even though she has 10 bighas of land. Even upper castes have recourse to the money-lender. Sajjan Singh, a Thakur landowner from Chapta village, Etawah district, Uttar Pradesh, says that in bad times he pawns his wife's jewellery against a loan.

The SWRC at Tilonia is trying to stop money-lending by having discussion groups on social customs and superstitions. According to SWRC activist, Khem Raj: 'We are trying to stop villagers from attending traditional death ceremonies so that they will not go to the money-lenders for the huge outlays required.'

Money-lending is rampant in tribal areas. The Tribal Development Commissioner, Udaipur, South Rajasthan, says: 'There are people in this region whose entire land is mortgaged to the money-lender because they have no money to repay loans. Seventy to eighty per cent of the land mortgaged to the money-lenders is never recovered.' A village survey of Shinghu on the Delhi-Punjab border about 15 miles north of the Indian capital showed that out of a total indebtedness in the village of Rs 164,525, 87 per cent had been taken from private money-lenders.[39] Another survey of Bhangarh, Rajgarh Tehsil, Ajmer district, Rajasthan, noted that the possible reason for the high amount of indebtedness 'is the full control exercised in the villagers' lives by the money-lenders . . . The simple villagers are nearly always cornered by their exploiters and find no way out of their predicament.'[40]

In fact the All India Rural Debt and Investment Survey of 1961/62 estimated that in 1951/52, 90.9 per cent of all borrowing in the countryside came from money-lenders while only 0.9 per cent came from commercial banks. In 1961/62 the figure had decreased to 67.4 per cent, while the share of cooperatives had gone up considerably from 3.1 per cent in 1951/2 to 15.5 per cent in 1961/62. By 1973/74 the All India Rural Credit Review Committee estimated that institutional agencies provided 38.4 per cent of the total rural credit. Most of the institutional credit benefits the wealthier class of peasants who have land to give as security. Money-lenders continue to be the main source of borrowing for the poorer sections of the peasantry and among the tribes. The All India Rural Debt and Investment Survey conducted by the Reserve Bank of India shows that 43 per cent of rural households were in debt at the end of June 1971 and the total debt stood at Rs 39.21 billion. According to the Rural Labour Enquiry conducted in 1974/75, 66 per cent of all agricultural labourers were indebted and of these 20 per cent were indebted to their employers. No other national surveys have been conducted on this subject since then.

Apart from commercial banks, credit cooperatives are supposed to form another major source of borrowing. In 1976 they had 40 million member households, but only 15 million were actually borrowing from them. Seven of India's poorest states with 58 per cent of the agricultural population received only 30 per cent of all credit. According to *The Economist*, London, 'The people who suffer most are the small farmers who have so far been lent very little by anyone except traditional money-lenders.'[41]

One of the consequences of traditional money-lending practices is the persistence of bonded labour, despite the fact that the practice was legally abolished by Article 23 of the Constitution in 1975. The most crucial aspect of the system is that the moneylender is not interested in recovering the capital as bonded labour provides him with a cheap source of labour and control over land. Numerous press reports have also highlighted the existence of bonded labour amongst migratory labour, where exploitation of workers is notorious. The Gandhi Peace Foundation, New Delhi, has claimed that there are as many as five million bonded labourers in the country. Until there is a more equitable distribution of land and assets, bonded labour, in its many forms, is bound to continue.

One may well ask whether in fact bonded labour has increased in the post-Independence years. Earlier indebtedness to some extent followed from the jajmani system. The landlord would advance seeds and loans to his labourers because he felt some form of moral responsibility towards them. Today, with the growth of the cash economy, bonded labour in its modern form consists of the deliberate suppression of groups to obtain cheap labour as a result of indebtedness. The conclusion of a study by N.N. Vyas of the Tribal Research Institute, Udaipur, entitled *Bondage and Exploitation in Tribal India*, supports this view. While it was found that all castes were indebted to the same extent, one middle caste of drumbeaters, *dhelis*, were protected from indebtedness because they still maintained a patron–client relationship with their landlord.[42]

The Supreme Court of India is now trying to take judicial cognizance of any reported bonded labour. Justice P.N. Bhagwati points out that such court action can have only limited value and that the real need is to change old patterns of thinking. To quote him from a personal interview: 'We must educate our people in the socio-economic realities of the country by exposing the drawbacks and deficiencies of our system. We are trying to do this by our judgments and speeches.'[43]

The government is fully conscious of the need to uplift the countryside. Mrs Gandhi, as Prime Minister, was the first leader to launch a national campaign for the abolition of poverty in the countryside in the early seventies. This tends now to be designated as a mere populist slogan. However, it was in the early seventies when the slogan 'Garibi Hatao' ('Banish Poverty') was first launched that programmes for the underprivileged were formulated. Since then there have been an increasing number of programmes to alleviate poverty and huge sums of money have been pumped into the countryside.

In assessing the impact of these programmes, which will be discussed below, one comes up against the dichotomy in the Indian mind. In this case there is a genuine schizophrenia on the part of the people at the top planning levels. Many of them have either experienced or have a deep understanding of practical conditions in the countryside. They evolve a sophisticated conceptual framework to tackle the problem. They even succeed in issuing the most comprehensive guidelines to take care of lacunae in implementation and to insist that the benefits reach the poorest. This very insistence presupposes their knowledge of the realities of the power structure in the countryside. The result is that one side of their personality is genuinely striving towards ideal programmes to improve the lot of the underprivileged. The other side, however, not only recognizes the reality of local power structures but, with the responsibility of avoiding administrative turmoil, is unable, or unwilling, to disturb this local structure too deeply.

It is only in rare cases where team work between political leadership and administrative implementation emerges that meaningful programmes of change are carried through. Such instances are becoming rarer due to the politicization of almost every activity and the overriding impulse of the leadership to cover themselves against criticism. Such criticism from the entrenched vested interests can and does result in a politician being toppled from power or an administrator being summarily transferred or entangled in proceedings against him. In very rare cases, usually after discontent has erupted into some form of violent confrontation, an intelligent and sensitive local administration can manipulate various forces in order to achieve some measure of redress for the rural poor.

The anthropologist Christoph von Fürer-Haimendorf has drawn attention to this factor in the handling of the aftermath of extreme Leftist Naxalite activity in the Srikakulam district of Andhra Pradesh in the late sixties.

The Naxalites are extreme Left-wing groups which were particularly active in the Naxalbari area of West Bengal in the late sixties. They have now revived in small rural pockets, especially in

Bihar, despite often ruthless attempts by the government to liquidate them. The basic Naxalite theory is that any compromise with the electoral system is fatal to a revolutionary movement. Some have taken to the path of liquidating class enemies – landlords and money-lenders – others believe more in mass movements. However, there is a tendency to describe any dissident activists championing the poor as 'Naxalite'.

In Srikakulam the poor peasants were ultimately able to obtain somewhat more benefit from the declared objectives of the programmes than those of Adilabad district in the same state where the entrenched power structure had not been weakened by radical disturbances.[44] It must be emphasized, however, that such a pattern is extremely rare and depends largely on the emergence of sensitive and dedicated individuals intelligent enough to manipulate a situation to the benefit of the poor. In many other cases disturbances merely result in a heavy-handed suppression on the plea of maintaining law and order as currently seems to be happening in parts of Bihar.

The indifferent success of these government programmes for the 'weaker sections', which were first launched in the Fourth Five-Year Plan in the early seventies, needs to be analysed less on the basis of their individual performance and more in the light of the original social limitations under which they were launched. They seem to have been pushed through for inclusion in the Fourth Plan against many objections and reservations of the Planning Commission and the Government of India's orthodox economic advisers. The orthodox economic approach cautioned against unremunerative schemes for submarginal farmers and agricultural labourers and continued to stress the economic goal of increasing as rapidly as possible the aggregate national growth rate.

In practice, under Indian conditions, this would merely have reinforced the domination of entrenched social castes and classes over the weaker groups. In particular there was resistance from the orthodox planners to the reversal of liberal industrial licensing policies in 1970. Mrs Gandhi, on the other hand, probably with a shrewder insight into the unstable foundations of a rapid orthodox growth rate, if these were laid on the quicksands of social oppression, preferred a series of measures targeted at the weakest sections of Indian society.

Amongst these programmes, dating from the middle of 1970,

were the pilot projects leading to the Small Farmers' Development Agency (SFDA). Under this small farmers became eligible for subsidized loans and investment capital for minor irrigation, land improvement and animal husbandry programmes. There was a separate scheme for the even worse off marginal farmers and agricultural labourers. To reinforce assistance to the latter a three-year Crash Scheme for Rural Employment (CSRE) was launched in April 1971 to generate employment for a thousand individuals per year in each district of the country. Although the overt opposition to such schemes was overcome politically after Mrs Gandhi's landslide victory in the 1971 elections, the programmes tended to become bogged down in obstructions and criticisms at the level of implementation. The fact remains that a beginning had been made by a courageous assertion of willpower against orthodox Indian thinking.

The original programmes have undergone changes in detail and conceptual sophistication. Yet they now form an essential ingredient of any political party's programme and the expectations which they have aroused can never again be lulled to sleep. Under the Janata government a sophistication of programmes for 'weaker sections' was termed 'Antyodaya'. The rural employment programme became the Food For Work Programme and, after the Janata defeat, was again renamed the National Rural Employment Programme (NREP). Critics in the early seventies could rightly point out that fund allocations for all the small and medium farmers and agricultural labourer projects were sufficient only to touch approximately three million agriculturalists over a five-year period, as against the 49 million who constituted small and marginal farmers alone. As regards the rural works project for landless agricultural labourers, the average budgeted outlays came to only Rs 500 million per year against the Rs 5 billion assessed as necessary to have a real impact.

Since programme evaluations from the field recounted the same stories of obstructionism year after year, new planning concepts were evolved for the Scheduled Castes and Scheduled Tribes. In 1977 Tribal Sub-Plans were launched in districts with tribal populations exceeding 50 per cent. The aim was to build up the infrastructure of these 'backward areas' and uplift the tribes through integrated programmes involving education, primary health care, job training and subsidized agricultural and animal husbandry programmes.

In 1980 a Special Component Plan was introduced for the upliftment of Scheduled Castes. The government acknowledged, in its Sixth Plan document for 1980–85, that the social and economic position of the Scheduled Castes has remained unchanged since Independence. This programme seeks to uplift them economically through programmes similar to those targeted for the Scheduled Tribes. Unfortunately, one of the problems this scheme may encounter involves the attitude of the extension worker. Generally caste Hindus feel too uncomfortable to establish any general rapport with 'Scheduled Caste' target groups.

Since the government is fully aware of the situation on the ground it should have a continued monitoring of effective means to overcome the impediments and obstructions in the field. Problems with the banking structure arise in every programme and their demands for mortgageable assets inevitably divert the benefits of the schemes to the relatively more affluent in the countryside. Added to this is the fundamental lack of conviction or enthusiasm which, to say the least of it, characterizes almost the entire machinery supposed to deliver results in the countryside. Too often there is downright obstructionism, especially in areas where the network of implementing agencies is closely interwoven with the dominant castes who stand to lose their dominance if the schemes are put through with a will. Ultimately, too, the control of vote banks by these same dominant groups necessitates compromises all along the line.

Recently the middle peasants and larger farmers' lobbies have achieved, through their vociferous complaints, a certain share in the special schemes. They complained that everything was being done by government for the weakest and poorest who could not deliver the goods and nothing for the real farmers who were contributing to India's self-sufficiency in food. The extent to which imaginative schemes can be frustrated in the field becomes evident on a visit to a typical block, the lowest unit of developmental implementation.

Bhagyanagar, a block in Etawah district, western Uttar Pradesh, is located in a sylvan setting away from any township. The Block Development Officer had evaded a previously planned interview. However, from the block office the following information was collected in relation to the Integrated Rural Development Programme (IRDP). The IRDP, launched in 1980, had merged the earlier programmes for small and marginal farmers, the SFDA and MFDA programmes. One of the IRDP's main components is the upliftment of three thousand of the poorest families in every block amounting to 15 million families for the whole country during the Sixth Plan. This is to be achieved through subsidies for wells and land improvement, animal husbandry and self-employment training schemes, etc.

The 1982/83 IRDP programme at Bhagyanagar was supposed to have 533 beneficiaries, including 287 Scheduled Castes. The breakdown was 114 small farmers, including 36 Harijans; 319 marginal farmers, including 193 Harijans; and only 69 agricultural labourers, including 5 Harijans. The plans included 53 pumpsets, 77 pairs of bullocks and 1 cart, and helped 29 rural artisans, including 8 Scheduled Castes. Actual achievements were impossible to identify and the talk centred mainly on the administrative confusion and difficulties. The sole viable project seemed to be aid in the shape of a loan of Rs 3,000 for handloom units to 21 families who live together in a traditional Muslim weaving community. The bank had arranged for the supply of yarn from a spinning mill cooperative.

In so far as other programmes were concerned there were endless difficulties. The Punjab National Bank was supposed to be not cooperating. Applications for projects were returned by them with the remark 'below norms'. They insist on a cultivator possessing a minimum of two acres before a plough animal scheme is sanctioned. It was generally accepted throughout the area that the bank staff have to get their cut on any application. The Central Bank of India is now the lead bank. The various regulations inhibit meaningful progress towards economic advancement. There is a ceiling limit of Rs 1,200 per buffalo and these have to be bought by purchase teams who go around cattle fairs with the 'beneficiary'. Since the government purchase teams are well known, prices shoot up and they cannot obtain good stock.

In so far as the Special Component Plan is concerned, the position is even more complicated. The block has a specific Assistant Development Officer for this plan who was 'on tour'. The mechanism for loans to Harijans is even more complicated. Under the general IRDP programme small farmers of whatever caste are entitled to an element of 25 per cent subsidy and marginal farmers to 33 per cent. This basic IRDP element of subsidy is drawn from the district rural development agency. A

Harijan, however, is entitled to an extra element of subsidy enhancing it to a total of 50 per cent. This extra element has to be drawn separately against the Special Component Plan central allocation through the State Scheduled Caste Finance and Development Corporation.

The actual progress was dismal. The Scheduled Caste Component Schemes only seem to have percolated to the block during the financial year 1982/83. Only two projects had been sanctioned but no budget allotment had been received until February 1983 (the financial year ends in March). Last year a token amount of Rs 2,340, plus 4 quintals of rice, was spent on making brick pathways through the mud in a village. The Harijan Development Corporation is also supposed to be constructing some shops to help Harijans in trade. This scheme involves 50 per cent outright subsidy and a 50 per cent loan recoverable in ten years without interest. The scheme is obviously liberal but no shop has yet been handed over to anyone. There is another scheme to purchase land for the landless up to Rs 10,000 per family but no purchase has yet been made. A third scheme for community tubewells is to be constructed by the Harijan Development Corporation to provide subsidized water for irrigation. The situation reported was that 'site selection is in progress but no construction has been made'. The position regarding schemes for individual beneficiaries, including Harijans under the Special Component Plan within the IRDP, has already been noted. More serious was the supercilious smirk of the Brahmin accountant when he said that: 'Harijans prefer buffaloes. It is easiest for them. They like tanning.'

A study sponsored by the Central Government[45] specifically entrusted the Indian Institute of Management in Ahmedabad with organizing a study of the SFDA programme by including academics, administrators and public workers. The study revealed interesting sidelights. A sample study in Sirkok, Andhra Pradesh, showed clearly that the real beneficiaries were those who had adequate land to benefit from irrigation schemes or loans. Case histories of the 'weaker sections', especially Harijans, who owned marginal, unirrigated plots, showed them unable, even after slight amelioration, to pay back the loans. Interestingly enough not a single tribal from this major tribal district, where tribals were the mainstay of the earlier Naxalite movement, found place in the survey.

There was a general problem regarding credit and lack of coordination between the loans supposed to be provided by banks and the subsidy element to be provided by the agency. One without the other would obviously totally disrupt any scheme to benefit an individual farmer. Banks were found to limit credit to farmers with more than 2.5 acres and in practice to pose all sorts of obstacles. It was found that to obtain a loan for a well they demanded a certificate from a geologist. How an individual small farmer was to find or persuade a geologist, even if helped by the Block Development Officer, is difficult to imagine. The study also found that:

> ... because of the technical rules and unlimited property rights, the small farmer is at the losing end. He cannot dig a well if it falls within a 600 feet radius of an adjacent well but the big farmer can dig any number of wells with his own funds without taking into consideration such technical ties.[46]

Too much fragmentation into small handkerchief plots was also mentioned as a barrier in preparing viable schemes for small farmers. Community solutions to many of these problems were felt desirable. Experiences of Orissa where community wells brought prosperity were highlighted. It was pointed out that 'there was no dearth of data and reports.' Feedbacks received from earlier studies 'could have been usefully applied for improving the programmes'. But limited powers in the hands of the project officer 'did not encourage such changes'.

The discussion also skirted another basic issue. It is recorded that the director of the Indian Institute of Public Administration, who at that time was an officer with long and practical field experience in frontier areas, made a passsionate plea for an organization of small farmers. He stated that nothing would happen unless those who want to benefit could organize themselves. The valedictory address, however, carefully sidetracked this dangerous thought by pointing out that bureaucrats were not the instruments for such action; that others would get into this business only when they found it necessary to do so; that democracy runs on the basis of pressure groups, apart from the enlightened self-interest of the society as a whole; and the realization that the vote matters.

The study highlighted the whole problem of the SFDA succinctly:

As regards the implementation of SFDAs several organizational drawbacks were highlighted. The first and foremost was the lack of proper communication with the target group. The unwillingness to cooperate and the hostility of certain dominant sections of society were referred to. The conflicting interests of landed farmers and poor farmers were noted. A project officer from Andhra Pradesh attempted in vain to motivate Scheduled Caste small farmers to take advantage of SFDA schemes. These farmers did not respond because they were threatened by non-Scheduled Caste groups . . . What was required was a motivated and committed project officer but social scientists are yet to come up with programmes to produce Gandhi or Mao.[47]

The concept of rural public works programmes is extremely popular among the poor in the countryside. This was especially the case when the Janata government introduced a system of wage payments in kind, thanks to the massive reserve of grains in the godowns accumulated by the previous Congress (I) regime. When the Congress (I) was returned to power in January 1980, it was incorporated into the Sixth Plan under a new name, the National Rural Employment Programme. An allocation of Rs 40 billion was made but, due to present grain shortages, wages are once again being paid in cash.

In areas where these programmes have not been thwarted by vested interests, they have helped to stave off hunger during the lean season. In Silora block, Ajmer district, in the heart of the Rajasthan desert, Bunker Roy, director of the voluntary organization, the Social Work Research Centre says: 'During famines government works do absorb labour from the poorest agricultural sector.'

In many cases, however, such public works programmes never get under way in areas where they are most urgently needed. The main reason is that vested interests thwart the programme in order to keep wages low and the demand for labour down. The tribal district of Banswara in South Rajasthan, inhabited largely by Bhil tribes, is frequently drought-stricken. Yet because most of the Bhils provide a cheap source of labour for road and dam construction sites in the area, neither the FFWP, nor its successor the NREP, was ever brought into the area according to tribals interviewed personally in two blocks, Ghantali in the western part of the district and Kushalgarh in the south. Even in April 1982, at the onset of summer, tribal women could be seen collecting roots from the stark forests to stave off hunger.

J.C. Jetli, Joint Secretary in charge of the NREP in the Ministry of Rural Development, points out that the scheme may have been under way in one of the villages in either of the blocks visited: 'The money allocated per block is about 500,000 to 700,000 rupees. So among 15 villages in a block the amount becomes very small. This means only a few schemes are possible. Moreover, the NREP is spread over a working season which is fairly long.'[48]

An evaluation survey carried out by the Planning Commission conducted in ten states showed that the programmes have not had any significant impact on wages and only a short-term and seasonal impact on the living conditions of its beneficiaries in the majority of areas surveyed. The study also noted that muster rolls had been inflated in some villages by fictitious names added by contractors and panchayats, or village councils.

The extent to which these public works programmes have made a dent in rural unemployment and underemployment is an open question if one considers there are about 120 million landless. In addition, according to the Agricultural Census of 1976/77, more than half of the 82 million farmers who own land depend on farms smaller than 1 hectare to support them at subsistence level. Many of these families are therefore also dependent on rural works during the lean season.

The dimensions of the rural unemployment problem are massive. Over fifty per cent of males in the labour force of 261 million work as farm helpers or casual labourers and have irregular employment.[49] Unemployment is a highly regional phenomenon. Six states – Bihar, West Bengal, Tamil Nadu, Kerala, Maharashtra and Andhra Pradesh – accounted for two-thirds of the person-days seeking and/or available for work in rural India in 1972/73. Kerala, Tamil Nadu and West Bengal continued to have the highest incidence of rural unemployment in 1977/78 according to the 32nd Round of the National Sample Survey.[50]

To provide employment on the scale needed would require political mobilization from the grass roots which could only be achieved under a Chinese-style regime. At best the present programmes are only palliative. Inderjit Singh's monograph dealing with Rural Works Programmes is not overly optimistic when it states: 'In the decades ahead even accelerated and optimistic agricultural growth rates will be associated with positive unemployment growth in rural areas.'[51]

These have been studies undertaken to assess ways of alleviating the unemployment and underemployment problems in the countryside. M.S. Swaminathan, former director of the Indian Council of Agricultural Research, has calculated that agriculture could provide additional employment for 40 million workers if the will was present in the administration. The Indian Agricultural Research Institute maintains that a scheme of multiple cropping could lead 'to a threefold rise in farm production and give jobs to a 17-million rural population within three years.'[52] It has been estimated that an irrigated hectare requires 122 person-days of labour as against 74 on a non-irrigated hectare. One study points out that in Uttar Pradesh alone there are 30,000 hectares of cultivable waste land.[53]

Such studies sound nice on paper but are based on fragmented economic assessments usually based on the pet project of the researchers. Triple cropping will undoubtedly provide more employment but an essential prerequisite is massive irrigation and fertilizer availability at economic rates to the small farmer. Irrigation potential conversely could be utilized more speedily by concentration on rural employment projects and on digging field channels. This in turn will require a coordinated drive to sort out land record problems and probably a certain degree of land consolidation. No simple facile prescription can therefore solve the problem with the rapidity it deserves. Although much lip service is paid to integrated rural development, in fact the IRDP scheme has merely developed into a limited sectoral programme without the prerequisite of either integrated planning, integrated supervision or integrated implementation.

One of the main reasons for the failure of the poor to benefit from rural development programmes is due to their lack of political organization. The political system itself operates through the network of traditional caste patronage. Therefore low castes cannot make independent demands on the system. They are only able to relate to the political process through the traditional dominant caste leadership.

The aspirations of the landless agricultural labourers and sharecroppers remain unarticulated by any political party and most peasant organizations. The reasons for this require deeper probing. Most of the leadership of political parties has ceased to be instruments of social change because the leadership is dominated by upper and middle castes. Since the landless lack representation at higher party levels, their aspirations are never voiced by the latter except to the extent that it suits their own interests.

Indeed there is a growing suspicion of a genuine lack of political will, not only on the part of government but of many of the parties and organizations purporting to champion the rural poor. In the final analysis the political parties to achieve power also have to strike an ambivalent attitude, on the one hand, publicizing postures of identification with the rural poor and, on the other, retaining the support of their oppressors who still largely control the vote banks. Even in the case of extremist groups, usually loosely branded in India as Naxalites, their overriding priority seems to be the utilization of pockets of discontent for their own political struggle rather than a coherently conceived programme for rural justice. The end result too often is that the poor villager is often encouraged by such organizations to stand up for his rights and then left in the lurch to face the dominant exploiters in his own village once the immediate political aims of publicized agitation have been met.

Most political parties of all ideological shades rarely have their roots in villages and generally do not go below the district level. Part of the reason may be that cadres are not willing to take responsibility at the grass roots. It appears that some minor efforts have been made through the Kisan Sabhas, or peasant organizations, of various parties like the Congress (I), the Communist Party of India (Marxist) (CPI(M)) and the Communist Party of India (CPI) to organize agricultural labourers. After 1969 the extremist pro-Maoist organization, the Communist Party of India (Marxist–Leninist) (CPI(ML)) established their own association. The Indian Trade Union Congress also has an affiliate for agricultural labourers. Despite these multitude of organizations very few of them are organized. D. Bandyopadhyaya, former West Bengal Land Reforms Commissioner, estimates that 5 per cent of the rural poor are members of these organizations but a Rural Labour Enquiry of 1974/75 revealed that only 1 per cent are unionized.[54] Nor does the leftist organization necessarily support the interests of the poor. During agrarian unrest in Patna district, Bihar in 1981, the CPI joined in an armed procession of landlords against the rural poor.[55]

In fact several studies conducted by the FAO, the ILO and the Indian Council of Social Sciences Institute show that organizations of agricultural labourers have only been effective in limited areas like the Kuttanad and Palghat regions of Kerala, in Tanjore district, Tamil Nadu and in some parts of the Punjab, Bihar, Maharashtra and West Bengal.

In the case of Kerala the Communist Parties were mainly responsible for the organization of rural labour. Their success was due to the fact that they formed part of the leadership in the broader nationalist movements and anti-caste movements. Their influence in Tamil Nadu has been localized to Tanjore because in this state the Communists had been isolated from the dominant Dravidian movement.

In the case of Tanjore there are several reasons for the successful organization of the landless labourers in the eastern part of the old Delta. The area is characterized by a rigid system of stratification. The Brahmins are concentrated at the top while the agricultural labourers, as Harijans, comprised virtually a homogeneous class at the bottom. The convergence of the Harijans as a class of agricultural labourers ensured the unity necessary for political action. The Harijans could easily be motivated in a situation of such inequalities, while the physical isolation of their quarters made it particularly easy for them to be organized into a class for political protest.[56]

Even where Harijan leadership has emerged at the village level, it has failed to organize agricultural labourers. Padirikuppam is a Harijan settlement in Puttur taluk of Chittor district, Andhra Pradesh. Even though the Harijans are not dependent on the caste Hindus at the village level: 'It is interesting that the emerging Harijan leadership has not been engaged in organizing agricultural labourers' households but has been busy instead trying to secure the government-sponsored programme for the weaker sections.'[57]

Generally, peasant organizations voice the demands of the richer elements. During the statewide Nasik Farmers' movement in 1981 in Maharashtra for higher agricultural prices, such demands put forward in the name of all the peasantry were actually those of the richer farmer. As journalist Gail Omvedt points out: 'The propaganda of the movement seems to be to convince the poor and middle peasantry to identify themselves as peasants rather than toilers and to see their poverty as deriving not from 34 years of exploitation but due to the low price of agricultural products and nothing else.'[58]

Similarly, the Thamizhaga Viva Sayigal Sangam, the Tamil Nadu Agriculturalists' Association, which has over 1 million members, is an organization solely for cultivators, and the president, C. Narayanaswamy Nadu, admits that the landless agricultural workers are outside her organization.[59]

Even the decentralization of political power to the three-tier panchayats in Maharashtra, which run parallel to economic institutions like cooperative banks and land development banks, has helped the rural élite, mostly sugar barons, not only to gain more political power at district and state level but in reaping all the economic gains: 'They have also "succeeded" in creating new glaring economic disparities and have often acted as instruments of economic, political and social oppression and injustice in the rural areas. The lot of the poor peasant shows hardly any improvement.'[60]

The law-and-order machinery is always very swift in declaring any activity to redress social injustice as a violation of Section 144 of the Criminal Code. This empowers the magistracy to prohibit meetings or gatherings of more than five people if a breach of the peace is likely to result therefrom. On 11 May 1983 the police had imposed Section 144 of the Criminal Procedure Code in a part of Gaya district, Bihar, following agitations by agricultural labourers for higher wages. A few days later the Mazdoor Kisan Sangram Samiti (Joint Workers' and Peasants' Association) working with the labourers began a two-day conference. The police broke up the gathering by resorting to beating up those present and other groups of police posted along the roads beat up anyone coming to attend the meeting. At least 100 villagers had limbs broken as a result of the police brutality.[61]

One of the factors responsible for the carnage at Pipra in Bihar, in which 14 Harijan men, women and children were butchered and their bodies thrown into their blazing huts on the night of 25–6 February 1980 was administrative collusion with the landlords. The *Economic and Political Weekly* editorial reports that: 'As agricultural workers organized themselves to press for better wages, the state government issued licenses for guns to the landlords.'[62]

This enabled 400 armed men hired by landlords to attack the Harijan section of Pipra village and to carry out the mass killings.

The present alignment of forces in the countryside bears no resemblance to those prevailing in pre-revolutionary Russia or in France before 1789. In both the latter cases the landed aristocracy was in an overwhelming minority, while the oppressed peasantry could ultimately count as allies a disillusioned mass of the aristocracy's own followers in the lower rungs of the army and administration. In India the old landed aristocracy has largely disappeared from the rural power structure after the abolition of the feudal estates in the early fifties. The struggle of the lowest rung of the peasantry is rather against a middle rung of peasant proprietors. In any class struggle the linkages both through caste and economic interest, and, in many cases by blood relationship, are firmly interwoven with the lower rungs of the administration, law and order machinery and judiciary. The landholding interests have generally been successful in crushing any protests of the poor. In some instances the magistracy may resort to the use of power to preserve the public peace by issuing orders against those who challenge the status quo. It also uses the power to issue restraining orders, to prevent danger or disturbance or injury, to protect the higher castes with whom the magistracy and police sympathize.

For example, the *Indian Express* of 25 May 1983 reports that in parts of Patna district, Bihar, landowners in November 1981 had begun organizing themselves against growing extremist political activists. These were organizing the landless agricultural labourers in the area. The report states that a procession was taken out by the landowners 'to symbolise their unity and strike terror into the landless labourers': 'They were armed to the teeth. Scores of elephants, camels and horses were taken out in procession in defiance of Section 144 of the Criminal Procedure Code.'[63] Yet the police or magistracy did not consider this intimidating demonstration show of force to be any danger to public peace.

On the other hand, a report[64] by the civil rights group, the People's Union for Democratic Rights, relating to events in Patna district, Bihar, in the autumn of 1981, highlights police collusion in suppressing the demands of the landless agricultural labourers over payment of legal minimum wages and redistribution of land. It shows that the police deliberately fabricated allegations that an extremist organization in the area had been instigating the poor to violence against landlords. This false accusation was used as a *sine qua non* for the campaign of repression, a wave of 135 arrests and firings which killed seven people.

There is a growing likelihood that, as the poor become more conscious and if they find, as they seem to be doing, that redress through constitutional channels is never forthcoming, there will be more and more recourse to violence. These will not merely be individual, impulsive outbursts of anger but acts of violence undertaken in conformity with extreme Maoist Communist philosophy that there is no other way of obtaining justice. The blame will have to be shared by all political parties, by the judicial system and not merely by the immediate executive which itself is also a victim of the system. Indeed the sober sociologist M.N. Srinivas himself visualizes increased caste conflict.

The future of the countryside will focus between the interplay of economic and social factors. There has to be a breakthrough in production and land use – in food and cash crops, including commercial forestry and ecology. But equally important is the future of the marginal farmers and landless labourers. In Indian conditions there will be growing pressure from the dominant caste lobbies, including the newly prospering middle castes, for programmes targeted at their concept of efficient economic growth and food production. They will argue persuasively the case for merely modernizing the old feudal and caste structure to organize efficient production. There seems to be growing agreement amongst economic planners that in this climate of thought the only real future for landless labourers lies in some occupational shift. Western-type industrialization hardly offers hope of absorbing more than a minute fraction of the labour force.

Gandhian programmes like the *khadi* and village industries network seem to have degenerated into mere mechanical organizations heavily subsidized and functioning in a rut. They are not economically competitive while actual social achievements are hard to identify. There are, however, indications, in certain states and areas, of genuine rural growth providing its own multiplier effect through economic forces which are difficult to document or quantify. For example, in the Punjab and Haryana there has been a shift in traditional occupations with a host of ancillary activities in the small-scale household sector contributing to a wider base of prosperity.

An indicator of this is the large rural market growing up in small country towns or larger villages. There is specific evidence that this market is even attracting the attention of transnational corporations. To some extent such islands of relative prosperity attract agricultural labour from really poor areas such as Bihar and eastern Uttar Pradesh. This migrant labour replaces the traditional local labour which has moved up the scale into newer ancillary occupations. The migrant labour is no doubt liable to exploitation. However, this exploitation is socially at least relatively lighter than in its abject poverty-stricken homelands in Bihar. The question arises as to whether the pattern of the islands of relative progress can be multiplied over wider areas of the country. If it can, this may be a potent factor in accelerating release from social bondage and allowing many families and groups to achieve an upward caste mobility outside the areas where their known origins inhibit their advancement.

Trends over the last decade, however, have shown the fallacy of assuming that purely economic factors will weaken the exploitative hierarchy of caste. Terminologies may change. New caste groupings may emerge. The exploitation and attitudes of superiority and inferiority may be disguised by astute intellectual analysis claiming that the process is one of an emerging class structure. Or that it is in the traditional Indian movement towards the modernization of the Sarvodaya concept – 'The Good of All' – buttressed, of course, by the 'necessary authority in decision-making and guidance'. Local rural tensions as they escalate into increasing violence may be sought to be defused by appeals to the wider danger facing the unity of the nation as a whole. The concept of nationhood in the Indian context may well, however, evolve differently from that of the Western nation-state and approximate more to a revivalist urge for strengthening the traditional structure of Indian society, especially its majority Hindu component.

At all events the change in the countryside since Independence has been very great, even if this change has not been entirely according to the patterns prescribed by planners, or claimed to be emerging by the government of the day. These changes have already produced a significant social ferment in the countryside. Its ultimate result may differ greatly from area to area. In some areas wise and effective leadership may guide it towards constructive advancement. In others there will be an intensification of local conflicts. Such a state of affairs is nothing new to India which has coped with them many times in its history. Galbraith's description of India in transition as 'a functioning anarchy' may be profounder than a mere paradoxical witticism. Local societies do seem to find their own way of functioning on totally different levels of concept and reality from the apparent anarchy in the 'normative order' or even from the 'models' of those who prescribe the norms.

CHAPTER THREE

Land: radical laws and tardy reforms

The measure of the resistance to an egalitarian rural society has been the failure of the government to effectively transfer ownership of the land to the tiller. Despite the government's oral commitment to such socialistic principles, some economists doubt whether the government's policy in implementing land reforms was to effect a total transformation in rural property relations. Land reforms have only resulted in a horizontal dispersion of holdings which some would argue accords with the government's plan to concentrate on commercial agriculture based on the middle peasantry which have been the main beneficiaries of land reforms in post-Independence India. The breakup of the very large erstwhile feudal estates, which had been operated in many instances by absentee landlords, resulted in twenty million tenants emerging as a new class of peasant-owners. This was in itself a major social change.

However, the land reforms did not provide any benefits to the bulk of the peasantry, to tenants cultivating land on the basis of informal oral arrangements, to sharecroppers and landless agricultural labourers. It has been estimated that 60 per cent of the agricultural labour force, especially the landless labourers, were unaffected by the abolition of intermediaries. In fact nearly all Kisan Sabha, or Peasant Organization, documents show that the slogan 'land to the tiller' was made the equivalent of the abolition of the feudal estates. In actual effect it meant the land was being transferred to the original occupancy tenant. It was assumed that a large class of sharecroppers and agricultural labourers would go on existing. Thus the long-standing inequalities in the village rural structure were barely touched.

The insecurity and loss of rights suffered by the peasantry began under British rule. From the end of the eighteenth century the Imperial rulers had imposed a Western-type land system based on private ownership which disregarded the distinction drawn in the traditional land system between rights to occupy land, to receive tribute from it and to dispose of it. Under the Moghuls the peasant had the right to use the land and occupy it so long as he was in a position to cultivate it. Thus the tillers had enjoyed *de facto* security in the land. Under the Moghuls the local notables acted as revenue collectors and had the right to retain a proportion of the taxes. However, no proprietary rights over the land were defined by written law.

One of the social consequences of the land tenure system imposed by the British, which was based on intermediaries and on an elaborate structure of rights and obligations defined by law and subject to court jurisdiction, was the breakdown of the earlier cohesion of village life. While the Moghuls did not interfere with customary rights in land and restricted their intermediaries strictly to the business of revenue collection, the new class of zamindars were now in a position to exploit the peasantry to any degree since their activities were no longer circumscribed by custom. As Béteille has pointed out, once the zamindars' independent rights over the land were recognized, it meant that to the British all cultivators were either owners or tenants. The corollary was that the latter were thus transformed into tenants-at-will and became subject to enhancement of rent and to ejectment.

The *zamindari* system distorted traditional customary rights in land because under Cornwallis' Permanent Settlement of 1893 the tilling of the soil was totally divorced from ownership. Villages were leased out permanently to zamindars who, at the end of every financial year, had to give a fixed rent to the British while any surplus was retainable. When subsequent laws were passed to define rights to the intermediary class which had developed, the zamindars found that the leasing out of land permanently to the former cultivators, who had been relegated to tenants, would place them at a disadvantage so they deliberately kept the system insecure. A chain of intermediaries between the State and the tiller emerged and there came into existence a chain of sub-proprietors or tenure holders under the zamindars who further reinforced the system of rent exactions. Altogether the zamindari system of land tenure extended over roughly 40 per cent of British India and prevailed mostly in the Bengal Presidency, parts of the United Provinces, northern Rajputana and smaller parts of the central and western regions and the Madras Presidency in the South.

At first, the condition of the peasantry was relatively better in the remaining part of British India, in the southern and western region, where a *ryotwari* system was introduced vesting property rights directly in the cultivator. However, since the peasant now had the right to sublet, mortgage or transfer his land by gift or sale, the money-lender had recourse to legal deeds of mortgage and the cumbersome judicial procedure where rules of evidence always operated in favour of the rich and influential. These had the means to pay lawyers over countless periods of adjournment and appeal and could tutor witnesses. Indeed the very possession of a legal title (*patta*) with the legal power to mortgage it increased the small holder's credit-worthiness and lured him deeper into debt. Unprotected tenancy developed on a large scale in all the ryotwari areas and, with the growing pauperization and expropriation of the small peasantry, bigger holdings continued to expand.

Thus the British legal system, far from benefiting the small landholder, now placed them at the mercy of a rapacious urban money-lending class whose manipulations of mortgage documentation could only be countered through lawyers in remote district courts. Earlier the village money-lender had, to some extent, been amenable to village public opinion, for the latter was aware of the truth about local transactions which rarely emerged out of the testimony of hired or tutored witnesses in legal court proceedings. According to the Deccan Riots Commission:

> In no part of India did indebtedness cause more misery than in the Deccan. Formerly the law or custom prevented a lender from more than tripling the original loan by compound interest; neither personal arrest nor seizure of property was allowed. The English law removing all such restraints caused much horror. To carry out the law judges had to strip old families of their ancestral homes.[1]

Such expropriation led in time to the emergence of many landowners drawn from the non-cultivating classes.

After Independence the National Commission on Agriculture studied this question. In its 1950 report it found that in the Bombay Presidency about five million acres passed out of the hands of small peasants into those of urban absentee landlords, traders and money-lenders. In fact the overwhelming number of tenants in zamindari and ryotwari areas were mostly sharecroppers whose rents in cash or kind constituted between 50 and 70 per cent of the gross product. Many illegal levies further re-inforced their servitude.

At Independence in 1947 figures for distribution of landhold-ings show a high concentration of ownership among a small percentage of the rural population. In the early fifties in Uttar Pradesh (UP), for example, the biggest landowners who paid more than Rs 250 as land revenue constituted 1.5 per cent of all zamindars in the state but held 58 per cent of the land. In the ex-Bombay Presidency in 1952–53 landholdings having up to five acres constituted 53 per cent of total landholdings, but the land held was only 15 per cent of the total. In Bihar in 1955 the poorest 50 per cent of the population owned 3.41 per cent of the land.

Soon after Independence the Congress set out to redeem its pledge to distribute land to the tiller. The first step was the liquidation of large feudal estates known as the zamindari aboli-tion. This succeeded in giving ownership rights to approximately 20 million tenant cultivators enabling a new class of peasantry to rise. But it did not create a socially homogeneous class of cultivators. As Béteille has pointed out, the legal definition of 'cultivator' had 'socially and economically a very wide range of referents'. Many 'cultivators' were in fact people with large landholdings operated by tenants-at-will. The land reform laws were in fact based in part on political compromise. Provisions in state laws allowed intermediaries to resume their land in their home farms in direct occupation for 'personal cultivation'. This resulted in the eviction of hundreds and thousands of tenants-at-will all over India, many of whom became sharecroppers or landless labourers. Francine Frankel is of the opinion that, notwithstanding the 20 million beneficiaries who acquired superior occupancy or ownership rights in land, these figures 'were outweighed by the numbers of tenants who lost their holdings to landlords under provisions permitting resumption for personal cultivation.'[2]

The laws were in fact ambivalent. For example, one of the crucial features of the Bombay Tenancy and Agricultural Land-holding Act, 1948, was the clause relating to the protected tenant and the fact that a tenant could claim ownership rights after proving he had cultivated it for six consecutive years. But the accompanying clause clarified that the onus of proof was on the tenant and that the landlord could eject tenants on the grounds of personal cultivation or for non-payment of rent. This is exactly what occurred. As Francine Frankel points out:

> The national leadership's inability to enlist the support of state leaders for the effective implementation of land reforms resulted in defective legislation that actually aggravated existing inequalities in the distribution of protected land rights enjoyed by landholders and those without land.[3]

Her valid but rather involved statement becomes clearer from examples in the field. As in Khalapur village, Saharanpur district, UP, during the Zamindari Abolition Act only four out of 6,000 acres passed into the hands of Untouchables even though many of them, especially the Chamars, the large Untouchable caste of leather workers, were tenant farmers.[4] Even today a Muslim from Chapta village, Etawah district, UP, recalls that: 'The fifties reforms did not result in any real redistribution of land.'

It took six years after Independence even to announce in principle the policy of ceilings on landholdings. Another three years elapsed before detailed legislation was recommended. The acts enabling the formulation of detailed processes and the implementation in the field were only passed by state legislatures in the early sixties. All this gave ample time to landowners to transfer or partition large holdings within their families or their own groups. Even the Planning Commission came to an early conclusion in its Panel on Land Reforms in 1961 that such transfers and partitions of land 'have tended to defeat the aims of the legislation' and that this legislation 'was not likely to yield any appreciable surplus for redistribution.'[5]

The net results in the field were even worse than the Planning Commission had feared. Not only was little surplus available for redistribution because most of the tenants found that their landlord meantime, after partitioning his estate, was on record as being within the legitimate ceiling; but in some cases the landlords were even able to resume plots from their tenants on the plea of taking it for personal cultivation within the lawful ceiling. The problem was compounded by the unreliability of land records, the failure to reconstruct these accurately, a rapid erosion of the periodical higher-level inspection system of such records and the onus placed on the tenant to prove his case legally in a revenue or district court. The fear that more tenants lost existing holdings than gained new rights finds support by a comparison of the National Sample Survey Reports from 1954 and 1961. In 1954, 12 per cent of rural households were recorded as leasing out land. This shrank to 7 per cent in 1961. During the same period the percentage of pure tenants dropped from 17 per cent to 8 per cent while those who operated mixed holdings or partly owned and partly leased-in land fell from about 23 per cent to 15 per cent. The total area under tenancy cultivation also dropped from 20 per cent to 12 per cent.

These statistics by themselves might indicate the success of land reforms in that tenants were decreasing because many of them had achieved ownership rights. But, in the absence of any countervailing figures to show such vesting of ownership rights and its redistribution, the only conclusion to be drawn is that in fact the landlords resumed the tenancies for themselves. In fact the economist P.C. Joshi has pointed out that: 'Almost all evaluation studies on land reforms have reported that land reforms legislation led to the eviction of tenants by landlords on a scale without precedence in recent Indian history.'[6] However, Joshi also points out that the original tenants, after being deprived of their earlier tenuous rights, continued to cultivate the land under much less favourable informal and oral arrangements.

The session of the 13th All Indian Kisan Sabha which had been working in the Thane district of Maharashtra, helping tenants obtain their legal rights, noted in May 1956 that mass evictions of poor peasants were 'increasing the number of landless, strengthening the hands of the landlords to increase their stranglehold on the tillers of the soil, and finally frustrating even the concessions secured by the peasant movement in the direction of land reform.'[7]

Similarly, according to the father of the Muslim pradhan, or elected village head, of Chapta village, Etawah district, UP: 'It was only in 1957 when verification of land records was going on that it was discovered that the landlords had managed to hold on to extra land. The meagre vested land was distributed among landless families much later and ultimately 10 to 12 Untouchables received small plots.'

West Bengal is usually held up as an example of relatively successful land reform. In this state the Estates Acquisition Act, 1953, which was to break up the feudal estates, had established ceilings on family holdings with the aim of acquiring surplus land to be distributed to the landless and sharecroppers. A special investigation undertaken by the Left Front Government when it came to power in 1967 revealed various subterfuges employed by the landlords to evade the laws. Some of the most common methods for retaining their lands were the creation of fictitious, backdated tenancies and undertenancies claimed to have existed in unregistered documents. *Benami* transfers in land to relatives, nominees, servants and agricultural labourers were made, often without their knowledge. Thousands of acres were registered as religious and charitable trusts which were exempted from land ceiling laws. For example, a landlord in Mathurapur in 24-Parganas district transferred 139.55 acres of excess land by executing fake registered trust deeds in favour of religious institutions.[8]

The situation appears to have been more favourable in Sripuram village, Tanjore district in South India, studied by Béteille.[9] By 1961 ceilings of 30 acres on wet land were effective in destroying the power base of the traditional landlords. A series of laws passed denying the landlord the right to arbitrarily evict a tenant from the land did ensure the latter security. But Béteille notes that a 'shrewd and powerful landowner is usually able to exploit loopholes in the law to his advantage'.[10] Furthermore, despite the land reforms, most of the land was still in the ownership of the former landowning classes. The land legislation passed in Tanjore since 1952 only served to undermine the position of the absentee landlord: 'Laws favour in some ways the growth of a new type of landowner, rooted in the village, tied closely to agriculture and owning a measure of land which is adequate but still below the ceiling.'[11]

In fact most of the state acts passed in the sixties with a view to imposing ceilings and to confer rights on tenants failed as there were so many loopholes in the laws. A renewed drive for land reforms was instituted or at least publicized after the state elections of 1972 when Mrs Gandhi was at the height of her popularity and had promised explicitly in her election manifesto a revision of land ceilings and a substantial programme for land redistribution.

Again, however, the programmes bogged down because of the considerable consultations needed with the State Chief Ministers and State Congress Committees, both of which, if not dominated entirely by landowning interests, at least knew that their own

survival through the vote banks depended on caution in antagonizing these dominant rural interests. As P.C. Joshi has pointed
out, political parties are aligned with powerful interests so that the
political will to implement land reform programmes is absent:
'They indulge in radical talk to mobilize the votes of the rural poor
but they allow a vast gap between words and deeds to preserve the
support of the rural rich.'[12]

An examination of the Karnataka revised ceiling act of 1974
shows how theory was totally divorced from practice. In actual
fact the revised ceiling law was merely a manoeuvre for political
ends; the substance of the revised laws was basically the same as
those of the earlier 1961 act: 'Changes were made in such a
manner that while the Act sounded more radical the real effects
were negligible.'[13] While the 1961 ceiling act allowed a family of
ten to hold 27 acres of the best-quality irrigated land through
private sources, the 1974 law allowed a family of five to hold 25
acres of first-class privately irrigated land. The law also allowed
adult sons to declare themselves a separate family and claim more
land up to the ceiling. Thus if a joint family had five adult sons, a
not uncommon feature in India, the family could keep up to 150
acres of first-class land irrigated through private sources.

In Andhra Pradesh the revised ceiling law, passed in 1973,
fixing ceilings on agricultural holdings, was meant to bring about
a 'revolution' in the rural areas. When the law was passed it was
estimated that there were at least 2 million acres of surplus land
available. Yet only 1,131,000 acres were designated as surplus
after 444,229 declarations were filed, of which only 59,054 were
found to be surplus cases. Out of these declarations 670,000
acres are covered by appeals before Appellate Tribunals, the
High Court and the Supreme Court. Of the 461,000 acres
available for taking possession, 360,000 acres were taken over. Of
the land taken over, 246,155 acres were distributed to 166,270
beneficiaries.[14] Most of this land was found to be of bad quality
and infertile.

Kerala had passed a ceiling act as early as 1969 under a United
Left Front government. However, delay in its implementation
and major loopholes in its provisions led to large-scale bogus
transfers to evade the ceiling laws; 115,016 acres had been
ordered for surrender but the only area available for takeover was
only 78,799 acres. Of the remainder taken, over 22,843 acres have
been stayed by the Kerala High Court, while 13,374 acres

are involved in disputes. Of the area available for takeover, 77,133 acres, or 97.90 per cent, have already been taken over. Of this 50,384 acres (or 65.31 per cent) have been redistributed amongst 80,825 people, with 0.62 acres as the average received.[15]

One of the major factors in all the states thwarting effective implementation of ceiling laws is the time lag, often two years or more, between the passage of a law by the legislature and its date of implementation. This means many landlords are able to make use of the time lag to 'adjust their holdings'. This poses no problem since the state governments are dominated by the rural landowning classes. One of the most widely used methods to evade ceiling provisions is tampering with records which is done by collusion with revenue officers. Even though acts often prohibit transfers of excess land after a particular date, many landlords backdate their sales.

All this again underlines the dichotomy between theory and practice, between the law and the actuality and between the guidelines of the planners and conditions on the ground. Numerous study groups and field investigations bring these to light. Directives or laws are amended accordingly but somehow these continue to be evaded and loopholes are found to restore the status quo of exploitation. Some of the studies will now be considered.

A study carried out by the Agricultural University of Udaipur, Rajasthan, entitled *Evaluation of the Implementation of Agricultural Ceiling Laws in Bhilwara district, Rajasthan* (1978) is enlightening on the subject. The reference period of the study spans 1970 to 1976 and the state ceiling laws of 1963 and 1973 were taken into consideration. The implementation of the 1963 law was delayed till 1970 because of legislative loopholes. Under both laws the surplus declared was only 26,244.68 ha and the study asserts that the figure given by Revenue Officials 'may not be correct'. After scrutiny 13, 198.44 ha, roughly 50 per cent, was ordered to be acquired under both laws. Finally, only 12,105.52 hectares were taken over under both laws: 'In various subdivisions of the district the area which has been taken under possession varies from 28 per cent to 54 per cent of the established surplus.'[16] Out of a sample of 252 allottees, 25 people declined to take possession of the land, while another 27 surrendered or abandoned the land as they found it unfit for cultivation. Out of the land allotted 89 per cent was barren and 11 per cent of this was uncultivable.[17]

Narendar Pani's study on Karnataka regarding the 1974 revised ceiling act found that as far as the distribution of land to the landless was concerned:

> In as many as six districts not a single acre of land had been distributed until October 1980. Moreover in 13 of the 19 districts in the state the rate of surplus land redistributed is well below 20 per cent.[18]

One of the main reasons for the evasions under ceiling laws are large-scale benami transactions whereby land is clandestinely transferred to relatives or individual nominees in anticipation of ceiling laws which are always publicized well in advance. Benami transfers were a recognized form of transfer under the British and such transfers are not illegal under the law. Only such transfers are to be treated as illegal as may have been done with a view to evading the land ceiling. Its mala fide intent has to be established which is extremely difficult to do in a court of law. According to A.R. Bandyopadhyay, Central Land Reforms Commissioner: 'This is why there are 40,000 land-related cases pending in the Calcutta High Court, to cite just one example. Some of these cases have been pending for the last 20 years or more.'[19]

The question arises as to why the law cannot be changed so that all benami transactions are made retrospectively mala fide to 1953 when the first major land reform laws were introduced. This is precisely what the present West Bengal bill, currently awaiting the President's assent at the Centre in late 1983, seeks to do. The bill provides that all land-related cases are to be re-opened and benami transactions are to be treated as mala fide unless proved otherwise. The Centre has kept the bill pending for two years, therefore further comment is superfluous.

A classic case involving all known devices to frustrate land reform programmes, especially ceilings by benami transactions, is that of a so-called religious foundation in India's backward state of Bihar. This religious land, comparable originally to the medieval landed estates of the Church in Europe, dates back to Moghul land grants. Up to 1932 this land seems to have been managed, again possibly not unlike the old European ecclesiastical estates, with a measure of certain feudal responsibility. In those days there was no single feudal *mahant*, or monastic head, and those in charge probably genuinely believed that they were administering the lands on behalf of divinities. Such a feeling still persists in the remote mountain valley village of Malana in the Himalayan state of Himachal Pradesh.

In 1947, however, the Bihar state government passed the Religious Trust Act to regulate and minimize excessive ecclesiastical holdings. The prospect of losing an enormous acreage, estimated at 17,000 acres covering 300 villages, spurred the management, under the newly emerging mahant, or religious head, to devote his entire energies to retain, and even strengthen, feudal possession by every possible legal, administrative and political device. First, he used the law to delay for ten years redistribution of a major part of the land by claiming that it was under private and not trust ownership. Simultaneously, during the currency of the case, he curried favour with all the elements of the establishment, including Gandhian movements. He was an early and generous donor of 8,000 acres to the Bhoodan, or 'Land Gift', Movement, involved the intellectuals by giving 300 acres to a university and, when the court case ultimately went against him, graciously donated to government 1,300 acres for distribution among the poor. As journalist Harji Malik wrily puts it: 'This voluntary donation must have been quite something.'

Ultimately in 1957 the mahant lost his court case. Mysteriously, however, the Bihar Government, instead of immediately vesting and redistributing all the property, 'came to a compromise'. This 'compromise' also was 'quite something', reminiscent indeed of the privy purses given to the erstwhile Indian princes when they signed the instrument of accession. It involved confirmation of sales or transfers of 9,903 acres to evade ceiling laws prior to 1957; for the mahant a personal annuity of Rs 200,000, a 'compensation' of Rs 1,000 per month and 240 acres for personal cultivation during his lifetime; and 2,300 acres in trust for the foundation, out of which he made the 'donation' of 1,300 acres to government.

The district magistrate, when questioned in 1980 about why all this happened, merely disclaimed any background knowledge but did not totally rule out some element of corruption. More likely any money that changed hands was the least part of the tacit deal. If strict action had been taken against the Math and its obviously shrewd mahant, he could well have pointed out, most inconveniently, the continuing existence of an enormous amount of other similar feudal estates owned under benami redistribution by influential members of the establishment. Even today the chief minister of Bihar, Dr Jagannath, who has recently dropped his Brahmin caste name, Misra, is generally recognized also to own several thousand acres under such transactions.

The Bhoodan land (8,000 acres) was taken over and assisted in land development by an organization known as the Association of Seva Farms, which canalizes foreign rural development donations. One of its local representatives, Diwakarji, remembers that on his first arrival in 1953 no Harijan could even walk past the fortified manor of the mahant's henchmen in daylight. The approach of this organization, however, is a quiet, non-violent and gradualist one. They take up schemes only where the title of the land is not in legal dispute and where other conditions in their opinion are favourable.

Part of the compromise achieved by the mahant in 1957 was that no redistribution transactions prior to that date would be reopened. His attitude even in 1980 is summed up by his arrogant confidence before investigative journalist Harji Malik. 'We give land to the government at our pleasure,' he said smugly.

Not content with his manoeuvres up till 1957, he began further transfers in the early sixties. This stirred up some sort of government reaction and the transfers were challenged in court. In the 1980s these cases are still going on. They involve 122 of his relations or henchmen. Even if each of these is allowed the land ceiling of 25 acres, this does still not account for all their actual holdings.

In the meantime in 1979, a whole generation after the land reforms had been initiated (and frustrated) a new element entered the scene in the shape of a radical activist organization, the Chhatra Yuva Sangharsh Vahini (United Youth Organization for Change). This had been developed under the inspiration of socialist leader, Jayaprakash Narayan. They were not content with a non-violent gradualist approach and began organizing the peasantry, especially on the land which still remained under the mahant's *de facto* control through his benami redistribution. In one particular village area in 1979, during the Janata Government, the cultivators went on strike and no crop could be sown. The mahant merely bided his time until the Congress (I) was returned to power the following year in 1980. Meantime the peasants were starving because no crops had been sown or harvested and the mahant, as the feudal landlord, would obviously not help them out with credit. Realizing belatedly the position of the peasantry, the Vahini activists changed their tactics and encouraged them to sow and harvest the next year's crop for themselves.

However, when harvest time came the mahant's henchmen moved in. It only needed six or seven of his armed followers in each sector of his estate, backed by their traditional feudal authority, especially over the lower castes, and by what everyone knew locally was the connivance of the 'forces of law and order,' to terrorize the peasantry. The police were called in to 'protect' the mahant's henchmen who, of course, on paper were the recorded individual owners of innumerable plots, each within the land ceiling. Cases were registered against the actual cultivators and their property attached. This meant forcible rounding up of all their immovable property, including even household utensils and buffaloes. In one extreme case even the wooden doors of a hut were taken away by the police. An individual who went into hiding was termed an 'absconder' and thus attracted the full weight of the law. All this led to women's demonstrations, publicity and visits by national journalists. The district magistrate, when interviewed, merely pointed out the technical legal position that 'if somebody comes and says that someone is threatening to loot my property, the DC has to act to maintain law and order.'

A later study by the then Land Reforms Commissioner of Bihar, A.R. Bandyopadhyay, now in charge of the Central Government's entire land reform programme, revealed the unpleasant truth, that according to land records the land in question was noted as being in the possession of over 1,900 smaller landholders, each within the prescribed ceiling, and that many of these in turn have subdivided the land for cultivation under various arrangements. According to A.R. Bandyopadhyay: 'The point to be noticed is that there has been a horizontal dispersion of much land. Even today the mahant is not the real beneficiary of all the land. The nominees, who are ryots, or owners, according to law get the produce, not the mahant.'[20]

This may well be the legal position according to records. On the ground, however, the actuality is totally different. After the agitation the Bihar government formed a 'committee' in which

Diwarkarji, the Gandhian worker, was associated. This committee summoned over 800 of the individuals who were on record as
owning the plots. Out of these about 200 refused to appear,
another 400 or so claimed that they were not involved at all. Only
200 or so brought their land title deeds.

The committee's report has not been published. It is supposed
to have recommended that the 600 or so individuals who refused
to appear or disclaimed involvement should have the land recorded against them and taken away by government for redistribution. Such action, however, by government, quite apart from
the government's political nexus with the landed vested interests,
would be obviously impossible under law based on the mere
recommendations of an enquiry committee who had also admitted the confusion on the ground due to the interspersing of
innumerable private plots and trust lands. Indeed the committee
was also constrained to suggest the appointment of a full-time
Additional District Magistrate to sort out the actual factual
possession. Thus, in the light of the ultimate study by the Bihar
Land Reforms Commissioner, one is back to square one.

Meantime the legal cases involving other elements of the
benami transactions in trust lands linger on. The mahant, to avoid
the ceiling of some 500 acres on such trust lands, claims that there
is no single trust but 18 quite separate trusts linked with 18
separate deities whose idols are strewn over the area. The
intricacy and confusion over the devious devices to frustrate land
reform for over 30 years would daunt even a most dedicated
investigative journalist. Harji Malik also discovered that all the
plots were inextricably intermixed. She found that a short journa-
listic visit was insufficient to obtain all the details and felt, but was
not sure, that the cultivators of the land could retain for themselves about one-tenth of the produce under various feudal
practices. She could merely suggest that a follow-up was necessary.

In the light of the history of the case one wonders who or what
agency could effectively undertake such a study of blatant benami
transactions when government agencies, gradualistic Gandhians,
radical activists, the judicial machinery and even investigative
journalists seem to have failed. The only sure and constant
element in this sordid history remains the mahant himself, vividly
described by Harji Malik as an 'obnoxious and vicious individual'
presiding confidently over the scene from the tiger-skin rug in his

mansion fortress guarded by a burly CID plainclothesman against 'intimidation', whether by the lower orders or by a minister whom he had sued! The final say remains that of the mahant: 'Many people who were making trouble for our people here have come to us saying, "We were misled" and have asked for our forgiveness.'

The example of the mahant illustrates to what extent the operation of the law favours the status quo. Another factor supporting the interests of the landholding classes is the fact that land ceilings refer to property held by a landowner. Therefore by definition they exclude any lands leased out by the landlord either to relatives, tenants, sharecroppers or agricultural labourers under various arrangements. D. Bandyopadhyaya, former West Bengal Land Reforms Commissioner, points out: 'Most of what are called operational holdings in national surveys are benami holdings. So unless you can make benami illegal no land reforms can be effective.'[21] In fact, Narendar Pani's study discovered that in both northern and southern Karnataka ownership holdings could be smaller than operational holdings and concludes that for land reforms to be effective ceilings would have to be placed on operational holdings.[22]

Indeed the scale of the evasion of land ceilings laws is well illustrated from a casual encounter. During a train journey from Chittorgarh to Udaipur in south Rajasthan this author was engaged in a conversation with a professor, a Rajput by caste, who teaches commerce at BN College in Udaipur. When asked how much land his family possessed, he openly admitted that his joint family owns 400 acres of land: 'Only 18 acres are officially declared in statistics. My family owns the rest in benami transactions.'

Estimates of surplus land to be vested as a result of the imposition of ceiling laws were based on land records and 'where the land records are not up to date, the record of possession available to the land revenue collecting authorities has provided the necessary basis for calculation.'[23] The government estimated from the land records that 5.3 million acres would be vested as a result of the 1972 revised ceiling laws, although Wolf Ladejinsky points out that 57 to 60 million acres should have been vested after the passage of the 1972 laws.[24] Yet only 4 million acres were declared surplus under these revised ceiling laws. As of 10 April 1982 only 2,737,354 acres had been taken possession of and

1,907,275 acres had been distributed to 1,370,825 beneficiaries.[25] As of April 1983 1.4 million acres were still tied up in court.

These figures are only a slight improvement over the distribution of surplus land vested as a result of the abolition of the feudal estates. According to an Agrarian Survey carried out by a team of eminent social scientists for the Asian Development Bank in 1977, it was found that in 16 states which implemented land ceiling legislation between 1958 and 1971 only 0.99 million hectares had been declared surplus by 1971, representing only 0.7 per cent of the net cropped area. Less than 0.49 million hectares had been distributed to poor farmer households and landless workers.[26]

Another important contributory factor impeding the progress of land reforms has been interference by the law courts, because the entire weight of the civil and criminal laws, judicial pronouncements and precedents, and administrative practices, upholds the existing social order based on the sanction of private property. Furthermore, the mass of writ petitions filed by landlords regarding the land reform laws and their application are awaiting disposal in High Courts. Thus landowners continue to be in possession of land held to be surplus and transferable to the landless. Tenants are also denied rights, to which they are entitled under tenancy laws, for long periods. Despite their poverty they are often involved in prolonged and costly litigation.

The outcome of a case may take years depending on the number of appeals and revisions involved. In some states judicial personnel are associated with the disposal of land reform cases at the appellate and revisional stages. These cases may be referred back by the High Court to lower courts or revenue tribunals. The delays can be further prolonged since the civil courts treat these cases like any other and do not assign them priority. On mixed tribunals evidence procedures can involve inordinate delays in their disposal.

The unsatisfactory progress in the vesting of surplus land is precisely due to the fact that all land ceiling laws are subject to the jurisdiction of civil courts in respect of disputes arising from these laws. Most of them have also been insulated from challenge in the courts of law because landlords invoke the fundamental property rights guaranteed in the Constitution. Within the administration there are top officials who feel frustrated by the obstructions placed by the judicial machinery. One of them was outspoken and said in confidence: 'It is only the High Courts and the judiciary which thwart the implementation of land reforms in a major way. That is why the thrust of all progressive people has been that the Ceiling Acts should be put in Chapter Nine of the Constitution so we can avoid judicial scrutiny.'

Another major impediment to effective land reform is the absence of land records in many parts of the country. This was admitted by the Task Force on Land Reforms appointed by the Planning Commission in the early seventies, both in regard to conferring rights on tenants and sharecroppers and in regard to the proper implementation of the ceiling laws: 'It is very difficult to find out from the record of rights itself how lands above the ceiling have been dispersed clandestinely for evading the expected ceiling law.'[27] Wolf Ladejinsky also attributes the failure of land reforms to the absence of proper land records: 'This explains the anachronism that while state after state continue to enact new ceiling laws, hardly any have gone to the trouble to put their land records in order to find out how much surplus land might be available for distribution.'[28]

When the American anthropologist, Joan P. Menscher, was doing research in Tamil Nadu her work was hampered by the absence of proper land records and she points out that if the Government ever tried to draw up a list of such land registers: 'It would certainly encounter a great deal of passive (and perhaps not only passive resistance).'[29]

During a visit to Chapta village in Etawah district, UP, in March 1983 the dimensions of the problem became evident. The headquarters of the *tehsildar*, the local officer responsible for land records, is literally miles away from the development office responsible for rural uplift. Village land records are supposed to be kept by the most junior revenue official called a *patwari*, or *lekhpal*, responsible for a small group of villages. He is hardly ever traceable in Chapta. Some record is supposed to be available with the panchayat (village council) secretary who is again totally elusive.

Even more serious than the unavailability of such records, either to the public in general or to a visitor, is the serious doubt that they are ever inspected at appropriate levels. During the British period it was one of the prime duties of the district officer (collector) to tour extensively, camp in villages and conduct on-the-spot verifications and inspections. Some states like the Punjab had very detailed questionnaires to be completed by him, including his assessment of the honesty of the patwari, the type of house which the patwari actually lived in, whether by local repute he had any other establishment and even whether he actually lived there with his family! It is common knowledge that under present conditions no district magistrate can possibly find time for such inspections today. No wonder therefore that there is a total lack of credibility about the up-to-dateness and accuracy of land records.

The most serious land problem in tribal areas regards the alienation of land to outsiders who are mostly intent on gaining the best land for settlement. This is in spite of the fact that sale of land by tribals to non-tribals is prohibited by law in many tribal areas. For example, in the tribal districts of Banswara and Dungarpur in South Rajasthan such a legal prohibition exists. Yet land alienation among the Bhils, the major tribal group of the region, to the landlord/money-lender is known to be very high. However, as N.N. Vyas, Principal, Tribal Research Institute, Udaipur, points out: 'If you look at village records in the area the land is registered as "belonging" to the tribals.'[30]

D. Bandyopadhyaya, former West Bengal Land Reforms Commissioner, believes that the only way to revise land records is to bring the entire population of a village, both the landlords and the landless, together. As he rightly points out, the only people who know the scale of the evasions in a village, apart from the landlords themselves, are the sharecroppers and agricultural labourers who cultivate their lands. He comments: 'The answer is to bring people together under a banyan tree and ask people to declare their holdings in the presence of everybody else and then follow it up by looking up your village land documents. The poor may be afraid to speak out against the landlords, they may not even tell the truth or even come. But a beginning must be made. The poor should be encouraged to congregate and speak in one voice.'[31]

Apart from the absence of up-to-date land records in many parts of the country, the reliability of statistics from the National Sample Surveys, All-India Debt Surveys and Rural Labour Enquiries, the three major national censuses carried out on landholding patterns in India, is open to question. Yet government studies and academic researchers cite data from these sources as these are the best available to date: 'The result of this uncritical use of biased sources is an underestimation of the power and wealth of the rich, an overestimation of the number and position of middle peasants and underestimation of the proletariat.'[32]

The fact is that landlords lie about their holdings, the more so since they are aware of the government's frequent revisions of land reform legislation. Even if these laws are badly implemented, the legislation still poses a threat to their traditional power base.

D. Bandyopadhyaya has his own telling comments to make regarding statistical figures on landholdings: 'In the rural areas nobody will declare land they hold beyond the ceiling to anyone. Even the landless will not say they are landless because a man without land is a non-person in the village. So both ways you get a cut-off. That is why in the agricultural statistics you have a bulge in the middle which on paper looks very egalitarian.'[33]

The Agricultural Census itself defines its own limitations. Its landholding is 'all land which is used wholly or partly for agricultural production and is operated as one technical unit by one person alone or with others *without regard to the title, legal form, size of location* [author's italics]'.[34] Even on the basis of declared holdings the situation remains totally weighted against the poor. The Government of India's own statistics admit that 25 per cent of the total area was operated by marginal and small farmers, although they accounted for nearly 73 per cent of the total number of holdings. On the other hand, the three per cent of 'large landholders' operated over more than 25 per cent of the area.[35]

Large and medium landholders in fact continue to be favoured by the government's agrarian policies, as, for example, in consolidation of holdings. Consolidation has now been completed in western UP, Punjab and Haryana, the three states where the Green Revolution has been successful. In consonance with its emphasis on increased commercial agriculture, the government has been promoting consolidation in other Indian states. The principle behind consolidation is that it makes for more rational and economic holdings for the application of modern farm technology. Traditionally landlords have held scattered plots which has made for informal tenancy and sharecropping arrangements, as well as for the use of hired labour. In other words, the inability of the landlord to cultivate his scattered plots himself helped absorb labour. However, once a landlord receives a compact plot less labour and managerial supervision are required and the landlord therefore goes in for mechanization.

While consolidation laws make elaborate provisions for updating land records, in practice this is frustrated by the vested interests in the village. Consequently, the landlords are able to acquire the best lands, while the marginal and small farmers are assigned poorer lands of inferior quality on the periphery of the village. According to D. Bandyopadhyaya, consolidation is 'totally anti-poor' and he comments: 'It makes the landowner much stronger because his land is much more homogeneous than before and his economic power has increased tremendously. The poor man will get land only on the margin of the village.'[36]

In a recent paper delivered at a Commonwealth Workshop on Consolidation of Landholdings it was pointed out that: 'In Bihar the rights of undertenants and sharecroppers are scarcely recorded in the record of rights. Consolidation has provided an opportunity for their unobtrusive eviction from land.'[37] The author of the article, A.R. Bandyopadhyay, is therefore against consolidation: 'In a country which is labour intensive and capital scarce surely mechanization of agriculture is the most irrational way of using scarce capital. The moment the people who were holding different plots of land through informal arrangements have to be shifted, that is the moment they get thrown off their land.'[38]

Thus it seems the poor lose out on all fronts despite the fact that from 1971 Mrs Gandhi was espousing 'socialist' programmes. Even between 1972, when the government revised the ceiling laws, and 1975, when the Emergency was declared, only 62,000 acres throughout the country had even been vested in the state governments, quite apart from any question of actual distribution to the poor. Under the total powers assumed during the Emergency, one would have expected a speedier progress. This in fact to some extent did happen, mainly perhaps because of the disability placed on landowners in moving courts for stay orders against awards by new local institutions known as 'Political Implementation Committees'. Those who attended successive chief ministers' conferences during the period and were at the helm in inner administrative circles remember clearly the urgency and stress at high levels for this programme. Such chief ministers, notably those of Karnataka and West Bengal, applied their minds forthrightly to detailed problems of implementation. There was much pressure on the local bureaucracy to cut down on red tape and reduce the time lag between scrutiny of landholdings, government takeover and actual distribution.

The result was that against 62,000 acres merely vested in government in the three years before the Emergency, an additional 1.7 million acres were vested in the year or so after the Twenty-Point Programme got off the ground in 1975. Out of this, 1.1 million acres were actually distributed. Much, however, depended on the commitment and efficiency of local authorities.

Nor do even these figures accurately depict the gravity of the situation at the grass roots. Under the 1975 land distribution programme 1,000 agricultural labourers in Silora block, Ajmer district, in the Rajasthan desert, had been assigned land. The voluntary organization, the Social Work Research Centre, based in the block, has found that 40 per cent of the allottees are involved in land disputes and therefore still cannot occupy their land. According to SWRC director, Bunker Roy: 'Of the remaining 60 per cent many do not know where the land is. Sometimes the land is located on the side of a hill, or the top of the mountain, in the middle of a sand dune or river. Sometimes the land exists on paper only. The land is usually very poor and full of rocks and stones. Thus the poor Harijan doesn't know what to do next.'[39] The visual evidence of the arid, infertile plots that he points out stare a visitor in the face in mute testimony to the truth of his assessment.

Four common problems hampered this distribution programme according to Bunker Roy. Much of the land distributed was already disputed; secondly, legal papers were given to the allottees but the land was non-existent; thirdly, the police failed to follow up reported cases of forcible harvesting by former occupants; and fourthly, some land came under court stay orders.

David Selbourne in *An Eye to India* also noted that a significant proportion of land distributed in 1975/76: '. . . included reserved common land, land unfit for cultivation, and land of even less substance, since not to be found on terra firma but only on paper.'[40] However, V.C. Pande, Adviser, Twenty-Point Programme, Planning Commission, is more realistic with regard to the power of vested interests at the grass roots and their ability to thwart land distribution. He rightly points out: 'If you think that the best land can be vested under the ceiling for redistribution to the landless, then one is hoping for too much. If you confine yourself to giving allotments of good land to the landless, then the vested interests will see to it that all land that the government seeks to acquire in the future is of low grade and that it is given to institutions, trusts and so forth and not distributed to the poor.'[41]

In fact, not everyone was a loser. In Chapta village in Etawah district, UP, where one-third of the population of 4,000 are landless and three-quarters of the holdings are below one acre, small portions of land between two to four decimals were distributed during the Emergency. A lot of the surplus land distributed in the village was scattered all over the place and the plots were not contiguous. Only four acres were distributed among 15 to 20 people, 20 per cent of whom were Harijans. Lala Ram, a wiry weather-beaten Harijan from Chapta, was fortunate enough actually to receive such a plot and not to be involved in any court case with the original owner. Yet he continues to face economic insecurity working as an agricultural labourer, as the allotment feeds him for only one and a half months, even though he has no family to support. Yet at least in his case the tiny plot, lush with tall green wheat, brings to his deprivation the first small glimmer of hope. The tragedy is that there are so few like him.

It became evident by hindsight after the Emergency that even the drive to bring about a transformation in the rural areas, as exemplified by the Twenty-Point Programme, although backed by unlimited theoretical power, could yet be frustrated to some degree again due to the basic control of all local levers of power in the countryside by dominant landowning classes. It is indeed open to question whether these were not as responsible through the local vote banks for Mrs Gandhi's defeat in 1977 as much as the more widely publicized excesses such as the sterilization programme.

Even in a remote Himalayan frontier village at 12,000 feet, beyond the district headquarters of Keylong in Lahul district of Himachal Pradesh, a Lohar, or Scheduled Caste, land allottee of the Emergency programme, who in 1978 had expressed fears that his land would be taken away following the Janata Government's victory in 1977, reported in 1981 that he was not firmly in possession. However, Himachal Pradesh during that period was not totally typical of the rest of the country. It had a committed chief minister who ran a well-organized team of administrators. However, the fear of the state allottee toiling up the slope to his village of Kolong, surrounded by a backdrop of jagged snow peaks, illustrates a very real problem faced after the Emergency. The very drive for speed and cutting of red tape often resulted in somewhat slipshod documentation of the new records, Full advantage was taken of this by the landowning classes once the courts' jurisdiction was restored and the Congress voted out of power.

Thus the Twenty-Point Programme, launched during the Emergency, failed for the same reason that earlier movements by voluntary organizations to uplift the poor had run aground. Even movements like the 'Bhoodan (land-gift) campaign' which had been inspired by Gandhian ideals were unsuccessful in their ultimate achievements. According to Lalu Singh, a close associate of Acharya Vinova Bhave, the initiator of the Bhoodan campaign: 'In many cases the land given to the landless was bought up by the middle peasant.'[42] The Bhoodan campaign was a movement which had been started to awaken responsibility of the rich to part voluntarily with some of their land for the benefit of society as a whole. It was envisaged as a vital component of the movement called 'Sarvodaya (the good of the whole)'.

A.R. Bandyopadhyay, former Bihar Land Reforms Commissioner, had deep personal experience of the situation in the field. Bihar was the centre of the activity where the movement claims to have taken 2.2 million acres for redistribution to the landless. A.R. Bandyopadhyay is sceptical not only of its claims but of its actual achievement in the field. Quoting his own experience he found that much of the land on inspection turned out to be of 'very poor quality and sometimes full of rocks'. He further notes that in the process of specifying and regularizing the transfer of land in government records that: 'What happened was that where good lands were given, a substantial part of them continued to be enjoyed by the donor/landlord, or people close to him, or people nominated by local Bhoodan movement workers, till a decision on their final distribution to eligible allottees was made.'[43]

The Sarvodaya movement, launched in 1968/69 under inspiration from the Bhoodan movement of the fifties, whose aim was to bring about an egalitarian order, was equally unsuccessful. In a study conducted by the A.N. Sinha Institute of Social Studies, Patna, on the application of the Sarvodaya in Musahari block in Bihar in 1969/70, it was found that the amount of land distributed in the course of this 'movement' was very small and nothing could be expected of it in the way of solving the problem of unevenness in land distribution. In a surveyed village of Musahari block, a little less than 10 per cent of households engaged in cultivation received Bhoodan lands and on average the distributed land came to a little less than 0.3 acres per household. Nor was it always the poorest who obtained these lands. Households with land formed the bigger proportion of the allottees. In a few cases allottees received land outside their own villages, implying that the landlords saw to it that donated lands were mainly distributed among households who were under their grip, even if they were located outside the village.

There is evidence to suggest that unevenness in land distribution continued to increase even after the Sarvodaya movement. According to the Agricultural Census, by 1971 about 50 per cent of the cultivating households in Musahari block operated less than one acre of land each. In 1961 the percentage was about 45 per cent. Where the Sarvodaya launched community irrigation schemes in the block, the major benefit has gone to the richer sections. It also launched a drive to distribute handpumps to provide the poor with drinking water. Here also the major benefit went to classes other than poor peasant households.[44]

While both government and voluntary organizations have failed to solve the problem of the landless, there is yet another class which suffers economic grievances. To date, laws on paper notwithstanding, the government has failed to solve in any large-scale manner the problem of insecure and informal tenancy which continues to affect millions and millions of tenants. Such tenancy generally arises where ownership of land is divorced from cultivation or where land hunger, due to a highly skewed distribution of land, is so acute that a vast population of landless and marginal farmers can find no alternative source of livelihood away from the land. As a result they will come to almost any terms, even with a cultivating peasant proprietor, to grow something to feed their families. Before land reforms, it was assumed that the terms of tenancy formed three descending rungs of insecurity. At the top were 'occupancy tenants' with recorded leases. These have generally been the main beneficiaries of land reforms after Independence. In the middle were tenants-at-will who could be ousted at the will of the landlord. And at the bottom were sharecroppers who tilled the land on purely oral understandings that they would pay a percentage of the produce to the landowner.

Below these were only the daily labourers. It is not possible to reach any dependable computation of tenancy or sharecropping in India because most arrangements are oral or, even more seriously, concealed. As the Task Force on Agrarian Relations points out: 'The position regarding the record of tenancies, particularly in the matter of entries relating to rights of sharecroppers is not satisfactory anywhere in the country and no record exists in some areas.'[45]

Francine Frankel has concluded that many tenants with registered leases were converted into tenants-at-will in the fifties by the landlords on the plea of resuming the land for 'personal cultivation', because of the landlords' fear that at some stage the government might transfer land to the tenants. In Sripuram village, Tanjore district, Tamil Nadu, Béteille had noted in the early sixties that the system of tenure and the recognized power of eviction kept separate families of non-Brahmins competing against each other for land and employment.

The position of sharecroppers was far worse than that of formal tenants for the land reform laws did not benefit them, even though those very laws sought to give them protection. Writing in the fifties on the situation in a UP village, the anthropologist McKim Marriott noted that for fear of the subletting clauses of these laws: 'They are moved about every year, or at the most every two years. Labourers are rarely kept by an employer for longer than the six months winter water period ...'[46] Nor has the situation changed in the eighties. Chhote Lal, a Thakur landowner of Chapta village, is a typical case in point: 'Our family does not lease out land to the same person every year. We may give it to a Thakur one year, a Muslim another and to a Chamar a third year.'

The Task Force on Land Reforms had noted that landowners frequently circumvent provisions of tenancy laws affording protection to sharecroppers by having recourse to the preventive sections of the Code of Criminal Procedure or to litigation in the civil courts. Moreover, there are numerous instances of land reform laws conferring rights on sharecroppers being negatived with the help of Section 144 of the Indian Penal Code. As Myrdal has stated:

All the significant policy measures for agricultural uplift – whether technological or institutional – have tended to shift the power balance of the rural structure in favour of the privileged classes.[47]

Even when sharecroppers are technically covered by laws, since they have no security of tenure they are in too weak a position to have legal rates of rent enforced.[48] This is the case, for example, in eastern and southern India where in some areas, 'fifty per cent or more of farmers cultivate wholly or partially leased lands mostly on oral leases', according to a Ford Foundation survey of tenurial conditions in India carried out in 1963. Furthermore, in eastern India National Sample Survey and micro-level enquiries, such as case studies of selected villages by agro-economic research centres and other agencies, show that tenancy in the traditionally rice-growing, densely populated areas of eastern India is of a subsistence character. This means that the landlord has full advantage over the tenant, the more so since the tenancy is largely of an oral character.

A.R. Bandyopadhyay recalls a study made of sharecropping in eastern India which highlighted the exploitative nature of the arrangements. According to the sharecropping laws the crop is to be divided equally between the landowner and the sharecropper on the assumption that both have invested in the inputs in equal parts. However, not only did the study find that the landlord failed to invest initially while still taking fifty per cent of the produce, but the sharecropper had no incentive to take another crop on double-cropped land because his share was further reduced to 30 per cent. A.R. Bandyopadhyay explains the situation:

> If the sharecropper wants to invest in a second crop, he has to put aside another 10 per cent from his first crop, further reducing his share of the first harvest by another 10 per cent. The landlord, however, will not invest in the second crop, although he will receive another 50-per-cent share of the produce. Therefore, unless the sharecropper is assured his right either by being recorded or given ownership rights, you cannot expect him to be induced to take the risk involved in a second cropping.[49]

The position of the sharecropper is much the same in UP, although the reasons for his insecurity and penury are different. They stem from the fact that since tenancy is illegal in UP, the sharecropper has no protection under the law. The practice continues to flourish clandestinely, especially in the more backward parts of eastern UP. This is brought out in a recent book on concealed tenancy in this state.[50] The study brings out the fact that time is fast running out for the government to confer rights on the tenants because, with the new technology being applied, it becomes more profitable for landlords to resume cultivation and use hired labour. Therefore tenants with formal leases can be done away with by reducing them to agricultural labourers, since even more surplus can be extracted by hired labour.

Béteille explains how the system works: 'Since sharecropping is disallowed, it is disguised in the form of a contract. A landlord engages in a contract with a sharecropper to give out some land in return for so much payment. It is called the *thekidar* system.'[51] For example, sharecropping was found to be very common in Chapta village, Etawah district, UP. Interviews with sharecroppers showed that the percentage each one received from the landlord depended on the relative strength of each party. Since sharecropping is not legally recognized, the sharecropper's bargaining power is minimized. Chhote Lal, a Thakur landowner of Chapta, rents out two bighas of land for which he receives two-thirds of the produce. In contrast in West Bengal, thanks to the movement for the recording of sharecroppers by the Marxist state government, the sharecroppers now receive 50 per cent of the produce according to state law. In the past, they often received only 25 per cent.

At the bottom of the agrarian hierarchy stand the landless agricultural labourers whom the land reforms have barely touched. Interestingly enough there are no exact official figures for sharecroppers or agricultural labourers, either as a group or as separate categories. The government constantly introduces new programmes to 'give land to the landless', yet its intentions are open to question. Commenting on the government's failure to carry out surveys to determine the exact number of sharecroppers and agricultural labourers in the country, Myrdal had this to say: 'Rigorous enquiries have not been sponsored officially, and one of the main reasons may well be that the authorities . . . have not wanted to risk stirring up the demand for agrarian reform that the release of such information must invite.'[52] Yet the Agrarian Reforms Committee as far back as 1950 had observed that '. . . to leave out the problem of the agricultural labourers in any scheme of agrarian reform as has been done so far is to leave unattended a weeping wound in the agrarian system of the country.'[53]

It is recognized that the proportion of landless people and those owning marginal land in relation to the total population is very high. According to the 1981 Census, out of a total agricultural labour force of 175 million, of which 91.4 million were cultivators, 55 million were classified as agricultural workers. The latter figure seems to be basically impressionistic. A.R. Bandyopadhyay, Central Land Reforms Commissioner, explains the problem: 'The classification "agricultural worker" includes whosoever is able bodied and has registered for work, or has worked at one time or another during the season. So my estimate is that there would be approximately 30 million such landless families. Some of these families will also have been noted as marginal farmers. We treat them as agricultural workers because according to the 1981 Census they have shown their principal source of earnings from agricultural wages.'[54]

The situation appears to have remained largely unchanged since the sixties when Myrdal estimated that at least one-third of the rural population relied 'for subsistence on wages as agricultural labourers'.[55] The situation in this country stands in sharp contrast to that prevailing in pre-1949 China where the percentage of tillers working as agricultural labourers was less than 2 per cent, according to several estimates.[56]

All over India's villages the demands of the poor are the same: 'Give us land.' Labourers from Chhatarpur district, Madhya Pradesh, are unanimous on this point: 'Most of all we want land.' In Banswara and Dungarpur districts, Rajasthan, the predominant Bhil tribal population ask for only one thing – land and irrigation facilities. Even when the landless are allotted plots, they are often apprehensive of losing them through harassment by former landlords. In the Bhilwara district of Rajasthan some landless allottees of surplus land abandoned their plots because they were afraid of the former landlords whose land the government had vested to distribute to these poorer sections.[57] In fact there is little hope of an equitable distribution of land when landlords continue to evade ceiling laws. Khem Raj, a social worker at the Social Work Research Centre, Tilonia in Ajmer district, Rajasthan, maintains that: 'Nine families in Kadampura village, Silora block, Ajmer district, possess 900 bighas, or 60 per cent of the land. Ten families have 70 bighas. The other 31 families have either small portions or land or are totally landless.'[58] There is obviously still scope for considerable redistribution of land to satisfy at least a proportion of the aspirants within the existing land reform policy. There is growing doubt, however, whether the realities of the rural power structure will allow this within the existing constitutional framework. However, the question also arises whether even effective implementation of the declared land reform policy could ever succeed in solving the problem of landlessness.

Many Leftists in India advocate a policy of land distribution to India's landless and marginal farmers. Some believe that, if the present land ceilings were properly implemented or reduced further, enough land would be uncovered to distribute two hectares to all landless families in the country. A.R. Bandyopadhyay, Central Land Reforms Commissioner, is the most senior Central Government official specializing in the land reforms programme. He maintains that the 1976/77 Agricultural Census report brought out the fact that there is a general scarcity of land for distribution: 'Despite a highly skewed pattern of landholdings, and considering that nearly 62 per cent of the land is unirrigated, there is an overall shortage of land. This is dismally clear. There can be no doubt about it.'[59]

Leftists, like the journalist Gail Omvedt, maintain that such statistics are inaccurate because of the large-scale evasions. A.R. Bandyopadhyay admits there is a great deal of evasion: 'The government knows that the landlords are keeping more land than they are permitted by the ceiling but, if one looks at the result of the variations in the Census undertaken in the Agricultural Census of 1970/71 and 1976/77 and the 26th Round National Sample Survey, the certain broad facts which emerge do indicate the margins within which evasions may have taken place.'[60]

Indeed other interviews at high levels show that some officials are even more frank and realistic in their appraisal of the progress in implementing the ceiling laws. One such disclosure was unequivocal: 'Except in a few states, despite the ten or twelve years that have gone by, we cannot say that the achievement is as impressive as it could be. Firstly you'll find that most of the state governments revise their ceiling act and each revision would mean a greater denotification of a greater number of areas. In many cases the act will be framed in such a fashion that more and more land has been left with the landowners and it allowed various relations to have some land. In this way the liberation procedure has cheated the poor of land.'

Thus despite recognition that some form of sharing of land in rural areas is necessary, such a change has not taken place. The government's present Sixth Five-Year Plan merely stresses that the present ceiling laws should be implemented and completed by the end of the Plan in 1985. Since the numerous drives in the past to implement ceiling acts have always come up against local vested interests, there is no reason to doubt that the present attempt will fail on the same count.

Even if the government were to further reduce the ceilings, some economists argue that this would hardly solve the problem of landlessness. There are several schools of thought on whether the lowering of land ceilings would still further reduce productivity and efficiency in Indian agriculture. V.M. Dandekar and Nilakantha Rath, in a well-known study,[61] rejected lower ceilings as impractical. They classified states into two categories, high-density and low-density areas. They calculated the ceilings that would be necessary if half an acre in the high-density areas and 2.5 acres in the low-density areas were to be distributed to every landless and marginal household with holdings under half an acre. The study argued that since the land vested would be of poor quality, no amount of long-term or short-term credit from cooperatives or national banks could make them economically viable. Therefore the study concludes that most of the allottees would sell their land. If this were prohibited by law, conditions would be such that they would lease-in their land, thus leading to the emergence of tenancy in reverse. Another well-known study by the economist A.M. Khusro, from another school of thought, argues that ceilings do not interfere with productivity but in fact promote higher productivity.[62]

Today it is generally accepted that small farms are just as productive, and usually more so, than large farms. For example, *The World Agricultural Census, Tamil Nadu*[63] has documented that those who own more resources in large quantities do not necessarily put them to optimum use. The study found that the gross cropped area as a percentage of the total area declines strongly as the size of the holding increases 'falling from 100 per cent in the case of very small holdings to less than 50 per cent in the case of holdings above 50 hectares.'[64] As V.C. Pande of the Planning Commission points out: 'If you distribute land to the landless you can still have a Green Revolution. Whether a person has one acre or ten acres make no difference.'[65]

Studies for 1980 on yields per acre, for example of wheat, in different countries show that large mechanized farms are less efficient than small farms using the same kind of technology. France and England, whose holdings are smaller than those of Australia and Argentina, are more productive. In 1980 the yields per hectare for France and England were 5,167 kg and 5,653 kg respectively, while those for the USA, Argentina and Australia were 2,249 kg, 1,567 kg and 939 kg respectively.[66] The yield per hectare on the Russian collective farm was 1,590 kg per hectare and on the Chinese comune it was 1,934 kg. The Soviet figures are, however, open to doubt, given the frequent grain purchases by the Soviet Union from the USA. The point here is that neither large-scale capitalist farming nor collective farms produce as much per hectare as a medium plot worked basically by family cultivators using modern technology.

Despite the theoretical possibility that modern technology can be applied economically on small holdings, the scale of the upheaval that would be necessary in India to achieve this last step of equitable distribution of land would be such as to be totally impossible within a democratic framework.

Thus despite recognition that some form of sharing of land in rural areas is necessary, such a change has not taken place. The basic reason for this is that notions of hierarchy are too deeply rooted in the culture. Given the intellectual commitment to modernization, policy framers have posed the question as to what is to be done about it. The assumption so far is that modernization would reduce these inequalities. However, this does not seem to have occurred to any significant degree. The rise of a new class of proprietors from the former tenant classes as a result of the zamindari abolition contributes a new class of exploiters for the subtenants, sharecroppers and agricultural labourers.

A final phase of land distribution of such a kind would in fact involve depriving an immense number of these middle peasant cultivators of plots which many of them would incidentally only recently have received from government after the break-up of the large zamindaris. Short of a ruthless Stalinist policy to liquidate millions of such middle peasants – which policy in the end backfired even in the Soviet Union – this programme cannot be considered more than theoretical. It is of significance that the Marxist Government of West Bengal has refused to fall into the trap, suggested by the Centre, to lower ceilings further rather than to reopen existing decisions to study whether there has been an evasion of objectives.

The only radical change that is realistically feasible will depend on massive employment programmes for the enormous mass of landless or virtually landless peasantry. This assumes vital importance when one considers the fact that, despite India's industrialization programme over the past 34 years, the industrial sector has been able to absorb only 4 per cent of the rural labour force. This shows the magnitude of the problem and the capital-intensive nature of India's industries.

In theory at least, there seems to be some realization regarding the need for massive programmes for rural employment in government circles. In the seventies the Congress (I) began the Crash Scheme for Rural Employment (CSRE); then under the Janata a variation was launched called the Food for Work Programme (FFWP), with the latest variation, the National Rural Employment Programme (NREP). However, all these have successively given the impression of having being half-hearted in implementation, again perhaps because of the distaste, obstructionism and specious criticism on the part of local vested interests whose hold on cheap labour at starvation wages would undoubtedly be weakened if such programmes achieved their aims.

Another problem has been the difficulties in uniting and organizing the rural poor, even to demand or make use of such existing employment programmes and other facilities. While rural works are necessary to provide employment to the landless and sharecroppers, the problems of the marginal and small farmers must also be effectively dealt with by the government. Especially necessary are service cooperatives to provide inputs and marketing facilities and a series of strong cooperative organizations to press for interrelated programmes of land consolidation and irrigation inputs. As has already been seen, too much irrigation potential is wasted due to two problems. Firstly, there are difficulties in planning a network of field channels to small holdings. Secondly, there are problems of investment in tubewells which normally cater only for larger holdings. A small or marginal holder therefore has to rely on the larger peasant holder for water from his tubewells which may not be available to an adequate extent in time.

The solutions to the problems at hand may therefore lie in the organization of some form of collective endeavour in each area to achieve this. The pattern may well have to vary from region to region. Stereotyped organizations of cooperative societies are unlikely to deliver the goods. Neither will doctrinaire attempts at Marxist collectivization. The first stirrings of new thought on these lines are beginning to appear in relation to the problem which is particularly acute in the Marxist state of West Bengal. Old traditional institutions of mutual self-help used to be prevalent, especially among the weaker sections of society. These will be discussed in the next chapter.

CHAPTER FOUR

West Bengal: a Marxist alternative

In the social ferment engendered by the mixture of traditional and modern values, one of the more potent catalysts is the rare phenomenon of a Marxist government administering a state the size of the United Kingdom within the framework of India's liberal federal constitution. This Marxist-run state of West Bengal is the only region in India to have carried out significant land reforms for the sharecroppers and landless agricultural labourers, the poorest strata in the agrarian hierarchy. Its agrarian reform programme emanated from its Communist ideology whose fundamental principle is that of wealth distribution. In a feudal-based economy this must take the initial form of land distribution. While in West Bengal land reform legislation has a long history dating back to British days, the Communist Party of India (Marxist) (CPI(M)) claims that it had largely remained on paper during previous Congress regimes and that only their present party leadership has possessed the political will to translate land reforms into one of India's most significant experiences.

The Marxists have had to implement their policies within the framework of a non-Communist parliamentary democratic constitution; therefore in assessing the land reforms one must recognize the constraints under which they have had to function. The first is a constitutional one. The Marxists in West Bengal claim that there is inadequate financial and policy autonomy for the states in the federal structure of the Union. The Centre, through its Finance Ministry and Planning Commission, has the ultimate say in the allocation of resources and the policy thrust of development programmes. Power for irrigation and grain allocations have been major bones of contention. However, land reforms are a state subject and, theoretically at least, have always been one of the main planks of Central Government policy. As will be seen, in West Bengal earlier spadework was far from insignificant.

The second constraint is juridical. The Marxist government

feels that the class orientation of the judiciary has played an important role in challenging or obstructing land reforms through legalistic challenges from landed interests. The third constraint is economic. India, although pledged to a socialistic society, has a mixed economy where private enterprise very much flourishes, influences government and provides election funds. The fourth is the apprehension, justified from previous experience in 1967 and 1969, always lurking in the background, that the Centre, on the plea of a breakdown of law and order, would install President's rule. Just before the state election in May 1981, Jyoti Basu, the Chief Minister was apprehensive that the Centre would make such a move, thus depriving the Marxists of access to the apparatus of state power to consolidate their hold.

Although the Marxists claim that their administration has implemented India's most significant land reforms to date, in actual fact Bengal has a long history of political and, to some extent, social awareness dating back to the days of the British connection in Bengal. The Bengalis, centred around Calcutta, were the class in India most receptive and longest exposed to Western thought. However, this was basically confined to an aristocracy, both of birth and culture. The Bengali renaissance from the mid-nineteenth century owed much of its stimulus to the impact of Western thought on Hindu values. From this sprang reform movements such as the Rama Krishna Mission, the Arya Samaj and Vivekananda. Economic pressures, especially the increasing number of educated unemployed, made many of the educated groups turn to Marxism, even in the British days. It was a Bengali, M.N. Roy, who was the first Asian member of the Third International.

In India land reform legislation was passed in all the states after Independence but remained largely on paper, except for mild reforms carried out by previous Left Front governments or Coalition governments in Kerala and Congress state governments in West Bengal. In West Bengal the earlier Congress regimes tackled land reforms on various fronts because Bengal has a certain tradition of advanced liberalism. In 1953 the zamindaries, or feudal estates, were abolished by the Estates Acquisition Act, land ceilings were imposed and surplus land was vested in the state for redistribution to the landless. Although land vested by the Estates Acquisition Act accorded no rights to sharecroppers on vested land, land vested under the West Bengal

Land Reforms Act, 1955, accorded the sharecroppers actual ownership of land up to 2.47 acres. It came to light that very little land had in fact become available for redistribution because the ceiling had been imposed on individual holdings. This enabled the landowners to parcel out their land to other family members by mass transfers.

In fact the most serious loophole in the land reform legislation in India was precisely the ability of landlords, once the ceiling was publicized, to transfer excess land to individual relatives or nominees, thus violating the entire aim of the legislation. In West Bengal the legislation was more realistic than in other states and the loopholes with regard to evasion of land ceilings were plugged by the West Bengal Land Reforms Amendment Act, 1972, passed under the Congress state regime. This law was made applicable retroactively to June 1969 to invalidate mala fide transfers. The Congress regime also fought out in the state high courts and the Supreme Court numerous tortuous legalistic challenges to frustrate the land reform legislation. Even after appeals had been taken out of the purview of time-consuming judicial procedures and vested in administrative tribunals, the landlords challenged the new legislation itself under an article of the Constitution affirming the right to private property.

In fact the Marxist regime inherited clear and effective legislation from the earlier Congress regimes to enable it to swing into action immediately after its victory at the polls in 1977. The Marxists also inherited considerable administrative machinery and functional experience in the field. The officialdom in West Bengal is less rooted in large family landholdings than in other adjacent states, notably Bihar, for many officials came as refugees from former East Bengal during the Partition of India in 1947. Lastly, West Bengal was the only state where the law recognized and provided security to sharecroppers who often tilled the land on payment of a percentage of the yield, often as high as 75 per cent, to the recorded owner. Indeed a beginning had already been made in the recording of sharecroppers and allotments of land and homestead plots to the landless, the latter being part of the plank of Mrs Gandhi's Twenty-Point Programme in 1975/76.

The Marxists, however, claim that the full implementation of the land reforms had never been possible under the Congress because the political will was lacking and because there was a class bias among the administrators and judiciary in favour of the landlord. The Marxists cite, for example, the method of recording the sharecroppers through the Revenue Courts which meant that the sharecroppers had to act on their own initiative as there was no government or administrative machinery to assist them; few sharecroppers were recorded since the majority feared eviction by the landlords. Or the fact that until the West Bengal Land Reforms Act, 1977, was passed, the eviction of sharecroppers could take place on the ground that the 'person owning the land requires it bona fide for bringing it under cultivation.' This could be interpreted to mean the landlord might engage wage labour and led to many evictions. This new law provides for eviction only if the landlord himself cultivates the land.

The Marxist land reforms launched energetically in 1978 had three main aspects: the identification and vesting of further surplus land; the recording of sharecroppers; and the distribution of title deeds covering up to one acre to landless agricultural labourers, or former sharecroppers. Implementation was through joint involvement of the official government machinery, Marxist party cadres elected in 1978 to the panchayats (village councils) and peasant organizations. Responsibility for initiative was fixed on the administration, both official and non-official, rather than on an individual sharecropper being expected to approach the Revenue Department to get himself recorded as in the past. The panchayats have been responsible for identifying deserving recipients of land title deeds.

The partial success of the reforms is thus due firstly to the presence of a strong political will and the Marxists' ability to arouse awareness both in the administration and amongst the illiterate masses; secondly, to the concept of group action publicized in an open forum which helped the passive and submissive peasant to overcome his diffidence. Up to 30 June 1981, 1,089,500 sharecroppers had been recorded, out of which 275,000 were recorded during the Congress regime. Out of this total 435,800, or 40 per cent, were Scheduled Castes and 196,100, or 18 per cent, were Scheduled Tribes. Up to 30 June 1981, 1,124,856 land title deeds were issued to the landless or former sharecroppers.

The philosophy behind the grant of seemingly uneconomic holdings to the poorest labourers has been questioned by economists. However, quite apart from the Marxist ideologues, the strategy evolved by their party in West Bengal has been understood and endorsed even within the Central Government's Planning Commission. V.C. Pande, Adviser, Twenty-Point Programme, Planning Commission, is categorical: 'The point is that the giving of one-acre plots in West Bengal was never carried out on the philosophy that the allottee will have a surplus. That one acre makes a human being out of him. He gets into government records, he can get a bank loan, he now has a future. I don't think that any Marxist ever thought that that one-acre plot would make him self-sufficient and help him to cross the poverty line.'[1]

Despite the Marxist state government's obvious goodwill the land reforms have created many new problems which the state government may not have foreseen, thus showing how difficult it is to try to bring about even a modicum of change in the agrarian structure. Organda is a typical village in Bengal. Like the rest of the state it has been under Communist rule for the last six years. On the surface it is steeped in halcyon calm. Spacious huts smoothly plastered with sunbaked mud and thatched with thick layers of straw line the main street. There is an aura of mellow neatness. On one flank, in a separate hamlet, stand the more humble dwellings of the lower castes, the former Untouchables. But new antagonisms are dividing the society as a result of the Marxist drive for land reforms.

A gaunt figure, Madhav Nayak, paces out the boundaries of his new land grant on the narrow embankment of the paddy fields. It is a minute plot, only a third of an acre, which could at best feed his family for three months of the year. He tells his story unemotionally with generations of endurance in his eyes. For he is a low-caste agricultural labourer whose ancestors have always tilled the soil for a pittance on the land of others. His plot, which could have been a symbol for a new hope, was part of a former feudal estate. The latter had been taken over under both the Estates Acquisition Act, 1953, and the Land Reforms Act, 1955. In 1981 the son of Madhav Nayak cultivated the plot but the paddy was harvested by Shodipada Loha who claims to have actually cultivated this land continuously for the past thirty years, and to have been recorded as a *bargadar* (sharecropper) under the Land Reforms Act, 1955. Since Shodipada Loha already possesses 4.5 acres of land, under the Act he has the right to this land. However, he has filed a petition in the Court under article 226 of the Constitution relating to fundamental property rights. On 9 September 1980 the High Court issued an injunction restraining the new patta holder, Madhav Nayak, from interfering with the possession of the petitioner.

Many new allottees are not contesting the claims of old bargadars so that the Marxists cannot effectively gauge the success of their reforms. About a kilometre away stands Organda II, a separate tribal village inhabited by Santhals, the largest and most advanced tribal group in the state. In India Hindus and tribals do not mix because of the strict pollution and caste rules prevailing in Hinduism. In typical Santhal style the outer walls of the rectangular huts have black wainscoting on the lower sections, while the upper portions are decorated with intricate geometrical designs. Barsa Soren, an agricultural labourer, squats on the mud verandah of his house as he talks. He was allotted half an acre in March 1981. This year his harvest was collected by Upendro Sahish, a lower caste, who claims to be a sharecropper on this land which was originally a part of a feudal estate. Barsa Soren has not submitted any application to the Junior Land Reforms Commissioner who is to settle such disputes since Shodipada Loha is organizing the bargadars against the patta holders and he is 'afraid of the other party'. The dispute appears to be on party lines, the bargadars being Jharkhand supporters, while the patta holders belong to the CPI(M) which is relatively weak in the village.

The tensions that have arisen in Organda reflect the types of problems being created in many villages across West Bengal. Since only 0.7 per cent of households in the state own above 10 hectares, the land reforms are pitting the middle and marginal peasant against those even poorer. Ramesh Hembron, a Santhal schoolteacher from Ranarani village, Binpur 1, in Jhargram, Midnapore district, has filed a case with the Junior Land Reforms Officer regarding three acres of land which he claims was gifted in the common knowledge of all villagers by the zamindar to his father, a respected educational pioneer. His father did not possess legal papers when the land was vested but he went on cultivating it. Meanwhile, many years later, the government has listed these 3 acres for redistribution to 25 people. The pattas have not yet been assigned.

The new types of land conflicts are also creating a certain passivity among some agricultural labourers. In Ranarani, a Santhal village in Binpur I, Chope Murmu Baskey, a Santhal pro-Jharkhand agricultural labourer, who earns Rs 4 a day, has not yet received patta land. He says: 'I haven't applied for any as I don't want to disturb someone already in occupation. I don't want to have a clash over land.'

Another type of problem is political in nature. In some cases a CPI(M) supporter is recorded a bargadar on land on which another bargadar has already been recorded under the Congress regime. Kundu Mahato, a landless Jharkhand party supporter from Chotodiha village, Jhargram PS, was recorded a bargadar in 1954 through the Revenue Court. During 'Operation Barga' Amulya Mahato, a CPI(M) supporter, was certified the bargadar of this disputed 3.63 acres. In 1980 the matter was amicably settled with each one receiving 50 per cent of the crop.

These cases came to light in an on-the-spot investigation undertaken in December 1981 in Jhargram subdivision, Midnapore district. Figures given by the Senior Land Reforms Officer for Jhargram subdivision fail to substantiate the claims of the Marxists asserting that they are the main initiators of land reform in the state. Prior to 1977, 36,099.16 acres were distributed to 17,914 Scheduled Castes, 21,264 Scheduled Tribes and 17,783 others under the Block Level Land Reforms Advisory Committee, a pre-Marxist institution; whereas under the present panchayat samitis since 1978, 12,145.15 acres were distributed to 7,963 Scheduled Castes, 10,366 Scheduled Tribes and 9,032 other castes. According to the same source only 7723.20 acres still remains to be recommended by the present panchayat samitis. In fact the lack of good vested agricultural land available for distribution may be one of the reasons that during my visits to actual plots in the course of my field investigation undertaken with Marxist cadres or members of the administration, not one patta holder was met who was not involved in a case over land or whose land was cultivable. It may be unfair to suggest general conclusions from these random visits. But it is significant that a formal evaluation study on Land Reforms commissioned by the West Bengal government in 1981 through the Socio-Economic Research Institute, Calcutta, found that in Birbhum district 25 per cent of sharecroppers were involved in disputes and specifically refrained from presenting data or commenting on the vesting and distribution of ceiling surplus land. Such a detailed study is clearly called for.

In fact, there have been accusations by the Opposition that the CPI(M) are recording their own supporters as bargadars. The government contests this. The Additional District Magistrate from Midnapore district thinks that not more than 5 per cent of the total bargadars recorded by the Marxists were even CPI(M) activists. The Settlement Officer (Midnapore) is claimed to have conducted a survey in which he estimated that not more than one per cent of recorded bargadars were CPI(M) activists. In the author's field study the trend seemed to be that the old bargadars are moving away to the Jharkhand movement.

M. Mathur, Secretary of the Jharkhand Party, Midnapore district, claimed in Jhargram that tribals are leaving the CPI(M) because they are not benefiting fairly from the land reforms. He claims that, although they constitute 29 per cent of the population there, only 20 per cent of them have received vested land. This perception from one set of statistics is, however, offset from another angle by the Subdivisional Officer (Jhargram)'s figures showing that out of 64,139 assignees of *khas* (special land reserved by the government for use as allotment at its discretion) and vested land, 24,157, or over 36 per cent, are tribals. In regard to acreage, a similar percentage holds good.

There now appears to be a scarcity of land available for allotment, indicating that the pace of land reforms may subside. The Marxists argue that much surplus land is still concealed in benami holdings and that they are counting on bargadars to bring these to the notice of the authorities. According to D. Bandyopadhyaya, former West Bengal Land Reforms Commissioner, only 9 per cent of the total arable land in the state has been vested under the Estates Acquisition Act, 1953, and the West Bengal Land Reforms Act, 1955, up to 30 June 1981. 'Our own assessment is that 18 per cent of the total arable land in West Bengal should be vested as surplus land,'[2] he comments. Out in the field, however, there does not seem to be much progress in discovering surplus land. In Jhargram subdivision there are only 7,723.70 acres left for distribution. In Binpur block, Jhargram, 290.38 acres remain for distribution under the Estates Acquisition Act, 1953, and 47.45 acres under the West Bengal Land Reforms Act, 1955.

According to Keshab Chandra Mandi, the *pradhan* (chairman) of gram panchayat no. 8 of Jamboni block, Jhargram, when the panchayat was formed it was only able to detect about 60 acres of surplus land. Out of that amount, 40 acres were distributed to 40 families and the remaining 20 acres, were distributed amongst 30 families. Out of the 70 beneficiaries, 30 were Scheduled Tribes and 7 were Scheduled Castes. Only 17 out of the 70 families received credit during the 1981 kharif season, according to the pradhan and these cases were selected by the panchayat samiti. Since 1978, 10 bargadars have been recorded through the panchayat according to the pradhan. Ten civil cases had been instituted. In three, ex-parte injunctions were issued in favour of the landowner; the other seven were settled in favour of the bargadars.

Figures for Binpur block show that the Congress record was significant, even though Congress' long tenure was largely taken up in formulating land reform legislation and plugging loopholes. In Jhargram subdivision under the Block Level Land Reform Advisory Committees (BLLRAC) which operated during Congress rule, 56,961 landless received pattas; during the present regime 27,961 landless received pattas up to November 1981. In Binpur the BLLRAC distributed 5,725.93 acres; under the Marxists 2,153.54 acres were distributed by the panchayat samitis. Under the Congress 1,313 bargadars were recorded on 769.02 acres; under the Marxists 377 bargadars on 236.27 acres were recorded.

The implementation of land reforms has also been consistently thwarted by legal obstructions. Up to December 1980 one-seventh of all vested agricultural land was hit by court injunctions. The state is contesting these rulings which means, however, that the distribution of land to the landless may be delayed over a period of several years. The former Land Reforms Commissioner of West Bengal points out that while the state High Courts have consistently favoured the original landowner, the Supreme Court has ruled in the government's favour in two important appeals. No effective legal option exists to solve the problems ascribed to the class bias of the High Courts. The state cannot pass an amendment setting aside all cases hit by injunctions because Article 226 of the Constitution guarantees private property rights.

Yet despite these impediments ascribed to class bias, the government has won some significant victories in the Supreme Court. In a judgment delivered on 9 May 1980 the latter upheld the Land Reforms Amendment Act, 1972, regarding the retrospective effect of the law pertaining to family ceilings, as against individual ceilings. It also upheld as reasonable the maximum land ceiling of 7 standard hectares in view of the pressure on land in West Bengal and the need for helping the landless. The second Supreme Court judgment delivered in February 1981 upheld the legal validity of the Land Reforms Amendment Act, 1955, ruling that in the event of a sharecropper abandoning the land, the landlord does not have the right to resume personal cultivation of the plot but has to get the land cultivated by another person approved by the Junior Land Reforms Commissioner. This leaves a loophole for induction of a Marxist supporter. However, questioning the basic equity of such a provision, the Supreme Court recommended its reconsideration by the legislature.

The Left Front Government has recognized that land reforms will have little effect without a programme for providing credit and inputs. Unfortunately, to date, progress on this front has been inadequate. During 1979–80, 103,200, or 6 per cent, of sharecroppers and patta holders received institutionalized credit through the state. In Midnapore district in 1979–80 only a little over one per cent of the beneficiaries received some kind of credit, even though Midnapore has the largest amount of recorded sharecroppers and patta beneficiaries.

D. Bandyopadhyaya, former West Bengal Land Reforms Commissioner, explained that government is fully alive to the problem.[3] Characterizing usury as the major source of rural exploitation, he recognizes that this cannot be broken unless banks and credit institutions intervene in a massive and coordinated programme. In so far as the weakest sections of society are concerned, the Congress in 1976 had already established the West Bengal Scheduled Caste and Scheduled Tribe Development and Finance Corporation to act as a financial catalyst for their economic development. However, during the six years prior to 1978 agrarian loans from the entire banking sector at differential rates of interest covered only 79,000 beneficiaries. In 1979 alone, the CPI(M) arranged coverage of a further 59,000, but it was only by 1981, through energetic and effective liaison with the banks, that they succeeded in clearing many of the procedural impediments and prejudices. A Scheduled Caste or Tribal sharecropper or land allottee can now obtain Rs 500 of credit per acre of paddy land. Of this Rs 250 is an outright subsidy; Rs 100 is interest-free margin money advanced by the Corporation; and the balance of Rs 150 is loaned by the bank at the easy differential interest rate of only 4 per cent per annum. There is even an incentive provision for subsidizing this interest, if repayment is within the stipulated period. The comparison with interest of over 150 per cent per annum charged by money-lenders is impressive. The CPI(M) also claims success in radically improving recovery percentages, which were earlier well below the all-India average, by advocating practical steps such as initiatives to contact loanees at harvest time itself. Their surveys incidentally show a better repayment record on the part of the poor than on the part of the more affluent.

All this augurs well for the future but the fact remains that in many parts of the state, especially in the west of Midnapore district where the quality of the soil is poor, the land reforms have yet to yield substantial economic improvement. Malati Mullick, a Lodha tribal woman from Pranabpally village, Jhargram PS, received a one-acre patta two years back in the adjoining village, Baharasuli, after applying through the local panchayat. The land is poor and in December 1981 she had not yet cultivated the plot as the land needed a large input of fertilizer, *bunding* (water-retaining banks) and water, but credit was not yet available in the area. Furthermore, despite the fact that Madhav Nayak, from Organda village, Binpur II, admitted receiving a Rs 170 loan from the government in July 1981, he admitted also having borrowed a loan from a money-lender the same year.

Apart from the problem of individual credit for inputs, the priority need of the Jhargram area is for irrigation. At present only a single rain-fed crop is possible. The major Kansavati irrigation project has so far benefited very few in the area. Changes in its planning design are supposed to have created problems, amongst them some major flood damage from the project itself. In any case, it holds out little hope for the much needed irrigation of a second winter crop. One aspect of the problem regarding a follow-up to land reforms is that of co-ordination. While the Marxists have rightly conceived of the district and panchayat samiti as the focal co-ordination points of development, vital projects like the Kansavati dam still seem to be highly departmentalized.

A comparison (see table on page 142) of landholding patterns on an All-India basis for West Bengal and for Purulia, Bankura and Midnapore districts clearly shows that the present land reforms are in many cases at the cost of the middle and marginal peasantry. According to the West Bengal Agricultural Census, 1976/77, large holdings above 10 ha in the state account for only

Landholding patterns for all-India, West Bengal and Western Plains of Bengal

		All-India		Western Plains of West Bengal*		West Bengal	
		% Holdings	% Land	% Holdings	% Land	% Holdings	% Land
Marginal	below 1 ha	62.62	9.76	74.96	29.9	66.8	27.8
Small	below 2.02 ha	78.11	24.44	90.89	58.77	87.03	55.68[1]
	below 4.04 ha	90.05	46.36	97.21	79.83	97.58	87.22[2]
Large	above 10.13 ha	2.22	22.91	0.21	2.64	0.03	3.44[3]

*These are the districts of Purulia, Bankura and Midnapore.

Figures for West Bengal are calculated on the following bases:
  1 2 ha and under
  2 4 ha and under
  3 10 ha and above

SOURCES: *All-India National Sample Survey conducted from 7/71 to 9/72.*
        National Sample Survey for the Western Plains of West Bengal 7/71 to 9/72.
        West Bengal Agricultural Census 1976–77

00.3 per cent of the total number of holdings and comprise 3.44 per cent of the land, while a National Sample Survey (NSS) conducted in 1971/72 indicates that 2.22 per cent of holdings above 10.13 ha account for as much as 22.91 per cent of the land. The chart shows that in West Bengal most of the land is held by small and marginal farmers: according to an NSS conducted for the districts of Purulia, Bankura and Midnapore in 1971/72, 97.21 per cent of the holdings were under 4 ha and accounted for 79.83 per cent of the land. Corresponding figures for the All-India NSS show that 90.05 per cent of holdings are under 4 ha but account for only 46.16 per cent of the land. Even before the Marxists came to effective power the trend towards smaller holdings was in evidence as is indicated by the percentage of variations between the Agricultural Census of 1970/71 and 1976/77. Thus, in this short period of five years, medium holdings of between 10 and 20 ha had decreased by 52.59 per cent and semi-medium holdings of between 5 and 10 ha by 38.29 per cent. Conversely, marginal holdings of below 1 ha had increased by 38.51 per cent, while minuscule holdings of below 0.5 ha had increased by 47.25 per cent. Therefore the Marxist government is only accelerating an existing trend at the cost of increasing tensions between the middle and marginal peasants and those even poorer.

The myth has long been exploded that intensive cultivation on small peasant holdings decreases yields in comparison with large 'well-managed' estates. But multiplication of really minuscule holdings, especially considering the constraints of rural credit and irrigation, definitely seemed to be affecting production targets in early 1982 while dehoarding and procurement drives simultaneously slackened. It is clear that the distribution of one-acre plots to the landless and the recording of sharecroppers will only acquire social and economic significance if perceived as a first step in far-reaching reforms culminating in consolidation of holdings and some sort of cooperative endeavour in farming. For the trend towards minuscule holdings has resulted in stagnation of agricultural yields.

Indeed in April 1983 a bill passed by the state legislature was awaiting President's Assent at the Centre. The bill, contained, among other things, provisions for consolidation of marginal holdings below 1 acre. According to D. Bandyopadhyaya: 'If people having land up to 1 acre in a village agree, they will be able to consolidate their lands so others will be thrown out. The poor will thus have a consolidated chunk somewhere and on that piece of land a mutual help society will be formed. Instead of implementing the North Indian type of consolidation, where the rich benefit and the poor lose their land, we say let the poor consolidate and throw out the rich and see what happens. Once the plots of the poor are consolidated they are very easy administratively to service. Previous attempts to service the poor on their dispersed holdings with credit and inputs was a herculean task. We just couldn't reach them.'[4]

However, given the distribution of holdings in West Bengal, it would appear that the middle peasantry, not the rich peasantry, will bear the cost of consolidation of marginal holdings. The concept of mutual self-help teams to be introduced seems to be along the lines of the Chinese self-help groups. This sort of system seems to be an extension of an old custom prevalent among the Scheduled Castes and Tribes of West Bengal which the state government merely wants to formalize. To quote D. Bandyopadhyaya again: 'We are trying to codify an existing practice which also already exists among the poor. Now the poor will come together not only on an aspirational basis but also on a hard economic basis. Therefore this consolidation among the poor, this organization among the poor will be more stable and law abiding than the emotional upsurge that occasionally takes place and fritters away. This will be a fundamental rock on the basis of which a very strong movement of the peasantry of poor peasants could develop provided there are people to develop.'[5]

The other major aspect of the bill causing problems for the state government is the retrospective effect of declaring benami lands illegal from 1953. According to D. Bandyopadhyaya about 1 million acres could be had for distribution to the landless if that law could be passed and implemented. However, the Central Government maintains that West Bengal has not been able to present it with any facts justifying such a conclusion. The West Bengal government presumably feels that loopholes in the two previous attempts to implement land reforms, both of which were carried out under Congress regimes, were unsuccessful, and possibly deliberately so, in unearthing evasions to the benefit of larger landholders. They feel it is essential that at least one more attempt be allowed to the present Marxist government to plug these loopholes.

The Central Government is most chary of conveying President's assent, which has now been pending for two years, to the bill because it claims it will undermine people's faith in the legal system and also, by the repeated reopening of old cases, would have serious effects on the stability of the whole agrarian structure which the country can ill afford. The Central Government also points out that there are 40,000 civil writ petitions pertaining to land reform cases in the Calcutta High Court still pending, and that some of them are more than twenty years old. The government is of the opinion that, if the Marxists are allowed to reopen old cases once again, for what will now be the third time, it will be difficult to resist a plea by any future government of West Bengal of a different complexion to continue reopening these old cases depending on their own political ideological stance. Similarly, whenever there is a change of government in other states, there will be similar pleas leading to a general atmosphere of insecurity of land tenure throughout the country.

However, on balance, it would appear that the West Bengal state government is justified in wanting to reopen cases because it is widely recognized that large-scale evasions occurred both when the Estates Acquisition Act, 1953, abolishing feudal estates, and the West Bengal Land Reforms Amendment Act, 1972, imposing ceilings on land, were passed. This has resulted in horizontal dispersion of holdings within kindred groups. Therefore statistics showing that only 0.03 per cent of holdings are above 10 ha, and that these account for only 3.44 per cent of the land, may present a distorted picture. Certainly the state government feels that, apart from the question of accuracy of statistics, there is a likelihood that a great deal of land, which really forms part of larger family estates and which ought therefore to have been redistributed, is in fact disguised in the records among holdings below 10 ha. Thus such statistics cover up the continued concentration of land among privileged groups. In effect the bill has far-reaching provisions in the sense that all benami transactions carried out since 1953 are assumed mala fide unless proved otherwise. The Marxists could also justifiably claim that factual assessment of landholdings on the previous two occasions was done without serious on-the-spot association of the really poor peasantry in the verification process. ·

The bill provides for the reopening of old cases where evasions had been suspected by local land revenue staff. Such a grass-roots study of the actual position on the ground, with the state government on the side of the rural poor and actively associating them in the revenue investigations to uncover the truth, is the only way to break the stranglehold of the network of vested interests that has so far impeded effective agrarian reforms. The stand taken so far by the Centre, that such cases have already been reviewed exhaustively on two separate occasions, and that a third review without defining new legislative criteria would be superfluous, ignores one fundamental aspect. On the two previous occasions there was no serious association of the rural poor in investigations at the grassroots level.

All this illustrates the basic problem of a Marxist state government operating within the framework of a non-Marxist constitutional and judicial system committed to an antithetical agrarian ideology, weighted in favour of existing powerful owner cliques who still dominate the vote banks. Within the existing electoral system all such land reform programmes in the ultimate analysis amount to political jugglery. If West Bengal were really serious in implementing far-reaching agrarian reforms the only logical conclusion, given the pattern of landholdings in the state, would be to move towards cooperativization. In the Indian context it is unlikely that terms like 'collective,' 'cooperative' or 'commune' would ever find acceptance. These terms are all associated with specific alien institutions. In West Bengal some new pattern of organization in agriculture will have to be evolved out of earlier rural traditions. It is among tribal societies and the lower castes, who constitute the bulk of the rural poor, that vestiges still exist of ancient patterns of mutual self-help. In West Bengal the word *gata* still connotes this. It remains to be seen whether the Marxists, who have received another five-year mandate from the electorate in the May 1982 state elections, can succeed in tapping these deeper strings of folk tradition.

CHAPTER FIVE

Caste: a factor affecting social change

This chapter will study to what extent the caste factor will determine current and future social change in India. While some schools of thought see caste as an impediment to social change, others see it as adapting itself and taking on new functions in the modernization process. There is general agreement in modern India that caste, far from withering away under the impact of Independence, modernization and economic change, still plays an important, if not decisive, role in almost all spheres of activity. In fact, traditional attitudes are conditioning patterns of change in new ways which are not yet understood. There is, however, disagreement among observers as to whether caste is weakening or, at least in the realm of power politics, intensifying. It may be nearer to the truth to view it as changing, as in fact it probably has changed and renewed itself throughout history.

It is fashionable today to give overriding stress to the economic and occupational background of caste. More important may be the ethnic origin of castes. The caste system may have arisen due to the interaction of Aryan dominance with the indigenous social structures. As the Aryans gained ascendancy over the autochthones, the latter were subjugated not merely by physical force but by the inculcation of an inferiority complex. The inculcation of this complex persisted long after the racial strain of the invaders had been diluted to the extent that even aspirants to power or status without a drop of Aryan blood, even those who might have possessed their own heritage of pride and power, would aspire to Aryan status.

It is sometimes argued that the colours of the varnas bear no relation to complexion. ('Varna' refers to the four theoretical caste divisions which, in hierarchical order are the Brahmin or Priest; the Kshatriya or Warrior; the Vaishya or Merchant; and the Sudra or Cultivator. The Untouchable, belonging to the fifth category, was 'a-varna', literally 'without caste'. For comparative purposes 'varna' can be equated in Western terms with class or estates. In English confusion is often created by the fact that the word 'caste' is used interchangeably to denote both 'varna' and 'jati' or the subcaste.) Brahmins are white and Sudras black, but Kshatriyas are red and Vaishyas yellow. This contrary argument would assume rather a symbolic significance the world over – white seems somehow associated with purity and goodness and black with darkness, fear and evil. Red for a warrior might be symbolic of blood and yellow for a trader's gold. However, the fact remains that there seems to be a drive throughout the *Rig-Veda* to exterminate the *dasyus* who are ascribed definite facial characteristics including darkness of skin. The colour complex indeed seems to be persisting longer in India than even in the West.

The earliest reference to the fourth varna is in a single passage of the *Rig-Veda* which is generally recognized to be a later interpolation in the main text. Some even dismiss it as a much later Brahminical forgery. There is also clear evidence in Vedic texts of a great mixture of varnas, even though this is lamented probably more from the angle of Aryan race obsessions than that of caste hierarchy. There are also passages to show that occupational caste was not hereditary. This fact is even recognized by an orthodox cultural history of India with regard to Vedic times. One of the sages is reported as saying that: 'He was a poet, his father a physician, and his maternal grandfather a stonecutter.'[1] The so-called rigidity of the caste system does not seem therefore to have existed even theoretically in these earliest times. But the classification of the varnas has remained identical in form right up to modern times, though with permutations, combinations and modifications in the contents of the categories.

The four varnas should be regarded as a theoretical framework for the division of society into four groups. The working basis of the caste system depends on the networks of subcastes, or *jatis*, which are governed by strict rules of endogamy and commensality restricted to each subcaste. Some subcastes are derived from tribal or racial elements, some are occupational, some are territorial, some religious and so forth. The caste system itself was based on the opposition between the pure and impure with hierarchy constituting the organizing principle within the caste and subcaste. Hutton believes the Aryan invasion had the effect of strengthening a tendency to associate differences of caste with differences of colour and also for castes to be organized according to a scale of social precedence. There are three principles governing caste: firstly, gradation of status; secondly, detailed rules aimed at ensuring their separation; and, thirdly, the division of labour and the interdependence which results from it.[2]

The vertical division of society facilitated the assimilation in later centuries of new ethnic groups. Each new group who entered India took on the characteristics of a separate subcaste and became assimilated into the larger caste structure. The position of the new subcaste in the hierarchy was dependent on its physical power, its occupation and its social origin.

The caste system is based on different principles from those of the class-based society of the West. Many of the characteristics of caste, such as its preoccupation with purity and pollution, may have arisen from the fusion between pre-Aryan and tribal elements. Hutton associates such notions to primitive ideas of magic which may have originated within tribal society.

It would be going too far to ascribe the origin of the caste system, as it eventually emerged, to pre-Aryan or tribal sources. Some scholars see in the Indus Valley civilization indications of a hierarchical grouping of buildings in these early pre-Aryan urban centres. However, material on which to assess the real social structure of Harappan urban society is still too scanty to warrant definite conclusions. Researchers from the South trying to trace back their original Dravidian heritage tend to claim, on the basis of their earliest traditional poetry and folklore, that the original 'Dravidian' culture was fundamentally egalitarian. However, this original Dravidian culture was itself in all probability a composite one involving both numerous tribal groups as well as perhaps some form of pre-Aryan leadership which had cultural, if not ethnic, links through trade with the earliest Mesopotamian urban cultures.

More interesting is Hutton's suggestion mentioned above that the rudiments of the caste system exist even in a number of tribal societies. This extremely perceptive insight is based on long experience on the North-Eastern frontier with tribes who, in those days, had absorbed practically no cultural influences from the Indian mainstream – notwithstanding certain Brahminical attempts to transplant for their own audiences Central Indian or North Himalayan traditions to the extreme North-East.

More telling examples of what Hutton probably had in mind are found in the social structure of the Apa Tani tribe of

Arunachal Pradesh which was unknown in Hutton's day. Quite apart from the usual clan structure, there are two definite divisions into endogamous classes known as Guth and Guci. In his earlier studies Haimendorf had translated these, although himself unhappy about the artificiality of the terms, as 'patricians' and 'plebians'. He also used as an equation for these terms the Apa Tani words *Mite* and *Mura*. However, the Apa Tanis themselves distinguish clearly the conceptual differences in their own terminology. Their own tribal understanding of its sociological implications are probably more profound than those of sociologists who continue to pursue arguments about caste and class. The terms Mite and Mura are strictly class definitions involving ownership of a slave or the existing actual status of a slave. Haimendorf has himself later clarified that the word Mura was not used for all persons of slave descent. However, in his own latest words:

> The division between Guth and Guci is considered unalterable and so far neither wealth nor education and political success have enabled a Guci to rise to the status of Guth except in rare cases of persons of mixed parentage. According to Apa Tani tradition all Guci were originally the slaves of patricians but even . . . in the 1940s there was a large class of Guci who had been free for generations. Even then the distinction between patricians and commoners was not overtly noticeable for there were some wealthy Guci who had gained prominence . . . Yet, the innate superiority of the patricians was never questioned and every Guci stood in a relationship of dependence to a patrician family which involved certain obligations of a ceremonial nature . . . We cannot rule out the possibility that the Guth and Guci represent two different, though largely assimilated, ethnic elements . . . There is no doubt that all foreign slaves ever acquired by Apa Tanis have been absorbed only into the Guci class.[3]

Apa Tani tribal society also had two interesting alignments dividing it into two other groups known as Assos. These cut across both villages and even across clusters of groups celebrating a major traditional ritual festival called Mloko. A major social crisis erupted some thirty years ago when the Apa Tanis incidentally were still untouched by any Hindu mainstream cultural influences. A prominent tribal priestly leader taunted two villages saying that they were not 'pure' and dependable because they were divided between two Assos. In a priestly chant he compared the two villages to ears of rice bearing white and black grains.

Haimendorf has also noted the existence of ritual taboos among the Gond tribes of Andhra Pradesh. These were maintained in their relations with other tribal groups with whom they lived in a close symbiotic relationship until recent times. The Gonds regarded themselves as a group which had to maintain its purity by avoiding contact with outsiders. One Gond told Haimendorf:

> In the days of our grandfathers we even washed our feet on returning from the market. But now who washes? . . . For that reason our clan god is weak. Before we were advanced, now we are backward. We are not following the ways of our clan gods. We are mixing.[4]

In the forties, when Haimendorf first began his work amongst the Gonds in Adilabad district in Andhra Pradesh, there was little contact in daily life with Hindus and no elaborate hierarchical structure had evolved. However, over the last forty years as roads were built opening up these previously inaccessible forest areas to the outside world, Hindu immigrants began entering the traditional Gond homeland. Vast tracts of tribal lands were alienated by various subterfuges; businesses and trade were set up and soon the Gonds found themselves outnumbered. As a result of this contact an overall pattern of change in relationships has taken place. A basically hierarchical model has emerged as a result of the social contact between the Gonds and the Telugu castes.

In this whole process of increasing contacts with other communities one may perhaps understand the beginnings of the early caste system before it became rationalized in the Brahminical texts. In the same work Haimendorf gives an example of a modern development which may be an exact replica of the process which began thousands of years ago as the tribes came into contact with outsiders. A sect leaning towards Hindu ideas emerged amongst the Gonds in Adilabad district. The sect began forming an endogamous group which forbade intermarriage with traditional Gonds. The Gonds of Adilabad traditionally sacrificed cows to their clan deities on certain ritual occasions. These sacrifices caused a great deal of local opposition from the Hindu immigrants. In this case the sect, whose leader emerged from within the tribe, probably arose when it was realized that cow sacrifice was detrimental to their social status. For ultimately it would have reduced them to the status of Untouchables in the eyes of the Hindus.

Such instances tend to support Hutton's thesis that the rudiments of a caste system may have existed in tribal societies before either Harappan urbanization or the Aryan impact. The stringencies and demeaning features of the later stratification propounded in the Laws of Manu and in subsequent Hindu society may not have existed. Tribal society, perhaps because of its environment requiring common effort to survive natural challenge, was certainly by and large egalitarian. But while the impact of Aryan migrations and racial fusion in other parts of the world undoubtedly produced racist attitudes and tensions culminating in the Nazi phenomenon and concepts of apartheid, the peculiarities of the Indian caste system, including its tendency even to extend in some form to Indian Muslim, Christian and Sikh groups whose religions specifically discountenanced them, may have deeper roots.

It is not so simple as the assertion of Aryan supremacy nor even the rational distribution of wealth through interdependent sub-castes. These were all aspects of a system rooted even more deeply in the original soil of India. As the system absorbed the tribes, it absorbed with them the rudimentary indigenous features which the system would claim to approximate to caste structure from within the tribe. Superimposed on the traditional hierarchy that might have existed from settled societies like the Indus Valley civilization would be the Aryan obsession with their racial and colour superiority. An added factor would be that pointed out by Sachchidanand Sinha, that many of the absorbed tribes possessed some special artisan skills, as in the case of the weavers and potters for example.[5]

All these added together would contribute the raw material for the intellectual framework ultimately designed by the Brahmin priesthood. This finally crystallized in theory, at least, into a rigid hierarchical structure also involving the added complication of the stigma of a low-caste person being born into a low caste as a punishment for evil deeds in his previous existence.

Too often the evil of such deeds was not based on universal

human codes of conduct but upon ritual offences challenging the presupposed purity or ascendancy of the Twice-Born in a previous existence. There is a growing school of thought which, while acknowledging a bid for pre-Buddhist ritual Brahminical supremacy, doubts whether this in fact was achieved. This school of thought would therefore visualize the ultimate crystallization of the caste system during the first millennium AD, less as a Brahminical revival or restoration, than as the first actual establishment on a wide level of the Twice-Born power combination of the Brahmins and Kshatriyas.

The caste system, as it evolved, is based on institutional hierarchy and for at least two millennia has been buttressed by religious law and used to justify and perpetuate the exercise of power and ascendancy of one group over another. During these two millennia caste has been the single determining principle underlying the organization of Indian society. Caste is not only an ordering of groups ranked high and low, 'it is a system of values in which the idea of hierarchy occupies a pivotal position.'[6] Hierarchy, unlike the concept of interdependence of caste, which is a less conscious aspect of the caste system, is one of the most conscious aspects. This is an extremely important point and helps one to understand the constant preoccupation of Hindus with status. As Dumont has pointed out 'hierarchy integrates society to its values.'[7]

Dumont's classic work, *Homo Hierarchicus*, has to some extent fostered Western assumptions regarding a fairly rigidly graded hierarchical order of ritual status which throughout history has impeded social change. Yet Dumont himself has recognized the subtle interplay of secular power and dominance with ritual hierarchy. This interplay has often modified earlier concepts. Modern Indian sociologists find Dumont's analysis and semantic definitions rather artificial. Yet the main value of his work is to focus attention on certain undoubted preoccupations which in India undoubtedly do seem to have transcended in a peculiar way the normal preoccupations of any human society with power, wealth, prestige and racial superiority.

The traditional Indian obsession with ritual purity and fear of pollution, as well as the ingrained antipathy to mixing equally with inferior persons or groups, has been evident and survived for centuries on end. Yet from the very beginning such mixing and change was all too apparent. Even in the *Rig-Veda* there is a verse describing the confusion of varnas: 'O Indra, find out who is an Aryan and who is a Dasa and separate them.'[8] It seems necessary therefore to reassess the insights and interpretations of earlier commentators and match them against visible signs in the India of the eighties.

Many Western scholars have interpreted the caste system through the classical scriptures or relied on Brahmin pandits for their interpretations of caste, neither of which have taken account of the realities on the ground. The caste system has always been characterized by a high degree of group mobility. Yet according to Hindu texts a man cannot change his caste and there is no theoretical scope for upward mobility. The Brahmins, because they were steeped in the classical scriptures and on account of their own existential base, were bound to present the caste system as rigid. For example, Dumont has shown how relationships are ordered and given meaning in the ideology of orthodox Brahminical Hinduism, but as Harriss points out:

> Whether or not relationships actually work in empirical practice according to the precepts of the ideology is quite another question; and the extent to which people believe in those precepts is another.[9]

There are indications that group mobility has always existed. Such a group, or sometimes even a family, by dint of its exertions or manoeuvres, would deny its former caste or subcaste affiliations. If, in addition to achieving economic or temporal power, it also adopted a nomenclature either new or affiliated to a higher caste and, if its way of life was then strictly adjusted to that of a higher status, with 'discoveries' of a remote ancestry to tally with this, there was a chance within a few generations of the group gradually enforcing acceptance of its new position, however theoretically impossible this might be. Such changes, however, were kaleidoscopic within the existing structure. The framework of the system remained unaltered. In a country constitutionally pledged to egalitarianism and a rationalized order, some would argue that social change presupposes the disappearance of caste so that all barriers inhibiting individual mobility may be removed. According to sociologist Srinivas changes today '. . . cannot be described as a simple movement from a closed to an open system of social stratification.'[10] He maintains the old system was not a closed one and notes that: 'Though the scope for individual and familial mobility has increased strikingly since Independence, caste continues to be relevant in subtle and indirect ways, in such mobility.'[11]

In Hindu culture religious views and obsessions with ritual purity, rather than economic criteria, determine the rank of each group, but in a secular state the economic factor prevails. But Béteille does not think the economic factor was unimportant in the past: 'It was just that economic advantages had always to be legitimized in a religious idiom. Just as in any medieval society it wasn't enough to make money, you had to legitimize it. I would not discount the material basis of these so-called inequalities of religion.'[12]

There is no real conflict between the two schools of thought, only a shift in emphasis. In a sense Dumont is correct in observing that the overarching feature of the caste system can be located in the ideology of purity and pollution which is schematized in a hierarchical form in day-to-day life. But in the modern context the ritual dimension has been considerably eroded and the significance of the secular dimension, with which power and wealth are associated, has certainly increased in the modern context. To argue, as some scholars have done, that the ritual dimension is the essence of the caste system and that its 'desacrilization' will mean the demise of the caste system is to fall into the trap of functionalism. Here one should look at the whole question of independence. One must recognize that both dimensions have a certain level of autonomy. Therefore it is quite possible that the power dimension can operate independently or autonomously from the ritual dimension. Dumont has recognized this when he brings out the bifurcation between the Brahmin and Kshatriya – between the Priest and King. Yet to acknowledge that there are dimensions of autonomy does not mean that there is no reciprocity between them. For, as an organic system, the castes are mutually interlinked by a principle of reciprocity.

What needs to be recognized is that both reciprocity and autonomy coexist. It is clear that in the modern context, notwithstanding an erosion of the importance of the ritual dimension, the caste system is very much present in everyday life. T.K. Oommen, Associate Professor of Sociology at Jawaharlal Nehru University, New Delhi, sees the secular aspect as the more important dimension today: 'For the vast majority of Indians today both in the urban and, to a certain extent, in the rural context, caste is not so much a matter of temple entry or of intercaste marriage as it was fifty years ago. It is linked rather to questions of personal dignity, to the casting of one's vote without restriction or intimidation, and to access to jobs without facing discrimination.'[13]

Another angle on the modern Indian's feeling about caste was expressed by a professor of commerce, a Rajput, during a train journey from Chittorgarh to Udaipur in Rajasthan. In response to a question as to whether a Hindu cared more about money or caste his response was unequivocal: 'We will die for our caste.' This confirms Hutton who in *Castes in India* writes: 'With many Hindus the highest form of religious observance is the complete fulfilment of the claims of caste. Most of them conceive of sin as a breach of caste discipline rather than of moral law.'[14]

Béteille disagrees: 'It can easily be argued that the highest form of religious life comes only when one is able to transcend caste. The example of the sanyasin, or renouncer, who at a certain stage in life renounces all concerns of caste and social responsibilities, is a very powerful example in Hinduism. Caste from a moral point of view is consciously regarded by Hindus as a compromise with the relationships of everyday life. Performance of caste duties is therefore not the highest form of religious experience. As regards sin being concerned only with the observance of rules of caste, I also don't think that is valid because in the Dharmasastra a distinction is made between two kinds of dharma, or rules of right conduct. Varnasrama dharma, the rule of right conduct appropriate to your caste; secondly, Manava dharma, or rules appropriate to all human beings. That distinction is certainly made. So it is not as if all rules of right conduct are rules of right conduct appropriate to one's station in life. There are also rules of right conduct which are rules irrespective of one's station in life.'[15]

The general Hindu feeling is that caste was established by divine ordinance. The *Bhagavad Gita* inculcates the supreme merit of performing duties appropriate to the caste which take precedence over all other obligations, including those of kinship. It is equivalent to dharma, i.e. religious observance, for it is said that perfection is only attained by those who do not deviate from the duties of caste. Brahmanic codes have insisted that every community should obey its own rules. Krishna, the hero of the

Mahabharata, says: 'Again, seeing thine own duty thou shouldst not shrink from it for there is no higher good.'[16]

The stress placed in performing caste duties rather than on bettering oneself has been pointed out by Western scholars and many have concluded that dharma, or rules of right conduct, imbues the individual with a fatalistic attitude towards life. Béteille does not entirely agree with this point of view: 'Certainly dharma has something to do with the rather half-hearted efforts to better oneself in the past. But I would also ascribe this passive attitude to material constraints. After all one can adopt a purely fatalistic attitude without subscribing to any coherent religious point of view. One just finds that economic opportunities are too few. So I would think of dharma as an active principle but I would also put by its side a kind of fatalism which comes from the scarcity of opportunities the lower down you go in the hierarchy. I think that despite that and despite all the things that are said about bottlenecks to development, people are less fatalistic today.'[17]

Dr Karan Singh, leader of the Virat Hindu Samaj, seeks to give a modern interpretation of the concept of dharma: 'Dharma means that which, in the social sense, supports society. In other words, it is the moral and ideological framework within which human society continues its activities. When the caste system was working, then dharma was largely divided into castes. But the concept of dharma itself is not necessarily linked with caste. In the same way that you have a caste dharma, you can have a human dharma.'[18]

One may interpret Dr Karan Singh as realizing the danger to Hindu society from present caste tensions. He therefore seems to be groping for a wider framework within traditional Hindu thought. This seems to be provided by what he called the 'Human dharma' which is none other than the Manava dharma mentioned by Béteille. Somewhere too in his Renaissance thinking there is probably the urge for consolidating Hindu society with that same measure of 'authority' which again derives from ancient tradition. This line of thought therefore coincides with that of V.C. Channa who, in company with other modern Indians, deprecates Dumont's interpretation of hierarchy and sees the authority enshrined in the original system as being intended to achieve harmony. This line of thinking could of course also be interpreted as a subtle way of restoring traditional caste authority by adapting it to a modern setting, in the same way as the system has adjusted itself to challenges throughout the centuries.

Much of the conformity in behaviour which has been stressed in the traditional caste system is linked to such concepts as dharma which applied to both the religious and secular realms. Even in ordinary daily conduct within relations in the kin group, there is a strong stress on abiding by customary behaviour. Relationships conducted with one's in-laws or with members of other castes tend to be based on stereotyped codes of behaviour.

A natural concomitant of the rigid rules governing caste is the stifling conformity one observes. Conformity can only be achieved by a certain amount of coercion and government by coercion has a long history. The *Arthasastra*, the Indian classic on statecraft, akin to Machiavelli's *The Prince*, stresses the need for coercive government. Lannoy has pointed out that Kautilya, the chief minister to the Mauryan king, Chandragupta, who reigned in the fourth century BC, and a modern village or caste council both speak the 'same language of power and conformist morality'. Such codes of behaviour are said to lead to the depersonalization of the ego: 'In interpersonal relations depersonalization is the ideal Indian habit. Depersonalization can best be observed at the opposite extremes of the caste hierarchy where the stress to conform to stylized behaviour is at its maximum.'[19]

Such patterns of interaction which were traditionally based on stereotyped behaviour need to be changed. Although traditional patterns of behaviour are being eroded they have certainly not altogether disappeared from the traditional village setting. Rather Hindu society in this regard may be said to be in a transitional stage where the more discrete details regarding patterns of behaviour are no longer observed. For example, traditionally the Chamar has been prohibited from wearing a turban or using a horse mount at a wedding. Today such prohibitions are to some measure honoured more in the breach than in the observance. If dominant castes resort to violence against lower castes for breach of traditional caste rules, the incident is treated as an aberration in the sense that the press will highlight the issue.

It is clear that some degree of progress has been made in removing some of the worst aspects of the caste system in the 34 years since Independence when democratic ideals of egalitarianism have underpinned the state ideology. Yet even today a caste mentality pervades the entire society. Lannoy rightly points out that in contemporary Indian society: 'The pyschology of the vast majority of the Hindus is still fundamentally a caste psychology whatever radical changes have affected their outward lives.'[20]

Dr Béteille finds the idea of a caste psychology rather difficult to accept: 'One can mean so many different things by this term. It could mean that people assign priority to the group over the individual – that they don't attach importance to the individual but think of a person as a member of a particular caste. Certainly that continues to be very important in many sectors of life. Then one can mean an obsessive preoccupation of ranking people high and low, whether in dealing with collectives or individuals. That also persists to a very large extent. But I don't know whether purity and pollution and other very specific aspects of caste hierarchy still survive to the same extent. I think that has altered to a very large extent.'[21]

Most analysis of contemporary change in India has generally ignored the role of ideology, which is largely responsible for the persistence of a caste mentality, in assessing social transformation. Such studies have dismissed caste as 'false consciousness'. In the Indian context, however, it is still the orthodox Brahmin ideology which dominates and studies like that of Harriss have brought out to what extent it permeates the thinking and attitudes of all castes, irrespective of their positions in the hierarchy. Therefore purely materialist theories such as those of the Marxists which argue that economic change will bring about social transformation are fallacious. Observers often assume that, when a modicum of change occurs underlying the caste system in some region, there will necessarily be a shift towards a 'class-based' system.

The essential character of social change in India is not the 'displacement' syndrome but rather the 'accretive' syndrome. To put the matter in a different way, it is not that caste will be replaced by class. There are essentially three elements around which the whole question of mobility operates – economic resources, political power, and social status. This in turn gives one a position of cumulative domination on the one hand and of cumulative oppression on the other. In the traditional caste system these three factors coexisted in the caste of the Brahmins and gave them cumulative dominance. At the other end of the caste spectrum the Untouchables were economically deprived, socially oppressed and politically voiceless.

Today the situation has changed to some degree because the

Harijan is gaining in some contexts, while the Brahmin is losing in other spheres. This becomes evident if one makes a comparative study of the composition of state legislative assemblies in the fifties and in contemporary India. While in the fifties the upper castes element would have prevailed in all the state bodies, since then there has been a progressive displacement of the Twice-Born groups by those below that. A similar change has taken place in landholding patterns. The monopoly of the Brahmins is by and large maintained in the bureaucracy and the professions where their monopoly remains disproportionate to their numbers. In other words, from a situation of cumulative domination there is an overall tendency in contemporary India towards dispersed domination.

Despite this shift in emphasis the overall structure of the caste system has remained unaltered. Therefore in observing the national scene in India today one may therefore ask what kind of change has in fact occurred since the caste system with its religious and customary sanctions have not disappeared. V.C. Channa, Lecturer in Social Anthropology at Delhi University, believes that: 'Caste is finding new political and economic functions. The traditional structures are changing. A lot of changes are occurring because of outside forces and a lot because of internal forces within the society.'[22]

Despite such an ongoing process of transformation the overall framework of Indian society has not changed. The Constitution should be regarded merely as a definition of objectives, for many Indians continue to feel that it is ideology, the ideology of caste founded on a Brahminical Sanskritic heritage, which preserves unity over and above regional differences. As Lannoy points out: 'The caste system was, and indeed still remains as inseparable and as fundamental a part of the social order, indeed a *valued* part by the great majority of Hindus, just as the principle of social equality is a valued ideal of modern democracy.'[23]

The idea of having one kind of normative order that applies to everyone is not part of the Indian tradition. The caste system has always been marked by a great deal of separatedness, and a certain autonomy with regard to behaviour and patterns of social control has been closely associated with this system. The influence of Christianity in the West provided a single code of ethics which applied on an open-ended basis to the entire society. One can argue that Hinduism provides a certain set of shared ideas in terms of pollution, hierarchy and so forth, but these act to sustain a framework. It is not applicable to persons across the board. This is in substantial contrast to the Western tradition where the evolution of a formal state apparatus, with supportive cultural traditions, provided a coherent set of general principles applicable to the community as a whole. In other words, while Christianity played an integrative role in Western society by helping to evolve common codes, the Dharmasastras, or traditional Hindu law codes, by emphasizing differences between the castes, created a gulf between the various elements. Those supportive cultural traditions which produced the kind of framework in the West for its institutions are absent in India.

Satish Saberwal, Associate Professor of Sociology at Jawaharlal Nehru University, differentiates between 'ingrained' ideologies and 'external' ideologies. The first are embedded in daily social relationships and forms of living, while the second may have accompanied an intrusive regime. The divergence between theory and practice at all levels stems in part from the dualism that pervades the modern Indian value system. For the British introduced a rational modern system based on impersonal codes. Indians have difficulty in working with its logic 'because of the very different logic which comes to us from our social heritage, especially the caste system.'[24]

The divergence between the normative and existential order can to a considerable extent be attributed to the caste system. The modern institutions are based on norms applicable to the society as a whole, while the caste system is characterized by a great deal of separateness. Associated with this is the existence within each group of a certain autonomy with regard to norms of social behaviour and patterns of social control. As Satish Saberwal points out: 'The idea that there should be one kind of normative order that applies to everyone is not part of our tradition as against Christianity in the West where one kind of ethic applies on an open-ended kind of basis to the entire society.'[25]

Further comparisons of Indian society with the West today have been dealt with by many sociologists, but this approach may not be entirely tenable. One should rather look at the West before it modernized because all pre-modern structures have both assets and liabilities. 'The ingenuity of a modernizing people depends on how they transform assets into the modern idiom and how they wash away their traditional liabilities', according to T.K.

Oommen.[26] The argument put forward by some sociologists that the caste system is hampering modernization because of the high degree of segmentation of caste may not be entirely valid because segmentation based on language and regionalism are very much present in Europe.

The problem in India today is rather that there are two competing value systems. The traditional value system, the ingredients of which are hierarchy, holism and pluralism, are juxtaposed to modern values espoused in the Constitution such as socialism, secularism and democracy. The problem facing Indian society today is one of how to transmute the set of values and to see in what manner the assets in the Hindu tradition can be utilized so that an institutionalization of modern values becomes possible. Caste segmentation continues to exist but this does not mean that political consolidation is not possible. The context in which caste will operate in the modern nation-state will differ from its traditional functions. The question is largely normative in the sense that caste will have to be redefined just as political norms and values can be redefined in the modern sense.

The emergence of the caste factor in politics took place after 1947. In transforming politics into their sphere of activity castes could assert their identity and aspire to capture positions of power and influence. As Rajni Kothari aptly points out: 'Where the caste structure provides one of the principal organizing clusters along which the bulk of the population is found to live, politics must strive to organize through such a structure.'[27] In the growing politicization of caste which began to take place was the tendency to transcend territories and for the creation of caste associations constituting several collateral castes to emerge. This in effect meant that caste groups were using the political process to organize their own power base in their quest for political and social aims. The emergence of the caste associations showed that caste was responding to new challenges of social change and modernization.

Experience has shown both in Tamil Nadu and Gujarat that the kind of fusion process characteristic of the caste associations did not last long. In the course of time, when development programmes were under way, it was found that the individual subcastes, or jatis, which had constituted the caste associations, had not benefited equally. This led to stratification within the caste associations themselves and, on that basis, tensions and conflict arose and many subcastes broke away. In this way the caste structure with both its larger organization and its smaller primordial existence showed a tendency towards a dialectical process of fusion and fission.

Politicians were quick to discover in the caste structure a ready-made organizational base highly suitable for their purposes. It was deeply embedded in the popular consciousness. Its structure both provided a hierarchical chain of command as well as lateral links to organize the electorate. Yet in its day-to-day working it had achieved and even articulated a more than adequate flexibility. In practice it had always been a well-oiled machine which could cater for continuous social mobility and cope with factionalism, cleavages, dissidence and realignment throughout the ages. Especially in areas where Brahmin dominance was less pronounced, there were ready at hand distinct landed castes of great social power whose absorption into politics with both vertical and intercaste ties provided ready-made cadres for political recruitment. In a sense too this ready-made structure inhibited the emergence of horizontal solidarity based on economic or genuinely ideological interests.

Contrary to what Rajni Kothari seems to envisage, it is less a question of politics leading to the secularization of caste than of caste swallowing and digesting alien concepts of political thought. The resultant metabolic processes are already transforming them beyond original recognition. Also the group segmentation which this transformation involves, far from leading to a secular society, is also tending to polarize the electorate not merely on caste but on religious lines. The real impact of modernization or secularization seems to occur only when a competing wider group ideology emerges, like that based on regional self-respect against central manipulations as in the case of the Telugu Desam phenomenon in Andhra Pradesh. An alternative pattern of competing group ideology would be that advocated by the Marxists on the basis of their ideology. Similar to the latter would be the aspirations of the younger Dalit groups, the most radical of the Harijan movements, who envisage some sort of horizontal linkages between all oppressed toilers.

It remains to be seen, however, how such movements stand up on a long-term basis to the blandishments of the more traditional group loyalties. Because these traditional loyalties have always provided both scope and experience of great finesse in the flexibility of manoeuvre, they show signs of being used in the modern context as a pre-emptive weapon against the escalation of dissent into any real challenge to the system. Indeed the basic theme of Kothari's stand as indicated in his publication, *Alternatives,* seems to be the study of alternatives to radicalism as part of an international endeavour to prevent the Third World, or its component nation-states, drifting into chaos.

The question as to whether caste is impeding social change is a very large one. To the extent that the caste system is pervaded by a concept of collective identity based on segmented ties, this interferes with the smooth functioning of what in the Western view would be a rational administration in which individual merit alone counts. In that sense it obstructs social transformation. On the other hand, it has been argued that rational forms of competitive selection and admission tend to favour those that are already advantaged.

Western observers often point out that Hindus lack a civic sense. This is because Indian society is more concerned with group, family or caste responsibilities which would always override those of a state system theoretically committed to equality of the individual in law and society or a municipal system supposed to cater for its citizens. There is a similar problem about the modern village system. Legislation and planning after Independence were based on the false assumption that revival of village panchayats, based on Western electoral patterns, would cater to the interests of the village community as a whole. In practice the ancient panchayat system was based on representation of all groups and castes, on a parallel and stronger caste panchayat system and on village consensus in respect of matters of common importance. Such a consensus, however, although idealized as a harmonious integration, was in fact achieved by the authority of the dominant castes.

The emphasis on the collective has led to the emergence of caste networks which operate at all levels of the society. There is indeed some truth that the operation of such networks is largely responsible for nepotism. However, the pattern of this network has to some extent been changed. For a long time the upper castes formed the most powerful networks. Today, however, the Backward Castes have gained considerable economic power and are using their networks to further their own kin groups. The caste network is accepted as a mechanism for advancement in India. It operates most pervasively in the informal lower and middle sectors of the economy where recruitment procedures are still informal. In recruitment to top posts where open competitive exams are held, recruitment was, till recently, largely on merit. Even here, however, there are growing indications that the decisions of Public Service Commissions are being increasingly manipulated and distorted by the influence of 'networks'. In the case of recruitment on a competitive basis economic and cultural advantages come into play so that the monopoly of the upper castes continues to perpetuate itself, although, in this instance, it is operating through universalistic principles.

Caste networks also operate at the grass roots and are largely responsible for thwarting government programmes. One of the reasons the Gonds of Andhra Pradesh lost their land to outsiders, for example, was the existence of politically and economically influential networks which had been established by the immigrant communities. The combination of financial resources and the monopoly of important posts like patwari, or revenue official, by the immigrants '. . . enabled such clusters of powerful families to outwit illiterate Gonds of modest means at every step and to sabotage even the campaign of the government to restore alien- ated tribal land.'[28] The ramifications of these networks based on community or caste will be discussed further when dealing with the problem of corruption.

Another factor closely interlinked with caste is the preoccupa- tion with status. Present caste groupings may not remain in the future but the ultimate reality is that of status and advancement. In order to maintain status one has to show one's superiority in relation to the next individual and to legitimize one's superiority. At cocktail parties in New Delhi one of the most interesting pastimes is to listen to opening conversations between wealthy upper-caste women who have just been introduced to one another. The first few minutes are spent questioning each other as to their respective husband's occupation, their residential locality, the number of cars owned and, most important, the family income. If either one discovers the other to be of inferior status the conversation is cut short.

The increasing number of dowry deaths is not a symbol of oppression against the Indian bride; rather the issue revolves around the question of status. The demands by prospective in-laws for huge dowries involving Western goods like cars, fridges, tape recorders and so forth have grown with the country's increasing stress on modernization. Incidents of bride-burning are generally related to cases of insufficient dowry. The perpetrators are always the in-laws, often in league with the husband, who regard the provision of handsome dowries as a means of raising their own status. The one indication that increased cases of bride-burning are a result of modernization and directly related to status is that modern occupations like engineers and doctors fetch the highest dowry prices. Furthermore, it is because each person is jealous of his status that he protects himself from 'ill-advised contracts and marriages'.[29]

Dr Béteille thinks that today people are no longer using the religious idiom to legitimize their status and that alternative criteria of status have developed: 'Srinivas has talked about Westernization and Sanskritization as being ways in which people legitimize their status. I don't think there are societies where people make more and more money and are satisfied just with a sheer accumulation of wealth. They want other people to recognize that they have a legitimate title to that wealth. That requires them to bring about some changes in their styles of life in terms of accepted canons of social respectability. The canons of the middle and upper middle urban classes today are somewhat different than was the case a hundred years ago.'[30] While today power and wealth are the main components of secular status, any status achieved by such means alone still seeks to be legitimized by acceptance into a higher-born social community or by the burying of one's true community or birth origins. These new principles of status thus operate contingently together with the caste principle of social stratification and only rarely do they operate autonomously.

The maintenance of such outward appearances is closely interlinked with status which in turn helps advancement. If one's income does not permit keeping up a certain style of life commensurate with one's status, it becomes necessary to resort to malpractices. Thus there is an element which differentiates corruption in India from corruption in other countries because in India the individual or group is always preoccupied with building up status.

V.C. Channa does not think Hindu society is more preoccupied with status than other societies. He thinks caste is an institution 'the likes of which are found all over the world.' He continues: 'It is a transmission of status. Why is Joe Carpenter's son in England called by the same name? Only because he is trying to transmit his status. He is trying to prolong his own identity into the future. Caste and kinship status and economic and political relations are all part of an individual's status which a person wants to transmit to generations to come. Brezhnev would not permit his son to become a factory worker because his own status and continuity are involved through his children. The difference between India and the West is that in the latter there are two ways of transmitting status: through inheritance and through control of marriage and children. On the other hand, with us the process is far more rigid for Hinduism permits your status to continue for generations and hundreds of years because of its ideology.'[31]

Displays of status take place on such occasions as caste feasts, marriage feasts and collective festivals. These institutions are a survival of tribal customs, although the check on ostentatious display existing in tribes like the Nagas is conspicuously lacking in Hindu celebrations. In tribal society the environment provided a check on the balance of wealth and power, although stress was given to these. An egalitarian philosophy existed in tribal society which checked the amassing of vast quantities of wealth and power. During the great Naga 'Feasts of Merit' when a man could rise to become a powerful chief, he could establish a new village and people would follow him. It was seen as a symbol of power and wealth. However, having amassed all this, he showed it off by giving huge lavish feasts. The heads of slaughtered animals were displayed on the house posts. These customs were adopted by Hindu society and their equivalents are the huge weddings with their multi-coloured tents and vast amounts of food and drink which present a scene of staggering waste and consumption.

While one might decry the overemphasis on status in Hindu society, more important are the traditional attitudes towards hard work, particularly manual labour, which are hampering the country's development. In the Hindu value system, which has prevailed for at least two millennia and which is still very much alive in the rural areas, the work ethnic has never received strong emphasis. According to Lannoy, the *Gita*:

... ignores the essential creativity of man ... It reveals an awareness of human responsibility and enjoins people in all walks of life to act from the highest ethical standards . . . But the Gita's emphasis throughout is on action without attachment to the fruit of one's labour. This is hardly an encouragement for a positive attitude towards work.[32]

This stands in contrast to the Western stress on performance rooted in Christian ethics. The lack of work ethic can be explained by the Hindu religious belief in transmigration which produces a more relaxed attitude in the face of time. Furthermore, the traditional aversion to manual work is counterbalanced by an exaggerated adulation of the thinker or intellectual.

Brahmins, traditionally the scholars and priests, are prohibited by tradition from touching the plough for, according to the Laws of Manu, 'the plough wounds the earth and the creatures which live in it.' This is an autochthonous concept which persists till this day. Dumont believes that this law may be a rationalization for a prejudice against an occupation associated with the land and the despised autochthones. Since Brahmins are prevented by religious custom from ploughing, even poor Brahmins lease out tiny bits of land to sharecroppers or have the work performed by farm servants. 'Through such strict observance they are likely to sink still deeper into poverty but this demonstration of orthodoxy may enhance the esteem in which they are held by the village people.'[33] Similarly in a study made in Nagar village in eastern UP in 1980, even today the Brahmins refuse to touch the plough or work as agricultural labourers, no matter how poor they may be. Poor Brahmin families employ permanent labourers, ploughmen to look after the fields as the task is degrading to their status. Although the Brahmins in the village mix freely with other castes 'they do not touch the plough or work as agricultural labourers no matter how poor they are.'[34] Such attitudes are reinforced by traditional Indian thought, from the epics to traditional literature, which stress that work should not be performed because there is fulfilment to be gained from such an exercise. Rather it is because life has nothing better to offer and otherwise one would starve. Not only have the Brahmins been traditionally debarred by ritual sanction from manual labour or field work, their attitude has been communicated to other groups seeking higher-caste status. In West Bengal Hindus from all castes are averse to tilling the land as soon as they have become landowners. According to a recent survey carried out in West Bengal, in near a quarter of the villages surveyed, male adult members of cultivating families do not perform any manual work on the farm. Sajjan Singh, a Thakur landowner from Chapta village, Etawah district, UP, admits that it would be demeaning to his status to work on the land of others: 'If I took up land on lease from another landlord I would have to perform all kinds of tasks. It is beneath my dignity to perform such tasks.'

In West Bengal higher and middle-class women are debarred from any kind of manual labour or field work. The survey quoted above shows that in 91 per cent of cultivating families female adult members do not work on the farm. Even among labouring families female members in 64 per cent of such households do not work outside the house. Similarly in Rajasthan upper-caste Rajput women observe strict purdah and are confined to the courtyards of their homes. Women seen labouring or working in the fields or working on construction sites throughout India are either low-caste, Harijan or tribals, for tribal society has no taboo on manual work. Even in Kerala, the most advanced state in India with a literacy rate of over 70 per cent, such taboos still remain. Marginal and small landowners who are upper-caste Hindus or higher-ranking Syrian Christian women do not work in the fields and males are primarily supervisors of labour and at most go out to plough the land.

The extreme conservatism of the school system is one of main reasons for the aversion to manual work. According to Myrdal: 'The existing education establishments are part of the larger institutional system which includes social stratification and this system is supported by people's attitudes which themselves have been moulded by the institutions.'[35] It is not only manual labour that is looked down upon but in addition there is also a stigma attached to wage labour. As long as such attitudes persist it is difficult to see how there can be any real long-term increase and improvement in agricultural production. As Myrdal points out: 'Long-term advances in agricultural output and efficiency can only be achieved if South Asian peoples can be brought up to accept the fact that wage employment is a normal and healthy feature of progressive economies.'[36]

It is not only field work or manual work that is looked down upon; even skilled work is held in contempt. Graduate engineers or technicians request desk jobs and express aversion to working in contact with machines. Most graduates prefer to join government service or public- and private-sector business enterprises. Such a situation produces alienation amongst the upper castes from the rest of society and, as a result of this process, there is a total lack of realism in government development programmes for the poor.

One of the reasons for the persistence of such attitudes is the fact that in an agricultural economy most manual workers are concentrated at the bottom of the social hierarchy. The government should make attempts, through a reform in the educational system, for example, to make people more rational towards manual work. Certainly when manual work is manifestly dirty it possesses one kind of value. In the West, during the early phases of industrialization, mining was rated lowest and the profession was also manifestly dirty. But today in some industries this no longer applies. For example, work in the processing or chemical industries is no longer looked down upon. It seems, however, that most societies harbour prejudices against manual work. For even the Soviets have tried very hard to equalize manual and mental labour, but their attempts have not met with much success.

One aspect of the caste problem which needs pointing out is that under the post-Independence assumption that caste would wither away under the impact of modernization, various administrative measures were taken to accelerate this process. One example may be seen in the discontinuation of references to caste in data collection of the censuses or in service records. Since Independence the only separate records that are kept relate to the broad division of the 'Scheduled Castes', 'Scheduled Tribes' and 'Others'. At present the assumption that such measures are assisting the disappearance of caste concepts is being belied, but there is no basic data left in which to study the actual progress, or the reverse, of equalizing economic and service disparities between castes.

André Béteille of the Delhi School of Economics asserts: 'All kinds of survey work regarding landholdings are carried out from time to time by various agricultural universities and agro-economic research centers but no all-India caste-wise studies have been carried out in recent years comparable in depth and scope to the 1931 census for the whole country.'[37]

Yet the continuing domination of upper castes is ascertained by personal observation. Srinivas has also noted: 'As far as Hindus are concerned, there was – and to a very considerable extent still is – a very broad and general correlation between traditional caste hierarchy and the new Western occupational hierarchy.'[38]

Impediments to social change are thus posed by dominant social élites controlling key positions in government and vote banks in elections. The dominance of the same social élites in all institutions which might otherwise provide checks and balances – the judiciary, the press, academia, industry, commerce, planning, even the revolutionary leadership – continue to be the preserve of upper and dominant castes.

One of the reasons for the Brahmin dominance at the upper echelons lies in the fact that not only were they the first to take to Western education in the nineteenth century, but the system, with its stress on literary subjects, favoured the Brahmins and other literary castes. The Madrasi and Bengali Brahmins led the way in the service of the British and also prevailed in the élitist Indian Administrative Service. However, Srinivas makes an important point, namely that:

> . . . an entire varna category is rarely found occupying only a particular stratum or a few strata in the new hierarchy. What happens is that in certain strata and occupations, members from certain local jatis are found much more frequently than are other similar jatis.[39]

In a study made by Béteille for the Madras Presidency, the sociologist noted that:

> between 1892 and 1904, out of 16 successful candidates for the ICS 15 were Brahmins; and in 1914 452 out of 650 registered graduates of universities were Brahmins. In 1918 the Brahmins in the Madras Presidency numbered 1.5 million out of 42 million but 70 per cent of arts graduates, 74 per cent of law graduates, 71 per cent of engineer graduates and 74 per cent of graduates in teaching were Brahmins.[40]

Nor has the position changed to any significant degree even at the lower levels of the administration today. Although as already stated there is no data whereby this may be verified, due attention paid to surnames of those holding such appointments confirms this pattern of domination. Caste has not been enumerated since the 1931 census and the practice was continued after Independence. For, in accordance with the declared principles of equality in the Constitution, caste was to be discounted as a factor. In fact the measure whereby caste is no longer noted in data collection merely camouflages the continued entrenchment of higher castes in all positions of higher power. Recently, the Chief Minister of Bihar, Dr Jagannath Misra, dropped his Brahmin surname and announced that henceforth he was to be referred to as Dr Jagannath. One suspects that, notwithstanding his declared intentions, the ploy is meant to conceal the continued entrenchment of Brahmins at the top. The position of the lower castes remains largely unchanged today. The *Report of the Commissioner for Scheduled Castes and Scheduled Tribes, 1977–1978* notes:

> Reviewing 28 years of experience the operation of constitutional provisions regarding various service safeguards for the Scheduled Castes and Scheduled Tribes, it is revealed that the position even today is most unsatisfactory and discouraging . . . Unless some drastic remedial steps are taken, these weaker sections of the nation are not likely to be represented in the services in the foreseeable future.[41]

It would be very illuminating if a survey was carried out today as to the percentage of upper-caste Brahmins who continue to dominate the levers of power. It would undoubtedly refute the claims that merit and efficiency are being jeopardized by the rise of the Scheduled Castes and Scheduled Tribes as a result of reservations.

At the grass-roots level upper castes continue to control the land and monopolize local, district and state government jobs. During tours of Bastar district, Madhya Pradesh, and Banswara and Dungarpur districts, Rajasthan, all of which have predominantly tribal populations, the local administration was dominated by upper castes. This could be ascertained by the surnames of officials with whom one came into contact. Even visits to academic institutions like the Agricultural University or the Tribal Research Institute in Udaipur, or the anthropology department at Ravi Shankar University, showed the same pattern of dominance persisting in academia. Even voluntary organizations, like the Seva Mandir in Udaipur or the Social Work Research Center at Tilonia, are headed by upper castes.

In Chapta village, Ajitmal block, Etawah district, in western

Uttar Pradesh, at least two-thirds of the land continue to be concentrated in the hands of Brahmins, Thakurs and Muslims. The latter continue to hold on to sizeable portions of the land because, till the fifties, the village was controlled by a Muslim zamindar. The greater proportion of villagers who have managed to secure employment outside the village come from the upper castes. Thakurs, the principal landowners, have managed to obtain most of the local government jobs. As one Muslim from the village commented: 'The high castes are dominating the government. They have no feeling at all for the lower castes.' The continued dominance of the upper castes is reflected in the educational pattern of the younger generation in the village. Most of the boys with high school passes or college education come from the upper castes. Two boys presently attending the local polytechnic doing engineering training are both Thakurs. The only two girls in the village with BAs are Brahmins. Out of 500 children attending school in Chapta only 30 are Harijan boys and girls, despite the fact that the Harijans consist of a sizeable proportion of the population.

Even the upper echelons of India's main Communist parties, the CPI(M) and the CPI, remain the preserve of the upper castes, although Béteille thinks today the parties are no longer the monopoly of the high castes as was the case with the undivided party in the early part of this century. One of the weakest points in Indian sociology is the failure to assess leadership patterns in all spheres of national activity, for Dr Béteille could not cite any study analysing shifts in caste representation in various sectors of national leadership including that of the Communist parties.

He comments: 'I wouldn't be surprised if in the beginning its ranks were not even more upper-caste dominated in their membership and recruitment than the Congress. I think there has been a general expansion of the social base of recruitment. It has certainly happened in Kerala. It is well known that a large number of members at the top and middle levels belong to the Erava caste which is a fairly low caste. In Bengal, which was very élitist in its recruitment, there have been middle castes, if not lower castes, who were important members. One must, however, remember that leadership depends a great deal on higher education, even at the middle levels. They have to be educated people and the educational system continues to be highly selective in terms of caste.'[42]

One would have to disagree with Béteille that higher education is the key to leadership. In West Bengal today there are many educated Santhal tribes but those who join the CPI(M) never seem to reach its higher echelons. In fact during a visit to the predominantly Santhal region of Jhargram in Midnapore district, West Bengal, in December 1981, Ramesh Hembron, a Santhal schoolteacher, admitted that the Santhals were being alienated from the CPI(M) and joining various other tribal parties. Bengali cultural chauvinism persists even amongst the Marxist cadres in the same way that the Chinese leadership continues to face problems with Greater Han Chauvinism at all levels of the Chinese Communist Party. During a tribal function publicized by the local Jhargram administration, it was all too noticeable that, even at the opening ceremony, all speeches were dominated by non-tribals even to the extent that the tribal panchayat members, or elected village council members, were not even present around the dais and were only located for interview with difficulty.

The domination of the upper castes is not only a political and economic one. Even today people examine the caste problem through the eyes of the Indian intellectual who, even if sympathetic to the lower castes, usually fail to bridge the gap of perception. From the angle of the Scheduled Caste the situation appears quite different. Jagjivan Ram is the foremost Harijan politician in the country, having served as Agricultural minister during the Emergency and in the subsequent Janata regime as Defence Minister. He comments: 'In India everybody's status and station is determined by the accident of birth. In Hindu society one cannot think of equality. Even when I was Defence Minister, a Class IV Brahmin employee working as a peon regarded himself as superior to me.'[43]

Chanderjit Yadav, an MP from the Backward Castes, expresses similar sentiments. His statement is all the more significant because the Backward Castes have acquired considerable economic and political power since Independence. Yet in terms of the traditional norms of caste their social status remains low. He maintains: 'The caste system has become so rigid in India that people are regarded as high or low on the basis of their birth. Even if a person from the Backward Castes is wealthy he is regarded as low. His social status is low. This is the worst kind of social feudalism that one can imagine. I think it has been more easy to abolish feudalism from our economic life but it is more difficult to abolish feudalism from Indian society.'[44]

Such feelings are entirely justified. The kind of attitudes which persist among the upper castes were expressed by V.C. Channa. He believes that the hierarchical structure of caste, contrary to hampering modernization, provides a ready source of exploitative labour: 'You cannot industrialize without caste. No country in the world has industrialized without an exploitative labour system and we have a ready-made exploitative scene with the existence of the lower castes. We can progress much faster because we can exploit them any time.'[45]

This kind of attitude was reflected in the traditional Hindu legal system which was based on inequality before the law. Punishments varied according to one's caste. Thus the preliminary kind of orientation towards working with legal codes for which in the West there exists a set of beliefs and values is absent in Indian tradition. Ancient Hindu law texts state: 'In a local dispute between a Brahmin and non-Brahmin the arbitrator or witness must speak in favour of the former.' According to the Satpatha Brahmana: 'A murder of a Brahmin alone is the real murder.' On the other hand, Manu says that the 'slaying of a Sudra is equivalent merely to the killing of a cat, a mongoose, a blue jay, a frog, a lizard, an owl or a crow.' The king was never permitted to sentence a Brahmin, though convicted of all possible crimes. The most extreme form of punishment was banishment with his property secure and his body unhurt. On the other hand, if a Sudra mentioned the name of a Twice-Born 'with contumely, an iron nail, ten fingers long, shall be thrust red-hot into his mouth.'

Ram Vilas Paswan, an MP elected from a Scheduled Caste Reserved Constituency of Hajipur in Bihar, points out that equality before the law was introduced by the British. He is openly sceptical of the extent to which this norm has taken root on Indian soil. There is certainly widespread feeling among the lower castes that the judiciary and administration, which are largely dominated by upper or dominant castes, display traditional biased attitudes in their judgments and actions.

In the past few years an increasing number of atrocities have been perpetrated on Scheduled Castes by both upper and dominant castes, as well as Backward Castes, in isolated incidents in villages mainly in Bihar, Uttar Pradesh, Madhya Pradesh and Rajasthan. In all the incidents Harijan men, women and children were butchered and their huts set on fire. Ram Vilas Paswan, one of the most outspoken of the Harijan politicians, points out that the state administrations were prompt in punishing the atrocities committed by Backward Castes in Belchi and Pipra

He points out that in Kahalpa, Almora district, Uttar Pradesh, where 18 Harijans were shot dead by upper-caste landlords for walking down the street in their section of the village, not a single sentence was handed down by the court for 'lack of evidence'. In a similar incident in Sadhapur, Deoli, Uttar Pradesh, 27 Harijans were killed by upper castes but not a single person was arrested. Ram Vilas Paswan recalls: 'I was a member of a parliamentary committee set up to look into the matter. When we reached Sadhupur the Superintendent of Police did not even turn up before the Parliamentary Committee. He was not even transferred. Within another month of the incident in the district a dozen Harijans were butchered. Subsequently a third mass murder of Harijans by upper castes took place in Rampura in the same region but no action was taken.'[46]

P.S. Krishnan, former Joint Secretary in charge of Scheduled Castes and Scheduled Tribes in the Ministry of Home Affairs, points out, however, that atrocities on Harijans are being increasingly punished. His view is supported by the fact that in June 1983 the Congress (I) lost a by-election in Bihar because of its swift action in punishing those guilty of killing Harijans. Even the *Patriot*, a Left-wing newspaper not known for its sympathetic stand towards the ruling party, commented on the result of a by-election in Bihar: 'It is no secret that the stiff action taken by the government against those who indulged in brutality against the Harijans and the poor at Belchi, Kaila and Parasbigha, as also against the communal riots, had angered the vested interests.'[47] P.S. Krishnan points out that between 1980 and 1982 there were more sentences than acquittals handed down by the courts in cases involving atrocities on Harijans in Bihar, Uttar Pradesh and Gujarat.

Some studies have, however, brought out the class bias of the judiciary, although it is this author's contention that traditional attitudes based on traditional precepts of Hindu law persist even subconsciously. The assumption is that the powerful and the rich can twist the law in their own favour. T.K. Oommen rejects this idea. He believes that the notion of equality before the law is accepted as a norm of justice: 'If a policeman or a judge shows discrimination of a lower caste, these public servants will at least be criticized, whereas earlier this would never have happened.'[48] Yogendra Singh, Professor of Sociology at Jawaharlal Nehru University, New Delhi, tends to agree with this view. He thinks inequitous justice today is more a function of class domination than of religious beliefs. He believes that upper castes get away with a crime not on account of their status but because of their wealth. He maintains that once the lower castes become organized they will be able to exert pressure on the system and get redress for crimes perpetrated against their community.

One of the reasons for the failure of India's leaders to do away with caste may be linked to the fact that secular power in India has always traditionally been subsumed to the ritual power concentrated in the Brahmin as priest. Although caste lost its quasi-legal basis in the Constitution of January 1950, this has failed to bring about a significant structural change in the caste system.

Today the ritual Brahmin ascendancy has been taken over by a new group of self-styled intellectual leadership which regards itself as no less infallible and contemptuous of the lower orders than the old Brahmin leadership. Added to this is a certain sense of continuity in that the dominant groups in the new élite are also derived from the former upper castes. In India one may observe something more than the usurping of privilege by a group akin to M. Djilas' 'New Class'. The phenomenon is rather that of the absorption into the new system and its subtle transformation by the traditional upper castes with an extension of their attitudes to any new entrant to the extended system. This after all has been throughout the centuries the traditional Indian response to new challenges of change through gradual and subtle accretions to the Brahmin and Kshatriya orders.

Such a case was encountered in March 1983. In the hamlet of Debriaka Parwa of Sehud village in Etawah district, UP, the most prosperous-looking house belongs to a man from the barber community, a low caste. When villagers were asked how a barber could have a Brahmin surname like 'Sharma', people just smiled and answered: 'He's come up in the world recently.'

Co-option has therefore been one method of diffusing any threat to the power base of the ruling élite. Tactical ploys of 'divide and rule' have been adopted and applied systematically for the same end since the earliest times with no less success. For throughout history the dominant group has always been plagued

by a sense of insecurity because of its numerical disadvantage.
Hence the fear of being overwhelmed by the subjugated people.
The British found themselves in a similar situation in the aftermath of the 1857 Mutiny. The sheer scale of the revolt and its
accompanying violence contributed to a new sense of insecurity
which led them to adopt similar ploys of divide and rule to
maintain their paramountcy.

This seems to have been the pattern in facing any challenge
throughout various stages of history. Similar trends seem to be
emerging today. All the historical experience of dealing with
people whom the dominant group considered barbarian invaders,
whether one is dealing with the élites of the first few centuries AD
or the Muslims or British, and all the experiences of defusing the
dangers of people preaching some egalitarian philosophy like
Buddhism, Islam or Christianity, will now be focused on similar
challenges today.

The coming of the vote, the potential rise of a barbarian power
struggle of a majority of lower castes are a direct challenge to the
power base of the dominant groups. Today the 'lower groups'
comprising the Backward Castes, Scheduled Castes and Scheduled Tribes, who form about 75 per cent of India's total
population, are beleaguering the intellectual and secular numerical minority of the upper castes. Similarly modernization, in the
inevitable spread of world thought, means a new challenge no
longer based on hierarchy but on egalitarianism. So this is the
challenge which the upper groups, which may or may not develop
into a new caste or class, are seeking to meet by traditional
techniques for their very survival. If all the lower castes really
united under any leader the ruling élite would have their power
base undermined. But in practice they have so manipulated these
various caste and tribal groups that today they are fighting
amongst themselves.

The classic example is the Mandal Commission Report submitted to Parliament in April 1982. The report recommends that
a total of 48 per cent reservations be allotted to the Backward
Castes which represent 52 per cent of the country's population,
without disturbing the Scheduled Caste and Scheduled Tribe
reservations. The voting power of the Backward Castes is so
strong that the government cannot openly reject or throw out the
report. On the other hand, the demand is striking at the very root
of the monopoly of their own power, for if 48 per cent of the seats

are reserved, the Backward Castes are in a position to challenge that monopoly. This is especially the case for, unlike the Scheduled Castes and Tribes, they have an adequate economic base. As a result of the abolition of the feudal estates after Independence, these Backward Castes, who were largely tenants, were transformed into *de jure* owners of their land. These groups are full of vitality and today the upper castes are trying to meet their challenge by setting the Backward Castes against the Scheduled Castes and Tribes.

The latter are fully aware of this and in April 1983 Chanderjit Yadav, a Backward Caste leader, organized a 'Conference of the National Union of Backward Castes, Scheduled Castes, Scheduled Tribes and Minorities' to counter the offensive. The resolution of the conference stated: 'The Conference cautions the people belonging to the Backward Castes, Scheduled Castes and Scheduled Tribes and Minorities to be on guard against the nation-wide conspiracy to set them against one another and to thwart the growing unity amongst them.'[49]

The government adopts the same kind of divide-and-rule tactics towards Scheduled Castes. When any person from this community begins to move up the scale thanks to the reservation facilities, loud protests are raised to the effect that a new élite of Harijans is monopolizing all the reservation facilities within their own society. Calls for the abolition of the reservations are made on the plea of egalitarianism. Since one cannot fault the argument intellectually an attempt will be made to amend the lists.

Even the reservations for Scheduled Tribes operate in such a way that some numerically large groups, like the Bhils of Rajasthan, are kept down. The Minas, who are Sanskritized Bhils, were co-rulers of some of the former princely kingdoms of Rajasthan. The inclusion of their group in the Scheduled Tribe list, together with the tribes of the North-East, makes both these groups monopolize the special facilities by dint of their greater level of advancement. Even in the élitist Indian Administrative Service the Scheduled Tribe reservations are being filled largely by these groups. The issue of reservation will be dealt with in greater depth in the next chapter.

It would be perhaps stretching the issue if one accused the ruling élite of intentionally pursuing divisive tactics or of devising elaborate devices to maintain the status quo. It may be more correct to suggest that the subconscious element is an important factor in inducing such moves. It must also be admitted that the caste structure offers tremendous leverage for this general kind of process. As Satish Saberwal points out: 'One needs to go back to the structure and recognize the enormous amount of variety of separations that lie in the caste structure which can readily be exploited. It is a separation across which there is a lack of contact, suspicion, there is antagonism and so forth. So it is lying there waiting for someone to come and turn one group against another. Such hostility between castes only tends to deepen the biases and thereby strengthen the forces working for segregation.'[50]

There is a growing debate among the Left in India over whether caste is being transformed into class. It will be argued that this thesis is erroneous and is probably the main contributory factor for the failure of the Left to make inroads in the country-side. Leftists have tended to adopt Western Marxist theories to analyse Indian society, all of which may not be suited to the objective and subjective conditions of the Hindu social structure. V.S. Naipaul has accused Indian Marxists of 'mimicry'. In *A Wounded Civilization* he comments: 'Even Marxism tends to be only jargon, a form of mimicry. "The people" so often turns out to be the people of a certain region and of a certain caste.'[51]

In fact in the reserved Scheduled Caste and Scheduled Tribe constituencies the CPI and CPI(M) have made no major inroads either in the 1971, 1977 or 1980 general elections. The Communists had about 11 per cent of the total Scheduled Caste reserved seats in 1971 but this had declined to 9 per cent in 1980.[52] The Communist representation in the Scheduled Tribe constituencies was far worse, with representation in the last elections being 0 per cent, 0 per cent and 3 per cent respectively.[53]

The Left has consistently failed to recognize that caste is the dominant ideology and therefore the dominant reality in terms of the number of people who live by it. Most Indians continue to inherit the basic framework of their identity and their basic ideas with regard to their relationships from the caste system. The caste system, with its ideological principle being the opposition between the pure and impure, is unique to India. People are made to feel inferior or superior by reference to criteria that have nothing to do with the level of their material possessions or earnings. This makes the problem of the abolition of caste extremely difficult and complex.

While it is true to say that the four varnas do correspond to the term estate as applied to pre-revolutionary France, the subcastes, or *jati*, a term which is often used interchangeably with caste, are status groups. While classes are based on external possessions, caste thrives on 'ingrained biases, exclusive identity and a sense of superiority.'[54] Caste differs radically from the Western concept of class in that its sanctions and structures have traditionally been backed by religion, law and custom, although in modern India the legal sanctions no longer apply. Religious law was used to justify the exercise of power and ascendancy of one group over another by conquest. Although the concept of class has undergone many changes during the last one hundred years, partly in response to the change in the structure of industrial society, classes are economic groups based on a rationalized order organized along the principles of equality. The caste system is based on ideals of hierarchy supported by religious, legal and customary sanctions. Hutton has pointed out that caste cannot be equated with class: 'Caste . . . is not a principle by which politico-economic groups are recruited nor does it organize relations between political groups, but it is an organizing principle within such groups.'[55]

Castes, in the sense of jati, are ethnic groups, endogamous self-contained units. They may be described as status groups. In India a man is born into his caste and marries into his caste. According to all canons of Hinduism a person cannot move out of his caste individually by hard work or acquisition of power through wealth. In the West there is a relatively large degree of freedom of movement between classes and the only laws a citizen has to uphold are those of the polity. Traditionally an entire caste could, however, over a period of generations, move up the scale either through a process known as Kshatriyization or through Sanskritization. A promotion into the Kshatriya, or warrior estate, has been the most common form of caste mobility prior to the British conquest when avenues of political mobility became frozen. A caste could thus by conquest and the acquisition of power acquire Kshatriya status. The historian K.M. Pannikar has argued that for the last 2,500 years there have been no real Kshatriyas and that most have been recruited from the Sudras, the fourth estate. Ultimately, however, the Brahmin was always the arbiter of status. Sanskritization, a term coined by the sociologist. Srinvas, means that a caste may over one or two generations move up the hierarchy by emulating the Brahminical way of life. This involves stricter taboos on food, adoption of ritual orthodox observances and sometimes occupational changes. One example of such mobility are the Satnami Harijans of Madhya Pradesh who, having Sanskritized their way of life in the nineteenth century, are considered superior to other Harijans. Prior to the arrival of the British Harijans would not have been able to rise within the caste system since they were on the wrong side of the pollution line. Sanskritization was a more common avenue of mobility for these depressed groups during British rule: 'In the first place there were few opportunities for Harijans to acquire wealth and political power and in those rare cases where they did acquire it, their being on the wrong side of the pollution line proved an almost insuperable obstacle to mobility.'[56] Sanskritization for Harijans became possible during British rule because the colonial power refused to give legal recognition to the disabilities traditionally imposed on Harijans. Through the process of Sanskritization the caste becomes ritually purer. Srinivas was himself never satisfied with the term but for want of a better word adopted it.

Béteille has argued that class can be defined in a number of ways and that the definition of classes as economic groups is one among many: 'It can be defined in terms of hierarchy, dependence or conflict, in terms of ownership or the control of property; in terms of interest or of consciousness; in static or in dynamic terms.'[57] Marx had highlighted the political aspect of class. If one adopts this criterion it is clear that caste is in no way equivalent to class. The main inhibiting factor in the organization of the poor against those who control wealth and money is precisely the cleavages which exist between castes.

In Bhojpur, North Bihar, the standard of life of the landless Harijans and the small and marginal caste Hindu farmers is almost identical. But this factor has not materially altered the line of cleavage. The real distinction is not the economic disparities that exist between them. Rather it is the symbol of superiority or inferiority in terms of caste status which marks the real distinction. A destitute Brahmin would behave in a similar manner towards a Harijan as a rich Brahmin. In fact the poor Brahmin feels a greater need to assert his status. The Marxists have in fact never cited one example of a poor Brahmin and a poor Harijan uniting against a landlord to gain better wages to support their theory that class has overtaken caste in India. Workers in a small-scale industry in Gujarat have been unable to unite with the low-caste workers who were landless for better wages. Those with land will work for any wage and when strikes occur they act as renegades against their fellow workers. Furthermore, the upper-caste workers fear that if higher wages are granted the lower-caste agricultural labourers in their villages would also demand higher wages.[58]

A recent village-level study from Tamil Nadu in South India carried out in the mid seventies underscores the fact that consciousness of caste identity remains strong. Harriss notes that in Vegamangalam village in eastern North Arcot the caste solidarity of the Harijan labourers and Harijan landowners overrides their economic disparities in spite of intercaste exploitation. Harriss points out: 'Even where principles of orthodox Hinduism and the actual social practices are less congruent . . . it does not necessarily mean that there has been a shift in consciousness of class identity.'[59]

In regions where the agrarian hierarchy closely correlates with caste there have been instances where agricultural labourers, all belonging to one caste, have organized themselves politically to demand higher wages from the Brahmin landlords as in Tanjore district, Tamil Nadu.[60] In another village in North Kerala caste rank was closely correlated with agrarian classes. The Brahmin and chieftain castes tended to be landowners; the higher Nair sub-castes were either landowners or non-cultivating sub-tenants; the majority of the upper polluting castes were landless labourers; while the lower polluting castes were serfs until the twentieth century.[61] Despite the close correlation between caste and class, there would be no chance of the upper polluting castes uniting with the lower polluting castes, or Harijans, for better wages. Traditionally all castes unite against Harijans who had no rights in the traditional system. For example, traditionally Harijans were forbidden to own land in the South.

Béteille gives another well-known definition of class which is described as a force that unites into groups who differ from one another by overriding differences between them.'[62] Using this definition one can also show the falseness of the claim that caste is becoming class. This can be illustrated by a recent incident. In Ahmedabad, the capital of Gujarat, the Patels, an upper landholding caste, attacked a Harijan basti to put them in their place. On the outskirts of the Harijan slum some migrant labour from

Etawah district, UP, and from Bhind district in Madhya Pradesh, had temporarily settled. Since their indigence matched that of their neighbours, if caste had been transformed into class, one would have expected both to override their differences in their fight against the Patels. However, casteism prevailed: since the migrant labourers belonged to a slightly higher lower-caste group, the Bhaiyas, they joined the Patels at the latter's instigation and attacked the Harijans.[63]

A recent study of the composition of the *vidhan sabha*, or state assembly, of Gujarat was made along caste lines, not according to class, 'because caste still remains the most compulsive and dominating factor in the personal life and family relations of Indians.'[64] The study pointed out the importance of caste for understanding the political and economic significance of social factors. During the Agra riots in 1978 the violence broke out along caste lines, the upper castes attacking Harijans in collusion with the police. The issue was not a class one between exploiter and exploited. The riots broke out because the upper castes could not tolerate the economic betterment of the Jatavs, a Scheduled Caste group of shoemakers, in recent years.

The myth of the caste/class theory is further undermined by a recent development in Tamil Nadu where more and more organizations are coming up along caste lines. Even the Reddy community, which in Tamil Nadu, unlike Andhra Pradesh, constitutes an insignificant upper-caste minority, feels the need for a forum on caste lines. The Reddis may have felt insecure as the Backward Castes had already organized themselves on a caste basis. As a group they are becoming more and more vocal as in the case of the Vanniyas from the northern districts. The Mukkulathas from the southern districts are now coming together under a cultural organization. The Gounders, who are largely agriculturalists from the western districts, were to have held a statewide conference in May 1982.

Most of these groups are listed as Backward Castes who feel they have been deprived of a legitimate share of political offices, of placements in education and access to jobs. They claim that it is mostly the Neo-Brahmins, the successors to the Brahmins in matters of power and position, who have not played fair by them. These Neo-Brahmins are themselves drawn from the educated non-Brahmin castes who benefited from the anti-Brahmin movement in the state during the forties. For in the aftermath of the movement many Brahmins moved out of their home state and joined Central Government posts. Their monopoly over the professions was thus ended.

The trend towards the formation of such caste associations in Tamil Nadu is surely evidence that the caste factor is as strong today as it ever was in the state, despite the fact that educationally the South is far ahead of the North.

One of the reasons for the persistence of caste as the dominant factor governing social relations, despite the changes brought about in the political and economic sphere since Independence, is the fact that such changes do not affect the structural elements of the system. As Lannoy points out: 'Social change has made very slow progress in India. The caste system is not only almost as strong as it ever was but it has exacerbated divisions within society, while traditionalism has retarded the pace of development.'[65]

Even the *Report of the Commissioner for Scheduled Castes and Scheduled Tribes, 1977–1978* supports the viewpoint regarding the persistence of caste. In Aurangabad, Maharashtra, for example, almost all the colleges have acquired a caste character and have become single-caste institutions. The Saraswati Mahavidyalaya College is dominated mainly by upper castes and non-Marathas; the Devagiri College is predominantly a Maratha institution; the Maulana Azad College caters mainly to Muslim sects; Vasantro Nasik College is managed by the Banjaras, a semi-tribal group; while Milind College, established by the great Harijan leader, Dr B.R. Ambedkar, is the preserve of the Scheduled Castes.[66] Given the situation in higher educational institutions one may question the validity of the assumption that education and modernization will dispel caste structures even if they accelerate mobility within castes.

A challenge to social stratification is emerging in contemporary India. The concept of equality before the law found effective formal fruition after Independence, especially for the Scheduled Castes. If it had not been for British rule the Constitution would never have been what it is now. On the other hand, British Imperial policy made it necessary not to interfere with the social customs of the country because the British relied on the native élites for the preservation of their rule. The British were not necessarily influenced by them but it certainly represented a certain coming together of interests. The net result was probably that during the British period a tendency arose for the caste structure to be frozen at the same time as certain ritual rigidities were relaxed through the modernization process.

After Independence came the real impact of British education and Western institutions which had produced an élite committed to democratic principles and to the whole apparatus of the Constitution, its declared objectives and special provisions, as for the Scheduled Castes. These measures and declared objectives could be seen in two ways. Either they were far in advance of the cultural actuality but represented some ideal through which the gap could ultimately be closed, or they could be seen as being fundamentally antithetical to Indian culture, thereby making it inevitable that there would be major antagonistic contradictions. The latter might seem to be a truer picture. It is resulting in fundamental antagonistic contradictions and, above all, it is another step in deepening the dichotomy of Indian thought. Satish Saberwal even doubts whether the commitment to equality is there to stay, for as he comments: 'The normative order as reflected in the Constitution is not self-acting. It has to be enforced and who is going to do the enforcing? In so far as it has to be done by people whose being there to enforce the Constitution is contingent on their being elected, you are back to the values in the society. And there are all kinds of ways to get around constitutional norms.'[67]

One now has to consider the likely trend of events and especially the response of the traditionally dominant castes to this situation. It is likely that the response will be derived from traditional cultural roots modernized to meet current challenge. The response therefore need not necessarily be a Machiavellian or Kautilyan one, but based more on subconscious instincts. It is likely to be founded on certain fundamentals of the historical process. The first of these, as has already been seen, is that, although the dominant intellectual and power group has pro- pounded rigid hierarchical structures, in actual fact there has always been considerable mobility. Such mobility has, however, only been achieved when the dominant groups have been faced with a serious threat to their own conceptualizations. Such threats have rarely if ever arisen on an individual plane.

Indeed the first response to individual challenges is usually an attempt at suppression, either intellectual or physical. A Buddha is dismissed as a false prophet divinely ordained to spread false doctrines which can then be refuted so as ultimately to strengthen the traditional fabric. An individual Harijan could, according to the Laws of Manu, have molten iron rammed down his throat for daring to talk about the Twice-Born. A low-caste or outcaste individual daring to encroach on traditional preserves in either temporal or spiritual excellence had to pay the penalty. The Nishada Ekalavya is tricked into forfeiting his thumb after achieving pre-eminence as an archer. Even Rama, the paragon of Ram Rajya, is supposed to have dealt brutally with a low-caste upstart who aspired to study of the Vedas. However, there are also instances where an individual challenger succeeds in articulating the feelings of a much larger group through a new charisma of leadership, thereby posing a direct threat to the system which cannot be met by head-on confrontation or suppression. To do so would break the traditional Indian concept of ultimate harmony, which itself, of course, is founded on the definition and administration of such harmony by privileged minority groups.

At this stage the second traditional strategy is employed. It may take the form of weakening the opposition through internal dissent. Later the original thesis of the reformer or challenger is transformed almost beyond recognition into something approaching the very antithesis of his original message. It can thus ultimately be incorporated into the 'tolerant, all embracing' traditional structure. This can be accompanied even by an apotheosis of the original challenger. The Buddha then becomes an incarnation of Vishnu.

There are already signs that this traditional response is well under way. Shivaji, a peasant who rose to be king, had the utmost difficulty in forcing his will upon the Brahmins to obtain a traditional royal coronation ceremony. One Brahmin from Benares was finally persuaded by a large donation, but even he could not overcome the opposition of his brotherhood to perform the ceremonies strictly according to Vedic rites. However, Shivaji achieved a fabricated lineage traced back to the solar dynasty and later was almost apotheosized as the champion of Hindu resistance to the Muslims. At least, however, he achieved *de facto* Kshatriya status for his hardy Maratha peasantry whom no one thereafter could seriously think of reducing to menial status. Even despite this, the same problem was raised some generations later by the Brahmins for the coronation of one of his descendants, the Maharaja of Kolhapur.[68]

In the current context from the same area of Maharashtra arose Dr B.R. Ambedkar, the single acknowledged leader whom the Scheduled Castes have produced so far. It would be a mistake to ascribe his rise purely to the impact of modernization under the British. His initial advancement, if it can be attributed in any way to Western values, was through the indirect influence of such values, comparable to similar influences on the leaders of India's Independence Movement. Dr Ambedkar achieved prominence in the service of the liberal princely state of Baroda. Yet he too faced during his youth, although coming from a 'respectable' family, all the ritual indignities of sitting separately in school, finding problems in obtaining a glass of water and, even after becoming Finance Minister of Baroda, in having files dumped on his table by subordinates who would not hand them over personally and so risk his low-caste contamination. The usual red carpet befitting his high office was rolled up in the mornings before he came to office to avoid the pollution of his feet. He found difficulty in finding a horse carriage willing to convey him through the streets. Ultimately he came to occupy a position still ambivalent in Independent India. He was cited as the shining example of a Scheduled Caste success story.

He was in fact, and not merely in form, the main drafter of the Indian Constitution. He never saw eye to eye with Gandhi, the great harmonizer, and probably understood, as deeply as Gandhi, the basically antagonistic contradictions in policy towards the Scheduled Castes. Gandhi, in all probability also, was shrewd enough to understand them but exerted all his influence to defuse them for the sake of national harmony in the Independence struggle by encouraging, through a missionary approach, the uplift of Harijans, but never specifically decrying the caste system as such. Ultimately, Dr Ambedkar was induced to sacrifice his own instinctive constitutional preference for separate Harijan electorates. Ultimately, too, he led several million of his followers out of the Hindu fold but again compromised for the sake of the 'national interest' in choosing Buddhism rather than the more uncompromising ideologies of Islam or Christianity.

The main impact of his career upon the Scheduled Castes was on his own Mahar group. This group, more than any other Scheduled Castes, had tended to retain some elements of tribal pride and cohesion despite the ritual indignities earlier inflicted on them. It is from this Mahar group that the largest elements of

'Dalit (oppressed)' activists have emerged. His wife in the 1980s has taken up the championship of this Dalit cause. The sociologically fascinating present position is that the main opposition to Dr Ambedkar's Mahars comes from the very Marathas who had received upward mobility under Shivaji's leadership.

Some Mahar elements would even claim that the name of the state, Maharashtra, is 'the realm of the Mahars', as against the traditional derivation of Maha-rashtra, 'The Great Realm', over which the Marathas earlier exercised dominance. There is a current still smouldering controversy leading to group violence between Dalit (mainly Mahar groups) who demand implementation of an earlier Maharashtra government resolution to rename the Nagpur University after Dr Ambedkar, and the Maratha lobby which insists on retaining its earlier name of Marathwada. Here one has a classic modern variant of an old theme in which ultimately the Twice-Born leadership will 'have to intervene' to compose the differences between the earlier-risen Marathas and the now-rising Mahars. Such mediation will of course only reinforce the ultimate supremacy of the Twice-Born leadership over both.

In other parts of the country there is little evidence as yet of any cohesive challenge from Scheduled Caste or tribal groups. Indeed in a number of cases subcastes or groups amongst themselves work out their own antagonisms as, for example, Chamars against Kurmis and so forth. In a sense and again, of course, subconsciously, the Marxist ideological dogma also works against a really cohesive challenge from the lower-caste groups which alone could achieve some amelioration of their group interests. The Marxists insist that caste is class, that the poor Brahmin must inevitably unite with the poor Harijan to further class interests and that struggles on a caste basis reflect outmoded feudal thinking. In practice this never seems to take place. There are signs of some slight rethinking within the extreme Left to recognize actual realities, especially in certain areas like Bihar where caste and class oppression are almost synonymous. Insistence on the class dogma and ignoring the caste factor might even be welcomed by the oppressors as it would weaken the actual bonds of cohesion among the oppressed.

Caste will play an important role in determining both ongoing processes and the kind of future changes which will take place in the country. The basic problem of caste is its societal totalitarianism. While caste is important economically and politically, its most oppressive dimension is in the social realm. This is particularly so with reference to the Scheduled Castes. For whatever degree of political influence or economic power a Harijan may possess, once he is identified as such his quality of life becomes affected. Indeed the Sudras and middle castes often feel a greater distance from Harijans than from the superior castes. Social intercourse betwen Sudras and the Twice-Born, except in matters relating to marriage, is largely accepted. But the Sudras avoid contact with Harijans to the same extent as the Twice-Born castes.

The argument that economic and political resources would compensate for the social oppression borne by lower castes and Harijans has little empirical foundation. The most effective means of emancipation for these groups is in their organized political mobilization. The present protests, as exemplified in the demand by the Backward Castes that the Mandal Commission Report be implemented, are perhaps the beginning of this emancipation.

In the modern urban context the ritual element is receding and a new emphasis in terms of the caste factor in relation to the secular aspect is emerging. Caste is playing a very important role in elections, in access to jobs, admission to colleges and in getting licences and promotions. Similarly, in the political context, caste is being systematically utilized by politicians for their ends. This does not mean that the ritual factor has been entirely displaced by the secular factor, rather that a weakening of the ritual dimension has taken place and that the secular dimension is becoming more and more important.

On the theoretical level what is required is a 'demystification' of some of the ancient values because all societies, in order to exist at a given point in time, require sacred values not in the religious sense of the term but in the sense that people attach great importance to such ethical principles. In the modern Indian context there is a need for a 'desacrilization' of some of the ancient norms associated with caste and a 'resacrilization' of modern values. In this context the question of democracy is relevant, for within the caste and tribe there has always been a strong element of democracy. This is most manifest in the system of caste panchayats. Democracy existed only in terms of the decision-making process within the caste group. In present day

India the democratic traditions arising out of this institution can be retained as a value but the process of recruitment of leadership and recruitment affecting a wider society will have to be changed and the process of arriving at decisions through consultation will have to be transformed into a more truly democratic consensus. It is at this level that manipulation in favour of vested interests based on dominant castes has emerged within the theoretically democratic structure of the Constitution.

In the same context one of the greatest assets in the traditional institutions and values is that the caste system allowed for a great degree of pluralism. Each caste was not only an occupational group but also a political group in the sense that its members made decisions pertaining to their own affairs. In the modern setting pluralism will have to be redefined and reinterpreted to suit the contemporary context. Another asset of the traditional system would be holism, that is to say, the priority given to the group over the individual, or to the wider society over the small group. In the traditional context the collective family or subcaste interest was always emphasized as against the individual. With the advent of democracy, however, it became difficult to operate because at the lowest level the individual became the unit of operation, while at the higher levels the postulated national interest rarely achieved priority over that of the subcaste group network. T.K. Oommen comments: 'There are many contexts in which individual autonomy and freedom ought to be given, but at the same time there is a strong case for retaining the collective orientation and collective interest. In the present context one needs a redefinition of the situation.'[69]

There is a reluctance, however, to spell out such a redefinition. The dangers of the present drift have certainly been articulated. The sober, elderly scholar, M.N. Srinivas, saw them clearly and shocked an anthropological gathering by specifically foreseeing increasing violence amounting to caste war. More recently, other commentators have noticed how every politician, including Mrs Gandhi herself, while deprecating casteism and communalism in theory, have used it brazenly to further their narrow political interests. To this extent they seem to have become prisoners of the political system deriving from the Constitution which, as already pointed out, deepened the chasm between the normative and the existential order.

There is growing realization that, although caste mobility may become more fluid under the impact of modernization and the more archaic and oppressive ritual symbols of oppression may be modified, the system itself with its preoccupations regarding hierarchical status is not likely to disappear so easily. Dr Karan Singh seems to recognize this: 'The caste system really cannot be done away with in the sense that it is there. I mean people may or may not have a feeling for it but it cannot be abolished.'[70] He, of course, would argue for a transformation into a wider, more liberal, concept of pluralistic groups working 'for the good of all'. However, there is little grappling with the problem about who will define the good of all and who will coordinate the contribution of the pluralistic groups. The present political system seems inherently incapable of achieving this and is indeed intensifying group contradictions. There is a tendency to blame this state of affairs on to the immoral cynicism of the present breed of politicians rather than on studying the inevitability of their emergence or corruption by the pattern of the system itself.

One Indian commentator has suggested that the time is approaching when the manipulation of caste group loyalties will become so complex that it will pass beyond the control of the manipulators by further fragmentation of mutually antagonistic groups becoming smaller and smaller as time goes by. Occasionally, however, situations arise when these small groups coalesce for temporary immediate interests.

A case in point is the emergence of three major conglomerations over the reservations issue. The Scheduled Castes and Scheduled Tribes of course desire a continuance of reservations and special facilities and can point out justifiably that they are nowhere near achieving the parity of representation which their numbers warrant. Occasionally a minority group such as the Muslims express similar views. The second main conglomeration is of the intermediate castes loosely described as the 'Backward Castes'. The Mandal Commission has forthrightly drawn attention to the domination even of these by upper castes and recommended 40 per cent reservations for them. The third major conglomeration is, of course, the traditional leadership of the Twice-Born which continues totally to dominate the higher echelons of administrative, intellectual and commercial life, as well as the law-and-order machinery. Their dominance and representation is totally disproportionate to their numbers as it is they who in the present situation ultimately call the tune and make the decisions. Everything depends on their response to the challenges which will continue to intensify.

The traditional response, as has been seen, would take the shape of fomenting the already deep divisions of interests along sub-groups of the two other major conglomerations. If, in the process of these manipulations, a new and fairly powerful new conglomerate began to arise, one could not rule out this being used, as happened in Indian tradition, to destroy the old power group and replace it by a new one. The legend of the extermination of the old Kshatriyas and the rise of the new Rajput clans under Brahmin tutelage comes immediately to mind. The question, of course, arises regarding the cohesiveness of the upper-caste conglomeration of power groups and their ability to hang together. It is a fact that this group contains many extremely perceptive and liberal individuals from whom the ultimate leadership and new thought will probably still be derived. A few of them may be found as the most articulate champions of the more depressed groups. However, it is a little too much to expect that the present power groups will surrender easily their total dominance over all positions of power and privilege. Few commentators face the fact that any reservation or economic betterment policy for the weaker sections will be at the expense of the entrenched monopolies of the present dominant groups.

An alternative scenario, which would also have its roots in Indian tradition, would be the emergence of a group of charismatic reformers with an appeal partly ideological and partly religious on the lines of the great wave of Bhakti reformers some five hundred years ago. Many of these were drawn from the lower castes but in their day also attracted a following from among the more liberal upper groups.

Another more dangerous scenario would be based on the recognition that the fragmenting of group loyalties can realistically only be transcended and overcome by merging them into a wider and more fanatical group loyalty. The time seems to have passed when the existing political leadership could have mobilized such a movement by a really sincere slogan of 'Garibi Hatao banish poverty)'.

There are signs that the next slogan may well be 'Desh Bachao (protect the Nation)'. Internal antagonisms will therefore be sought to be defused by the harping on an outside bogey. There is already much talk about foreign hands being responsible for every conceivable ill in the country. No doubt such agencies – like the CIA – dabble consistently in manipulating other countries' problems according to their perception of their own country's interests. There is, however, the equal danger, especially given the present climate, both within India and Pakistan, of the leadership of both countries discovering a mutual advantage in precipitating confrontations which they could then use to defuse internal dissent by appeals to the wider national interest. In the South Asian context there would be the added complication of religious confrontation.

Whatever pattern ultimately emerges – and it may well be a mixture of the various scenarios – there can be no doubt regarding the increase in the ferment of the caste structure which in itself is one of the most important components of Indian society. The outlook need not necessarily be pessimistic. The society has faced such periods of ferment in the past. Dr Karan Singh when advocating his theory of Renaissance probably focuses in his mind on the artistic and intellectual achievements of the Western Renaissance era. It is easy to forget, in nostalgia for the Renaissance man, that he could not have come into being without the ferment produced by the barbarian sack of Rome and the ethnic tumult of the Middle Ages. The word 'medieval' does not in itself signify anything which is traditional or barbaric. It merely means the transition between two eras.

The present ferment in India has been started not merely by the catalyst of foreign concepts of modernization but by the resurgence of very old forces from within India's own tradition. By this is meant not merely the élite tradition but the tradition of large groups in the countryside. Much will depend on the capacity of India's social and political scientists to recognize at each stage the exact temperature and components of the catalysts so that the process of ferment produces worthwhile new elements and avoids an uncontrolled explosion.

CHAPTER SIX

Corruption: a factor affecting social change

There is a great deal of talk about corruption in India, not least among Indian commentators. The all-pervasiveness of corruption is now taken for granted and indulgence in malpractices has become institutionalized. It may therefore be useful to examine whether there are any special features in the Indian scene which contribute to the feeling that corruption is somehow endemic in society.

One important reason for the prevalence of corruption is the tremendous force of extended family ties in a society which is now expected to operate through an impersonal system in the administration and various other spheres of public life. Primary loyalties are accorded to family and kin groups, to caste or ethnic groups. Formal standards of public behaviour have not been widely internalized and perhaps subconsciously are regarded as alien. Strict enforcement of such theoretical norms clash with the demands put forth by the traditional group as a stronger social obligation.

Such ties are more compelling and immediate than administrative rules and procedures. Caste groups do not view the behaviour of officials from their own caste group as corrupt if it helps their group, even if such conduct deviates from the formal duties of public affairs. The norms operate according to different standards: it is rather that anyone not acting according to community principles would be ostracized, while, as a concession to 'modernization', nepotism, or furtherance of kindred interests, has to be condemned. The kind of corruption arising from nepotism is therefore rooted in the collective orientation of Indian society. In other words, the transfer of values is incomplete and social tensions arise.

In India, as in many developing countries, government embodies a concentration of power with its scope of responsibilities encompassing social welfare, development planning and actual production. Officials, however, live in a social environment where tremendous emphasis is placed not merely on 'getting ahead', but on acquiring more status and more money as a passport to this. White collar jobs in government not only offer great power and prestige but also provide vast opportunities to improve the wealth and status of one's kinship and caste group.

The rapid expansion of government activities in new fields after Independence, involving huge outlays, gave unprecedented opportunities for acquiring wealth by unscrupulous methods. Today there is an intense pursuit of wealth untrammelled by moral considerations. Money has increasingly become a criterion of a person's social status.

The amassment of wealth leads one to avenues of power, and such political power is largely obtained by money. Today expenses for running for a Lok Sabha or state assembly seat run into several hundred thousand rupees. Despite the existence of pre-scribed statutory limits, the expenses incurred are grossly under-estimated when returns are filed. The statutory limit for a Lok Sabha seat is Rs 35,000 and limited companies are not allowed to contribute to the election expenses of any candidate. Yet it has been estimated that the sum spent in the 1980 general elections for the 540 Lok Sabha seats and 3,200 seats in the state assemblies may have cost ten billion rupees. Most of this money was financed by black-money holders and those who required political patronage to obtain economic concessions at the cost of the public exchequer.

There has been a series of government reports on corruption which have made recommendations for the curbing of malprac-tices in politics. As early as 1964 the Santhanam Committee Report recognized the prevalence of corruption at the political level and concluded that: 'Nothing but a total ban on all donations by corporate bodies to political parties ... will clear the atmosphere.'[1]

The Direct Taxes Enquiry Report of 1971 recommended that various limits be placed on donations to political parties. Yet Shankar Acharya, an economist from the National Institute of Public Finance and Policy, New Delhi, estimates that approx-imately five billion rupees are donated illegally to various political parties every year. The close linkages that exist between black money and politics mean that legislation which seeks to regulate economic activity, with various controls and forms of taxation, cannot be implemented.

The sums donated to political parties are used not only for the running of party affairs but vast amounts are utilized to induce defections and floor crossings from opposition parties. The defections which occur after general and state elections not only undermine political stability but are also an important link in corruption. For a large number of legislators are appointed to ministerial offices and others are appointed to posts in corporate state undertakings. A Home Ministry Study for 1967 showed that a substantial proportion of defections were motivated by the lures of office and not ideology. To date the government has failed to pass legislation to stop defections. The excuse for failing to do so is the need to allow a healthy polarization of political forces.

Despite the pervasive corruption in politics and the administration, people from such circles who are speaking out against these corrosive practices are quoting Indian sources in support of a return to ethical norms of behaviour. The chief minister of Andhra Pradesh, N.T. Rama Rao, stresses the need to return to the traditional Hindu outlook which places great stress on moral character and human service to God. After his victory in January 1983 he expressed traditional Hindu thinking when he said: 'The main blame for corruption must be placed on the head of the state and not on civil servants. The leader must set an example.' He had constantly denounced the unprecedented level of corruption prevailing in the Congress state ministry during the state election campaign. Yet the overwhelming electoral support in his favour was more a reaction against constant interference and encroachments by the Centre into the running of state affairs than an expression of public disapprobation against corruption.

Quite apart from the ethical issues involved in corruption, there is what Mydral calls the 'folklore' of corruption. This undoubtedly has a corrosive influence on national life and impedes social change by tolerating and accepting its existence. The folklore of corruption concerns people's belief about corruption and the emotions attached to those feelings. The folklore easily leads people to think it inevitable that anybody in a position of power is likely to exploit this in the interest of himself, his family or other social groups to which he feels loyal. Another point should be mentioned in regard to Myrdal's concept: the belief held by the poor that slackness and corruption are the natural order of things. Their only points of reference are the government delivery system at the village level which has never operated without discrimination, favouritism and patronage.

The situation at the grass roots is a reflection of conditions in all spheres of national life. In one sense democracy is threatened by its prevalence because it results in the malfunctioning of the state. As long as the individual believes the powerful and rich will get away with malpractices, his belief in the polity will be undermined and cynicism bred. Even the late prime minister, Indira Gandhi, while inaugurating a conference of officers of the Criminal Bureau of Investigation in 1981, admitted that the feeling prevailed amongst members of the public that the powerful and influential escaped punishment for corrupt practices and only the small fry were caught.

Furthermore corrupt practices are highly detrimental to any efforts to achieve modernization ideals and social change. Myrdal points out:

> The prevalence of corruption raises strong obstacles and inhibitions to development. The corruption that is spurred by fragmentation of loyalties acts against efforts to consolidate the nation. It decreases respect for and allegiance to the government and its institutions. It often promotes irrationality in planning and limits the horizons of plans.[2]

To the extent that black money leads to conspicuous consumption and to investment in non-productive assets like precious metals and stones, it reduces the government's potential resources for investment in productive assets. Francine Frankel argues that the impact of black money on government policies is disastrous. Attempts by the government to impose selective credit controls in the late sixties consistently failed because of the availability of alternative credit markets for the black economy. This economist estimates that in 1968/69, when total private investment in industry was well under 5 billion rupees, the money value of transactions involving black income was estimated to have reached 70 billion rupees.[3]

Today economists argue that the black economy is closely interlinked with the white economy. This means that there are natural constraints which limit the government's compulsion to curb its activities. Certainly black money has become a vital and dynamic component of investment in the private sector. Some of the most common forms of transforming black money into white constitute key elements of the private economy. Investment in real estate provides lucrative financial returns in the form of rent. When the Delhi Development Authority, a public sector body, auctions off land, large amounts of black money get mopped up. Investment in inventories and subsequent underestimation of fixed capital equipment provides another avenue of transforming black money into legal channels. The transformation of black money into legal avenues is facilitated by the existence of a vast informal sector which remains largely untaxed.

There are great difficulties in studying the parallel economy because it operates outside the law. There have been innumerable attempts to quantify it. Black money was estimated to constitute 6 per cent or GNP in 1953/54 and by 1968/69 it was estimated at 9 per cent. Two economists, V.S. Mahajan and V.K. Mahajan, in a recent article estimate the black money economy at between 75 billion rupees (6.8 per cent of the national income at current prices) to 250 billion rupees (23.7 per cent of the national income at current prices) in 1981.[4] The economist Shankar Acharya has reviewed all estimates of the volume of the black economy and found that, depending on the criteria selected and methods of computation used, percentages for 1976/77, for example, varied from 5.7 per cent of black money as a percentage of GNP to 37.6 per cent.[5]

A report of the National Council of Agriculture and Economic Research (NCAER) estimates that black money worth 8.4 billion rupees was created in the Indian economy from 1965/66 to 1974/75 as a result of the operation of price controls in respect of six commodities including steel, cement and urea. The study pointed out that after the 1980 general election, as a result of control on sugar and corruption in the public distribution system, 4 billion rupees was generated in 1979/80. In its May 1979 Report the Dagli Committee had also concluded that price and distribution controls have led to the generation of black money on a large scale.

The repercussions of pervasive corruption means that 'money' power becomes more and more powerful in determining the nature of the polity and the nature of public policy. It is highly detrimental because all acts of public policy – questions of foodgrain prices or those relating to the level of import liberalization, for example – can in principle become the subject of behind-the-scenes auction among key participants. There is

every possibility that such activities will be merely serving section-
al rather than national interests.

The Direct Taxes Enquiry Report had recognized that corruption was not merely concerned with tax evasion, smuggling or
even undisclosed wealth. It recognized the role of the very
complex network of deals within a parallel economy where white
income could be used to generate more black income. However,
this report, although recognizing the enormous ramifications of
the parallel economy, seemed to assume that it merely enhanced
inequality through a greater burden on the honest and led, in its
own words, 'to a concentration of wealth in the hands of the
unscrupulous few'.

The ramifications may be much wider, permeating the whole
of society with the exception of the absolute poorest. Even these
tend somehow to be dragged into it. It seems to be a classic
illustration in the field of economic structure of a total divergence
between the normative and existential order. In other words, not
just of a divergence which exists in all tax evasion, power influence, etc., and of a small professional class using its influence to
evade the law, but of an existential order in the economy that
provides at all levels a totally separate reality from the declared
norms.

It is not just a question of big contractors getting contracts and
evading taxes. Right down to village level there are networks –
sometimes even within a family or, if not, within a social kindred
group – whereby petty officials, bank staff, court staff, law
enforcement machinery and contractor or supplier are all linked
in a network of deals in what has now become not so much a
deviation but a parallelism of norms; that is, in certain districts it is
known exactly what bribe is the norm right up to the level of the
minister for appointments or transfers at every level. Cuts are
expected on every engineering or irrigation project in terms of a
known local percentage. The precise amount for obtaining a
subsidy or Scheduled Caste bank loan is known. Usually the
anti-corruption machinery catches up only where there is a
deviation from these parallel existential norms. For example, if, in
return for a favour or contract, the quid pro quo is not delivered or
if the cut is not that promised.

Anti-corruption machinery can also be used against any naive,
idealistic social worker or forest official who might try to organize
a genuine cooperative or Food For Work Programme to help the

people. Inevitably then the vested interests plant charges of corruption or crime against that particular official or social worker. The book of rules is always quoted against anyone who tries to interfere with the parallel economy. If a genuine cooperative is established, trucks will continually be checked and will not be reloaded. Others who work according to the parallel economy will not face such harassment.

If one multiplies the volume of black market transactions throughout the whole spectrum of social activity it becomes clear that it is one of the main contributory factors to what has now become a free-wheeling economy. Therefore, if this parallel economy were somehow abolished, the entire economic structure might collapse. It has therefore become a strange and unevaluated ingredient of social change.

Social regulation probably does occur on some level. Everyone knows how much to pay for a service just as was the case in princely India. According to British norms these practices were regarded as corrupt. In a sense they were not because they were regulated. Therefore some new adjustment may take place in the future but the difficulties cannot be underestimated. Every new government coming to power at the Centre or in the states pledges itself platitudinously to curb corruption. When there is occasional evidence of sincerity by a 'new broom' such as N.T. Rama Rao, who was elected on a regional party ticket of self-respect for the people of his region, he too has to face threats of destabilization, hints of 'regionalism weakening national unity.' Such a party, or individual, then faces for its own survival the temptation to use in its defensive tactics the same weapons of corruption that are being used against it.

CHAPTER SEVEN

The Scheduled Castes

One in every seven Indians is born into a family that only a generation ago was classed as 'Untouchable'. At the time of Independence the new leadership, largely upper caste, had had its conscience so stirred by Gandhi that liberal provisions were written into the Constitution to redress the oppression which had lasted for over two thousand years. However, it was not only upper-caste altruism under the influence of Gandhi which contributed to the resultant social ferment.

One of the motivations was hard-headedly realistic. A national independence struggle cannot achieve success without the involvement of the masses. The dominant castes who led it had no alternative therefore but to offer them some amelioration of their lot, perhaps hoping that their awakening would not really involve a restructuring of society. Also at this time the Untouchables themselves had produced a charismatic leader, Dr B.R. Ambedkar. He never believed in the sincerity for reform of the Hindu upper castes and disputed and suspected the role of even Gandhi himself. His emergence as the undisputed leader of his community and his uncompromising stand were probably responsible for keeping alive to this day the case for the reform of Hindu society to wrest an equitable existence for the groups who had meantime been notified as Scheduled Castes.

There is otherwise every likelihood that the initial twinges of conscience which had moved the leaders of Hindu society would have been soothed into total forgetfulness. The future of the Scheduled Castes is indeed the touchstone on which India's future in the modern world and perhaps its whole political system will be tested. For the question of the Scheduled Castes is but one segment of the dilemma facing Hindu society in the attempt to restructure for India its ancient eroded foundations. Traditional attitudes towards the Scheduled Castes are merely an extreme example of attitudes towards other minority or linguistic groups. The whole question of the plurality of Indian society and the achievement of a new harmony no longer dependent on hierarchy will depend considerably on the capacity of upper-caste leadership to restore confidence among the Scheduled Castes.

The downtrodden position in which the Scheduled Castes continue to find themselves cannot be attributed merely to their minority status. For the Brahmins, who manipulate and control the levers of power, have always themselves constituted a minority, yet achieved dominance. Once the Scheduled Castes came to acquire substantial economic resources and political influence, the traditional kind of social oppression meted out to them may almost disappear. They will, however, never quite be accepted into any inner social circle or be treated as equals. As yet they have developed no networks through which to further really effectively the interests of their own group. Their advancement is further hindered by the discrimination they continue to face in their daily lives.

Conceptually the Hindu regards the Scheduled Castes as *a-varna* – literally 'without caste'. He is outside society; beyond the pale of Hinduism with all the absence of rights this entails. It would seem that India is still far away from the government's declared aim of giving them an equal place in Hindu society. Their social, economic and cultural marginality in society is reflected in and reinforced by their peripherality in the village settlement patterns. Unlike the tribes who are largely concentrated in the hilly forest tracts of Central India and the border areas of North-Eastern India, Scheduled Castes coexist with caste Hindus in almost every village. Despite social legislation prohibiting the practice of Untouchability, they continue to face discrimination in their daily lives. Over ninety per cent of the Scheduled Castes are concentrated in rural areas and live below the poverty line. In most villages they are still debarred from access to wells and temples. The government's own Sixth Five-Year Plan document for 1980–85 admits:

> Three decades of development have not had the desired impact on these socially, economically and educationally handicapped groups. Their problems cannot be resolved through the percolation of general economic growth. The majority of the Scheduled Castes and Scheduled Tribes, who form one-quarter of the population, are below the poverty line ... Continuing to pursue traditional occupations, they are unable

to participate fully in the process of modernization. The practice of Untouchability against Scheduled Castes is a special handicap for them and even the few educated groups amongst them are unable to compete for job opportunities created while Scheduled Tribes still remain outside the mainstream of development mainly because of their relative isolation and their exploitation by outside agencies.[1]

The few Scheduled Castes who receive an education and rise socially tend to leave their villages. This leaves no leadership at the grass roots. In industrial areas they tend to be concentrated in low-status jobs and live in their own separate quarters. The few who come up are ashamed of their ancestry and abandon their society. An inferiority complex and feeling of inadequacy accompany them throughout their lives. Their instinctive reaction is to blot out the memory of their Untouchability and to acquire new identities. Even the more radical of the urbanized Scheduled Caste groups, like the Dalits of Maharashtra and Karnataka, lack tenacity in their fighting spirit.

Dalit literature tends to be abusive rather than defiant and challenging. The economic position of the more advanced groups, like the urbanized Neo-Buddhists of Maharashtra, has not improved. Lack of resources and cleavages within Scheduled Caste groups have therefore diminished any chance they have of posing an effective challenge to the entrenched interests of the dominant castes, whose tactics of divide and rule, which are instinctive rather than contextually Machiavellian, have been effective in keeping the Scheduled Caste leadership split. Historically this has always been the subconscious reaction of the dominant castes. By exploiting the old caste system of division in the majority society they were able to maintain their monopoly of power by their pretensions to indispensability for composing such divisions and ensuring 'harmony' in society.

For example, in the sixties the Republican Party of India (RPI), a Scheduled Caste political movement, made up largely of Scheduled Caste Buddhist converts, did show promise of creating a base for itself on the question of land distribution in Maharashtra. But Y.B. Chavan, a Congress politician, started placating some of the prominent leaders and their followers with lures of positions of power or offices at different levels. This tactical ploy led to the disintegration of the RPI. By the early seventies a more militant organization, known as the Dalit Panthers, representing a younger generation of Scheduled Castes, emerged. This party soon succumbed to similar enticements from the Congress party. As a result today the Dalit Movement in Maharashtra is politically fragmented with its several factions toeing the lines of different political parties, and even divided on the trend of their future social religious or ideological affiliations.

The application of the manipulative policy can be seen most clearly in the electoral framework of reserved constituencies where the Scheduled Caste candidate always has to make some deal with upper or middle castes to get elected. Therefore he is never in a position to serve his community. In May 1981 in Karnataka the Dalit Sangharsh Samiti (Committee for the Struggle of the 'Oppressed') protested against the ineffectiveness of their Scheduled Caste legislators, MPs and ministers in the wake of growing atrocities against Scheduled Castes. The organization called upon its members and sympathizers to demonstrate against the indifference of their leaders and openly recognized the alienation of the Scheduled Caste élite from the masses.

In regions where the Scheduled Caste population is low they remain underrepresented in politics because they do not have numerical strength in any constituency. In Gujarat the backward castes and lower castes are either not represented at all in the state assembly or else very poorly represented in the legislatures. On the other hand, there is a striking overrepresentation of Brahmins and Banias, or merchant castes.[2] The labour force in both the organized and unorganized sectors, made up largely of lower-caste and Scheduled Caste groups, forms nearly 38 per cent of the working population. Yet it remains largely unrepresented in the state assembly.

In regions where Scheduled Caste political organizations are backed by religious reform and revivalist movements, they have made some political impact. In states like Maharashtra with a large concentration of educated urbanized Scheduled Castes, like the Mahars, their influence in politics has grown. This has been due in some measure to the establishment of their own educational societies, economic cooperatives and Dalit literary organizations.

Where the Scheduled Castes are numerically strong, they have been able to exert some influence in local politics. Dr Nandu Ram, a Scheduled Caste lecturer in sociology at Jawaharlal

Nehru University, says that in his native village in Ghaziapur, eastern Uttar Pradesh, the upper castes have come to recognize the importance of Scheduled Caste votes in local panchayat elections. Consequently candidates are careful to look after their interests. However, this influence does not extend to state and general elections unless they are able to strike a deal with another group or party. In that case the rival group or party may well entice some sub-group to split their solidarity.

The Left has failed to address itself to the Scheduled Caste problems. Both the Communist Party of India and Communist Party of India (Marxist) still consider caste to be a facade for class and the complex nature of the Scheduled Caste problem is ignored by both parties. They have been largely unsuccessful in mobilizing the large mass of landless labourers because their mechanistic transposition of Marxist class analysis to the Indian countryside reflects a complete misunderstanding of local conditions.

There is hardly any hope that the aspirations of the Scheduled Castes can be realized merely through electoral representation. The Scheduled Caste candidate elected from a reserved constituency is unable to look after the interests of his people. In other constituencies there tends to be a clash of interests between Backward Castes and Scheduled Castes. This cleavage is always exploited by the upper castes in their tactics of divide and rule. Some sort of united front has been achieved only where a larger tribal identity has been retained, as with the Mahar community in Maharashtra. A growing awakening is evident among the Scheduled Castes in Bihar where extreme Leftists seem to be recognizing that the bond between large castes is stronger than that of ideology, and where a large enough group of Scheduled Castes like Chamars is found in a definite area sharing similar economic conditions. The reaction of upper castes to this newly emerging threat to their own power base and authority is to warn against the dangers of casteism in Indian society. This is merely a tactical ploy to preserve their privileges, for it is always the lower castes who are accused of casteism and who pose a danger to the unity of the country.

The strength of the upper-caste lobby in all the national forums is evidenced increasingly in every political development. Most significant was the case of Dr Jagannath Misra, chief minister of Bihar. For over two years the documented evidence of total misrule, corruption and state oppression in Bihar was ignored by the Central Government. Rather Misra was supported to the hilt as a stalwart bulwark for Mrs Gandhi. Suddenly, however, in mid-1983 he changed his tactics and local alignments, perhaps realizing the strength of popular opinion. He withdrew a controversial Press Bill and, in an anti-corruption drive, sacked not merely a token minority of ministers but major elements in his cabinet. Simultaneously, he began going all out to implement the declared central policy of upholding the interests of the weaker sections and minorities.

Effective action was at last initiated against the mahant of Bodhgaya whose sordid history has already been recounted. In the periodical publicity blurbs advertised in newspapers regarding the state government's developmental progress, he emphasized action in favour of weaker sections and minorities. Incautiously he not only quoted some effective prosecutions launched in Bihar for atrocities against Scheduled Castes and the stiff sentences of rigorous imprisonment awarded, but let out that Bihar was the only state in India where such crimes had actually been punished! Finally he had the temerity to announce acceptance and local implementation of the Mandal Commission recommendations for Backward Classes.

The latter had earlier won unanimous 'appraisal in principle' by Parliament in an exercise of lip-service which was not apparently meant to be taken seriously. The Centre is still dragging its feet and attempting to delay implementation. These seem to be the real reasons for his ouster, despite the fact that he continued to enjoy the support of the majority of his legislature party. His successor was foisted on the party by the Centre, the decision having been announced even before the election which was manipulated by party whips as 'unanimous'.

A similar situation arose in Gujarat. Dissidence within the party crystallized along caste lines. The then chief minister was Madhavsingh Solanki. Solanki is named after one of the blue-blooded Rajput clans, although some say that the adoption of his clan name derived from upward social mobility. His challenger was one Darji who has a record of passionate involvement on behalf of Scheduled Castes, tribals and other weaker groups.

At executive levels it has now become commonplace for any local official administrator who dares to implement seriously the theoretical objective of safeguarding and developing the weaker sections, to the distaste of their local upper-caste oppressors, to be transferred at short notice.

The measure of resistance by the dominant castes and the increasing incidents of violent confrontation between Scheduled Castes and others has a twofold significance. It shows that the beginning of a major social transformation is under way and that the system is unable to absorb such rapid change. In the case of certain large Scheduled Caste groups, like the Jatavs of Uttar Pradesh and the Mahars of Maharashtra, their growing awareness is largely due to urbanization. This consciousness among the leadership of certain groups of Scheduled Castes is attributable to the policy of reservations which has enabled them to rise socially and economically. The attitude of these groups is that caste must be attacked and destroyed. The violent reaction by upper or newly risen castes to any assertions by Scheduled Castes is based on the feeling that their own power base and privileges are being threatened.

The root causes behind the spate of massacres against Scheduled Castes in recent years, which were largely concentrated in Uttar Pradesh, Bihar, Madhya Pradesh and Rajasthan, can be traced to such attitudes. In the case of the Deoli village massacre in Uttar Pradesh which left 24 Scheduled Caste men, women and children dead, the upper-caste Thakurs felt that since the early seventies their own economic and political power base had been eroded. In the 1972 local elections the Jatavs, a Scheduled Caste group, dared to vote for their own candidate, thereby breaking the Thakur monopoly, and in 1973 their elected leader had begun distributing village land to the landless Scheduled Castes.

In other incidents both sides have fought back. One such case occurred in the temple town of Mangadu, Chinglepattu district, Tamil Nadu, when violence broke out during a week-long festival celebrated during August. The dispute arose between the caste Hindus and Scheduled Castes who insisted on taking part in the upper castes' firewalking ceremony. The caste Hindus retorted that it was not a village festival but a community festival, celebrated by upper castes at their expense. The Scheduled Castes interfered in the ceremony which the upper castes then cancelled. The next day Scheduled Caste agricultural labourers boycotted the fields of the caste Hindus, but the latter began harvesting their own crops. Subsequently 500 Scheduled Castes armed with sticks and stones came to the fields and pelted stones at the caste Hindus. When the police arrived one thousand Scheduled Castes, including women, were throwing stones at them.[3]

Violence has not only been restricted to the countryside alone. In Agra city in April 1978 fighting broke out during the annual procession taken out by the Scheduled Castes in honour of their leader, Dr Ambedkar. The rioting, which soon spread to several localities, erupted when upper castes threw stones upon the image of Dr Ambedkar. The Jatavs responded by attacking caste Hindus and wrecking the office of the Additional Magistrate. The rioting spread to several localities when the police force, made up of upper-caste Jats and Backward Caste Yadavs, began participating in the violence against Scheduled Castes, and looting and plundering their localities.

The growing violence against Scheduled Castes in many parts of the country is not a mere law-and-order problem. It is a symptom of the growing aspirations of the Scheduled Castes and the reaction by other castes to this self-assertion. Every year atrocities against Scheduled Castes have been mounting and the *Report of the Commissioner for Scheduled Castes and Scheduled Tribes 1977–1978* admits that the Scheduled Castes in many parts of the country '. . . are humiliated, insulted, man-handled, assaulted, burnt alive, tortured and their women folk molested. Their miseries are aggravated when they are boycotted socially and economically.'[4]

The caste violence has been steadily increasing in the past decade. Official statistics for atrocities on Scheduled Castes in 1976 put the toll at 6,197 and at 10,879 in 1977, a 75.55 per cent increase over 1976. In 1978, atrocities mounted to 15,059, a 142.91 per cent increase over 1976, and partial figures from the Commissioner's report for 1978–79 show 13,426 atrocities against Scheduled Castes. In 1979 the highest number was reported from Uttar Pradesh with 4,102 atrocities, Madhya Pradesh with 3,866, Bihar with 2,152, Rajasthan with 760. This report notes that: 'The atrocities were acquiring the dimension of organized aggressiveness on the part of the perpetrators and were drifting towards a class war.'[5]

The latest report (1979–81), released by the government in 1983, points out that figures for 1981 are incomplete because some state governments did not supply figures to the Commissioner's office. Comment is superfluous.

Most of the atrocities categorized as major crimes such as 'murder', 'grievous hurt' and 'arson' were especially marked in Bihar, Uttar Pradesh and Madhya Pradesh. The figures reported can only be a mild indicator of the violence for several reasons. Firstly the Commissioner has admitted his inability to supply accurate figures for 1981 because state governments do not bother to respond to his requests for statistics. As one observer has noted: 'Harijans have never been on the priority list except before elections.' Many cases reported are never registered and investigated; in others complainants are turned away. The police may minimize an act by registering Indian Penal Code offences as minor ones. More important, the level of violence reflected in the statistics merely indicates that violence against Scheduled Castes is a fact of life in certain parts of the countryside, but it cannot in any way be said to approximate to its intensity.

Legal protection of Scheduled Castes is covered by the Protection of Civil Rights Act, 1976, which made discrimination against Scheduled Castes more stringent than the earlier Untouchability Offences Act, 1955. Yet it is well known that most of the cases of Untouchability offences registered under this law go unreported to the district authorities as the victims do not dare come forward for fear of reprisals. The Report of the Commissioner for 1977–78 notes that:

> The district authorities who are charged with the responsibility of enforcement of the Protection of Civil Rights Act, 1976, have not lived up to the obligations enjoined upon them to protect the civil rights of the weaker sections. No one familiar with the social climate in the rural areas would assert that there has been a decline in real terms.[6]

The Twenty-Seventh Report (1979–81) points out that in 1979 out of all cases pending in conviction only 71 convictions were handed down out of 2,982 cases tried regarding atrocities on Scheduled Castes.[7] The report states in regard to Gujarat that: 'It appeared that most of the offenders were able to get acquittals even in murder cases. In fact 95.5 per cent and 91.4 per cent respectively were the acquittal rates in murder cases of Scheduled Castes and Scheduled Tribes.'[8]

Even in registered cases, protracted delay has been found to substantially reduce the chance of convictions and government legal aid to Scheduled Castes is insignificant and poorly distributed.

The Protection of Civil Rights Act provided for survey and identity of regions where disabilities against Scheduled Castes are widely practised, the setting up of special courts, summary trial in cases under certain sections of the Act and imposition of collective fines. The same dichotomy reasserts itself in the Government's attitude towards crimes against Scheduled Castes. It has never attempted to implement these remedial measures. No state governments have yet set up special courts nor gone in for summary trials or the imposition of collective fines, even where large-scale acts of physical violence were committed against Scheduled Castes. *The Report of the Commissioner for Scheduled Castes and Scheduled Tribes, 1978–1979* has even noted that:

> There are many areas which can be easily identified as incident prone areas and it will not be wrong to surmise that these occurrences reveal a failure on the part of the revenue, police and development departments in promptly attending to the grievances of the weaker sections of society.[9]

Despite such legislation and administrative measures, atrocities continued unabated. A Home Ministry study on atrocities on Scheduled Castes between 1974 and June 1976 revealed that 70 per cent of the crimes were socio-religious in nature, that is they related to Untouchability such as the right to use wells, enter temples, etc.; 27 per cent were due to economic causes; 18.6 per cent to land disputes. Forcible harvesting accounted for 7 per cent; wage disputes to 7.2 per cent; bonded labour to 7.6 per cent and indebtedness for 4.1 per cent.[10] The more recent Commissioner's Reports state that clashes over land, payment of legal wages, etc., have become the most frequent causes of violence.

The police have consistently failed to defend Scheduled Castes against crimes about which they were forewarned, have themselves been perpetrators of violence, or have failed to take proper action against the accused. The recruitment pattern which is drawn largely from upper and middle castes is largely to blame. For example, in the police force of Uttar Pradesh there are only 1,600 constables, 15 officers in charge of police stations, 8 inspectors and 4 commissioners from the Scheduled Castes, despite the fact that the Scheduled Castes constitute a sizeable percentage of the state's population of 120 million. One can do no better than quote the Commissioner's report for 1975–76 and 1976–77 on the role of the police in perpetrating atrocities against these weaker sections: 'It is rather unfortunate that the police personnel who are supposed to be protectors of the weaker sections of society against atrocities by the influential people, should themselves indulge in atrocities against them.'[11]

One telling incident was the Marathwada riots in July 1978, launched by the Scheduled Caste Student Action Committee, demanding the honouring of a government decision to rename Marathwada University after their leader, Dr Ambedkar. This demand resulted in an orgy of violence by caste Hindus lasting over two months. The violence engulfed five districts of Maharashtra, spread to 1,200 villages, 1,000 people became homeless and 25,000 were totally demoralized or helpless. During the entire orgy of violence the police, teachers and local village workers failed to take preventive action to stop the atrocities. As yet the university has not been renamed.[12]

In fact Scheduled Castes continue to face discrimination at various levels. During elections it is common practice for Scheduled Castes to be debarred from voting. During the last 1980 general elections the Chief Election Commissioner received reports from many constituencies about intimidation and assaults on Scheduled Castes and lower castes. In Katha village only 30 km from the capital, New Delhi, Scheduled Castes were chased away from the special polling booth set up for them and told their votes would be cast for them.[13] In Haryana in thirty villages in Rohtak district, thirty villages in Sonepat district and fourteen villages in Mahendragarh district polling booths were captured and Scheduled Castes were stopped from voting.[14] Similar complaints were received from the Election Commissioner at Baghpat, Meerut and Muzzaffarnagar in Uttar Pradesh. In some instances they have been stopped from voting with the collusion of police officials.[15] After the carnage at Pipra, Uttar Pradesh, in 1980, Scheduled Castes told reporters who visited the village that they had not gone to the polling booths since 1952, though their votes had been cast for them by others.[16]

If one examines the conditions of the Scheduled Castes from around the country a familiar pattern of poverty, exploitation and humiliation emerges. The bulk of the labourers and sharecroppers come from the Scheduled Caste and Tribes and other lower-caste groups. According to the 1971 census 52 per cent of all Scheduled Caste workers were landless agricultural labourers. K.S. Krishnan, former Joint Secretary for Scheduled Castes and Scheduled Tribes, Home Ministry, believes that most of the Scheduled Caste cultivators will be getting the major source of their income from agricultural labour.

Despite all the government's welfare programmes no census data is collected on an all-India basis showing this convergence. Although elaborate schedules are canvassed to show separately the position of Scheduled Castes down to the district and block level in literacy, share in government employment, etc., statistics relating to their basic inequalities in life such as infant mortality, life expectancy, their percentage below the poverty line or land-holding patterns, are, however, not maintained. Yet every micro study seems to yield a monotously similar finding of continued grave inequalities and, in some cases, even the widening of such inequalities.

The Sixth Plan document (1980–85) has recognized this and for the first time the government has launched a programme called the Special Component Plan for Scheduled Castes with an allocation of 40 billion rupees from the Centre and an additional annual 6 billion rupees from the states. Its declared aim is to help the Scheduled Castes stand on their own feet economically. The Scheduled Caste hamlet rather than the individual has been made the target of development. There are special programmes for the installation of separate wells, for electrification and improvement of roads in Scheduled Caste hamlets. The approach may perhaps be criticized for its endorsement of continued segregation. Yet it is probably the only practical one in the light of current social realities. It was conceived, according to planning directives, to allow the maximum of flexibility in formulating detailed schemes to suit local conditions and local community needs.

A major impediment to success is the problem of contact. Most village extension workers find it distasteful to stay or work in a Scheduled Caste hamlet. Even if the rare village extension worker is free of such inhibitions, he tends to follow the line of least resistance through stereotyped schemes that excite no controversy from dominant groups. To fulfil targets he may sink a well or distribute buffaloes without ascertaining the real needs of the target groups or their capacity to benefit from them. Sometimes the livestock finds its way into the hands of the 'masters'.

The government's first priority to uplift the Scheduled Castes should rather be debt relief, the distribution of land and insistence on its undisturbed possession. Past and ongoing programmes to achieve this continue to fail. The fact remains that, until the present power structures are destroyed, no programme for the upliftment of weaker sections is likely to succeed, however well conceived it may be in theory. Its local implementers and the controllers of local vote banks are both bound by the same self-interest to preserve the status quo of Scheduled Caste dependency.

The Sixth Plan document acknowledges that for the most part conditions among Scheduled Castes have remained the same as in 1947. In many cases agricultural labourers do not even own the hovels they live in. They are frequently indebted and sometimes a debt is carried over to the next generation. Scheduled Castes are made to carry out the most degrading tasks such as scavenging, sweeping and skinning dead animals. They are also made to do the most degrading agricultural tasks like hoeing, digging and carrying earth. Most Scheduled Caste families are so poverty-stricken they need every spare hand to earn a livelihood to keep their families from starving. This means they cannot afford to send their children to school and those that do manage to attend school do not get enough food, clothing or a proper place to sit and study. Frequently they have nothing to read, nor even a kerosene lamp, and no one to help them at home. These facts are borne out by numerous surveys and personal observation at the grass roots. A recent study found that poverty was the single most important reason for the Scheduled Castes leaving primary school.[17] Another Uttar Pradesh study found that one Scheduled Caste in ten was doing an adult job before reaching their teens, while many of their upper-caste peers were left free to study.[18]

One telling indicator of their continued backwardness are the comparative literacy figures for Scheduled Castes and non-Scheduled Castes. According to the 1971 census the literacy for Scheduled Caste males and females was 14.67 per cent. The comparative figure for non-Scheduled Castes and non-Scheduled Tribes stood at 33.8 per cent. Scheduled Caste male literacy stood at 22.36 per cent and for females at 6.44 per cent. The literacy for non-Scheduled Caste, non-Scheduled Tribe males was 44.48 per cent and for females 22.25 per cent.

In some states the general literacy among Scheduled Castes continues to be much lower than the all-India average for Scheduled Castes. For example, in Bihar, according to the 1971 census, it stood at 6.53 per cent; in Uttar Pradesh it was 10.2 per cent and in Rajasthan 9.14 per cent. Some of the highest figures for Scheduled Castes were Kerala with 40.21 per cent, Gujarat 27.74 per cent and Maharashtra with 25.25 per cent.

Despite these dismal figures the situation has improved considerably since pre-Independence days. In the 1931 census overall Scheduled Caste literacy was 2 per cent. Briggs writing in 1911 reports that the literacy rate for Chamars per thousand was 2 per cent for males and 0.2 per cent for females.[19]

As bad as conditions are today, the more violent forms of pollution are quickly disappearing. Two generations ago Scheduled Castes were almost totally banned from attending school. The few that did manage to acquire an education were made to sit outside the classroom. Dr Ambedkar was not even permitted to learn Sanskrit and had to take Persian as a second language. By the time of Independence a greater number of Scheduled Castes living in the more accessible villages were permitted to attend school and to enter the classrooms. They were, however, made to sit separately. Today, by and large, in the more accessible villages children of all castes sit together, although Scheduled Caste children may still not be allowed to use a common drinking water source.

Even today in the more inaccessible areas age-old traditions are gradually dying out. When a primary school was opened in a remote Himalayan village called Malana in the state of Himachal Pradesh a few years back, classes were held in the house of one of the dominant clan families. Scheduled Caste children were banned from classroom attendance. By the early eighties the school building was completed and Scheduled Caste children were permitted to attend classes, although at first they had to sit separately. In 1981, however, the author noted that all the school children were sitting together.

Interestingly, now that the school doors have been opened to the Scheduled Caste children of Malana, it is they who are forging ahead in primary classes past the innate conservatism of the traditional leadership. Whether they will be able to reap the fruits of their education and enter the corridors of power and influence remains however to be seen. The father of the two brightest children is a Scheduled Caste artisan, Sangat Ram, who migrated some years ago into the village. Because of the especially unusual pollution rules in this fascinating semi-tribal village, many tourist trekkers can enter only the house of Sangat Ram who has been enterprising enough to tap this new source of economic activity.

Even in urban schools and colleges where more liberal attitudes might be expected, Scheduled Castes often face humiliation at the hands of higher-caste students and teachers on campus. The *Economic and Political Weekly* reports that: 'There is an instance in the medical faculty of an SC student accorded a high percentage of marks in the previous exam and failing in the first year of the MBBS exam, but passing smoothly after he got his surname changed into that of a higher caste.'[20] The same report notes that Scheduled Caste students who could easily have been admitted through the open competition exams, decided to apply through the reservation. At the interview they were told to their faces they should become sweepers and scavengers, not doctors. There was a case in an Engineering College where Scheduled Caste students had to pay a special unofficial mess fee for the 'privilege' of eating with upper-caste colleagues.[21]

Nandu Ram, a lecturer in sociology at Jawaharlal Nehru University, who is himself from the Scheduled Caste community, acknowledges that they face discrimination in their daily lives. He claims that approximately 55 to 60 per cent of Scheduled Caste graduates are unemployed compared to 30 to 40 per cent for non-Scheduled Castes. He points out that there is a qualitative difference between the two groups because the majority of non-Scheduled Castes have additional resources to fall back on in such periods.

His contention is borne out by a survey carried out by the 1961 census for Uttar Pradesh, correlating the percentage of unemployed Scheduled Castes and others by educational levels per 10,000. The greatest gap in unemployment rates was in the category of urban unemployed matriculates and above. While 160 non-Scheduled Castes were unemployed, the figure for Scheduled Castes was 514. Unemployment rates for those who were literate without any educational level in the urban sector was 266 and 60 for Scheduled Castes and non-Scheduled Castes respectively. In the rural areas the corresponding figures were 13 and

10. The smallest gap was in the category 'illiterate' where the rural unemployment rate was 3 for Scheduled Castes and 2 for non-Scheduled Castes and the urban unemployment rate was 50 and 20.[22] This merely shows that, once the Scheduled Castes try to move out of their traditional occupations, they face discrimination.

Nevertheless, the impure occupations with which the Scheduled Castes were traditionally associated in the past and which were responsible for their low status are to some extent disappearing. The Chamars, who were traditionally shunned as unclean because they were associated with work in leather and to the carrying away of dead cattle, are now largely agricultural labourers. Indeed they were always basically agriculturalists. Only in a few cases are traditionally impure occupations still followed as subsidiary to a main occupation. Although the older generation are generally still involved in traditional occupations, many middle-aged groups, particularly those in urban areas, have shifted to other occupations, low in status but with less of a stigma of pollution.

Even in rural areas a slow process of transformation is beginning to arise in pockets where government development programmes have made some impact. Nandu Ram returns to his native village in Ghaziapur, eastern Uttar Pradesh, every year. He recalls that in his own childhood in the fifties there were no educated Scheduled Castes. Yet today one Chamar has become a Block Development Officer, another has become a telephone operator and a few others are working in family planning. Some Scheduled Castes in the village are even building brick houses, a sign of status and wealth in rural India. In most of these cases Scheduled Caste families who have bettered themselves have usually had a substantial economic base in the shape of several acres of land. Economic advancement, however, has not removed traditional pollution taboos for they are still debarred from the sanctum of the village temple.

Yogendra Singh, professor of sociology at Jawaharlal Nehru University, points out that even where a Scheduled Caste has obtained a new identity through a government programme or education he still suffers from a degree of alienation of which he himself is not conscious. Yogendra Singh has studied change among Scheduled Castes in several villages in eastern Uttar Pradesh, a region generally considered to be one of the most backward areas in India. He found that upper and middle castes still harbour 'intense prejudices' against Scheduled Castes and in instances where a Scheduled Caste has achieved some sort of improvement a 'backlash psychology has emerged'. According to Yogendra Singh: 'The Scheduled Caste who has marginally improved his position is still living below the poverty line. He does not have enough money to send his children to school or to take care of his health. In such times of crisis he will be alienated in the village.'[23]

Most articulate Scheduled Castes are of the opinion that, while a few of the cultural idioms of prejudice have changed, the basic content of prejudicial attitudes has remained the same. Certainly pollution rules have not broken down completely in the villages, although they are far less stringent than in previous decades. Numerous reports of the Commissioner for Scheduled Castes and Tribes confirm that in most of rural India the Scheduled Castes are still debarred from access to the village wells and temples; that the services of barbers and washermen are denied to them; and that many times they cannot be served in local teashops or walk down the main village street. In the greater number of villages a Brahmin would not admit a Scheduled Caste to his house. As one sociologist has observed: 'You may feel that pollution and Untouchability is all rubbish, but at the same time you would not like them to get too uppity. That feeling is very strong in large areas of India. You would still like to keep them down.' Even Jagjivan Ram, the foremost Scheduled Caste leader in India, recalls a public insult made against him when he was serving as Defence Minister in the Janata regime: 'I had performed the unveiling of a statue in honour of a former chief minister of Uttar Pradesh. One of the politicians present at the ceremony proceeded to wash the statue in public to remove the pollution of my touch.'[24]

The measure of the intensity of continuing practices of Untouchability and discriminatory practices in the countryside can be gauged by the recent spate of mass conversions to Islam in South India in 1981/82. Buddhism, Christianity and Islam have constituted one historical avenue of escape from the humiliations and social disabilities imposed on Scheduled Castes. A spate of mass conversions in 1981/82 re-raises an issue in the interpretation of earlier Indian history. How much were Islamic conversions in India attributable to the sword and the weight of power and how much to a passive willingness to escape from an oppressive social system. One theory today maintains that Islam spread rapidly in Bengal as a backlash to the Brahminical revival when the Sen dynasties imposed a new social rigidity after the earlier Buddhist liberalism.

In more recent times the Scheduled Caste leader, Dr Ambedkar, who was the first law minister in Independent India, had contemplated conversion as far back as 1927. But it was not until 1956 that he converted to Buddhism along with almost three million other Scheduled Castes. His decision to convert was made after experience led him to the realization that Scheduled Castes could never gain an equal place in Hindu society. During 1927 to 1930 Dr Ambedkar participated in protest movements at various temple-entry promotions for Scheduled Castes in which he had to face the violent reactions of orthodox Hindus.

A series of incidents associated with his efforts at lifting the ban on temple entry, convinced Dr Ambedkar and his followers, that they could not gain elementary rights within the Hindu fold. In 1929 a resolution was passed asking Scheduled Castes to accept any other religion of their choice if they were unable to bear their sufferings. In 1935 Dr Ambedkar publicly denounced Hinduism, its customs and traditions and swore that: 'Even though I am born a Hindu I will not die a Hindu.' After his conversion of 14 October 1957 Dr Ambedkar said he felt as if he had been released from hell.

Buddhism's appeal lay in the fact that it stood for a casteless society. Historically in India it was associated with the pre-Aryan system which challenged the hierarchical imposition of Brahminical Hinduism in what was then the cultural frontier zone of Magadha, roughly corresponding to present day Bihar.

Dr Ambedkar asked his followers to embrace Buddhism because in his view Hinduism had perpetuated the most inhuman form of apartheid against the Scheduled Castes. The continued desperation of his adherents was underscored in February 1981 when a spate of mass conversions took place in Meenakshipuram and Kamanathapuram in Tamil Nadu. Conversions to Islam in the area by Scheduled Castes has been going on for many years but this was the first time mass conversions took place.

The choice of Islam shows that the more educated groups among the Scheduled Castes are developing a militant posture. The violent reaction by the caste Hindus against the conversions came about because Islam is the only religion that has struck at the root of hierarchy. Its fundamental ideology is one of the equality of man, whatever historical divergencies there may have been in practice. The mass conversions symbolized the revenge of Scheduled Castes against Hinduism and an attempt to achieve psychological emancipation. To quote B.P. Maurya, a Scheduled Caste MP of the Rajya Sabha, India's upper house of Parliament, who is himself a Buddhist convert: 'Conversion helps the person psychologically. The inferiority complex disappears from his mind even though there is no change in economic status.'[25]

The villages where the conversions took place were geographically close to Kerala, a stronghold of the Muslim League and the scene also of much earlier Christian conversions. The ritual distance between the Brahmins and Scheduled Castes is far greater in southern Tamil Nadu. The region used to be economically more backward, socially more orthodox and politically less affected by the activities of Leftist extremists such as Naxalites who only have a foothold in northern parts of the state. The Scheduled Castes' lives were governed by a cruel system of apartheid. They were barred from temples, teashops and hotels, had separate barber shops and drinking water facilities and were not permitted to wear sandals. A Scheduled Caste driving a cart through a village had to dismount.

Most of the converts came from the educated groups among them who had risen socially and economically thanks to government reservations. They felt that as Islam did not recognize caste distinctions their children at least would benefit even if they themselves could not escape their past. Many converts said the loss of 'reservation' privileges meant little to them compared to the social equality which Islam brought them. This shows that the intensity of the social indignities heaped upon them are so harsh as to render mere concessions unattractive.

The mass conversions in the South soon led to a spate of others throughout the country. In May 1981, following the caste struggle in Ahmedabad, Gujarat, over reservations in post-medical institutions for Scheduled Castes, about 7,000 families converted to Buddhism. Their choice of Buddhism is significant in that it symbolizes their public repudiation of Gandhi and Hinduism and their support of Dr Ambedkar. In July 1981 the Karnataka Dalit Action Committee, a radical Scheduled Caste organization, threatened to make Independence Day 'Quit Hinduism day' by organizing mass conversions of Scheduled Castes and Other

Backward Castes to Islam.[26] Fresh conversions also took place in Nagpur, Maharashtra, and in other parts of the country various Scheduled Caste Action groups threatened to convert if their conditions did not improve.

It is highly significant that the Scheduled Castes chose to convert to Islam rather than Christianity for the South is known for its very early Christian tradition ascribed to the time of St Thomas. In fact, apart from the greater militancy of Islam, the Christian Churches of South India have not in practice proved a good leveller of inequalities. Separate churches and separate burial grounds tend still to be maintained for upper castes and Scheduled Castes.

It is difficult for a non-Scheduled Caste to grasp the tremendous sense of deprivation and resentment that pervades the more educated sections of Scheduled Castes. In many cases they are no longer prepared to accept the inferior status their ancestors assumed was part of the unchanging social order. The regional director of the Jaipur State Employment Insurance Scheme, a Scheduled Caste called Bhagwati Parshad, made a significant statement which shows a certain desperation even among those who have risen professionally: 'If there is no alternative in the present system, we'll convert to Islam,' he asserts. It proves that legislation against Untouchability is inadequate to deal with the behavioural patterns of Hindus which have deep psychological and social roots.

The wave of conversions to Islam, which started at Meenakshipuram in February 1981, sent a shock wave through the Hindu religious leadership more violent than Dr Ambedkar's conversions in 1956. Islam has always stood in violent antagonism to Hinduism and almost a thousand years of Islamic rule in India has left a legacy of Hindu hostility. At Meenakshipuram the caste Hindus were so taken aback by the conversion that social barriers were removed and segregation in teashops and hotels was ended at least temporarily. The Tamil government began launching a campaign in August 1981 reassuring Scheduled Castes of equality. All temples in the state would organize special worship for Hindus on Independence Day followed by a common meal. The government even said temples would organize intercaste weddings between caste Hindus and Scheduled Castes. The RSS, the extremist Hindu organization, reacted violently. In its newspaper, *Organizer*, dated 19 July 1981 it stated: 'These conversions have shocked Hindus and brought various castes and sects together.' The newspaper stated that the RSS, its affiliate the Vishwa Hindu Parishad ('United Hindu Congress'), the Arya Samaj and many other organizations were 'studying the problem to nip the mischief in the bud'.

Following the conversions in the South the Vishwa Hindu Parishad, (VHP), a revivalist Hindu solidarity movement, launched a campaign to preserve the faith by a return to its version of its original ideals. After Meenakshipuram the VHP had asked the caste Hindus in the villages where the conversions took place to treat the Scheduled Castes as equals so that converts would return to the Hindu fold. The caste Hindus said nothing when the VHP led the Scheduled Castes into the temple. However, as soon as the representatives left they were again debarred entry.

The VHP also set up mobile vans containing Hindu deities which visited the areas where the conversions had taken place. For the first time this allowed Scheduled Castes to worship freely as they were barred from temples. Another Hindu organization, the All India Sanatam Dharma Pratinidhi Sabha ('The Association Representing the Religion of Eternal Values'), announced in August 1981 that Scheduled Castes would be allowed to participate in special prayers at the main temple in New Delhi.[27] After fourteen Scheduled Castes converted to Islam in Rohtak, Haryana, in August 1981, a Hindu religious organization began launching a campaign to counter the conversion. Darshan, or 'the viewing of the deity', was performed in the village and the sacred thread, traditionally only worn by caste Hindus, was offered to every Muslim convert.[28]

The VHP soon started an active campaign against conversions. It held a huge rally in both New Delhi and Ahmedabad in December 1981. The organization appealed for funds 'for saving Hindu culture'. Some leaflets were distributed quoting the Hindu reformer Vivekananda to the effect that 'a person leaving the Hindu fold is not merely a loss of one Hindu but adding one more to the enemies of Hinduism'.[29] This statement explains the historically unprecedented concessions which Hindu organizations seemed prepared to make.

In July 1982 over a hundred preachers were to go to various parts of the country to try and bring about a religious renaissance in which casteism and factionalism would have no part.[30] In September 1982 the RSS in Karnataka told sweepers in the colony that all were children of Hindu society and there was no high and low among Hindus. Most Scheduled Castes were surprised: 'Your words that we are all equal has brought me a sense of self-respect. Till now wherever I used to go I would introduce myself as a Harijan. That would make me suffer from an inferiority complex.'[31]

The spate of recent conversions was an attempt to rise socially and escape from the stigma of Untouchability. There is no question that the Scheduled Castes need to destroy the hold of Hindu caste oppression to achieve emancipation and only a threat of conversion to a forceful religion like Islam can achieve this. In the past many Scheduled Caste converts to Islam or Christianity have managed to remove the stigma of Untouchability in one or two generations. It is highly significant that for the first time the caste Hindus made immediate concessions in the wake of such conversions.

The marginal improvement in the conditions of certain Scheduled Caste groups is thus due in part to the fear that they may be lost to the Hindu fold. However, they will now have to contend with the more subtle attempts by the caste Hindu leadership to juggle with the whole situation and find some form of 'compromise' which will probably merely lead to a transformation of the caste system into new patterns. These will retain the fundamentals of the old system, i.e. some form of hierarchy and some form of lower orders whose work will be at the disposal of the ruling élite and be organized for their benefit. In this process of transformation groups of the present Scheduled Castes, especially those with the education or organizational capacity, which might otherwise pose a challenge, will be lured into the system, accepted under new jati, or subcaste, names and be recruited to assist in the exploitation of their erstwhile colleagues.

It is thus difficult to be optimistic about the future of the 110 million Scheduled Castes. Some proportion will escape from their lot by different strategies such as traditional methods like 'Sanskritization' or conversion or, where they are a united and politically conscious community, by agitation. It is difficult to see, however, how the bulk of them will better themselves unless massive new employment opportunities develop through which they can cut away from their original disabilities. Even here, however, the dice are always loaded against them.

CHAPTER EIGHT

Reservations

At Independence, due to the Gandhian influence, the upper castes were somewhat imbued with the feeling that they had a duty to help the poor Scheduled Castes and neglected tribals. No one seems to have foreseen that, if the egalitarian principles finally prevailed in the face of the totally contradictory attitudes of Indian tradition, the dominant élites which had hitherto monopolized all key posts in both the public, private and professional sectors would be reduced to a minority of approximately 20 per cent. It is difficult to recall any instance where such a totally dominant minority élite has ever relinquished voluntarily the levers of power.

The situation in India has now become acute. Partly this is because, in the case of the most underprivileged groups, the Scheduled Castes, there is a growing awareness of constitutional and legal rights and the will to achievement. Now, however, there is a growing realization that even in relation to the intermediate Backward Castes and, to some extent, the minorities, the dominant minority upper-caste élite continues to monopolize all key positions to an extent totally disproportionate to their numbers in society. The time is now passing when this could legitimately be explained as a carry-over from the old regime during the transition time which would inevitably be needed for underprivileged groups to obtain for themselves adequate education, training and seniority.

The controversy has been accentuated by the report of a commission (the Mandal Commission) appointed to go into this problem. This spotlighted a situation whereby the monopoly by a dominant élite of less than 20 per cent could only be broken by extending the reservation, totalling 22.5 per cent, for the most underprivileged communities, groups largely drawn from what in Hindu traditional society would have been termed 'clean Sudras'.

The Report pointed out that to achieve real social justice at least 80 per cent of all seats ought to be reserved. However, the

Supreme Court had earlier ruled that reservations could not exceed 50 per cent without attracting valid criticism of discrimination (even if the intention was to redress much greater earlier discrimination). The Commission therefore recommended reservations up to 47 per cent and listed as beneficiaries 3,743 castes.

The reaction of the dominant élite was predictable and their tactics are now becoming clearer. They have obvious difficulties in rejecting outright the principles established by the Commission. Indeed the Report's first reception by Parliament was at least, in lip service, almost unanimously favourable. On the other hand, categorical acceptance would sound the death knell of the dominant élite. There are practical differences in the safeguards programmed for the lowliest underprivileged communities and those which, it is proposed, should be extended now to the Backward Castes. These Backward Castes are in a much stronger position educationally and even economically to take advantage of them and to organize themselves to insist on their implementation.

The tactics and arguments of the dominant élite to scuttle the proposal follow certain well-defined lines. Firstly, they turn to their own dialectical advantage the complaint that even the reservations for Scheduled Castes and Tribes, with all the interpretative refinements embodied over the years to plug loopholes in their evasion, have been somewhat ineffective, especially in so far as key posts are involved. This reaction, of course, ignores the caste and community networks which operate in almost every organization to frustrate entry of even qualified individuals despite 'reserved vacancies'. Figures for educated and even graduate and technical unemployment amongst the underprivileged classes demolish this line of argument.

Often the impediments are procedural. In Jhargram subdivision of West Bengal's tribal area, unemployed tribal graduates, including one medical graduate, had been unable to obtain even vacant reserved posts in the main employment market, Calcutta. This was because of rules necessitating their registration in a Calcutta employment exchange and not in their own area. Even assuming that such underprivileged candidates could raise the financial resources to travel to the metropolis and live there whilst seeking employment, their registration at a Calcutta employment exchange was inhibited by another rule demanding production of a ration card. Obtaining a ration card in turn demands evidence of long-term residence at a particular address.

Instances are multiplying also whereby inner circles of dominant élite groups within any organization or office infiltrate their own candidates through selection procedures and frustrate others, even though the latter may be equally or even more technically qualified. A few such instances have been brought to light in the annual *Reports of the Commissioner for Scheduled Castes and Scheduled Tribes*, but these seem only to be the tip of the iceberg. At a recent seminar in the prestigious Jawaharlal Nehru University Fellowship organization a question from Uttar Pradesh brought to light, to the discomfiture and annoyance of the Union Home Secretary, a situation whereby in this state, with every change of ministry or chief minister, the recruitment of even a sub-inspector of police would veer overwhelmingly towards the caste group of the élite temporarily in power. Even for the lowly post of peon in the Central Secretariat of New Delhi where, there being hardly any tribal population in the vicinity, tribal reservations usually remain unfulfilled, a tribal candidate fully qualified found immense difficulty in obtaining employment and only did so ultimately through pressures from a senior tribal officer.

This brings one to the next tactical argument used by the dominant élite. It complains that, if the goal is an egalitarian society, there must be equal care to avoid or actively discourage the emergence of new élites among the underprivileged groups who collar all the vacancies at the expense of the poorer and more deserving. In a highly élitist society it seems inevitable that the first step towards advancement of an underprivileged group will be the pressures applied by its own new élite, once a few have succeeded with difficulty in reaching positions of some influence. The dominant élites therefore try to meet the challenge of a minority élite by raising bogies of economic restrictions on the more affluent of these, from whom alone in the existing pattern of society an effective leadership challenge might emerge.

The next bogey raised is that of lowering standards and denying due place to merit. There is widespread feeling among upper castes that the Scheduled Castes and Scheduled Tribes hold their jobs less on merit than by virtue of positive discrimination in their favour. Scheduled Castes and Scheduled Tribes are not only assumed to be incompetent but incompetence itself is identified with them. In a study of highly placed bureaucrats at Gandhinagar and Ahmedabad, Gujarat, in charge of development activities, more than 50 per cent believed that efficiency in the administration had been reduced by the job reservation policy. They believed that Scheduled Castes and Scheduled Tribes lacked the appropriate background.[1]

It is correct that in some cases rather thoughtless extremes have been resorted to in certain states, probably to pander to local vote banks or spread the image of populist liberalism. For entry into medical colleges, for example, at one stage Madhya Pradesh lowered the qualifying marks for tribal candidates to 28 per cent, when other candidates would often have to be refused admission even with 75 per cent and above.

There has been little attempt, however, to study the real dimensions of this problem. If underprivileged communities show inferior academic performance, it seems largely due to the social as well as economic obstacles which they face right from the beginning of their primary education. When Scheduled Caste or tribal candidates somehow manage to enter élite schools with the economic backing to maintain the children's position in an élite society, they tend to do just as well. However, such individuals again earn the envy and hostility of the dominant castes for breaking into élite circles, especially if they do not subscribe to the dominant caste norms.

Currently the Mandal Commission Report is likely to be scuttled after a considerable political furore, not by outright rejection, but by the Centre pointing out the lack of unanimity or acceptance by the various states and lack of agreement on the precise communities to be listed. At the same time attempts will be made to defuse the controversy by a restudy of the whole reservations issue on the basis of economic criteria.

Despite all the literature on social stratification and social trends in India, no coherent study yet seems to have been made of the caste and community composition in key sectors of the political, administrative and economic establishments. Such a study would be difficult. When it comes to a school admission forms mysteriously usually have a column requiring caste to be filled in. No caste statistics, apart from the general category of Scheduled Castes and Scheduled Tribes are, however, maintained either in the Census or in government records. Such general projections as are possible hark back to the 1931 Census.

Yet a visit to any organization shows that the names of the overwhelming majority of those in key positions are from the Twice-Born upper-caste groups as evidenced by the sub-caste name appendage which approximates in India to the Western use of a surname.

It might have been expected that the system of reserved constituencies for Scheduled Castes and Tribes would help bring about upward and social and economic mobility for both these groups. Unfortunately, this has not been the case. In the Scheduled Caste reserved constituency the candidate always has to make some deal with the upper and middle castes to get elected, because Scheduled Castes rarely form a majority. The system of reserved constituencies has only led to the emergence of a Scheduled Caste élite which has developed a vested interest in perpetuating the depressed conditions of the Scheduled Caste masses so that provisions for reserved seats continue. Moreover, in single member reserved constituencies various Scheduled Caste groups often work at political cross purposes. Studies show that Scheduled Caste representatives tend to trade their political base for personal gain.

The growing influx of non-tribals into tribal pockets is eroding the numerical dominance of the tribes in their own homelands. Consequently the tribal candidate in the Scheduled Tribe reserved constituency will become more and more dependent on the non-tribal vote. There has already been a decline in the influence of tribal parties at the regional level as Scheduled Tribe candidates have been drawn more and more into the all-India parties. This is a natural development as, with the influx of outsiders into tribal areas, the Scheduled Tribe candidate needs the support of the non-tribals to get elected. The feeling also prevails that, to improve conditions in a constituency, the support of the ruling party in power at the Centre is required.

The system of reservations, whereby 15 per cent of posts for Scheduled Castes and 7.5 per cent for Scheduled Tribes are allotted in higher educational institutions, Central and state government posts and in public sector enterprises, has proved equally ineffective in its aim of uplifting these communities. The underfilling of quotas year after year, especially in the case of the Scheduled Tribes, reveals the half-hearted manner in which these provisions are implemented.

In 1959 Scheduled Caste senior administrators made up 1.18

per cent of the total. In 1969 they constituted 1.77 per cent, although they made up 17.24 per cent of peons in 1959 and 17.94 per cent in 1969. The record of public sector enterprises according to the Elayaperumal Committee Report, 1969, is even more abysmal. In 1965 Scheduled Castes filled 0.2 per cent of class I posts in the public sector, 1.07 per cent in Class II posts and 0.92 per cent in Class III posts. The tribal record was even worse.

On 1 January 1979 things had improved somewhat, although under 10 per cent of Scheduled Castes and Scheduled Tribes were represented in the élite Indian Administrative Service (IAS) and Indian Police Service (IPS). In eight Central Government services their representation varied between 5 and 8 per cent, in six between 2 and 5 per cent and in three none at all. Scheduled Tribe representation was below 1.4 per cent in eight Central Government services; and below 1 per cent in five and none in nine. On the same day representation of Scheduled Castes and Scheduled Tribes in classified posts in 55 Ministries/Departments of Government was 4.75 per cent and 0.94 per cent respectively. In Central undertakings the position in Class I was worst, being about 2 per cent for Scheduled Castes and under 0.5 per cent for Scheduled Tribes on 1 January 1978. In these and other categories their quota was nowhere near complete, except in Class IV.

The record in state government posts is even more abysmal. In 1977, for example, representation of Scheduled Castes and Tribes in Class 1 posts for selected states with considerable Scheduled Caste and Scheduled Tribe populations was as follows: in Madhya Pradesh figures were 0.93 per cent and 0.03 per cent respectively; in West Bengal 1.35 per cent and 0.12 per cent; in Orissa 1 per cent and 0.2 per cent. The best representation was in Rajasthan with 8.6 per cent and 9.7 per cent respectively.[2] The representation of these groups in the judiciary is not better. In mid-1978, out of 313 High Court Judges in India, only 4 were Scheduled Caste and none were Scheduled Tribe.[3]

It is widely recognized that a deliberate policy of quiet discrimination operates surreptitiously at various levels. Recruiting boards are generally dominated by upper castes who tend to favour their own group. Scheduled Caste or Scheduled Tribe candidates available for posts or promotions are often overlooked. Seats are de-reserved and filled by general castes. Rosters for the backlog of unfilled reserved vacancies are not kept. The arguments put forward by upper castes, that quotas remain unfilled for lack of qualified candidates, does not stand up to scrutiny because from 1964 onwards all quotas for the élitist Indian Administrative Service (IAS) and Indian Police Service (IPS) were filled. The most serious underfilling of seats has been in public-sector undertakings. As of 1 January 1978 Scheduled Caste/Scheduled Tribe representation in the latter stood at 2.03 per cent and 0.47 per cent respectively in Class 1 posts.[4]

The Commissioner's Report for 1977–78 found deliberate thwarting of reservations in all the public-sector enterprises it investigated. In Coal India Ltd, Calcutta, no rosters were maintained as required for posts filled by promotion. There was evidence of deliberate thwarting of various reservations through 'non-action'. Copies of vacancies circulars were not forwarded to recognized Scheduled Caste and Scheduled Tribe associations. The Food Corporation of India said it was ignorant of a government order that sweepers must be promoted to Class IV posts. In the Garden Reach Shipbuilders and Engineers Ltd, Calcutta, in April 1978 the low level of representation of Scheduled Castes and Scheduled Tribes was explained by the fact that the company maintained it had to compete with private-sector industries so they had to take the best candidates in the market. The company had failed to implement reservations in promotions. In Hindustan Aeronautics, Bangalore, on 17 January 1978, there were 12 Scheduled Caste workers in the aircraft and engine division and not a single tribal. The same pattern emerges in all the enterprises studied by the Commissioner's annual reports. Furthermore, one may even doubt the figures given as being truly representative of the Scheduled Castes and Tribes, since it is acknowledged that many clean castes procure certificates to get reserved seats in institutions of higher learning[5] or the professions.

The benefits of reservations have largely gone to the more advanced groups among the Scheduled Castes and Scheduled Tribes who have come to monopolize all the facilities.[6] Statistics cited for Scheduled Castes as a category show considerable variation among the separate castes for the category. Those who have benefited from reservations were those who were first exposed to non-traditional occupations and acquired jobs, albeit low down, in industry. This is borne out by a study[7] showing that the percentage of literacy among fathers of Scheduled Caste children in schools and colleges was far higher than the total

Scheduled Caste literacy. Findings show that the fathers had moved out of their traditional caste occupations and they were classified under the category 'services', thereby indicating that a minimum of two generations is required for the Scheduled Caste to better himself. The study shows that, although according to the 1971 Census 85.3 per cent of the Scheduled Caste population in the country was illiterate, only 50.3 per cent of the fathers of those students covered by the national study of 1975 was illiterate. A similar pattern was found to prevail in Orissa where, according to the 1961 census, 88 per cent of the Scheduled Caste population was illiterate. Yet the study found that only 10 per cent of the schoolgoers and 17 per cent of college students had illiterate parents. The study brought out another important point, namely that the majority of school and college students had some financial support from home. In fact they could not have made good without it.

In northern India the Chamar and Jatav castes have benefited most by virtue of their numbers and higher rates of urbanization. The IAS reserved seats for Scheduled Castes are largely monopolized by a handful of castes: the Chamars, who form one-quarter of India's Scheduled Castes, the Nama Sudras of West Bengal, the Mallahs of Andhra Pradesh, the Mahars of Maharashtra, the Pullayans and Puraiyans of Tamil Nadu and the Polaiyas of Kerala.

In the case of the Scheduled Tribes certain small groups like the Minas of Rajasthan, a group of Sanskritized Bhils, and a few of the more advanced Christianized tribes of the North-East monopolize the bulk of the reserved seats. In the political realm it is only the upper strata of Scheduled Castes and Scheduled Tribes, irrespective of their numerical strength, who have risen to position of influence.

This trend is widely stressed by the opponents of the reservation policy. However, as long as élitist trends in education, influence and power persist among the dominant castes who determine the norms of society, it is inevitable that any advance by the tribal and lower caste groups can only be through their own new élites. So far the tensions produced within their own societies as a result are negligible compared to the resentment againt the continued monopoly of the dominant castes and attempts by the latter to frustrate the emergence of any independent thinking and leadership among the underprivileged. There has been little attempt at district or lower administrative levels to identify promising candidates from the most underprivileged groups and make especial efforts for their advancement through the same institutions and adolescent environments that groom the future leaders among the dominant castes.

Indeed the issue of reservations has now become a controversial one with members of the dominant élite arguing that recognition needs to be given to merit. It is asserted that even socialist countries gave weight to this claim. Yet merit itself is subjective, since it is the cultural élite itself which determines the criteria of what constitutes merit. The case for a meritocracy runs counter to the whole philosophy behind reservations which argues that, in a highly inegalitarian society, the more backward members need measures of positive discrimination to help them compete. To achieve any kind of equality it is necessary to restrict the positions of influence held by the élite approximately to its percentage among the total population. Reservations are one way of attempting this. Unless these provisions for the Scheduled Castes and Tribes are continued indefinitely and extended to the Backward Castes, India can never hope to live up to the ideal of equality embodied in the Constitution.

CHAPTER NINE

The tribes of India

The culture, religion and history of India have been formed from the mutual acculturation of the Aryans with pre-Aryan and tribal elements through a continuous process of assimilation since the earliest times. It is only when this point is understood that one can grasp the two mutually contradictory features of India, her diversity and simultaneous unity. If one adheres to the traditional interpretation of history which ascribes India's historical and cultural development to the Aryan invaders who brought their own superior culture, India's complexities can never be grasped. The view taken in this book finds support in four fields: cultural history, history, anthropology and assessments of the folk culture.

Richard Lannoy in *The Speaking Tree* stresses the mutual acculturation that has taken place throughout Indian history between the Aryan and pre-Aryan tribal elements. Indian society retains its 'profoundly archaic, not to say primitive foundations'. D.D. Kosambi in his work, *The Culture and Civilization of Ancient India in Historical Outline*, which is acknowledged as a work breaking new ground in historical research, stresses the extent to which the tribal culture has contributed to Indian civilization. Kosambi points out: 'The entire course of Indian history shows tribal elements being fused into a general society.' J.H. Hutton in *Caste in India* stresses the degree to which Hinduism is infused with rituals and symbols of tribal origin. Pupul Jayakar in her book, *The Earthen Drum*, has broken new ground in linking myth and ritual to the ageless art forms of rural India. She found through this rural tradition a unity which transcended and bridged the geographical fragmentation of the land. In other words she found a unity among the so-called 'Little Traditions'.

An earlier concept put forward in the early part of this century more or less recognized the fusion between the Aryan and the non-Aryan. However, while recognizing the contribution of other elements, especially the native civilization of the Indus Valley and the so-called Dravidian heritage, the subconscious assumption still persists that the Aryan dynamism was the key factor in establishing the admittedly composite Indo-Aryan culture. There is an implicit value-judgment in the linguistic equation of the term 'Arya' with nobility. A sort of cultural inferiority complex is sought to be unloaded on other groups. Even today there is the assumption of a cultural 'Great Tradition' deriving from the Aryanization and Sanskritization of numerous local 'Little Traditions'. This Great Tradition arrogates to itself alone the maintenance of Indian unity, while conceding, somewhat condescendingly, the necessity of India's background for some sort of diversity represented by the Little Traditions. It is only in very recent years that there have been the beginnings of some introspective research into whether the pre-Aryan tradition was in fact so barbarous and fragmented or whether it did not in fact represent the true mainstream of the cultural tradition of rural India, no less significant than the Great Tradition of the dominant upper castes.

There is no question that a process of mutual acculturation has taken place between the tribe and non-tribe right from early times. The *Mahabharata* tales show that the wives of some kings were non-Aryans. The Emperor Ashoka's father was a Brahmin while his mother was a 'naga', a generic name for certain tribal groups, not to be confused with the Naga tribes of the North-East. This shows the mobility that existed in those times, as well as the process of mutual acculturation that was under way. Kosambi cites evidence for this when he maintains that the tales in the *Mahabharata* sprang from three native sources: the Puru-Kuru War ballads, aboriginal myths and the Yadu sagas.[1] Lannoy points out that every case of 'great Indian power' shows evidence of contacts with the 'non-rational culture of excluded peoples and classes.'[2] Proof of the tribal and Aryan admixture can be found in the religious symbolism which emerged simultaneously with a unified society in the earliest times. Kosambi notes that:

> The divine family and entourage is an historical phenomenon marking the emergence of a unified society out of different tribal elements which were formerly not united. To justify such a combination the Brahmin books . . . record specially fabricated myths.[3]

The denigration of the autochthonous culture manifested itself in many ways. The religious symbols, concepts or rituals which had too powerful an influence over the popular masses to be ignored were assimilated. In the early stages some of the most powerful amongst them, after an initial period of denigration, finally achieved a new ascendancy. In the latter case, however, there were numerous subtle changes totally transforming the old concept. A classic example is the deity Shiva. His iconic likeness has been identified on the Indus Valley seals. Pupul Jayakar has rightly pointed out the identity of his headdress with that of the tribal Bison-Horned Maria Gonds of Bastar in Central India. Shiva is claimed by tribals of Maharashtra and Gujarat as their first ancestor. The earliest traditions of Shiva also depict him as a wild and crude individual who, for this reason, was considered by his first father-in-law, Daksha, as unfit for his daughter.

Later, however, the very power of this deity elevated him to the inner Hindu trinity with the title Mahadev, or Great God. His current urbanized image, often seen in front of Delhi buses, depicts him as fair-skinned with a serene or enigmatic Aryan countenance. In his association with the high peaks of the Himalayas and his white consort, Gauri, he becomes totally Olympian. Pupul Jayakar notes that as he is absorbed into the Brahminic pantheon: 'His appearance alters, he becomes the young, fair god of devastating beauty and his abode shifts from the dark forested Vindhyas to Kailasa, the Aryan homeland in the snow clad Himalayas.'[4]

However, what was probably his original *alter ego* became termed as Bhairava or Bhairon, sometimes considered a separate manifestation of Shiva himself and sometimes as the sentinel at his gate. It is with Bhairava, or Bhairon, that the lower-caste or tribal folk deities tend first to be assimilated in their identification.

The example of Vishnu illustrates the technique of defusing tribal loyalty to ancient Hindu traditions. For the very concept of Vishnu also underwent a subtle transformation in his rise from being a relatively minor deity in Rig-Vedic times to one of the three dominant manifestations of the later Hindu trinity. Perhaps more interesting than the purely philosophic question of his balance with Shiva, wherein the two aspects of destruction and preservation, mutually antithetical in Western thought, are harmonized in the Indian concept as two sides of the same coin of divinity, is the practical development of these two aspects of thought and the followers which they attract. The Brahmin intellectual will, of course, claim that there are no warring sects as such, and indeed Shiva has been claimed as a 'protector of Brahmins'. The fact remains, however, that throughout history his image as the passionate ascetic, the divine dancer who shakes the world, and his association with non-Aryan elements, seems to have attracted as his devotees the less orthodox or sophisticated elements in society. The mendicant babas, or *sanyasis*, who often have recourse to drugs to heighten their perceptions, derive from all segments of society.

The equations with the male manifestation of Bhairon and the various female attributes of Bhowani, Kali and, through them, with the very ancient tradition of the Mother Goddesses, some- how qualify him, along with his consort, as still the main real folk deity of the masses. It may be objected that Vishnu in his incarnation as Rama and, more especially Krishna, qualify equally in this regard. But there is a subtle difference. It seems fairly clearly evident from studies of the evolution of the Vishnu concept that his last three incarnations are conscious Brahminical attempts to synthesize, for the benefit of their hierarchical domi- nance, important elements of popular adoration.

Hence the virtual deification of Rama, the prince of what was probably the fairly recently Sanskritized kingdom of Ayodhya. The Rama tradition probably goes much further back into remote layers of pre-Aryan folklore from the days of tribal struggles between Austric groups in the Gangetic Valley. The word Ganga itself has been identified linguistically with a non-Aryan Austric word signifying merely a 'river'. All this may account for the seeming paradox whereby the suffix 'Ram', which ought to denote a blue-blooded Kshatriya prince, tends in modern India to be that of the lower castes. One of the children of Rama, Kusha, derives his name from the Kusha grass out of which in legend he was created as a companion for his older brother. Kusha grass again has especial pre-Aryan ritual significance among Austric tribes allied to the Mundas and Santhals who probably form the basic population base of the Gangetic basin, though many of them have now been reduced to low-caste groups such as the Chamars. There is indeed a folk tradition that the Chamars were at one stage a part of this much greater Austric tribal group.

In the case of Krishna the evidence is even clearer with his

Brahminical metamorphosis from what Kosambi aptly describes as 'the dark hero of the Yadus' through a 'foster adoption' by a nomadic pastoral tribe to the philosophic preceptor through whom the message of the Gita was ultimately delivered.

By absorbing these two powerful folk-hero traditions into the Brahminical scheme as incarnations of Vishnu large segments of the population were sought to be won over. Yet in both cases elements of the original folk tradition were too strong to be totally submerged. Within the *Gita* itself they surface, even if ambivalently, as indicating that any form of ritual from any individual or class of persons surrendering to the lord is acceptable.

In medieval times great devotional poetry and songs revived in the folk idiom of regional languages (as opposed to Sanskrit) in the name of Krishna. Less successful was the move whereby a potentially dangerous source of heresy was removed, after attempts to depict him as a devil's advocate, by incorporating the Buddha as another incarnation. Yet in a sense the strategy was successful in that, although the Buddha incarnation never achieved the sort of folk worship in India that Krishna or Rama did, it did avoid confrontation and defused any dissent from the hierarchical order.

Future developments will be interesting. The intellectual élite will, of course, deride any simplistic interpretation differentiating aspects of the same divine unity. At the social level, however, one cannot help noticing a tendency for Vaishnavite shrines and rituals to become, especially in rural India, the mark of a rise in social status, while adherence to the rituals of various aspects of Shiva and Kali are somehow associated with the lower strata. It is interesting that, at a time when Communist Kampuchea is reviving and reinterpreting the Ramaya ballet, no such delving back to cultural roots seems to be within the programme of Indian political activists working among the 'weaker sections'.

Even today, while some anthropologists and historians regard the relationship between the highly civilized Indian culture and the primitive tribes as one of 'mutual need',[5] caste Hindus vehemently deny any such link with the tribal culture. The Westerner who suggests any such link is dismissed as one without any knowledge of Indian history. Kosambi notes that references to the primitive influences in Hinduism 'infuriates most Indians of the middle class who feel their country ridiculed or their own dignity insulted.'[6] Few would admit Sinha's assertion that certain upper-caste groups possess tribal ancestry, as in the case of the Bhumihar Brahmins of North India. He notes that, since such groups rising in the social hierarchy would try to suppress all indications of links with their former tribe, 'This may also explain the vehemence with which such connections are denied.'[7] Kosambi also points out that it is not only Indians who choose to blank out this aspect of their cultural heritage but that most Indian observers miss 'the reciprocal influence of tribesmen on the Indian peasant and even on the upper classes.'[8]

Although the racist attitude of the caste Hindu towards the tribal is ancient and runs in the blood, these attitudes emerged at a relatively later period in history. Before the *Rig-Veda*, the earliest Indo-Aryan record, was composed, Indian society was fluid and as Lannoy points out: 'Aryanization included the assimilation of peoples of diverse origin. The history of Hinduism and the caste system is one of a long and incomplete process of detribalization.'[9]

Kosambi has himself pointed out that racial purity was hardly observed by the early Aryans. It was only after repeated conquests that the word 'dasa' came to mean a slave or helot, or member of the Sudra class, or fourth estate. For at first the term was applied to a hostile non-Aryan people who were dark-complexioned. It was only in the classical texts of Hinduism like the *Rig-Veda* that contemptuous references are made to the black colour of the autochthones. In the late Puranic legends which give an account of the origin of the Bhil tribe, the latter, as in the case of other tribal groups and dynasties, are invariably referred to in derogatory terms in the sense that their ancestry is ascribed to some form of sin or lower status redeemed by godly or high-caste favours. According to the Puranic account, the Bhils (Nishada) are said to have sprung from the thigh of a sage from whom sprang 'a man charred like a log with a flat nose and extremely short'.[10]

Even today the association of black skin with menial tasks remains unchanged since ancient times. The sacred books contain many racist citations: 'Like a vaisya . . . tributary to another, to be eaten up by another, to be oppressed at will. Like a Sudra . . . in the service of another, to be removed at will . . . to be slain at will.'[11] Kosambi notes that these two castes were to be enclosed between the two upper castes during the sacrificial procession of the whole tribe 'to make them more submissive'.

Pupul Jayakar says cultural roots may be lost under two

conditions: 'Firstly, when the necessity to nourish the inner spirit gives way to material values, then the real destruction starts. Secondly, when the cyclical time of rural India gives way to the linear stream of progress.'[12] One cannot but agree with Pupul Jayakar that India's age-old heritage – both the Great and Little Traditions – may be lost under the impact of modernization. However, throughout Indian history there have been deliberate attempts to denigrate and devalue the autochthonous Indian tradition.

The first stage seems to have been the denigration of the Mother Goddess whom Pupul Jayakar links with the Harappan culture. During this period of synthesis between the nomadic Aryan religion connected with the worship of the male deity and the earthbound female deity of the Harappan culture, the indigenous deity, the Great Mother Goddess, acquired a consort. In the course of this union she becomes a minor deity in relation to the consort who becomes the main divinity. Kosambi points out that the various marriages between the different gods in the epic *Mahabharata*, traditionally considered a Hindu classic, were 'a vital step forward in assimilating the patriarchal Aryans to some matriarchal pre-Aryans.'[13]

Recent scholarship shows that the Kula Devata, or household deities, which form the most important aspect of worship in north and central Bihar, have tribal origins. The form in which the deity is worshipped by the Maithili Brahmins in Bihar is Adi Bhagwati, or 'Primeval Goddess', who, Sinha asserts, is 'a syncretised deity of the pre-Rig-Vedic inhabitants of India among whom worship of the Mother Goddess was widespread in different forms.'[14] He points out the strong possibility that these household deities were once worshipped over large parts of India under different names 'and were driven to the inner sanctuary of the home as Brahminic Hinduism became dominant.'[15]

The second stage of denigration occurred with the attempt to absorb the traditional tribal societies, whose religious rituals were by and large iniconic, into the fused Indo-Aryan pantheon which by now had had to accommodate both the Deva and Asura traditions. The pattern in India, and one that is still going on today, has largely been that, in the interests of integration, one must Sanskritize the tribes. In practice this means the transference of the whole Indo-Aryan concept of the male deity and of legends like Shishupal, the antagonist of Krishna, and hero of the 'Yadas', who were a shepherd tribe to tribal religious imagery.

Today there are stirrings of a rebellion against this Sanskritization. Even the non-tribal Meithis of Manipur in North-East India, who were Hinduized in the seventeenth century and were earlier considered staunch Hindu Vaishnavites, have been searching back towards their different ethnic roots and their own original pre-Hindu traditions.

In the process of her own journey of discovery in the search back for roots, Pupul Jayakar found that the great art forms of the Little Tradition have been formed by the comingling of the settled village society and the tribes. She points out that the household worship of the five main deities – the 'Panch Devatas' – which are integral to the orthodox ritual of Hindu worship, represents a fusion of many streams, 'the tribal origins of some being indicated by the symbolic forms of worship.'[16]

Pupul Jayakar believes that two of the five main deities worshipped in the Hindu home – Shiva and Ganesh – are of tribal origin. She traces the iniconic forms in which the five deities are worshipped back to their places of origin. Shiva is worshipped as a lingam 'which usually comes from the bottom of the river Narbada, the very heartland of Central India where the tribes dwelt'.[17] Ganesh, who only became a respectable god in the Hindu pantheon much later, is worshipped as a red stone whose territorial ancestry she also traces back to the same place of origin. As evidence of his tribal origins she points out that Ganesh is worshipped by the tribes of Nasik in Maharashtra as well as those of Gujarat.[18]

Pupul Jayakar points out that the Atharva Veda, compiled after the Rig-Vedic Hymns, contains very archaic elements and is possibly the earliest 'record of the beliefs, the imagery, the rituals and worships of the autochthonous people of India as they met and transformed the conquering Aryan consciousness.'[19] Furthermore, one of the earliest vernacular texts was a group of Buddhist Charya songs composed around the seventh or eighth century by Savara tribal poets who were reputed to have been great adepts at both Buddhist and Saivite Tantric ritual.[20]

While the influence of the tribes on Indian civilization have often been ignored, the tribes have been no less influenced in the reverse direction. As Kosambi points out, when a more advanced civilization comes into contact with a more primitive society, the former tends to obliterate the latter. This is a Marxist interpret-ation of history, the underlying assumption being that the more advanced form of production supersedes the less sophisticated economy. Thus the superstructure of the more primitive society becomes transformed. In Lannoy's terms this means that the tribe becomes a caste. It loses its language and adopts the institutions of the more sophisticated Hindu religion. It changes to settled agriculture, accepts caste rules regarding marriage, diet, pollution, joins Hindu sects and loses its tribal name in the process.

Not a single tribe in the great central and southern belt has been unaffected by Hinduism because of contacts with settled village societies. The Bhils and the Satnami Harijans of Central India are excellent illustrations of this process of transformation and Sanskritization. The Bhils have now lost their original language and many now speak a dialect akin to the Gujjars, a shepherd caste, from whom they learned to keep cattle.

One can view the entire span of tribal and caste societies as a continuum and, as Hutton noted, it is difficult to differentiate between Hindu and tribal elements. Lannoy also notes that 'the Indian tribe and non-tribe have been defined sociologically as a continuum'.[21]

Primitive ideas of magic peculiar to primitive societies survive in Hinduism. Hinduism also contains many very ancient and primi-tive beliefs which in some cases constitute its major element. As Pupul Jayakar says: 'India carries her stone age along with her.'[22] This is not surprising considering that wherever hill or forest tribes have lived in permanent daily contact with Hindus, their religion generally rapidly assimilates itself to that of the neigh-bours. In this process, however, the old ways of thought remain unchanged because caste itself has an inbuilt tendency to 'con-serve, rather than transform, primitive tribal elements which have been assimilated into it.'[23]

If one compares Indian civilization in general with modern Western society, Lannoy notes that Hinduism is not free to the same extent from the subjective limitations of its own thought processes. Its primitive thought patterns remain and are '. . . the cause and the effect of the social coexistence of the tribes, the partially detribalized and the completely detribalized in physical proximity.'[24]

During this process of mutual acculturation tribes which were in contact with the settled village societies were assimilated into the caste system, although there has never been an organized attempt to bring the tribes into the fold of the caste system as separate endogamous units. Hutton believes that caste differences, in so far as they are racial, are rather differences in degree of mixture than absolute differences of race or type. Lannoy believes castes and subcastes derive from tribal groups of different origins. In some places it is certainly easier to differentiate between a specific racial type by area than by caste. Kosambi notes that often peasant castes bear the same name as an aboriginal tribe in the same region.

When only a section of the tribe became integrated into the caste system, a breach was created in the tribe itself. At different periods other sections of the tribe also became assimilated into the caste system, although with a different status and name. Sinha believes the Bhuiyans, who now constitute landless labourers in Bihar and who are listed as a Backward Caste group in Assam,[25] contributed a strain to the Bhumihar Brahmins of North India: 'In the case of the Bhuiyans we see a total tribal strand running from the caste of Musahar, counted among the lowest of the Scheduled Castes, through the Khandaits right into the Rajput and possibly the Bhumihar Brahmins.'[26]

Numerous castes of Gujarat and Maharashtra like the Koli are more dark complexioned and possess coarser features than the higher castes. According to Hutton they 'look like the jungle tribes and Bhils'.[27] Many of these lower-caste groups are cultivators, fishermen or work as manual labour in the mills. In Tamil Nadu low castes like the Badaga and Paliyans were formerly tribes as were the Musahar and Agariya castes of Bihar.[28] It appears that the Kabuis of Manipur were in the process of becoming a caste in the thirties. In contrast the process of Hinduization of the Meithis had been going on for about 700 years, and the ruler could bestow on non-Hindu tribes the caste rank of Kshatriya.[29] In 1960 it was less than 250 years since the Maharaja had abolished ancestor worship and dismissed the indigenous priests of the temples of local deities and replaced them by Brahmins. Some tribes like the Gonds and Bhils of present-day India, while being classified as tribes, are in the process of being assimilated into Hindu society.

Many of the Scheduled Caste groups represent tribal groups who were conquered and subjugated. Tribes who once ruled over kingdoms have become Scheduled Castes. Kosambi cites the example of the Bhar caste, or tribe, which sank to the status of labourers. Yet at one time they ruled over parts of Bihar. Many old forts and reservoirs have in fact been attributed to them.[30] Kosambi claims that caste developed within the tribe and that the Sudras 'were helots who belonged to the tribe or clan group without membership rights.'[31] This historian believes famine caused the creation of the slave castes.[32] The Chuhra, a scavenger caste of the Punjab, are 'remnants of an aboriginal tribe'.[33] Hutton also believes the Doms, who have been scavengers and sweepers for centuries, may represent a 'once respectable tribe'. He notes that in the 1940s the Doms living in the Himalayan foothills of Kumaon and Garhwal had retained a higher status and a part of their tribal organization had been preserved.[34]

The proof that Scheduled Castes may in some instances constitute tribes that have become assimilated as they settled on the periphery of settled village societies is indicated by the fact that they often act as watchmen and are considered experts on village boundary lines. According to Hutton, this suggests that they are the oldest inhabitants of the area. In his day Russell noted that the Mahars of Maharashtra, a former tribe who became Scheduled Castes centuries ago, were often authorities on village boundaries.[35] The thesis of tribal origin for many Scheduled Caste groups has found reinforcement in the latest study of Sinha.[36]

Hutton notes that the 'bulk of the Muslim population of Bengal are no doubt of more or less aboriginal extraction.' The bulk of these Muslims, who are concentrated in present-day Bangladesh (former East Bengal), are dark skinned and flat nosed. Their conversion to Islam took place as a reaction to attempts at reimposing Brahminical orthodoxy after the more egalitarian Buddhist period. The conversions may therefore represent an attempt by these assimilated tribes to escape from the rigidities that had crept into Hinduism.

The tribes who continued to live in the forests and hills have never been part of the Hindu caste system and in that sense their social position has never been defined in relation to Hindu society. According to Hutton, from the earliest times the primitive tribes who remained unassimilated were never downgraded to the rank of low castes. Russell makes the same point and notes that the 'Untouchables' were in an inferior position socially to the tribes.[37] The main reason being that the tribes 'lived apart in their own villages in the forest tracts and kept possession of their land.' On the other hand, occupations performed by the Scheduled Castes are degrading according to Hindu law and therefore polluting to the Brahmins.

As already pointed out in a previous chapter, the institution of caste may be rooted in tribal India. Hutton believes that since the institution is unique to this geographical region it is necessary to look for its origins within the subcontinent. He believes that the caste system arose as a result of a mutual intermixing of tribal institutions and ideas with those of the Aryans. Tribal notions of magic, taboo, pollution and purification were fused with the 'hierarchical policies adopted by the Rigvedic invaders and their successors to the communities they found in the land.'[38]

Hutton believes notions of hierarchy were absent from the system as it developed and suggests that the ideas of soul-force were fundamental to it. Even though some of the remoter Naga tribes in North-Eastern India had had no contact with the outside world in 1948, yet the institutions throw light on how the system developed.[39] One observer quoted by Hutton reports that in Gujarat taboos are stricter as one goes down the scale. The high-caste Hindus were less particular about their water than the lower castes and 'restrictions on intercourse increase as one goes from the top of the caste system.'[40]

Thus throughout Indian history there has been a continuous assimilation of various groups. It is owing to the continuity through the overlapping of layers of tribal groups that India has that sense of unity which otherwise is difficult to account for, considering the diversity of languages and customs on the sub-continent.

In fact there appears to be strong evidence that the *gotra*, or Brahmin exogamous clan, is an Aryan institution derived from the clan organization of the early tribes. More to the point, in early legends the progenitors of the Brahmin gotras show Asura affiliations. According to Kosambi, the institution was assimilated by the Brahmins who intermarried, as ancient texts themselves have recorded, with tribal women.[41] It was subsequently adopted by the Kshatriya and later absorbed by the lower castes in an attempt to raise their status. Hutton disagrees with this and offers a different point of view, maintaining that the lower-caste gotras may actually represent a pre-Hindu exogamous unit, although he too attributes the institution to tribal culture. He maintains that in many parts of tribal India the 'village or locality tends to supersede the clan or sept as the exogamous unit. Thus many of the gotras of the Golapurab caste of Agra district are named after villages and after occupations.'[42]

Kosambi gives specific examples from archaeology to support his thesis. The Brahmin gotra derived from the name Sigru, which is mentioned in a Kushana inscription at Mathura and means a 'drumstick tree'. He concludes that: 'The totemic nature of such tribal names is not in doubt.'[43] Similarly the only survival of the name Bhrigu today comes from classical Sanskrit. It is one of the main exogamous clan groups which has maintained its power and importance. Yet in classical texts the name Bhrigu appears as the enemy of the Aryan king Sudas and Kosambi maintains that this was 'obviously then a tribe'.

The mutual acculturation of the tribe and non-tribe has also resulted in a sort of symbiotic relationship between the two worlds. For Indian civilization the tribe represents a 'negative identity'. Members of the former imagine tribal people to be 'lazy, feckless, libidinous because it confirms their self-image as industrious, orderly, adult and socially organized.'[44] Lannoy concludes that the primeval stratum fulfils an emotional and psychological need for Indian civilization. This is rather a complicated Western conceptualization and should rather be interpreted as the fear of the open tribal society. The indigenous gods of India, while denigrated, are propitiated because they are feared for their 'evil potentialities'.

The fact is that there is a tremendous sense of insecurity in the upper castes because they have always constituted a minority on the subcontinent. This psychological malaise is one plausible explanation for the fact that the most ruthless degradation of tribes and the most violent forms of caste pollution were practised in the South. Not only did the Brahmins constitute a smaller minority than in the North, ranging from three to five per cent of the total population, but a much higher concentration of non-Aryans was to be found in the Peninsula.

Despite the ruthless subjugation and assimilation of the autochthones which occurred in the South, a strong sense of individualism was preserved. Lannoy attributes the vitality of the Shaivite sect which sprang up in the South to tribal influences. He notes that the sect's devotionalism had a vitality which was quite different from the ecstatic fervour normal to the Bhakti movement[45] when it entered its third phase with the spread of Vaishnavism to North India. The same kind of vitality can still be observed in the tribal dances performed by the tribes of Bastar district in Central India.

The religious and mythical influences of tribes on Hinduism are manifold. The impact of such ideas is most evident in the Little Traditions of rural India. Lannoy equates possession by spirits, found among lower-caste sects, to tribal animism. Many local village cults may also possess primitive tribal origins. Some goddesses with strong localized cults, yet whose names have no known etymology as, for example, Mengai, or Udalai, often represent 'some vanished tribal or clan group', according to Kosambi. Many of the gods riding different animals or birds were once tribal totems.

In fact, while scholars differ on the origin of totemism, most agree that it is rooted in tribal culture. The animal vehicle for Hindu deities and animal incarnations may be totemic as are tree and snake worship: ' "Tree marriages" performed among both the tribes and higher castes; Shiva's horrendous dance in a skin of a flayed elephant suggest tribal Shamanism.'[46]

Hutton believes totemism originated in the Proto-Australoid tribes. Strong traces of totemism are found among the lower Telugu, Kanara, Maratha and Central Indian castes.[47] Lannoy is of the opinion that totemism was borrowed from the non-Aryan societies before the sixth century BC when all societies, including the Aryans were tribal. It appears that totemism is less prevalent among the upper castes.

Many lower-caste groups often preserve tribal rules, images and myths. An example is cited in Briggs' work, *The Chamars*, regarding the Madiga, a great leather-working caste of the Telugu country. Briggs noted that in some parts they 'help remove demons of disease and perform the bloody parts of sacrifices.'[48] The women were often dedicated to temple service. There is every likelihood that, in the original tribal tradition, the woman was the interpreter of divine earth and that subsequently this notion became overlaid by the more sophisticated temple concept of the 'dedavasi', which after all only means 'servant of God'.

Primitive tribes themselves often worship the gods of a village and a village recognizes their deities as well. Lannoy maintains that country festivals, which attract villagers from afar, can often be traced back to primitive tribal origins, though the actual tribe may have vanished. Some traces of common worship 'may still persist, particularly of mother goddesses with peculiar names not known in other villages'.[49]

The most important place of public worship in Bihar and eastern Uttar Pradesh takes place at the ancient shrine finally dedicated to the sun god, Surya. Sinha traces its origins to the Chero, a former tribe, who have now become a very low caste.

Several of the existing holy places of Hinduism are located outside the Brahmavartta, or 'Land of the Creator', where one might have expected to find them if it were really the fact that Hinduism actually arose in that area. While to find them elsewhere is consistent with a view that these places were regarded with devotion by the pre-Aryans. To quote Sinha:

In the caste system the tribes find their old identity preserved and their old gods reconstituted in a syncretised form. The gods of their forefathers appear to have been reincarnated in the Brahminical gods and thus the great places of pilgrimage offer to them a double attraction and hence to visit them becomes a life's yearning for every Hindu.[50]

This point is emphasized by the existence of Hindu shrines where priests and custodians are not Brahmin but some pseudo-Brahmin or Sudra caste. One example are the Malis who are officiating priests of some Orissa temples. Pupul Jayakar upholds this view and notes that the:

Primordial sense of unchanging holiness of the site that survives the changing gods is also evident in tribal people who remain the main servitors of important holy Hindu shrines.[51]

At one of the most important pilgrimage spots of Hinduism, the Jagannath temple at Puri in Orissa, the Savara tribals have free entry to the inner sanctuary where the 'Blue God' is worshipped as Jagannath.[52]

The cult of Jagannath is an example of the syncretism under discussion. The process of this evolution has been analysed by a German scholar, Anncharlott Eschmann, who shows the affinities between the deities of tribal peoples of Orissa with the

Navakalevara ritual of Jagannath. She has shown how the wooden post worshipped by tribals subsequently becomes transformed into a Hinduized god or goddess.[53]

One has already seen that most of the early *rishis*, or holy men, from whom the Brahmin gotras, or clans, were descended, probably derived from pre-Aryan ancestry and how, to retain their moral and spiritual ascendancy, they allied themselves with any ruling groups of the day and manipulated the power struggles of these ruling groups to strengthen their own ascendancy. Towards the end of the first millennium BC their position, however, again became precarious. In the 6th century BC temporal power passed into the hands of dynasties centred on Magadha (present-day North Bihar) whose lineage, according to Kosambi, was aboriginal. In earlier religious texts, although praised for the beauty of its women, the Magadhans were regarded as impure and beyond the Aryan pale. The rulers of these dynasties, culminating in the Mauryans, often sprang from among the Sudras, the fourth estate. Indeed Kosambi points out that Brahmin records speak of the Magadhan dynasty with contempt as the lowest of kingdoms.

Worse was to follow. The architect of the new Mauryan power, Chandragupta, who was reputedly the son of a Sudra serf, also involved himself with cultural links with the Greeks after Alexander's invasions and opened up whole new relationships with Hellenized West Asia. Next his grandson, Ashoka, embraced Buddhism with its more egalitarian precepts. Even his grandfather, founder of the dynasty Chandragupta, is believed to have deliberately sought *samadhi* by starvation to identify himself with his subjects who were affected by famine after the break-up of the Mauryan Empire. During this period Ashoka extended his influence by renouncing conquest of tribal groups on his frontier, approaching them instead with a message of *dharma*, compassion and equality.

After the break-up of the Mauryan Empire the Indian subcontinent fell prey to a succession of marauding groups from the West and from Central Asia, like the Sakas, Kushans and Huns who had scant respect for any hierarchical Brahmin pretensions. It seems to have been during this period that the edifice of a really exploitative hierarchy was created again by the manipulations and winning over of the turbulent power groups of the day under Brahminical leadership. It is probably in this period that many much more ancient folk traditions, such as those embodying the epics of the *Mahabharata* and *Ramayana*, as well as the various *Puranas*, were subtly recast with a dominant theme of re-establishing or, as some would have it, creating for the first time a total ascendancy of Brahminical preceptorship in its equation with the temporal ruler.

Again it is probably to this period that one owes the similar redrafting in favour of an élite hierarchy, and the backdating to time immemorial, of the Laws of Manu, as well as a document on statecraft called the *Arthasastra*, ascribed to the Kautilya, minister to the much earlier founder of the Mauryan Empire. The Laws of Manu prescribe most draconian differentiations in punishments operating against the higher and lower castes. Until recent years, at least in theory, the Laws were revered by the upper castes as the epitomy of Hindu law and custom. They are similarly reviled by the lower castes as an instrument of oppression and on occasions have been publicly burnt. The *Arthasastra* also stresses the benefits of oppressive policies and the eleventh book has some interesting prescriptions for breaking up traditionally democratic tribal societies, many of which are still in use today.

The *Arthasastra* made several recommendations to this end:

The main technique was to soften them up for disintegration from within, to convert tribesmen into members of a class society based upon private property. So the leaders and the most active elements were to be corrupted by cash bribes, ample supplies of the strongest wines, or by encouraging personal feuds. Dissension would be sown by spies . . . Senior members of the tribe should be encouraged not to eat at the tribal common table . . . Royal agents could needle the younger people, who were allotted a minor share of tribal lands and revenues by custom, to question the apportionment . . . The king of the Arthasastrian state would intervene directly with armed force. The tribe was to be fragmented, the tribesmen deported to be settled upon distant lands in units of five to ten households, well away from each other.[54]

At a time when India is searching back for her cultural roots, there are obvious difficulties therefore in adjusting tribal policies to the age-old traditions. There was indeed some attempt during the Nehru period when a genuinely sensitive and liberal policy was being formulated to hark back to an edict of the Emperor

Ashoka. Dr Verrier Elwin, an English missionary whose work with the Central Indian tribes later drew him close to India's Freedom Movement and led him into the realm of anthropology, and who ultimately died a Buddhist, quoted Ashoka as having compassion towards the forest dwellers on the borders of his kingdom. This may have been a useful political ploy to try and derive ancient sanction for a modern liberal policy. Unfortunately it turned out, under scrutiny, that vital passages of the edict had been omitted. The original, despite the idealizing of Ashoka's Buddhist background, was much sterner and might have been a textbook for firm administrative no-nonsense paternalism, whether British or that of post-Independence Indian administrators, in dealing with restive tribes: 'The beloved of the gods conciliates the forest tribes of his empire but he warns them that he has power even in his remorse, and he asks them to repent, lest they be killed.'[55]

However this may be, Nehru's Five-Point Policy, formulated after consultation with Elwin, read as follows:

1. People should develop along the lines of their own genius and we should avoid imposing anything on them. We should try to encourage in every way their own traditional arts and culture. 2. Tribal rights in land and forests should be respected. 3. We should try and build up a team of their own people to do the work of administration and development. Some technical personnel from outside will, no doubt, be needed, especially in the beginning. But we should avoid introducing too many outsiders into tribal territory. 4. We should not over-administer these areas or overwhelm them with a multiplicity of schemes. We should rather work through, and not in rivalry to their own social and cultural institutions. 5. We should judge results, not by statistics or the amount of money spent, but the quality of human character that is evolved.[56]

The tragedy is that, except for a limited period, in a limited area centred around the North-East Frontier Agency (now Arunachal Pradesh), which incidentally is the only area of North-Eastern India so far virtually unaffected by insurgency, the directive was more honoured in the breach than in the observance. In fact, in most areas the reality on the ground was the total opposite and, after Nehru's death, even the lip service which had been paid to the policy began openly to be questioned. Despite the fact that the official policy of the government has been one of tolerance towards the beliefs, customs and way of life of the tribal people, many state governments have exhibited less sensitive attitudes to the right of tribal communities to follow their traditional way of life.

The policy of divide and rule which the Hindu rulers have traditionally adopted since ancient times began once again to reassert itself after Nehru's death. Since there is always a tendency for tribal groups to fragment, this has always been exploited by the Hindus. During the Magadhan empire in the 6th century BC the Licchavi tribe was broken up from within by methods described in the *Arthasastra*. Today the government has succeeded in breaking up the Jharkhand movement which was demanding a separate tribal homeland in eastern Central India by exploiting the traditional animosities prevailing amongst the different tribal groups as between the Santhals and Oraons. Even the original founder of the movement, a Christian tribal, Shibu Soren, came to an understanding with the Congress (I) in the 1980 general elections.

The *Arthasastra* suggested ways and means of breaking up the tribes in which the king 'might settle a whole tribe upon the land in one region, in detached farming units of five to ten families each.' A similar policy was followed by the Indian Army in Nagaland during the fifties when the Naga insurrection movement went underground to fight for an independent state. In order to break up and crush the rebels the Indian Army began forcing the Nagas into strategic hamlets on the lines recommended by Briggs. 'Malaya' Briggs was the original author of the plan to group villages as part of the strategy against Communist guerrillas in Malaya. It was later implemented by General Sir Gerald Templar when the latter took over as Military Governor of Malaya after World War II. Although in 1957 Nagaland was made into a separate state, the Nagas never succeeded in gaining their independence from India. Once again the government was partially successful in dividing the tribal leadership by exploiting intertribal divisions as between the Sema and Angami Nagas.

The government is following the same policy of divide and rule in Assam today. The 15 March 1983 issue of *India Today* reported the government as saying it would divide up Assam.

The Congress (I) has succeeded in exploiting conflicts of Hindus against Muslims, tribal against Assamese, Bengalis against Assamese, etc., thereby exacerbating tensions in this strife-torn state.

The real aim of the government today is the promotion of national integration to ensure that no minority, tribal or otherwise, remains dominant in any particular area. The North-Eastern region inhabited by Mongoloid tribes has been a particular source of anxiety for the Hindus who feel the tribes are unreliable. Just after Nehru died, when Charan Singh was Agriculture Minister of Uttar Pradesh, he sponsored a lobby to keep the North-East, especially NEFA (now Arunachal Pradesh) bordering China, safe for India by inducting hardy peasantry. These would be fighting farmers who would defend the frontiers. His idea was to resettle ex-servicemen there, the accent being on North Indian servicemen.

The content of this strategy may be compared to the policy of the Israeli government of establishing Jewish settlers in the West Bank to break up the unity of the Arabs. There was one such resettlement scheme in Arunachal Pradesh but nothing actually came of it. In fact, Charan Singh's idea was never translated into practice, as saner counsels prevailed. Such ideas, however, were even formulated in pre-Independence days during the Freedom Movement. For example, Rajendra Prasad, who later became President of India, had advocated in the thirties a scheme to combat Muslim immigration into Assam. He actually tried to organize groups from his home state of Bihar, but nothing substantial came of it.

Similarly in the fifties, again within the Congress, Sardar Patel, the first Home Minister, drew attention to the dangers of the North-East with the implication that some racial dilution was desirable through settlement in the wake of the Chinese moves towards Tibet.

These attitudes, although rarely expressed openly, and disclaimed by continuous references to the Hindu tradition of tolerance and universality, do seem to permeate the traditional policy. Haimendorf has noted with reference to tribal languages that, notwithstanding the voluminous works by Tribal Welfare Departments, little attention has been paid to this subject and notes: 'It is difficult to avoid the conclusion that politicians and officials alike regard their ultimate disappearance as inevitable and even desirable in the interest of the integration of the tribes with the majority community.'[57] A Planning Commission official with long experience of tribal administration and development plans recently remarked that: 'We have to be wary of the arrogance of the dominant groups, of an internal colonialism.'[58]

In actual practice there is indeed a tendency to permeate all tribal and minority areas, while at the same time claiming that in reality it is the Hindu majority that is being eroded in strategic pockets. Such claims are found on detailed scrutiny to be totally false, contrary to the general impression created among the public. For example, census figures show an actual decline of the Muslim percentage in Assam between 1961 and 1971. Similarly there is a decline in the fairly narrow Sikh majority of the Punjab. In the tribal areas the situation trend is accelerating even more rapidly. Tripura, a tribal-ruled state at the time of Independence, was reduced to a total tribal minority by 1971. The tribals constituted fifty per cent of the population in the 1931 and 1941 censuses. It was reduced to 37 per cent in 1951 and to 32 per cent in 1961. By the 1971 census the figure was 29 per cent and it is expected to have dwindled further in the 1981 census, figures for which have not yet been made available. The impression gathered on a tour of Bastar, the district with the largest tribal concentration in India, is that the same trend is under way with the likelihood of the tribals soon being reduced to a minority.

One suspects that a subconscious element is at work. For despite detailed planning and huge allocations for the development of the tribes, in practice these have remained largely on paper because of frustration by different elements. These include social attitudes towards tribal people, obstructionism by vested interests who have traditionally benefited from the exploitation of tribes and a corrupt and slack administration which, even in tribal areas, is dominated largely by caste Hindu officials.

The concepts of the Tribal Sub-Plan first formulated in 1977 is one of the most advanced in the world. Conceptually there is meticulous thinking down to the most practical details. If this planned strategy had been backed by any genuine conviction on the part of the implementers of the Five-Point Policy originally enumerated by Nehru, a genuine social and economic transformation would have taken place in tribal areas without destroying the fabric of the tribal societies, a process that is taking place today.

The Tribal Sub-Plan, the main instrument for tribal development, covers 65 per cent of the country's total tribal population in 17 states and union territories. The Sixth Plan is supposed to be helping over half the population living in the Tribal Sub-Plan areas, totalling 530,000 families, of which 80 per cent live in abject poverty, to cross the poverty line. Forty billion rupees have been set aside for this purpose during the 1980–85 period.

Yet despite such huge allocations, the tribal populations have remained exactly where they were at Independence. The total lack of will displayed by the Central ministries and state governments in effectively implementing programmes was brought out by the Parliament's recent Committee report on the welfare of Scheduled Castes and Tribes. The Committee found, for example, that the government of Madhya Pradesh, a state with the largest tribal population in India, numbering 9.8 million according to the 1971 census, instead of conducting bench-mark surveys in all the villages of the tribal development block, had carried out surveys in only five villages in each development block. Yet detailed plans for projects in Tribal Sub-Plan areas are supposed to be based on these bench-mark survey reports.

It is significant that a report of the Comptroller and Auditor General of India submitted in the first half of 1983 severely criticizes the failure of the administration to implement tribal schemes. The report notes that Central Government funds for various programmes have remained unutilized and deficiencies were noted in all aspects of Tribal Sub-Plan programmes including priority sectors like drinking water, irrigation, education health and agricultural programmes.

An added complication is the fact that, although the Tribal Sub-Plans for their development were targeted at areas where the tribal population was still concentrated in a fairly homogeneous fashion and formed a considerable rural percentage, the net result of 'development' seems to be that, even in these small pockets, the percentage of non-tribals is rapidly increasing, as was pointed out above, so that all over India there will soon be no homeland left for these groups. This is despite the fact that quite apart from any question of modernization, the tribes used to possess both cultural and linguistic traits to qualify them as national minorities.

On top of all this, their little remaining land, despite all policies and enactments to the contrary, continues to be alienated whether to non-tribal settlers or to increasingly rigid forest regulations. It seems to be largely in tribal areas that huge dam projects inundating their traditional land have been initiated, while mining and industrial towns have also been established as, for example, in South Bihar, Orissa and eastern Madhya Pradesh. Such industrial projects when formulated are usually supposed in some way to contribute to the modernization and economic betterment of isolated tribal communities. In practice they only seem to contribute to their pauperization.

With India's growing stress on industrialization, the future of the Indian tribes is likely to be undermined. Despite the threat posed to their way of life, there is little likelihood that the 45 million tribals will be assimilated into the larger society in the near future. Attempts at integration through development programmes and educational policies have so far been ineffective. Future patterns of assimilation may well follow classical lines of absorption through the bottom of the caste hierarchy, with the present-day Scheduled Castes and Tribes poised to become the Sudras, or 'working class', of the modern industrialized Indian nation in the coming decades. The exception to this pattern will be small pockets and groups where a tribe has retained its own language and its land and where it possesses at least the basis of an educated group within its own community. Such small groups will adjust themselves to the system.

CHAPTER TEN

Losers in the development process:
Bhil tribals of South Rajasthan

For centuries the Bhils have inhabited the once dense forest
tracts of south-west Central India which border on the Indus
Valley. The Bhils are one of the oldest tribal groups in India and
were referred to in ancient Sanskrit texts of AD 600 as 'Nishada',
with traditions going back centuries earlier. In this early period
some Bhil clans ruled over parts of Rajasthan, Gujarat, Madhya
Pradesh and Maharashtra. The extent of the forest in the old days
is illustrated by the Indus Valley seals depicting the rhinoceros
whose habitat is swampy jungles. As these remote frontier areas
inhabited by the autochthones were being opened up during the
period of expansion of the Hindu kingdoms in the medieval
period from AD 400 to 1000, the process of Hinduization began.
Many tribal chieftains achieved Kshatriya status in exchange for
giving protection to the Brahmin preceptors meditating in the
forests.

The Bhil contact with the Hindus, unlike that of most of the
other tribes, was one of collaboration. This was true especially of
the Bhil relationship with the Rajputs, the rulers of Rajasthan
since medieval times, many of whose dynastic founders sprang in
part from Bhil ancestry. In the sixteenth century Bhil clans fought
side by side with the Rajput kingdom of Chittorgarh in its war
against the Emperor Akbar who was trying to extend centralized
state power, based in Delhi, over large parts of India. The degree
of cooperation between the Bhils and Rajputs is symbolized in the
state emblems of the Rajput kingdoms of Kushalgarh and Mewar
where the Bhil chieftains and the Rajput princes appear side by
side. However, in the course of the seventeenth century, when the
Rajput principalities elaborated court ritual and hierarchy, especially after they had to recognize some form of paramountcy
elsewhere, the tendency intensified for social distances to be
widened. The Bhils sank in status. Much earlier they had been
outside the caste system. Now gradually, without formally being

admitted into it, all but a few of the more successfully Sanskritized groups tended to be reduced in status to the lower rungs of Sudras. By the eighteenth century, under the protection of the Rajput administration, the region was opened up to commercial castes, and peasant and artisan castes also gradually moved in to settle the upland valleys. As a result the Bhils were pushed back further and further into the forests.

The introduction of a market economy by the British in the nineteenth century, which superseded the barter system prevalent among the Bhils, began the process of economic deterioration in which the Bhils of Dungarpur and Banswara districts in South Rajasthan find themselves today. The British took away their traditional land and forest rights and introduced a new land-tenure system based on private property and centralized land records under which the Bhils were allotted small plots. As moneylenders, contractors and traders entered the region, mortgages, indebtedness and its concomitant, bonded labour, became endemic.

The Bhils, one of the larger tribal groups in India, were expected, like other tribes, to benefit from the liberal and thoughtful policy framed in the early fifties by Prime Minister Nehru. All over the country numerous development programmes were framed for such groups. Performance has been so patchy as to invite serious criticism of their failure. One reason for the failure of such government development programmes involves the theoretical base from which planning operates. A fundamental premise of some policy-makers assumes that economic change by itself will bring about a transformation in traditional attitudes and institutions. This belief is based on the Marxian postulate that base determines superstructure. It has been taken over by Western economists and become so much a part of institutionalized economic thinking that, in turn, Third World Planners have adopted the theory in their own development programmes. In fact, economic development without a simultaneous programme for social progress leads only to social disequilibrium.

This is exactly what is happening in the 'backward' districts of Dungarpur and Banswara, which are both under the Tribal Sub-Plan. Tribal Sub-Plans, which were launched by the government in 1977, seek to uplift defined 'backward' areas with majority tribal populations through specific integrated development programmes. Unless there is a simultaneous attempt at social development – stress not merely on formal education but on training for leadership, awakening of awareness and breaking the barriers of mistrust, despondency and inferiority complexes – development programmes will never benefit the recipients.

The other factor responsible for the negative outcome of programmes, as demonstrated in Dungarpur and Banswara districts of South Rajasthan, is the failure of the administration to mobilize people's participation in their own development. Lip service is always paid to this concept but planning still takes place at centralized levels without any real consultation at the grass roots as to villagers' priorities. There is not even a practical paternalistic understanding of them. There is also the usual lack of coordination between departments. A vital component of any programme may thus languish to the jeopardy of the entire programme. Programmes are implemented by petty officials at the lower levels who manifest an open contempt for villagers, particularly Harijans and tribals. This widens the communication gap further. In many instances the indifference amongst officials is such, as in the Tribal Welfare Department in Dungarpur, that bureaucrats cannot even produce figures showing progress in current programmes. One social worker in Banswara described government programmes as a 'dumping process' which was instilling a 'beggarly attitude' among the Bhils. Schemes are processed within routine departmental frameworks without concern for the target groups or their real needs.

It is extremely difficult to assess the extent of land alienation among the Bhils because transfers from tribal ownership to the landlords/money-lenders are never incorporated in land records. For example, in an investigation undertaken by a statistical assistant of the Tribal Research Institute in Udaipur, seven cases of illegal transfers from indebted tribals to money-lenders were noticed in Kanba village, Dungarpur, for which no official entries had been made. Once the land is mortgaged against security for a loan, the tribal becomes an agricultural labourer on his own land and *de facto* possession passes to the money-lender. One of the reasons for the poverty and consequent indebtedness of the area is the small size of the average holding among the Bhils and the lack of irrigation facilities. According to the *tehsildar* or circle revenue officer's records in Dungarpur, the average holding is three bighas in Rajasthan (2.2 bighas equals one acre), while fifteen bighas is considered an economic holding for a family of five. The average holding amongst the Bhils of Banswara, according to the Bench-Mark Survey, 1977, is 1.69 ha, while 60 per cent of their holdings range between 0.5 and 2 ha. Although according to the 1971 census 72.93 per cent of the Scheduled Tribe population of Banswara and 63.64 per cent of the Scheduled Tribe population of Dungarpur were classified as cultivators, the majority of such cultivators also work as agricultural labourers.

According to the 1971 census the Scheduled Tribe population of Dungarpur constituted 242,917 out of 337,480 people, or 71.9 per cent of the total population. In Banswara the figure for the Bhil population was 437,261 out of a population of 477,369 and constituted 91.6 per cent of the total population. In 1971 the literacy rate among the Bhils in Dungarpur was 6.8 per cent and 5.7 per cent in Banswara. However, even this compares favourably with the average Bhil literacy of 3.7 per cent. Among Bhil females it is still lower, as in Kushalgarh, Banswara, where it is reported to be 1.27 per cent. According to the 1981 census the populations of both districts have doubled to 680,865 in Dungarpur and 885,701 in Banswara. No further breakdown is yet available. At the most the tribal population could have increased by 2.5 per cent over a decade; therefore the only conclusion is that there has been a large influx of outsiders as a result of increased development activity. Thus the Bhils are being reduced to a minority, even in their last strongholds, with the added menace of further loss of their land to outsiders.

An important contributory factor to the growing impoverishment of the Bhils during the past thirty years has been the ruthless destruction of the forests and with it of the traditional tribal forest-based economy. According to the Project Report, Tribal Sub-Plan (1980–1985) for Banswara, out of a total forest area of 115, 468 ha, only 28,400 ha of wooded area remain. The report does not say over how many years this destruction was wrought. It is difficult to say who is responsible for this plunder. It is usual to blame the tribals for their improvidence but most field studies show that they are the least to blame, even if they actually work as woodcutters. It is usually as underpaid labour for exploitative contractors. The director of the voluntary organization, Seva Mandir, in Udaipur, who has been working with the Bhils since Independence, feels that a good deal of havoc was wrought by some of the petty princes and their feudal underlings about the time of the merger of their states with the Indian Union. They had no more interest in forest conservation at that time and auctioned off all the timber for immediate profit.

The Bhils have been hardest hit by the resulting devastation brought on their environment. Hurma Mangla Damor, distinguished by his white turban, is an elderly Bhil from Jalu Kuwa village, 20 km away from Dungarpur, the district capital. He remembers how twenty years ago the village was surrounded by thick jungle and tigers used to roam nearby. Manga Haru from the same village is busy executing traditional Bhil wood carvings on the beams of his house. He laments: 'I feel sad the jungle has gone. We have lost the animals, the grass and trees. We have lost wood for our houses, for our woodcarving and for our household crafts.' Today the vegetation around Jalu Kuwa is sparse and arid and villagers have to walk many miles to collect firewood.

The Bhils have had to adjust to the introduction of a monetized economy. There are still groups, however, who derive their main source of livelihood from the forest but because it is shrinking daily they are falling further and further below the poverty line. The Kathodi tribe near Gujarat earn their living from the forests for eight to ten months of the year. Today the chillum workers who migrated to South Rajasthan from Maharashtra fifty to sixty years ago have no employment because of massive deforestation. As a result of the destruction of the tribal economy thousands of Bhils come to Banswara and Dungarpur, the district capital, to seek work on daily wages, the only available, and return to their villages in the evening.

One reason for the poverty is the lack of a basic infrastructure in the region. In Dungarpur about 10 per cent of the cultivable land is irrigated, while in Banswara the figure is 13 per cent. In Banswara only 13 per cent of the total area is double cropped. In Dungarpur up to 1976/77 there were 17,299 wells out of which only 8,081 had water. Though according to the revenue record there are 18,342 wells in Banswara, only 8,644 are working; the other 9,698 are out of order, having insufficient water or no water. To resolve this problem deepening of wells is to be undertaken free of charge in both districts as most tribals are burdened with overdues. Moreover, out of 2,419 villages in Banswara only 256 had a double source of water, including wells, according to the 1977 Bench-Mark Survey for Banswara According to the same source 507 villages out of 2,419 are still to be provided with water. In Dungarpur up to 1981, 344 out of 834 villages were electrified and in Banswara, as of 31 December 1979, 410 out of 1,462 villages were electrified.

The aim of the Tribal Sub-Plans has been the removal of poverty and unemployment in a definite time frame by investing in agriculture and by improving the infrastructure, for example, by building dams and setting up industries. In this regard, as of 31 December 1978, 1,440 small and cottage industries had been registered in Banswara, providing 4,746 people with employment. It is estimated that 50 per cent of the Bhils live below the poverty line. Such schemes as the Integrated Rural Development Programme (IRDP) involve subsidized schemes to the tune of 50 per cent for tribals for digging wells, for pumpsets, bullocks, seeds and fertilizers, etc. Under the Training Rural Youth for Self-Employment (TRYSEM) scheme the Bhils are taught such skills as carpentry, *bidi* rolling, *durrie* making, etc. with the aim of doing away with underemployment and unemployment. Social forestry has also been taken up. When the IRDP was first started in 1978, only 58 families in two blocks in both districts were covered. In 1979/80 it was extended to 850 families in Dungarpur out of which 707 were Scheduled Tribes and 12 were Scheduled Caste families. In 1980/81, 1,556 families in all five blocks of Dungarpur were taken up, of which 986 were Scheduled Tribes and in 1981/82 3,000 families were to be benefited. The same scheme is supposed to be going on in Banswara.

From 1981/82 onwards under the same programme, six hundred of the poorest families in each block of both districts are to benefit from the schemes over a period of three years. The project involves land development, installation of pumpsets, animal husbandry programmes, TRYSEM, etc. The *gram sabha*, or village council, is to select the families, the criteria being landlessness or possession of a minuscule holding, no animals and an annual income of Rs 700 or less a year. Since 90 per cent of the Bhils find themselves in this position, competition for these programmes can only create divisions within Bhil society. Nani and her family, who are landless Bhils, are to be beneficiaries from 1982 onwards. For the past 13 years Nani has been working in an upper-caste household in Peeth, a large village with many brick houses and a busy bazaar area. Peeth was once part of a feudal estate before Independence. Nani, a dark, willowy woman, who was sweeping her masters' courtyard with a palm leaf when the author passed by, talked about her plight. She says she sweeps the courtyards, cleans out the cattle shed and does other menial tasks for Rs 50 a month in addition to receiving food and clothing. Her husband works as a sharecropper for one-fifth of the total produce. The agricultural extension worker said he thought this Bhil family had probably become indebted to this family 13 years ago and were probably still working to pay off the interest. Nani's case is a typical one as far as being a nominee for this government programme. No one, however, seems to have taken the trouble to consult her and work out in detail what practical help can be fitted into the scheme in order to increase her earning power.

Statistics showing the success of these programmes tell one story. Field tours of Dungarpur and Banswara reveal quite another picture. Firstly, if government programmes were having an impact on the countryside, the level of migration would be reduced. Yet the level of migration reported from every village visited is an indicator of the continuing distress in the area.

Traditional seasonal migration amongst the Bhils of this region has been intensified over the past fifteen years. Partly this is attributable to periodical droughts and resultant famine. Every third year is said to be a famine year, but between 1971 and 1980 there have been seven such years. In all the villages visited many people said one or two family members migrated every year. In Jogarimal, a remote village in Banswara near the Madhya Pradesh border, the *sarpanch*, or elected head of the village council, said there was hardly anyone in the village as one or two people from every household had gone to the adjoining state of Gujarat for two months. Other village members are working nearby on the Mahi dam site. Yet Food For Work Programmes (FFWP) were started in Banswara in 1978/79 while the district statistical officer, Banswara, maintains famine relief works started in November 1981 have benefited 4,834 people.

It would appear that, despite the fact that the Jogarimal area is one of the poorest in the district, it has been neglected in public work programmes. For even the sarpanch said one of the reasons for the high rate of migration was the absence of government relief programmes nearby. In the neighbouring village of Khotan, where the land is arid and the vegetation sparse, poverty is such that a lot of people migrate for seven months from November to June.

In Jalu Kuwa, a compact village near Dungarpur which seemed

comparatively well off, Manga Haru says: 'If there is no rain, we wander here and there.' In 1980 his family worked for Rs 5 daily wages in government relief works, raising stone boundaries in forests, and in soil conservation programmes. Havaji, a youth from the same village, has been migrating to Sabarkatha in Gujarat for the last four years as an agricultural labourer. Last year he went for two months and brought back Rs 300, earning Rs 5 daily. He built himself an unauthorized hut but did not suffer harassment by the police. Dhuli, with her crimson and yellow sari tucked in, petticoat-style, at her waist in the traditional Bhil manner, puts down the basket of manure she is carrying to her fields and joins in the conversation. She recalls earning 25 paise daily as a migrant labourer before 1947. According to the Social Work Research Centre, a voluntary organization, based at Mada in the same area, at least 60 per cent of working men and women in this region migrate for three to four months every year either to find work in the mills of Ahmedabad or as agricultural labourers.

Migration is also reported from mixed villages. Punja, a Scheduled Caste from Peeth, migrates to Gujarat annually as an agricultural labourer as 'there is a third crop in Gujarat'. Hujia, ex-sarpanch of Jorawar Pura, Dungarpur, belongs to a subcaste of the Bhils. His land yields only enough food for six months, so for four months he also migrates to Gujarat in the same capacity. Chokla, a Bhil from Dhelwara in Banswara, also migrates to Gujarat annually for three months.

Given the situation of dire poverty in both districts, the question arises as to what extent programmes like IRDP are helping to uplift or at least relieve the Bhils. Even though an actual daily wage is only Rs 5, it compares favourably with conditions in other states. But in Jalu Kuwa the Bhils said they had no belief in government programmes 'because there is no follow-up'. Dhula Gala, a middle-aged Bhil clad in a dhoti, wants a well but complains of the endless forms and formalities involved. 'All functionaries ask for bribes for doing this,' he complains. He recounts how one relative a few years back took out a Rs 5,000 loan and 'had to give Rs 1,000 to officials.' However, on the positive side, his family has obtained a loom through an Oxfam scheme with the help of the local Nehru Yuvak Kendra worker. The latter is a national government-sponsored youth organization. The SWRC at Mada provides them with raw material and markets their products. If they work eight hours a day, they can supplement their income by earning Rs 5–6 daily. This helps them as 'if nothing is grown in our fields, we need money to purchase ghee, cloth and salt in the market.'

His neighbour, Hurma Mangla Damor, has ten bighas of unirrigated land but has not applied for a loan for a well because of past bitter experience with government schemes. Five years back he took out a Rs 1,000 loan from the Bhumia Vikas Bank, or Land Development Bank, for purchasing bullocks. He claims he only received Rs 500 of the total amount, while the accounts recorded Rs 1,000 against his name. 'They told me they would give me the other half but never did,' he says. Meantime he has been made liable for the whole amount as the subsidy element of the scheme does not seem to have been operative at the time to cover the balance.

A recent corruption case at the local cooperative covering seventeen villages in the area was very much on the villagers' mind. In 1981 the chairman, Valama Labana, and secretary, Bala Vira, were suspended for signing up for loans under unsuspecting villagers' names. The false loans were obtained by collecting thumb impressions from any villager and presenting the forms to the bank for approval. Two years or so later many such villagers were confronted with repayment schedules.

Banswara district appeared to be far behind Dungarpur in on-going government schemes. Most villagers had never even hears of the IRDP schemes. At Dhelwara, the headman, Mogji, a fine-featured man from a dominant peasant caste of Gujarat, knew nothing about various programmes, as was the case with other villagers. In Jogarimal, whose only source of drinking water is a stream which dries up in periods of drought, no one seemed to know about TRYSEM or social forestry schemes and reported that no agricultural extension workers had even visited their village the preceding year. 'If we apply for seeds and fertilizers, the assistance only comes when the crop is ripe,' was the recurrent complaint. They claimed there was nothing in the cooperative when anything was required. They did know about subsidized loans for bullocks but had not applied for any. No one had ever explained anything to them regarding short-term loans from the cooperatives: 'We have never seen the face of a village-level worker.'

In the adjoining village, Khotan, Tejiya, an elderly Bhil, says he obtained a pump, which irrigates his three bighas, from the cooperative. He has to repay the loan over a period of five years and reports that he was 'just given the pumpset and told the conditions.' The dealer obtained it from the cooperative and presented him with the papers on which to place his thumb impression. 'I sign whatever papers they give me,' he says. He said he knew about the TRYSEM scheme but was not interested in it.

Proposals have apparently been prepared and submitted for social forestry programmes but so far 'nothing has happened.' On the positive side Khotan may soon be supplied with drinking water, as in 1981 investigations were undertaken, and in April 1982 drilling machines boring wells were operating in the area.

The same story is repeated at Ghantali, a remote area near the border with Madhya Pradesh which is inhabited almost entirely by Bhils. According to the director of the Social Work Research Centre at Ghantali, which has been working with the Bhils for about five years, the TRYSEM scheme has completely failed. In 1981 during April, May and June some Bhils were persuaded to stay and not migrate for work, so as to be trained for self-employment under TRYSEM. Despite repeated requests at several echelons by SWRC for the tribals to receive payment on time 'to stop them from starving', payment only materialized six months later, in December. This dooms TRYSEM since other tribals 'will never be persuaded to join the programme the following year,' reports Srilata Swaminathan, the director of this SWRC centre. As for the local LAMP cooperative: 'It is always shut or out of stock at the proper time, so the Bhils have to go to the traders and pay higher prices.'[1] The social forestry programmes in Ghantali have so far failed 'because saplings which are supposed to arrive at the outset of the monsoon instead come in October when there isn't any rain.'

In fact, Bhils at Jalu Kuwa said they thought government programmes had only benefited non-tribals. This is confirmed by N.N. Vyas, Principal, Tribal Research Institute, Udaipur: 'Generally it is the non-tribals or the influential tribal minority who grab the facilities.' If a handpump is to be installed, 'the sarpanch or landlord wants it near his house so the tribal might have to walk two kilometres to fetch water.'[2] Seva Mandir, a voluntary organization based in Udaipur is headed by a Gandhian of Nehru's generation. He feels that government programmes are having little impact in tribal areas. K.L. Kothari, an anthropologist from the district capital of Dungarpur who has carried out studies on the Bhils in the region, claims the caste Hindus are the indirect beneficiaries from programmes 'due to cash payments in the form of bribes.'[3]

N.N. Vyas' contention is borne out at the grass roots. The one village visited where programmes were in evidence was in the large and thriving mixed village, Mandla, near the Gujarat border in Dungarpur district. It is evident that the Patidars and Patels, both upper landholding castes who originally come from Gujarat, were the greatest beneficiaries, although the Bhils and lower castes were also reaping some benefits from the government schemes.

Motu is a tall fine-looking man, typical of his caste, the Patidars, who are known for their skills as cultivators. Motu has a lift irrigation system costing Rs 30,000 which he obtained through a long-term loan from the Primary Land Development Bank. Altogether there are 28 lift irrigation systems in Mandla belonging mostly to the Patidars. Ram Lal Nanalal, another Patidar, with 40 bighas of land, ten of which are irrigated, has his own lift irrigation system. He obtains three crops a year from his land as a few years back, thanks to a World Bank Programme, he started cultivating summer groundnut as a cash crop. Being a wealthy landowner he has no trouble repaying the loans for fertilizer and seeds to the cooperative at 6.5 per cent interest per annum.

In contrast, Heera Dhai and Kaja Bhai, darker and wiry, are Damars, a sub-caste of Bhils, who also live in Mandla. They own two acres of land, one of which is irrigated from a well they own jointly with three other farmers. They also work as agricultural labourers and depend on government relief programmes during the lean season. Both said during the last season they had taken seeds and fertilizers on credit from the LAMP cooperative and as a result their yield had increased. They are subsidized to the tune of 50 per cent for tribals but, being a short-term loan, if they fail to repay the balance with 6.5 per cent interest after the first season, they cannot obtain another loan for the following year.

While the tribals recount tale after tale of corruption and incompetence, the district administration have their own story to tell. The manager of the Central Cooperative Bank, Dungarpur, which has 32 PAK cooperatives under it, talks about the problems of recovery. From July 1980 to 31 March 1982 the rate of recovery on loans from all castes was 22 per cent. The situation is such that, at present, the Reserve Bank of India is considering writing off tribals' overdue loans from cooperatives up to Rs 500 and advancing them interest-free ten-year term loans. This loan would go toward repayment of overdues to enable them to avail themselves of the facilities of future loans and to repay the new loans in easy instalments. It seems even the minimum assets required for short and medium-term loans (the bank does not give long-term loans) do not seem to provide the bank with a solid guarantee. The borrower must have at least ten bighas to qualify for a well, five bighas for bullocks, but no land is required for sheep and goats as these are self-perpetuating units.

In Khotan the sarpanch admitted that villagers in general were defaulters on loans and therefore could no longer obtain loans the subsidies. According to N.N. Vyas, Tribal Research Institute (TRI), Udaipur, more than 70 per cent of tribals in Dungarpur and Banswara are defaulters on cooperative loans. Thus they cannot obtain government loans as they have to obtain no-due certificates. N.N. Vyas maintains that a tribal who defaults on a short-term loan will obtain a medium-term loan out of which he will pay half as adjustment against the last loan. 'Now the stage has come where tribals find it difficult to obtain loans,' says N.N. Vyas. One reason for the large-scale defaulting is the mechanical pursuance of the programme merely to fulfil targets. He further comments: 'An agent approaches the tribal and gives him a loan, although he doesn't want it.'

Many times diesel pumps will be installed for a few minutes and then removed, just to fulfil paper targets, according to S.N. Samadani, a researcher at the TRI, Udaipur. The tribal does not need the pump as he does not have the economic viability. Moreover, S.M. Samadani raises the question as to the reason why the subsidized pumpset costs more than the current open market price. As for the subsidy element for the pumpset: 'Fifty per cent of the loan is disbursed and the agent keeps the balance,' asserts N.N. Vyas.

All this has resulted only in landing the Bhils into still deeper trouble. In Dungarpur there are thousands of cases of summons on various points relating to outstanding debts on government loans. The money-lender comes into the picture to repay these loans, when in fact these loans were designed to assist the tribal to become independent of the money-lender. If a co-operative society begins a 'one-hundred-per-cent recovery' campaign, N.N.

Vyas maintains the tribal is trapped in a vicious circle as often the later will have to mortgage his land to the money-lender to repay such loans.

According to the Block Development Officer (BDO), Dungarpur, often no water is struck in the well but the tribal is still liable for the loan. Furthermore, at the time of digging the well, they cannot obtain a blasting unit as they are all engaged. According to the BDO, both government programmes and the cooperative movement are 'a one-hundred-per-cent failure in Dungarpur because the Bhils are one-hundred-per-cent defaulters.' He cites the example of the bullock programme. Since most Bhils obtain one crop a year, the bullocks are not required for a good part of the year. But they still have to feed them, although they cannot be put to other use. Since no regular working capital is generated, the tribal is never in a position to repay the loan.

Fulia is an elderly Bhil from Chikli village in the western part of Banswara. The poverty of the area is attested to by the fact that large families of Bhils can be seen gathering products from the forest to stave off hunger. Fulia says he is not interested in loans, as these have to be repaid, only in subsidies. He says he prefers government loans to village money-lenders but complains: 'Government attempts at recovery are too strong.' He was forthright in admitting that he was not in the habit of repaying loans and said: 'We have to face a lot of difficulties in getting and paying back loans.'

The present system of loans and subsidies was designed to do away with the cruel exploitation by money-lenders, but in fact the opposite seems to be happening. Mathu, a Bhil, with eight bighas, took out a Rs 1,000 loan for fertilizer but says: 'We have to borrow from the moneylenders to repay government loans so there is no security.' Punja, a Scheduled Caste, from Peeth village also admitted borrowing from the money-lender to pay back the first instalment on a well. Since he had failed to pay the first instalment he incurred an 18-per-cent-penalty interest on the instalment due.

This is confirmed in a study made by S.N. Samadani in a paper of the TRI, Udaipur, entitled 'Alienation of Tribal Land and Prospects for Remedial Measures' (1980). The paper states that, in Kanba village, Dungarpur, where the study was carried out, 'Whenever institutional agencies take some strict action against the defaulters, the tribal debtors borrow money from the local money-lenders. This vicious circle aggravates the problems of land alienation as the land is continually mortgaged to money-lenders and such transactions are not recorded anywhere except in the bahis (registers) of the money-lenders.'

In fact, there does not seem to be any evidence of a significant decrease in dependence on traditional sources of borrowing. According to the 1977 Bench-Mark Survey for Banswara, about 51.9 per cent of tribal families surveyed, or 33,328 out of 64,227, were indebted to traditional money-lenders, traders, landowners and others, while 47.1 per cent of tribal families, or 30,899, were indebted to banks, cooperatives and to the government.

The 'irresponsibility of the tribal' towards government loans is borne out by several officials and academicians. According to the Additional Magistrate, Banswara, tribal defaulters take loans in other family members' names. According to R.S. Mann, an anthropologist from the Anthropological Survey of India (ASI), Dungarpur, government loans are used for death feasts. K.L. Kothari, anthropologist, maintains that 'if a tribal gets a cash loan more than fifty per cent goes for marriages or feasts.' Om Srivastava, deputy director, Seva Mandir, Udaipur, says the Bhils often sold their pumps because they were not economically viable.

On the other hand, officials also admit the existence of corruption in the administration. The Additional Magistrate, Banswara, estimates that five to ten paise in every rupee reaches the grass roots, an estimate concurring with that of the director, SWRC, Ghantali. K.L. Kothari's estimate is Rs 30–40 out of Rs 100. S.S. Pandhya, Nehru Yuvak Kendra worker in Dungarpur, thinks 60 to 80 per cent of wells are not completed or there is insufficient water for irrigation. According to Om Srivastava, Seva Mandir, the tribal has to obtain a certificate in order to receive the final instalment for the well. Om Srivastava maintains the bank official only agrees to come to the village in return for a bribe.

The BDO, Dungarpur, describes the 'typical situation' prevailing amongst the Bhils in the district. Most are agricultural labourers, even if they possess small holdings, so they have no time to dig a well on their land. Indeed many may not even qualify for a loan because of their minuscule plots. Even if a Bhil possesses two acres of land with a well, his holdings are often scattered on undulating ground, therefore water from the well cannot be taken to all the plots. Since most holdings produce only one crop a year, the yield suffices for barely three months. This traps the Bhils in a permanent cycle of borrowing and indebtedness to the local money-lender who lends him grain for nine months of the year, often at 100-per-cent interest. The level of indebtedness is confirmed by R.S. Mann: 'Often, all that they raise on their land goes towards paying off debts.'

According to a Lead Bank Survey Report, Rajasthan has the highest number of money-lenders in the country amounting to 15.08 per cent of the total. The Dungarpur tribal district alone accounts for 8.9 per cent of the total licensed money-lenders in the state, although it contains only two per cent of the state population. According to a report of the Agricultural Survey, 1972, out of 660 families surveyed in the region, 538, or 81.52 per cent, were indebted.

In his book, *Bondage and Exploitation in Tribal India*, N.N. Vyas thinks that new employment opportunities in 'government relief works, migration to Gujarat and a general awakening' have broken down the former dependence on the village and that bonded labour is not as pervasive as before. On the other hand, the introduction of cash crops has not changed the extent of exploitation since a new form of 'bondage has emerged in the form of sharecropping'. In twelve villages in Dungarpur, revisited in 1976 after an eleven-year hiatus, the study found that in some cases bonded labour was being replaced by daily wage payment for labour. From the bonded labourer's own statements this is a negative development, since he loses the security on which he had come to depend. In fact, the study concludes that one of the reasons bonded labour is continuing in both districts, despite the 1975 Amendment to the Rajasthan Sagri (Bonded Labour) System Abolition Act, is precisely because 'ties of security are assured'.

Independent attempts to assess the extent of bonded labour proved futile because Bhils will rarely reveal their plight on account of their dependence on the money-lender in times of distress. In all the villages everyone vehemently denied the existence of bonded labour, while money-lenders, as for example in Peeth, refused to be interviewed. The director, SWRC, Ghantali, however, thinks land alienation through mortgage transfers is very high. As for the existence of bonded labour, the director asserts: 'The Bhils are born in debt and die in debt.'

The foremost exploiter for the Bhils is the police official.

According to Bhils interviewed at Ghantali, the police beat up tribals on any pretext. 'They threaten to arrest them, making up laws as they go along to extract money, chickens, goats, etc., knowing that the tribal will do anything to avoid jail,' says the director, SWRC, Ghantali.

The main reason for the tribals' vulnerability is their general state of illiteracy and ignorance. Government programmes like the National Adult Education Programme (NAEP), launched by the Janata Government in October 1978, was declared a dismal failure in its attempt to raise the level of literacy in the country-side. Apart from the operational and administrative flaws, the task is complicated by the attitudes and problems of villagers which are rarely understood by planners. Age group differences among class attendants can lead to conflicts. Illiterate men and women who in daily life enjoy the community's respect, despite their lack of education, suddenly find themselves sitting with and being instructed by people younger than themselves. When such men and women participate in the NAEP, they naturally feel their status is being undermined. Seva Mandir, which was involved in implementing the programme, thinks that functional literacy classes are not enough. According to Om Srivastava: 'If there is to be a social benefit, literacy must mean bringing people into the process of development.'

Even the present educational system fails to do this, one prime example being the level of educated unemployed in the country. One of the few tribal boys from Jalu Kuwa who has completed high school, for example, cannot find work so he is employed in the Adult Education Centre of the Nehru Yuvak Kendra in the village. In fact, one can argue that the present kind of education being inculcated has a negative social impact. The peasant boy who attends primary school refuses to touch the plough, regarding it as beneath him to do so and he 'forgets to pay respect to his father.' Yet he cannot obtain employment.

This is what Om Srivastava calls 'skin deep modernity'. To illustrate his point, he recounts an incident that occurred at a *mela*, or local gathering, in Kherwara, Banswara, a few years back. Seva Mandir has put up an exhibit showing the kind of work the organization was doing in the area. One social worker had taped a lot of traditional Bhil and other tribal songs and proceeded to play them over the loudspeaker. According to Om Srivastava, several Bhils were angered by this reminder of their cultural identity: 'We don't want to go back to that,' they told him. Similarly, during the nocturnal festivities preceding the marriage of the young girl, Miraka Damor, in Jalu Kuwa, it was evident that the boys, who were all school-going, were losing their cultural roots as they were unable to perform traditional Bhil dances.

The Bhils are not only losing their cultural roots under the impact of the modernization process; even the traditional Bhil councils, or *gametis*, have been undermined since their replacement in 1958 by the introduction of the statutory panchayat raj, or three-tier system of self-government.

The failure of government to take the traditional institutions into their confidence has undoubtedly contributed to the failure of government programmes. According to N.N. Vyas, the Bhils' attitude towards government schemes is one of 'non-participation and non-response'. This is hardly surprising since, even in mixed villages with a Bhil majority, the leadership is often non-tribal, as is the case in Dhelwara, Banswara, where the sarpanch is a Patel, a higher caste, although 90 per cent of the village is tribal.

Several dams are under construction as part of the development plans for the region. Ironically such schemes are supposed to bring economic benefits to the tribals but the impact of such projects is generally adverse. The most controversial scheme in the region is the Mahi dam presently under construction in Banswara. The project involves two masonry dams across the Mahi river and 578 km of canal system. Thirty-five thousand people will be affected and 93 villages in Rajasthan and 23 in Madhya Pradesh will be submerged, some only partially; 19,124 acres of private land will be submerged. The project will generate 140,000 megawatts and will irrigate 200,000 ha in Gujarat and only 80,000 ha in Rajasthan. As one official put it: 'Banswara will be the sacrificial lamb for Gujarati agriculture.'

Since the cost-benefit considerations of building the dam are such that the premium value of water is very high, therefore in purely economic terms it is obvious that, from the Mahi dam's inception, the capitalist agriculture of neighbouring Gujarat and the Patels and Patidars owning the best land in Banswara are to be the main beneficiaries. The tribals are supposed to receive land in the command area but N.N. Vyas maintains that the process of alienation gets under way precisely as lands develop in the command area of a dam, when land purchases in benami transactions begin. To support his claim N.N. Vyas says alienation is much higher in villages where irrigation has been developed in the past ten to fifteen years. 'All this alienation cannot be quantified on the basis of official data because on official records they are low,' according to S.N. Samadani, TRI, Udaipur.

As for the compensation paid to the tribals for the loss of land to any dam project, the director, SWRC, Ghantali, states that the tribals are 'very lucky' if they actually received Rs 1,000 as compensation for their land 'when they should receive Rs 32,000.' As one example, the social worker cites the accident which killed two Bhils while working at the Mahi dam site. Their families were awarded Rs 10,000 but they barely received Rs 1,000.

The measure of a programme's success can be gauged by responses at the grass roots. In different villages in both districts reactions were generally negative. According to the sarpanch at Jogarimal, Banswara: 'In twenty years there has been no change in the level of poverty. Our clothing is better but our food is worse. Many people are starving as they only get one meal a day.' For Dhuli, an elderly Bhil lady from Jalu Kuwa, Dungarpur, government programmes do not appear to have made any impact: 'The best things that has happened since Independence is that *begar*, or forced labour, has been abolished.' In Khotan and Jogarimal, two adjoining villages where the land seemed especially arid, everyone unanimously agreed that they wanted irrigation most of all. The sarpanch of Khotan, Banswara, said that, if any kind of government programme was in progress to provide local irrigation: 'I will work for less than the prescribed wages as the project will bring so much benefit to everyone.'

It would appear from the villagers' response that planned change has not brought about any significant improvement in living standards. An officer of the Tribal Development Commissioner's Office, Udaipur, makes a similar assessment. He maintains that the qualify of life for the Bhils seems to have deteriorated over the past twenty years. The official admitted that, because of the depressed economic situation, the area has a great potential for Naxalism because of the level of migration from villages to the mills of Ahmedabad where political awareness is strong. According to an independent academic source in Udaipur, there have already been minor incidents involving Naxalites in Dungarpur, but these have been hushed up by the district administration.

What is needed is a reassessment by the government of the underlying premise behind planning for development and a new approach governing implementation in the field. Many of the programmes are in themselves excellent, but only officials who are truly interested in uplifting the rural areas should be placed in charge. Above all, they must be supported when, in implementing declared governmental policies for weaker sections, they disturb, as they inevitably must, the exploitative power structure which dominates the rural areas and controls the vote banks. If few individuals can be found who dare to do so, it is a commentary on the lack of training, posting or orientation programmes for attitudinal change. There is increasing evidence that 'tribal development' founders not on the 'tribal problem' but on the problem of the exploitative vested interests and their attitudes of disdain. At least equal attention needs to be paid in rational planning towards reeducating the 'stronger' sections of society as towards uplifting the rural poor. There must also be better coordination between departments, and villagers should be made to feel they are participants in their own future. Before this can happen and before development programmes can yield positive results, functional literacy and education to awaken awareness must prevail. Surely in all the model textbooks of the Central Department of Education one simple arithmetic lesson could be founded on the daily statutory minimum wage of an agricultural labourer or the criminality of denying access of a Harijan to a village well. Only in such ways can corruption and exploitation be reduced and evolutionary social and economic change be ensured.

The question remains regarding the dichotomy of intention. There is growing realization of another reality behind the programmes: a limited aim of merely defusing incipient unrest by the exploited, while at the same time cultivating the elements who determine the power structure and are themselves the exploiters. Can such a 'synthesis' in policy really restore 'harmony' in society?

CHAPTER ELEVEN

Losers in the assimilation process: the tribals of Chotanagpur

'An inferiority complex runs in our blood,' says Father Albinus Minz, a Roman Catholic priest from the Oraon tribe of Chotanagpur and a practising lawyer of Ranchi. He would trace the Hindu perception of the autochthone as an outcaste from the times of the earliest Aryan invasions into the subcontinent which he claims pushed the aborigine further and further into the forests, into pockets of isolation, as the Hindu kingdoms expanded and developed into centralized states. However, there is considerable evidence to show that there are many strong tribal bloodlines in the various Kshatriya dynasties in the first millennium AD and even earlier. But the fact that many aboriginal chieftains and their followers felt it necessary to 'achieve' Kshatriya status and a revised ancestry traced back to reputedly Aryan lineages by the Brahmin preceptors shows that even then there was a sense of inferiority which had somehow been inculcated in them.

The tribal problem today, as it presents itself in South Bihar in its dual interrelated aspects of erosion of tribal culture, mainly from industrialization and the problem of assimilation into the mainstream through the very bottom of the caste system, reflects a worsening of the tribal position socially and economically in relation to the dominant castes and classes. For previously, as D.D. Kosambi has shown, many Rajput families had a tribal ancestry. According to this source, a tribal chieftain would feel intellectually inferior to the Brahmin priest meditating in the forest and would often adopt him as a preceptor and fountainhead of the modern knowledge of the day. The situation of the tribals in South Bihar may even be worse today in comparison to earlier times because, contrary to what Father Minz believes, the tribals were never classified hierarchically, since they were never considered part of the Hindu social system. In fact the tribals were left much to themselves until the advent of the British when the capitalist economy brought the contractor and money-lender into the forest and this contact with a more advanced mode of production doomed the more primitive tribal way of life, as Kosambi has shown.

The history of the Chotanagpur Hills since the British began administering the areas in the late 18th century has been one marked by resistance and rebellion from the tribals, particularly the Hos. Several agrarian revolts took place in 1831–32, the Santhal Rebellion occurred in 1857 and the Kol rebellion among numerous others. All of those revolts were directed against the 'dikus', or outsiders, who had entered the areas as money-lenders, businessmen and officials. It was also during this period that the demand for a Jharkhand state, which was again being vociferously revived in 1980, developed and in the 1840s the Lutheran missionaries were actually fighting alongside the tribals for a state of their own.

At the time of the reorganization of the Indian State, the break-up of the Chotanagpur Hills to make up four other states is viewed by some educated tribals as a deliberate step by the politicians in 1954 to prevent the tribals from consolidating themselves. Since then the government has adopted a systematic policy of colonizing the area to bring the percentage of tribals down through construction of industries and importation of a workforce from outside, as well as through the appointment of officials from North Bihar. Even business and trade are almost entirely run by traditional merchant groups like the Marwaris and Gujaratis. Twenty-five years ago the percentage of tribals in Ranchi district was 52 per cent but in 1980 it was 48 per cent. Comparison of the 1961 and 1971 censuses shows a decline in the tribal population of all six districts of South Bihar, the greatest fall in the percentage of tribal population occurring in Dhanbad where it fell from 61.61 per cent to 58.08 per cent.

Dhanbad is the most industrialized area in Bihar and the Bokaro steel plant, which supplies 25 per cent of the coking coal in India, is the biggest steel plant in Asia. The fact that the biggest decline in the percentage of the tribal population in relation to the total population took place here proves the Marxist MP, A.K. Roy's contention that the large industries, both public and private, are bringing in outsiders at all levels and the tribals do not even constitute 50 per cent of the unskilled labour force, despite being expropriated of their lands to make way for these industries.

According to A.K. Roy, who has been elected from the Dhan-bad constituency, Bharat Cooking Coal Ltd (BCCL) dismissed 6,753 casual labourers between 1 March 1977 and 1 January 1981, while the managerial and supervisory staff increased from 22,749 to 23,557 for the same period, and the time-rated staff also increased from 53,900 to 61,819. This retrenchment of labour has been due to mechanization in the nationalized coal industry. Despite the creation of skilled jobs on account of the mechanization none of the weaker sections were trained for the jobs, but between 1 April 1977 and 1 April 1980, when mech-anization was completed, according to figures from a review by the Ministry of Energy on the Rajadhyaksha Committee Report, 8,380 casual labourers were retrenched. But during 1980–81 almost the same number of extra staff were hired on piece rates to man the mechanized coal mines. A.K. Roy feels that these figures represent the replacement of poorer weaker sections of society, predominantly Harijans/Adivasis by more dominant castes, favoured by the officers.

The first workers in the South Bihar coal mines after Inde-pendence were tribals and semi-tribals, who generally worked in the unskilled mining jobs, together with weaker sections from other states, especially from eastern UP and western Bihar. However, when some of the facilities increased, safety measures developed, job pay increases occurred and mechanization started, other higher-caste people began pushing for the jobs and removing the unskilled labour. Even today not a single executive position in any industry or mining enterprise is held by any tribal man or woman.

Over the past three years there appears to have been abuse of rules in the coalmines of Coke and Coal Limited (CCL) at Hazaribagh and Kuju in the number of persons replaced under a special scheme whereby sons and sons-in-law of Harijans or Adivasis have a right to the job of the relative retiring. At Hazaribagh out of 268 persons retired between 1978 and 1980, 80 were replaced by non-Harijans and non-Adivasis who were appointed as 'dependents' of Harijans and Adivasis. In Kuju, out of 602 persons retired, 112 of those replaced were non-Harijans/non-Adivasis, appointed as dependents of Harijans and Adivasis. If these 'dependents' were sons-in-law, one cannot but suspect large-scale marriages of convenience or wonder how long these lasted before the Harijan/Adivasi wives were abandoned after the jobs were secured.

The large-scale concentration of heavy and light industries, mines and coalfields in South Bihar has meant that there has been an acceleration in the erosion of the tribal culture compared to other tribal areas of India, for example, Koraput district, Orissa or Bastar, Madhya Pradesh. The primitive and the modern world, which has doomed the tribes of Chotanagpur, coexist side by side in Jamshedpur, with its giant steel mill. Near the steel plant, hallmark of twentieth-century progress, tribal women can be seen putting dung patties to dry on walls of urban hovels. In October 1980 lepers were living in tents nearby. With large-scale expropriation of land for the construction of industrial complexes, the great influx of outsiders from North Bihar and other states and the domination of Marwaris and Gujaratis in trade and commerce, the tribals and Scheduled Castes, which together comprise 42 per cent of the population of Chotanagpur, have been deteriorating steadily in numbers over the years as the industrial sector, the most concentrated in the country, has been expanding rapidly. Giant projects in the area consume the majority of the electricity while only ten per cent is available to the local inhabitants for domestic consumption. The level of rural electrification, amounting to five per cent, is the lowest in the country.

While the government's developmental efforts in the region have been almost nil, the expropriation of tribal land has proceeded apace unabated. In 1943, 293 acres out of 643 acres of Adivasis' family land at Rajhanka village in Singhbum were expropriated to build a cement factory. Although some compensation and some factory jobs were given at the time, 33 years later, despite all the government welfare schemes for tribals, no one in the village has benefited from them so as to qualify for white-collar or skilled labour employment at the factory. Sikhs on motorbikes and other 'outsiders' can be seen around the factory. The latter is ruining the rest of the village land by the effluence of white smoke from its chimneys which settles on vegetation for a few kilometres around.

To build the public-sector complex, the Heavy Electrical Corporation (HEC) in Ranchi, 20,000 tribals were uprooted, no adequate compensation was paid and of those promised jobs only about 50 per cent received appointment. The project was completed in 1959 when about 16,000 workers from South India and

West Bengal were brought in to fill the managerial, technical and skilled jobs. The tribals received no compensation for their land when it was expropriated in 1954 as HEC construction began, but only after three massive demonstrations were organized before the HEC office in January 1962, May 1967 and January 1976, over 16 years later. According to Dr S. Mukherjee, a well-informed citizen of Ranchi, with a social conscience, the Adivasi families each received only Rs 800 – 1,000 for their land. According to N.E. Horo, leader of the Jharkhand Party, HEC has expropriated thousands of acres which he claims will remain unutilized over the next 50 years. Some of the land is in Palamau and Hazaribad. D. Minz of Ranchi claims no record exists of the resettlement of expropriated tribals and many go deeper into the jungles, as has happened in Palamau, east of Chandwa.

In fact, instead of improving, the situation of the tribal population situation appears to be getting worse. After the nationalization of the coalfields in 1971, there was a large-scale retrenchment of unskilled labour and in a single week 50,000 Adivasis and other weaker sections lost their jobs and were replaced by people mainly from the Bhojpur region of North Bihar. During the 'efficiency drive', enjoined during the Emergency, thousands in mines were retrenched and, with rare exceptions, they were all Adivasis or Harijans, an example of how directives from above are perverted into exploitative trends at lower levels.

Since the nineteenth century when the British began exploiting the forest wealth of Chotanagpur, the tribals have, little by little, had their land encroached upon. With the introduction of the capitalist economy the British allowed money-lenders and contractors to enter tribal areas to exploit forest resources. Various devices were used to deprive them of their land.

So much land was being alienated from tribals to money-lenders and contractors that the British passed the Chotanagpur Tenancy Act, 1916, which forbade any tribal land being sold without the consent of the Deputy Commissioner. But means were devised to evade the law through 'collusive title suits'. In 1969 the Chotanagpur Tenancy Act was amended by the Land Restoration Regulation under which any land alienated in the 30 years up to 1969 in violation of the Chotanagpur Tenancy Act would be restored to the tribals if the latter applied for restoration in the courts. The courts have begun restoring some land alienated by money-lenders, contractors and other outsiders, but due to flaws in the law, after lower courts had restored land, many parties appealed to higher courts. According to a report in the *Statesman*, dated 31 August 1980, out of 40,000 petitions disposed of in Bihar nearly 16,000 went against the tribals. In fact, despite this Act, expropriation of land continues unabated. In Ranchi itself tribal land is being acquired by the government for the building of residential houses for the employees of the public-sector enterprises. A confidential document of the Home Ministry states quite frankly: 'In some cases land has been requisitioned for one purpose and used for another; in some others, land much in excess of the requirements of a project was acquired.'

About 1905, when the Land Survey was made, most of the forest areas were under tribal occupation. Later, when the Indian Forest Act was passed, most of the areas were taken over by the Forest Department. As more and more areas are auctioned off to forest contractors and with the loss of curtailing of traditional rights to use the forest for firewood, hunting and gathering of produce, the tribals have become poorer and poorer and sunk deeper into debt.

The Forest Department is in fact the tribals' main enemy as it is slowly strangling the Adivasis to death. Most of the forest areas in Singhbum were under sal trees which provided the tribals with fruits and seeds, their main source of nutrition in times of famine. But the forests are now being cleared by the Forest Department to plant teak for a World Bank Project. Worse still, most of the villages in the forest area around Gua and Singhbum are not revenue villages and therefore not under blocks. Thus they cannot get loans or development aid and find themselves at the mercy of the Forest Department.

While the tribals are accused of destroying the forest and illegally chopping down trees, huge parcels of land are expropriated for mining purposes. In Saranda can be found the best sal forest in Asia which the Adivasis have been accused of destroying. But 7,000 ha of their land has been taken for two big iron-ore projects at Kiriburu and Meghatuburu and 'allotted' and another 300 ha have been taken over for the depositing of iron tailings, a scheme that will pollute the tribals' drinking water and further denude the forests.

The Divisional Forest Officer has certain quasi-judicial powers regarding complaints of illegal tree felling. But contractors are rarely fined. If caught they have little difficulty in paying the fines. But thousands of tribals are caught and fined or jailed for forest offences every year, simply because the forest has been their means of livelihood for centuries. Worse still, in view of the loss of forest, is the government's refusal to concede the tribals' demand for the release of portions of forest land for agricultural purposes. With the whole machinery of the state against them, the tribals are waging a losing battle with the Forest Department. Documents released by the Janata Ministry in 1978 list about 50,000 cases of forest offences by tribals of which 45,000 were finally dismissed. About 1,000 tribals were in jail at the time, half of them being Pahadias of Santhal Parganas. This whole state of affairs is not unknown to government and is indeed reflected in their own officers' reports. One such report of a senior officer stated: 'The contact at the level of forest division had been very unhealthy so far as the tribes are concerned. The agencies the tribesmen have come in contact with not only take away their material wealth but also exploit the tribal men and women morally and psychologically.'[1]

Denied their traditional rights to the forest, landless, the tribal has been forced to fell trees for the contractors for a pittance merely to survive. The government gives contracts to fell areas where trees are old but the Marwari contractors tell the tribals to cut trees in other areas in Singhbum and to bring the trees to the areas assigned by the government. This is done in collusion with government officials who are paid off, according to an independent Tamil source in Chaibasa.

About three years ago, partly for economic reasons, the tribals of Singhbum began going back deep into the forests to their ancestral graves from where they had been moved by the British in the last century and resettled in villages on the outskirts of the forest. After their return there they began cutting the trees and claiming the land as their own and at this point the contractors began encouraging the tribals to cut more trees for money, according to this same Tamil source. In this way millions of rupees of timber were cut down. Such acts can only be regarded as self-destructive because sal trees take twenty years to grow. Many have begun abusing their collective tribal right, *khunt katti*, to land which belongs to the clan or village. Since they are apprehensive that one day they will find the Forest Department cutting down trees on this land, they themselves cut them for fear that they will lose everything. On the train platform at Ranchi, between 5 and 6 a.m., many tribal women, or 'headloaders', carrying bundles of firewood can be seen. Four to five sticks sell for two rupees and they have to bribe the police on the platform with 10 or 20 paise for each headload. Sometimes these women have to travel as much as 50 to 60 km every other day. Another problem afflicting the Hos of Singhbum, the main tribal group there, is the division of family land among sons causing fragmentation of land and making them almost landless. Their destitution is such that a weakening of the Ho family unit is occurring, as many can no longer afford a traditional marriage ceremony and take to casual affairs started at weekly markets.

The 31 different tribal groups of South Bihar are heterogeneous, both ethnically and in their mixed levels of economic advancement. While most of the tribes such as the Mundas, Hos and more primitive tribes are of Austric stock, the Oraon language belongs to the Dravidian family. While there are eight primitive tribes in Chotanagpur, some at the food-gathering stage, at the other extreme are the Christianized tribals, mainly Oraons and Mundas of Ranchi or the Santhals of Santhal-Parganas who are now largely settled agriculturalists. The eight primitive tribes are the Asurs and Birjiyas of Netarhat, the Birhors of Hazaribad, the Mal Paharias and Sauria Paharias of Santhal Parganas, the Hill Kharias of Singhbum and the Korwas and Parahiyas of Palamau.

The influence of the Christian missionaries on the tribals of Ranchi district, where the majority of the missionary educational work was concentrated, has been a progressive one for the tribals. Most of the reservation quotas for the Scheduled Tribes are being filled by the Christianized tribals of Ranchi as opposed, for example, to the more backward Hos of Singhbum district where missionary activity was never strong. Out of 300,000 Catholics in Chotanagpur, 200,000 are Oraon and 50,000 are Munda, the rest mainly Kharias, whilst out of 65,000 Anglicans, 45,000 are Munda and out of 150,000 Lutherans the majority are Munda.

The Jesuits have been responsible for building up the institutional infrastructure of the Catholic missionaries as it stands today, which the editor of the *New Republic*, the main Ranchi English daily, refers to as an 'empire'. The Catholic tribals can borrow money from the Catholic Cooperative, a credit society, which has a capital of Rs 30 million. It was founded in 1908 by one of the greatest of the Jesuit missionaries, Father John Hoffman, who is also the author of the classic multi-volume work on the Mundas, the *Encyclopedia Mundarica*. The cooperative society functions in all the parishes and each village unit has several members. Although the bank's director is a Jesuit, 'it is the money of the aborigines', according to one Jesuit missionary.

However, the influence of the missionaries is resented by many caste Hindus who claim that it is preventing a rapprochement between tribals and non-tribals. According to Uttar Sen Gupta, editor of the *New Republic*, Roman Catholic, Anglican and Lutheran missionaries have built up powerful empires in Chotanagpur founded on the massive conversion of tribals. On this account a fusion between Hindus and tribals at this point would weaken the missionaries' institutions, one of the leading ones in Ranchi being the Jesuit St Xavier's School for Social Work.

Despite the excellent education given by the missionaries, Father Albinus Minz is adamant in the belief that all tribals have an inferiority complex when they come face to face with the Hindus. As one example he cites the case of fourteen to fifteen tribal advocates in the Ranchi court who are considered third class because they do not have the gift of oratory. He claims they are too frightened to speak in the court because they are hampered by their inferiority complex. But the tribal élite of Ranchi seems to have acquired the traits of the Hindu mainstream they have joined and have failed to address themselves to the problems of other tribals. One such example is T. Bodra, former State Forest Minister, one of the richest among the tribals holding properties in Nayatoli, Ranchi. He has been accused of carrying out benami transactions in hundreds of acres of land.

The tribal élite is not alone in its loss of identity. In fact the erosion of the rich and varied tribal culture of Chotanagpur can be seen around Murmumela, an Adivasi *mela*, or local gathering, held annually about 30 km from Ranchi. One sees few tribals in costume and the poverty of the Adivasis can be seen from the scarcity of items for sale. There is a lack of spontaneity in the dancing and most of those attending the mela are dressed in shirts and trousers, an indication that the tribal culture is dying out.

Precisely on account of the indigence, the Christian influence notwithstanding, the Left is making new inroads into South Bihar. The influence of the Marxists has developed over the past five years in eastern Ranchi in the Bunur area, in Sonathalu and

Tamanu. According to N.E. Hero, the Marxists began support-ing the demand for a Jharkhand state made up of the original Chotanapur Hill tracts because they have found that unless they support this demand they will not have an impact. The Naxalites, the extreme pro-Maoist organization, have also begun activities in the Singhbum area, the Binod Mishra faction being active in Madhya Pradesh and the Satya Narayan Sinha group in Sing-hbum and West Bengal. The extent of this activity is hard to ascertain. A government document states: 'In fact, some tribal leaders thought that what was dubbed as extremist activity was really the assertion of a few tribal groups contesting the occupa-tion of tribal land by others.'[2]

An attempt was made to gauge the state of the tribals of Chotanagpur and the impact of government programme for the settling of nomadic tribes by visiting several villages at various locations in Ranchi district. Ichadaf village, near Ranchi, has approximately 400 people divided into five castes – Rajputs, Kurmis, Lohars, Yadavs and Harijans, as well as Adivasi families. Most of the land is owned by the Rajputs. While several of the Harijan families interviewed possessed land and others were landless agricultural labourers earning Rs 3–4 a day, all the Adivasi families interviewed were in debt, one family being bonded labourers. One Harijan, Ramga Ragwar, possesses six acres of land and works in the post office.

One Adivasi, Bandu Mahli, has bonded himself for one year to a landlord for a share of food grain and between Rs 250–300 a year. He says he has enough to eat for nine months of the year but during June, July and August he has to weave baskets for a livelihood. His father is living in a village in the interior of the forest. Bandhu Mahli's aim is to educate his children.

Another Adivasi, Punit Mahli, has become a bonded labourer as a result of a Rs 200 loan he took 19 years ago. The landlord let the debt accumulate into accumulated interest until he could take over two out of Punit Mahli's five acres of land to cover the loan and interest. Today his family works on this land and the landlord still gets the produce after 19 years. The loan was taken to perform the *shraddah* or traditional death ceremony. So as not to starve Punit Mahli gets odd jobs such as road repairing and sells *kendu* leaves.

Many of the villagers are in the clutches of South Indian money-lenders from Madras as well as Punjabi money-lenders, who stay nearby and spread out into the villages. If a villager fails to pay his debt after a ten-week period, the money-lenders come and take the villagers' utensils away and threaten them. This is substantiated in a report of the Ministry of Home Affairs written after a tour of Chotanagpur in the late seventies: 'A network of what are known as 'Madrasi' moneylenders has got established in this area in the last decade or so; they advance small loans at exorbitant rates of interest, up to about 400 per cent which is realized with a considerable amount of harshness if necessary.'

Health care is very difficult as the nearest dispensary is 8–10 km away and one baby has advanced polio but has never been to a doctor.

In eastern Ranchi, where many of the villages are very poor, many families go to Punjab and Assam, and earlier many went to the Andamans Islands, to find work in a bad crop year. In the Adivasi village of Chingri near Netarhat, made up of several tribes, although many have land, they do not work as they are too poor to buy ploughs. There is no government school. In the summer of 1979 five families went to the Punjab to work as servants, although the village chief, a naukri, admitted that they only go as servants when there is famine. Other families have earlier gone to the Andamans to work as coolies or cut wood in the jungle and brought back money. One family has been there for 13 years.

In one of the poorest villages, called Akir, in the same vicinity as Chingri, visited in October 1980, four tribal girls had been taken away by some men about six months ago, according to the mother of one of the girls. While three of the girls had returned claiming they worked as bricklayers, they do not know where they were taken. They say they were separated and paid Rs 4 a day for bricklaying. The mother of the missing girl, who is called Gormi Basanti, has no other relatives.

A few kilometres away from Chingri are two villages, Beti and Jehengutua, where the government has settled Birhors and Asurs, primitive tribes at the food-gathering stage who used to live in the jungles. At Beti, a Birhor village, the government has built mud rectangular huts which have been crumbling for the past seven years. The Birhors have sold the tiles of the roofs of the huts and have replaced them with the traditional roofing of leaves. Out of the 30 families originally settled here, 14 have gone back to live in the jungle. In the process they sold the cattle and goats the government gave to each family. However, in the winter some of the families return 'as life in the jungle is too hard then'.

According to one social worker working with the Birhors in Beti, they have little patience to cultivate and instead make string from sahir which they sell at Rs 1 for a batch of string. Although the government provides seed for sowing, it is subsidized and never free. The Birhors claim that sometimes they have no seed to cultivate on their plots of land and go without food. This is probably because like other primitive groups, such as the Wa of Yunan province in China, they eat up the seed and feed it to their animals at one go when it is available. The Birhors are in the hands of South Indian money-lenders based in Benari village nearby because they find the procedure for filling out forms for low-interest bank loans and the requirement of a guarantor too difficult to fulfil, according to the social worker. But now the Block Development Officer is preventing them taking loans from the money-lenders, according to the same source.

The welfare officer said it is difficult to tell whether there is any corruption on the part of the Block Development Officer at Bishunpur in charge of the area because 'whatever comes from the government goes to the block itself so we only see what they bring to the villages.'

Although the Birhors are materially better off than when they were living nomadic lives in the jungles, the fact that over half of those originally settled at Beti have gone back there permanently has a significance that should not be missed: namely that a way of life close to nature, providing few material goods, has more value to certain societies than life in an ordered state where material goods and comforts are available. In fact, the term 'backward' used to describe tribals, and particularly the more primitive tribes, is based on a value judgement founded on a misconception which consequently has endowed the term with negative connotations. The tribal way of life, close to nature, is conceived as something barbaric, a 'life in the dark', which is as unrealistic as Rousseau's conception of the 'noble savage' was over-romanticized. Government officials and bureaucrats in India are convinced that, by elevating the tribals by 'detribalizing' them through education and bringing them into the Hindu mainstream, they will contribute to their mental and physical well-being. But nothing could be further from the truth, as a visit to one of the few remaining secluded primitive tribes, the Upper

Hill Bondas of Koraput district, Orissa, demonstrates.

The money economy has barely penetrated this matriarchal tribe and only a few of the wealthier families walk the 15 km down from the hills to the local Sunday tribal market. Even here the goods for sale are few compared to remote rural markets in other parts of India. But precisely because the 50 square miles of hills and forests in which the 31 Bonda villages are located have never been encroached upon by government (for example, the area is still unsurveyed), the Bondas, unlike the tribals of Chotanagpur, have retained their wealth based on their land, mostly paddy fields, and their unlimited rights to the forests. Lack of material goods, education and health care, which we equate with progress, has nothing to do with the advancement of mental and physical well-being with which ironically the term 'progress' is equated with in the modern world.

However, if their per capita income is calculated it would be negligible. But they have plenty to eat being expert rice cultivators and having plenty of forest land which provides a balanced diet. They live in spacious warm dwellings and their clothing, however scanty, is adequate to their needs. The basic human requirements of food, shelter and clothing are thus met, and they are far better off than the residents of an urbanized slum. Even more important, their quality of life produces an exuberance that is sadly lacking in the careworn struggle for existence of the pavement and slum dwellers.

The greatest loss to which a tribe, clan, or nation can succumb is the loss of its culture and traditional values, for this necessarily leads to its demise. This is precisely what had happened gradually to the tribals of Chotanagpur over the last two centuries. But the situation would be somewhat attenuated if the society eroding their culture could give them an equal place in the new order, and if the latter constitutes elements which form a genuine synthesis and does not make them ashamed of their own traditional basic values. Unfortunately, attitudes of superiority, which are strengthening more than at any time since Independence, mean that the educated, 'detribalized' tribal joining the mainstream loses not only his identity but his self-worth as he joins the lowest ranks of the Hindu hierarchy. Even the exceptions who rise higher do so at the cost of losing their own cultural roots, becoming ashamed of these and thus developing an inferiority complex.

CONCLUSION

The correct definition of present Indian society is 'medieval', in its true sense of transition between two eras. A medieval society, as in Europe, is always in a state of flux. Traditionalists bemoan the 'barbarian' element, but it was out of medieval European societies that the vitality for the Renaissance was born. Preoccupation with hiatus and dichotomy is the hallmark of the traditional intellectual who feels puzzled by the state of flux because inherently a state of flux cannot conform to any recognizable framework. It is a natural process of ferment.

Caste, which has formed the structural base for the organization of Hindu society for at least two millennia, has evolved from a theoretically rigid but practically flexible system of hierarchy to one of dispersed domination. Techniques of social control are beginning to shift from a total cultural superiority of the upper castes. Earlier their dominance was unquestioned. In the old days it was considered a sin to go against them and the wrongdoer felt a pang of guilt. In some areas of the country there is probably still a remnant of this feeling of the divinity of the higher castes but such attitudes are now much less in the mind. In fact an element of resentment is developing among many lower-caste groups. However, a feeling of hopelessness remains that they are unable to act with success against the élite strata. The other factor operating against them is the economic stranglehold of vested interests owned by the same groups.

The main techniques of social control in ancient India were through ideology and cultural conquest. The root word of Brahmin 'brh' means to grow or spread. Balakrishna Nair in his book, *The Dynamic Brahmin*, argues that the urge for social control in the beginning was not necessarily a rational impulse but rather a primeval urge or instinct. It is possible that the elaboration of various stages of social control must have been a conscious or rational process, what Nair calls: 'The result of an instinctive propensity controlled by a conscious and rational direction to safeguard the Brahmin's status.'[1]

Social control methods have differed in each culture. In nineteenth-century England they were primarily economic. In the United States they were complicated by the racial issue. In Russia the feeling of the divine right of the Tsar and the religious acceptance of inequality reflected similar methods of social control as in India. Today the Soviet Union and the People's Republic of China are both grappling with the problem that inegalitarianism is inherent in the human system. However, under these Communist regimes a certain equality of opportunity has really taken place at the cost of considerable initial force. Yet in this system the worker or peasant who becomes a member of the Presidium still tries to perpetuate his power through favouritism displayed to his family. New élites have emerged in these societies. These could, perhaps, crystallize in time into a new aristocracy based on birth. Yet the Soviets and Chinese have been so imbued with Marxist thinking that probably any attempt to perpetuate such a trend would provoke a strong reaction from within society. The reaction in China against special schools for children of the cadres is an example.

In India the old élite continues to perpetuate itself by adaptation and fresh absorption. Brahmin ideas and ideologies have expanded to many sectors of social life since Independence. One of the main reasons is their dominance in all levels of control. The continued entrenchment of Brahmins and other upper castes in the higher levels of the bureaucracy means that a large number of posts are actually distributed by status groups within the administrative apparatus to members of their own group. This leaves only a margin of seats for genuinely open competition.

Furthermore, bureaucracy has allowed scope for the advancement of group interests and narrow cultural goals and thus reversed the advantages of a supposedly equitable system of administration bequeathed by the British. Bureaucracies everywhere have an inbuilt mechanism to resist change. In India there is a further social impediment on the bureaucracy acting as an instrument of transformation. Its cultural content exercises a pernicious influence on the official structure, not only by reason of its continued expansion, but due to the unabated influences that it is subjected to from the society at large. For the bureaucracy to act as an instrument of social change it would first of all have to be purged of its caste gradations.

Some sociologists believe caste will not necessarily be retained in the political and economic context in coming years. Rather certain customs only would be preserved in the realm of social interaction such as commensality, marriage and patterns of worship. In other words, the socio-cultural aspects of caste will be maintained while its political and economic basis will be eroded. This is a moot point as, in the past, many notable scholars like R.V. Russell also erroneously foretold the demise of caste. Writing in 1916 Russell remarked that with the spread of education and growing communications 'the life of the caste system is limited.'[2]

The continuity of the caste system is a testimony to its strength in meeting challenges and threats and of its flexibility in resolving contradictions which have arisen at different points of time. Srinivas has remarked on the built-in resilience of caste which has enabled it to adapt to a variety of forces brought about by British rule and Independence, 'thus implicitly questioning long-held beliefs about the institution's rigidity'.[3]

The caste system has evolved simultaneously in several directions and even adjusted to an ideologically antagonistic system. The modernization of caste has meant that ritualistic considerations in ranking of hierarchy have become less effective. With growing urbanization and modernization the new attributes of caste status may seem to be higher education, success in business, prestige white collar jobs and moneyed wealth. In one sense the process of urbanization and capitalization of the economy are destroying the old sub-features of caste.

However, the concept of self-contained groups functioning in isolation seems so ingrained that even in the modern context new such groups keep on forming. Again an interpreter has to be careful of going to extremes. Departmentalism is rife in bureaucracies the world over. In India, however, the tendency which some would ascribe to the British legacy seems to have been aggravated since Independence. The traditional ways of thinking and instinctive attitudes may have contributed to the virtual impossibility of any programme being effectively coordinated between various departments. These attitudes have to be recognized in order to understand fully the seemingly extraordinary antics which increasingly pervade the administration.

At the time of writing a crisis is developing in the top echelons of the railway administration– the railways constituting India's major employer. The equivalent of a caste or sub-caste war is raging as new incumbents on the railway board seek to fill the top posts of zonal general manager from the contending clans of the 'mechanical' and 'traffic' cadres. In the field, although district collectors or *zilla parishad* chairmen are theoretically supposed to coordinate development activities and indeed hold almost unending 'coordination meetings', each department continues in practice to obtain its own financial allocations and to determine its own priorities in its own way. The so-called Integrated Rural Employment Programme does not integrate all aspects of rural development and in practice is confined to a few specific programmes. Nowhere does one find land records staff, panchayat raj staff, block development staff, rural employment staff or the departments of irrigation (major and minor), agriculture and public works working together or along with supply agencies like the cooperative department (which handles fertilizer inputs), or the Food Corporation of India (which procures from villages). It is only very rarely, when an exceptionally strong chief minister emerges for a time, that something tends to be achieved in a state's programme. Patterns may vary as between a dynamically ruthless P.S. Kairon or Bansi Lal in Punjab and Haryana, a benevolent but undisputed leader like Dr Y.S. Parmar in Himachal Pradesh, or other effective leaders like Devraj Urs in Karnataka. There is a growing tendency, however, these days to suspect and destabilize any forceful leadership which might emerge anywhere.

The nature of the political system that has emerged in post-Independence India is such that it is unable to carry everyone together. The system is dominated by a kaleidoscopic coalition of the élite belonging to all sections and the same pattern prevails in all political parties. In each of these groups, whether, for example, Brahmin, Muslim or Scheduled Caste, there is a critical élite which is posing as spokesman of its respective constituency. Blame cannot be placed on a single party nor is it true that these politicians are necessarily using their respective constituencies merely to feather their own nests. In some instances they do mean to do something for their constituency; but somehow things fail to get done. To analyse why this is so, one has to get back to the grass roots. The reality on the ground is that power relations, notwithstanding the minor changes that have taken place, have substantially reinforced traditional power alignments. One of the main problems is that politicians are not in a position to find alternatives that would be likely to change the situation in the immediate future.

Substantial changes have taken place if one looks at the situation on the ground in states where Communists have ruled for some time, or where they have been in Opposition, as in Kerala and parts of Andhra Pradesh. At the same time in some states like Karnataka, where the Communists have never held power, substantial changes also came about under the Devraj Urs Congress ministry in the first half of the seventies. The question here relates not only to ideology or party, but as to whether any party is in a position to implement, with even fifty-per-cent success, what is already accepted as the ideal or objective. The entire land reforms programme in India, for example, was not a Communist idea. As early as 1936 in a Congress meeting the maxim was accepted that land should belong to the tiller. The only difference is that in this context the provisions were more or less implemented by the Communist parties. The point is not one of ideological variation but of an implementation lag. In this context one gets back to the uses of power and in this regard the position has varied from state to state. West Bengal and Kerala have a much better record on the agrarian question than Bihar or Uttar Pradesh.

One of the reasons the Left has not made more inroads in India is that for a long time the Communist movement did not recognize the unique nature of Indian reality. Members of both the CPI and CPI(M) tended to be more bookish than sociological. They engaged in discussions on Lenin's *What Is To Be Done?* rather than in an analysis of the actual social structure of the Indian village. However, there have been some policy reformulations in recent months. The CPI(M) has now recognized the importance of caste and said it should be treated as a special institution in mobilization.

In certain areas the caste structure, despite its theoretical diversity, became, in the common perception, fundamentally dualistic.[4] In West Bengal Béteille notes certain congeries of rural categories in very broad and general terms. In popular parlance the division was between the *bhadralok* (the gentry) and the *chotolok* (the small people) who were despised and looked down upon. The relatively early break-up in Bengal of the large landed estates also facilitated mobilization by the CPI(M) of the chotolok, with especial emphasis on the rights of sharecroppers. Where a multiplex caste structure exists and where there is an intermeshing of a strong peasant caste culture as well as those of weaker classes, there is such a complex criss-crossing of loyalties that mobilization becomes a difficult task. The problem is one of ideological pluralism rather than polarization. This situation prevails in the whole North Indian belt. However, in recent years there has been a growing polarization of forces in pockets of Bihar, largely confined to the tribal and Scheduled Caste belts. This new development does indicate that India is in a transitional stage.

The growing tide of regionalism culminating in the sweeping victory of N.T. Rama Rao and the Telugu Desam Party in Andhra Pradesh in early 1983 is another sign that new political trends are emerging. There is a growing feeling among non-Congress-ruled states that powers are too heavily weighted in favour of the Centre. Recently states like West Bengal, Tamil Nadu, Jammu, Kashmir and Andhra Pradesh have been voicing demands for a redefinition of the federal structure. Their main demand, led by the Marxist state of West Bengal, has been for a devolution of financial powers. Certainly 36 years of almost uninterrupted Congress rule have allowed the Congress to acquire a dominance for Central Government organs beyond constitutional prescriptions.

The Central Government formulates certain subsidiary laws or rules. For example, income tax is constitutionally a Central subject but the revenue from it is divisible between the Centre and the states. A complaint of the states is that when the Centre decided to increase this revenue it did so not by enhancing income tax, which would have involved a proportionate increase also in the revenue of the states, but had recourse to imposing a 'surcharge', all of which went to the Centre.

However, in the last resort, this whole question of Centre–state relations largely boils down to a matter of attitudes rather than of tight legal or constitutional provisions. Recently the Centre has appointed a commission to study the problem or, as critics would carp, to delay and confuse it. The commission has asked the states to point out specific instances whereby existing provisions have been found to be detrimental. Such instances like those of the income tax controversy and the earlier Central suggestion to substitute for sales tax (a purely state revenue) an enhanced excise duty at source (a Central revenue divisible with the states) may be few and far between.

More important is the insinuation regarding the Centre–states' relationship of the attitude of hierarchical superiority in all fields. For example, there is nothing in the constitution to insist that the Planning Commission be the ultimate arbiter of financial allocations for development to the states. Resentment has also arisen when Central technical agencies like the Electricity Authority or the earlier Water and Power Commission arrogate to themselves the attitude of being the sole technical arbiters of policy without concern for specific needs or conditions.

Recent developments in the Punjab and the North-Eastern state of Assam, each located at the extreme corners of India's frontier, are a symptom of the ferment and cultural disintegration taking place in Indian society. At the outset of the Sikh unrest in the Punjab the press failed to report the growing tide of resentment. It was only when violent activities and pronouncements reached a peak that the Punjab hit the headlines. This illustrates either a lack of sensitivity or lack of communication even amongst the press and media. After the problem was published, and even till this day, the assumption amongst non-Sikh commentators seem to be that the solution lies in some form of detailed compromise formula involving sharing of river waters, the status of Chandigarh, which is presently shared as a capital with Haryana, and the various claims for transfer of territories.

The other part of the problem is classified as religious demands which the government claims to have conceded involving Gurdwara (temple) management, media arrangements for religious broadcasts, the right to carry *kirpans*, or traditional Sikh swords, even specifying the measurements of such weapons. The government stand also points out that when the Akali party, the Sikh group now behind the movement, was in power in the Punjab during the Janata regime, no such movement on these specific issues was pressed.

The real problem, however, is hardly ever mentioned. It is part of the same uneasiness that is plaguing all national, cultural and linguistic minorities and the suspicion that the dominant elements in Indian society are basically insincere in the lip service that they pay to concepts such as secularism and the plurality of Indian society. The Sikh issue is a case in point. The demand for Khalistan is an attempt to safeguard the Sikh self-identity and self-interest. Such groups have come to feel that their communities or distinctive cultures must always accept a subordinate status and that, although some of their representatives may achieve nominal high office, decision-making is always the prerogative of some inner circle from which they are emotionally, if not physically, excluded.

Indeed this is exactly the same trend which, before the Partition of India, led the Muslim leadership which, it is too often forgotten, was initially part of the united anti-imperialist Congress party, into forming their separate organization. When such a development occurs there is always the tendency to seek a scapegoat in the shape of the imperial divide-and-rule policy, or, nowadays, a 'foreign hand'.

There is little introspection as to what continually alienates such communities within the Indian social system. Even granted that such alienation can be exploited by outside elements, it has to exist before such exploitation is possible. Once the community suspicion develops towards the basic system it becomes practically impossible to classify members of such a community into watertight compartments such as extremist, separatist, loyalist or secularist. Each individual is torn by different pulls which may vary from time to time under the impact of day-to-day events and reactions. A person may be ninety-nine-per-cent loyalist one day, yet with one-per-cent subconscious community pride in the assertiveness of the extremists and, on another day, as suspicion or resentment at a particular incident mounts, be swung towards a different frame of mind.

The government line is that the Sikh extremists who demand a separate sovereign state outside India represent a totally insignificant foreign-based minority. This is probably in the ultimate analysis still true. It is doubtful if an opinion poll among the Sikhs would opt categorically for a separate sovereign state. However, everyone shies away from mentioning the fact that the overseas Sikh, Jagjit Singh Chauhan, the leader of the secessionist movement, was earlier a minister in the Punjab state government. Jinnah too was at one time a Congress leader and in those days the idea of a future separate state of Pakistan would have been considered among undivided Indian Muslims as the practically unsound dream of an insignificant lunatic fringe.

Matters have not been helped by insistence among Hindu intellectuals that Sikhs are really a sect of the Hindus. Historically there is an element of truth in this, though the derivation of separate Sikh religious beliefs from other sources, not excluding Islam, has been underplayed. What matters is the way a community looks at itself. Ultimately, as a minorities movement develops, all manner of grievances are rationalized and argued about. They are basically, however, peripheral to the main issue. For example, the Sikhs are one of the most dynamic and economically advanced groups in modern India. If, even in the face of this obvious fact, a now sizeable body of opinion amongst them feels in some way suspicious or resentful of being second-class citizens, the root causes in attitudes require deeper analysis.

Another area in the recent news was the state of Assam. The government machinery over the past few decades has been deliberately ignoring here the basic nationality issue because of the fear of losing vote banks. The Assam tragedy, culminating in the massacre of Muslim immigrants from Bangladesh by tribals at Nellie in March 1983, and of counter killings elsewhere, has been largely due to the manipulation of communal feelings in the state by the Congress (I) and BJP for their own electoral gain or party interest.

Quite apart from the absence of political will to arrest the flow of immigrants, the Assam issue illustrates an important point which the Indian government has failed to recognize. It substantiates Spengler's view, expressed in *The Decline of the West*, of the inevitability of the organic making of history. Human migrations have been going on for centuries. Yet once immigrants settle down in a new land, after two or three generations they come to claim themselves as native sons of the soil, even though they retain their original language and culture. Nationality laws and other legal provisions have been unable to stem the flow of impoverished Bangladeshi families, Hindu as well as Muslim, in search of land or avenues of employment. Once they establish a foothold, they attract and harbour more of their kinfolk. The parallel with Mexican immigration into the USA springs to mind. Attempts to analyse, justify or criticize actions by quoting (or selectively suppressing) legal and constitutional provisions ultimately founder. They come up against a stronger reality in the organic growth and ferment of society which pays no heed to the laws of rationalists.

There are two ways of responding to such a ferment. The first is to join it gladly and, understanding the elements involved, offer oneself as a catalyst to contribute to the ultimate solution, knowing that one's own element will be unrecognizably transformed in the new society. The second and more common reaction is to deplore the seeming chaos, destabilize the more effervescent elements and 'restore order' in society.

During much of 1983, rather than living up to the national principle of 'unity in diversity', the then prime minister, Indira Gandhi, followed a policy of destabilization in states not ruled by her own cadres. In the 1983 Jammu and Kashmir elections Mrs Gandhi made a serious bid to weaken or defeat the regional party called the National Conference. This had earlier proved impossible due to the stature of its leader, Sheikh Abdullah. It was assumed that his son, a relative political novice, Dr Farouq Abdullah, would fall easy prey to destabilization through local dissensions and the weight of Mrs Gandhi's electoral machine. The result was interesting not only for the Kashmiri rebuff but for the campaign of disinformation to which a sizeable section of the press lent itself.

Their motivation was complex. It would be unfair to attribute to them the simple role of being stooges of the ruling party. The editors and reporters concerned probably functioned more from a subconscious will to believe that the largely Muslim National Conference was a danger to Indian national unity. Fortunately, a more vigilant section, led by reporter Arun Shourie, but also backed by several prominent and respected journalists, protested at the false picture presented by reporters based merely on Congress(I) handouts, unsupported by personal local investigations.

This led to a split and controversy between journalists belonging to an organization known as the Editors' Guild of India which disputes the original reporting regarding the National Conference violence and other reporters including those of influential agencies like the Press Trust of India. One of the reports of the latter was that the Congress(I) headquarters in Kashmir had been attacked and set on fire by an unruly mob led by Dr Abdullah himself. This later turned out to be false and there is growing evidence that the whole incident, including the fire, was stagemanaged on the lines of Hitler's Reichstag fire in the 1930s.

Now the whole background is sought to be further obfuscated by an inquiry as to whether the initial reporting was coloured by political bribery or bias. This in fact was never an allegation. The real issue being merely the truth or the falsity of the reports and the professional weaknesses or prejudices that might be deduced.

At the Central level the issue tends to be viewed as one of

political manipulation with one or the other group seemingly gaining the upper hand. It tends to be forgotten that the reality will always be known locally and that, even if the Central machinery seemingly succeeds in gaining the upper hand by manipulation or disinformation, the local resentment and opposition will only deepen through knowledge of the local reality.

These examples and the many diverse trends described in this book are but a few aspects of the fascinating vitality in the ferment of Indian society today. It cannot be understood, nor its results predicted, in terms of neat ideological terms largely borrowed from Western thought: democracy versus a dictatorship, whether of the right or of the proletariat; contradictions, antagonistic or non-antagonistic; or syndromes in a 'social, spatial and temporal continuum'! The ferment will determine its own processes, as it has done throughout history since the first legend of the 'Churning of the Ocean'.

Optimists, who are too often mere propagandists, nostalgic for the old order, will deny that there is any real disintegration in progress. India, they rightly claim, is very much alive almost a quarter of a century after its 'dangerous decade'. A microscopic 'eye to India' can dissect, with great labour and accuracy, the distempers in its body politic. Yet it fails to interpret the Indian capacity to drift into 'Emergency' rule, divest itself *electorally* from 'authoritarian dictatorship' and finally re-elect the same 'dictator' for a further perfectly constitutional tenure. 'Corruption' may be mounting. Social injustice remains acute. Yet large groups from the 'static society' have moved up both the economic and social ladder with rapid mobility. Even 'black money' generates its own dynamos of development. These viewpoints are valid.

The pessimists too sound valid warnings. 'Akhand Bharat' (United India) of pre-Independence has actually split, not once but twice within half a century. Neighbours who were culturally close in history, like Nepal and Sri Lanka, prickle with suspicions of Indian hegemony, or demographic infiltration. There are ominous trends in Central relations, whether with Punjab and Kashmir in India or with Sind and Baluchistan in Pakistan. There is increasing restiveness among minorities and the underprivileged Scheduled Castes and Tribes. Above all, they no longer take it for granted, as they used to, that the present leadership is the sole custodian of their interests and their protection for survival. The feeling that rival political parties offer little, if anything, better, does not cancel out this erosion of confidence. There is growing cynicism that 'national interest' and 'national danger' are catch-phrases arrogated by the ruling coterie as synonyms for their own 'danger' or their own interests. Appeals in their name may no longer evoke the spontaneous magic of the 1962 confrontation with China.

Beyond these viewpoints the single fact of ferment remains. It has already engendered, beyond the point of no return, potent chain reactions in all the elements of Indian society. The classic total dominance over all spheres of life by a 20-per-cent minority of the Twice-Born castes, the monopolists of thought, power and money, is being challenged. In human history no such minority has ever parted with power willingly. In almost any other country, revolutionary violence could be assumed to be inevitable. The Indian response, if the leaders of thought follow their own traditions, will be partly to divide the opposition by every known device including that of disinformation; but also to widen their own circle of the dominant minority to absorb into their own culture and system the remaining potential leadership of dissidence which they have not succeeded in discrediting.

This leads ultimately to a renewal of the old order with accretions in ideas – perhaps even in carefully doctored values – from those whom it has absorbed. Eventually the very details of the original confrontation are lost in myth. Such a pattern is already discernible in the establishment's policy towards the Backward Classes Movement, composed mainly of erstwhile clean Sudra castes, many of whom are well on the way to becoming the new Kshatriyas, with the Brahminical policy-framers also, as in fact they have done throughout history, taking new accretions into their ranks. The money power of the new élite, not only among the captains of industry and commerce but among the money-spinning petty traders and successful artisans, would form the third prop of the new alliance.

The real test will be the relationship between such a new alliance of interests 'to save society from chaos' and the remainder of the really underprivileged: the exploited Scheduled Caste wage labour and the tribal population of the central belt of India which is rapidly losing its land to industry, power projects and state forest restrictions and is also descending to the status of Scheduled Caste wage labour, to be hired, fired and exploited at will. The dreams of a renaissance and transformation of Hindu society into the ideal of 'Sarva Dharma (responsibility towards all)' has already been propounded by intellectuals, partly perhaps to defuse the rising tide of dissidence. It is unlikely to be realised by them. Some form of new Bhakti movement might contribute towards its achievement especially if new 'extremist' Leftist cadres at the grass roots could evolve their own theoreticians who would give adequate importance to devotional dedication rooted in India's deepest folk culture. Such a possibility at present sounds totally implausible, not to speak of being 'deviationist'. Yet it would be in one of the streams of Indian tradition.

However, present indications are quite to the contrary. The erstwhile Backward Castes on their way up the hierarchical ladder are often the main instruments of oppression, at times savage in its brutality, to keep the lowest orders in their place. Perhaps further blood sacrifices will be needed to produce the final revulsion in society. In the meantime the cycle of decay, rebirth and rejuvenation will continue. It will be influenced by the political leadership from time to time. But ultimately it will determine the course of its own organic evolution.

The tragic assassination of Mrs Gandhi on 31 October 1984 at the hands of her two Sikh bodyguards, marked the passing of a generation that had brought India to Independence. Mrs Gandhi's last four years in office were her most difficult years as prime minister, but it must be said that she was herself partly to blame for the deteriorating situation on the national scene. It was a period characterized by growing political unrest, increasing public cynicism regarding politics and politicians and dangerous religious violence which ultimately took her life. Instead of trying to assuage the growing restiveness and upsurge in violence, Mrs Gandhi was beginning to transform the entire political process into a battleground for all-out confrontation and was constantly calling attention to instability, the 'foreign hand' and the threat to the country's unity. Her violent death underscored the extent to which she had eroded the democratic foundations of the State, especially in her last years in office, by her determined policies of destabilization of non-Congress(I) state governments and by her artful manipulations of ethnic and religious communalism, ever latent beneath the social fabric, for short-term political gain. Her assassination must be seen as a symbolic warning that India is facing a political crisis whose repercussions, if left unresolved, could augur badly for India's survival as a secular pluralistic state.

The Punjab issue remains the most serious challenge to India today. A government White Paper, released on 10 July 1984, has sought to depict the Punjab problem as a crisis of national integrity, while many observers have described it as a crisis of growing communal hatred and a cult of violence. But it remains essentially a political crisis which has arisen as a result of the tussle between the three-year old Akali-led mass movement based on certain grievances of the Punjab and Sikhs and the attempt by the Centre to curb and divide it. Communal tension and terrorist activities are merely a symptom of the problem.

The violence in the Punjab would not have developed on the scale it did if the Congress (I) had not encouraged the Sikh terrorist leader, Jarnail Singh Bhindranwale, to contain the Akalis three years before.[1] Nor did the government's undermining of the moderate Akalis stop there. It underwrote state repression against the peaceful Akali agitators and encouraged fanatic Hindu organizations to 'teach the Sikhs a lesson'. At first the demands for a separate Sikh state of Khalistan were limited largely to Sikhs living abroad, one of the main protagonists being London-based self-styled Khalistan leader, Dr Jagjit Singh Chauhan, a former Punjab state finance minister. The demand for secession inside India emerged after the preachings of the fiery religious figure of Bhindranwale had caught the imagination of young Sikhs who saw in him a great hero calling them to arms. As the extremist Sikh violence mounted, especially from the end of 1981 onwards, when individual citizens became targets of attack when Bhindranwale's programme to eliminate opponents, both Sikh and Hindu, gained ground, the violence acquired communal overtones as Hindu extremist organizations began retaliations. The point of no return was reached on 9 September 1981 with the murder of Lal Jagat Narain, one of the most important Hindu leaders of the region, by Sikh extremists. From then on the state was witness to a wave of terror that culminated in June 1984 with the despatch of Indian Army troops into the holiest of Sikh shrines, the Golden Temple in Amritsar, to wipe out Bhindranwale and his armed followers.

The Akalis had not remained bystanders in this drama. Once Bhindranwale and his cult of selective murder came to be widely propagated, the Akalis kept their party alive by launching peaceful agitations for fulfilment of various territorial, religious and political demands so as not to be undermined. By February 1984 the government was ready to sign a settlement with the Akalis after successful private negotiations which had been going on for over a year. However, on the day of the meeting the chance of peace was lost as the extremist Hindu organization, the Hindu Suraksha Samiti (Hindu Safety Organization), apprehensive that the Akali–Congress(I) settlement might be at the cost of the Hindu community, indulged in a day-long orgy of murder and terror against the Sikhs in the neighbouring state of Haryana. A collapse of the talks ensued as did the chance of any settlement.

This merely played into Bhindranwale's hands. Since taking refuge in the Golden Temple, a place which was exempt from the laws of the land until the Indian Army operation in June 1984,

Bhindranwale and his men had stockpiled weapons, stacking them in underground vaults with or without the permission of the Akal Takht, the highest Sikh religious authority. As weapons were amassed in this sanctuary, unhampered by the authorities, hit lists of selected Hindus were drawn up and death squads dispatched to liquidate chosen targets.

From April to June 1984 terrorist activity had increased to such an extent that arms were being dispatched daily out of the Golden Temple for use in carrying out Bhindranwale's policy of selected murder. A flashpoint was reached on 1 June when an exchange of fire between Bhindranwale's heavily armed men on the periphery of the Golden Temple complex and the police forces stationed outside, left 11 people dead. At this point Mrs Gandhi was left with few options but to make the fatal decision of ordering the Army, in a mission codenamed 'Operation Bluestar', involving several thousand troops, to flush Bhindranwale and his more than a thousand armed followers out of the sacred complex in an encounter that took four days and cost several thousand lives.

The Sikh community was outraged. Sikhs from all over the country felt that a great injury had been done to their faith. Several thousand Sikhs from different regiments around the country mutinied. It was felt that the army had used maximum rather than minimum force and that the cost of exterminating the terrorists had been too high. Thousands of pilgrims, including women and children had been killed, the Golden Temple complex badly damaged and the Punjab placed under army rule.[2]

For as 'Operation Bluestar' got under way, the army raided 40 other places of worship in the state while 70,000 troops and paramilitary forces took up predetermined positions in the streets of Punjab and fanned out along the thousands of kilometres of roads that linked the state's 12,168 villages. Virtually the whole administration of the state was placed under its control as curfew was declared in various parts of the Punjab. Although the civilian administration appeared to function, the whole operation of the state administration, railways and transport was carried on or suspended according to the army's needs. The state police virtually ceased to exist as its various functions, such as its power of searching and arresting persons, were taken over by army personnel. The most galling aspect of the military presence, as the army combed the villages, was the reign of terror unleashed in the countryside. In continued police and army operations innumerable young Sikhs were subjected to third-degree methods of torture to extort confessions in the search for arms and terrorists. Many were arrested and locked up for further questioning in police stations.[3]

The increasing use of the army to quell civilian disturbances is regarded by many observers as a dangerous trend for which they blame the government. The use of the armed forces in the Punjab to restore law and order in the state is only the latest example of its intervention in civilian affairs. For the past two years it has been similarly deployed in Assam. Since 1955 it has fought an intermittent secessionist movement in Nagaland and similar burgeoning ones both in Manipur since 1966 and subsequently in Mizoram. Today the army is still present in these three North-Eastern states. Lt.-Gen. J. S. Singh Aurora, the Indian Army commander in charge of the Bangladesh operation in the 1971 Indo-Bangladesh War leading to an Indian victory, believes that continual exposure of the armed forces to civilian life could seriously undermine discipline and could weaken civilian administration and the police. Political scientist Rajni Kothari is particularly critical of the government's role in this regard: 'The army has been called in place after place as the government has failed to provide for law and order or they themselves take part in the disturbances. In this matter, Mrs Gandhi and her politics are to blame. In Punjab the government tried to discredit the police and the Border Security Force (BSF) to make a case for the army to move in.'[4]

To assist in the task of curbing terrorism and violence in the Punjab the Centre introduced a number of draconian laws which are almost a replica of the bills passed to deal with the earlier secessionist movements in the North-East. The latest bill, the Terrorist and Disruptive Activities (Prevention) bill, passed in May 1985, provides the death penalty for terrorist activities and redefines the term 'terrorist' in a broader manner, although by July 1985 the earlier legislation – permitting the authorities to make arrests and carry out searches without a warrant, hold closed trials in special courts, and laying the onus on the person accused of being a terrorist to prove otherwise – had been held in abeyance in the wake of the government's negotiated settlement with the Akalis. Before this agreement there were widespread fears that these provisions would lead to an escalation of terrorism in the Punjab and during the time that they were applied they helped transform the Punjab into a police-military state devoid of human rights along the same pattern of Nagaland earlier. Many expressed the fear that the army's overt presence was creating a Northern Ireland type of situation in this strategic border state. A People's Union for Democratic Rights (PUDR) fact-finding team sent to the Punjab in March 1985 to investigate the effectiveness of such laws found that '. . . not only were the laws ineffective with regard to the stated purpose, but worse are helping to further communal alienation and creating a favourable climate for communal terrorism. Thousands of Sikhs have been under detention, thousands more have become fugitives from army and police terror while others have been killed in false encounters and torture has been widespread.'[5]

General Aurora was right in his assertion that the continued presence of the army in the Punjab and such legislation could only alienate the Sikh community further. 'Operation Bluestar' could be mounted successfully because the terrorists in the Golden Temple were an easily identifiable target enabling the armed forces to deal with them swiftly and directly. The fact remains, however, that most of the terrorists were, and still are outside the gurd-waras. With the Sikhs so embittered, the ranks of the terrorists would swell, especially as in the aftermath of his death, Bhind-ranwale had become a cult hero, a status denied to him in his lifetime. Even recent Akali politics have surrendered to this trend with Harchand Singh Longowal for a time displaying an increasingly extremist stand during an internecine struggle for leadership in May 1985 in an effort to pander to outraged Sikh sentiments. If the Sikh population in the Punjab turns hostile it could provide a breeding ground for new terrorists for, with popular support the extremists could more easily conceal themselves and make the army's task of identifying and dealing with them more arduous. If events ever reach such a point the government will have a full-scale insurgency on its hands with the possibility of the movement spreading to neighbouring Kashmir. This would entail a semi-permanent army presence in the vital and strategic North-West, similar to the current state of affairs in the North-East.

Political scientists like Rajni Kothari have commented at length on the growing use and endorsement of violence by the State. Nowhere is this more aptly illustrated than in the wave of terror against Sikhs in New Delhi and 84 towns and cities which lasted four days and nights in the aftermath of Mrs Gandhi's tragic assassination on 31 October 1984. It was a massacre, the worst since Partition in 1947, in which the Sikh community had no chance to defend itself and which took a toll of 3,000 Sikh lives.[6] Some 1,200 women became widows in a matter of days. Over 50,000 Sikhs became refugees in Delhi with thousands of others crammed into makeshift refugee camps in other riot-stricken towns. Over Rs 100 millions' worth of property was looted and burned.

The pattern of violence underlying the events was one of calculated state terror. The carnage was not communal rioting but politically inspired violence against the Sikh community, with many Hindus coming to the defence of their neighbours. During three days of terrible killings in Delhi, the administration failed to take drastic action as mobs set upon helpless Sikh men, women and children, shops were looted, cars burnt, markets destroyed and houses gutted. The worst violence took place in the slums, or resettlement colonies, of New Delhi where local Congress (I) political functionaries in local blocks were largely responsible for instigating the reign of terror.[7] In the Trans-Jumuna slum localities of the capital, like Mongolpuri and Trilokpuri, mob fury was unleashed against the Sikhs in many instances by local Congress (1) activists who led crowds of lower castes and Harijans from neighbouring villages, identified the houses of Sikhs by means of voters' lists and supplied the mobs with kerosene to let loose a reign of terror to 'teach the Sikhs a lesson'.[8] The common pattern of violence took the form of lynching and burning alive of Sikhs. To quote from the joint commission of inquiry carried out by the New Delhi-based civil rights organizations, the PUDR and People's Union for Civil Liberties (PUCL) into the November riots: 'In all the affected spots, a calculated attempt to terrorize people was evident in the common tendency among the assailants to burn alive the Sikhs on the public roads.'[9] In the midst of the reign of terror unleashed on the capital, not a single political party tried to intervene to stop the rioting. It is a sad commentary on the state of India's politics when one recalls that in 1947 Nehru chased Hindu and Sikh rioters through the streets of New Delhi as they set upon the Muslim population.

Congress Party, police and administrative collusion in orchestrating the violence has been pointed out by a number of independent commissions of inquiry. In a report prepared by Rajni

Kothari entitled *Who Are The Guilty?*,[10] a large number of people, all belonging to the ruling party, have been accused, among others, of murder, rape, arson and loot. They include H.K.L. Bhagat, presently a member of Rajiv Gandhi's Central Cabinet and two MPs, Jagdish Tytler and Lalit Maken (in late July 1985 Lalit Maken and his wife were murdered in New Delhi by two men (at the time of writing their identity is not known), armed with semi-automatic weapons, and police believe he became the victim of Sikh terrorism for instigating the November riots). Even eminent Sikhs, with a longstanding reputation for distinguished service to the country like Lt.-Gen. Aurora, have been led to comment: 'The massacre of the Sikhs by hoodlums who had been led by certain functionaries of the Congress (I) party and the chance given to those people to pillage, burn, loot and kill people . . . That a government should permit such outbreaks of violence is something that is almost unheard of. But the government failed to combat the situation and, in certain places, the police encouraged the mobs and took part in it. The fact the government refused to hold an enquiry for six months is clear proof of Congress party involvement, if any proof is required.'[11]

Police and administrative collusion in the violence has also been documented. The *Report of the Citizens' Commission*,[12] which included in its team such eminent public figures as Justice S.M. Sikri, a former Chief Justice of India, Rajeshwar Dayal, a former Foreign Secretary, and Govind Narain, a former Home and Defence Secretary, states that police personnel at times deliberately misled army units who asked for directions to the riot-stricken areas. It accuses the administration of tardy deployment of the army, lack of effective coodination between the Delhi administration, the police and the armed forces, and is critical of the inadequacy of the army strength initially deployed. Despite the shoot-at-sight orders and the imposition of curfew the army was left with a lack of information from the police on the exact location of the riots. Even an ex-Inspector-General of Police commented in March 1985: 'The inactivity of the police during the holocaust in Delhi following Mrs Gandhi's assassination could not have taken place without political signals.'[13] Indeed the police bear a substantial measure of responsibility for inflaming passions. In certain localities police vans used loudspeakers to spread deliberately fabricated rumours that the Sikhs had poisoned the city's water supplies and that trains coming into New Delhi station from the Punjab carried the bodies of murdered and mutilated Hindus.

The pogroms against the Sikh community soon led to a new cycle of violence with the spate of bomb attacks by Sikh extremists in Delhi and other North Indian towns from 10 to 11 May 1985 which cost upwards of 80 lives. In a highly efficient synchronized operation Sikh militants placed bombs, concealed in transistor radios, in buses, trains and crowded localities. The areas selected as targets had seen some of the worst massacres of Sikhs in the November riots. Even the Punjab, despite the army's presence, was still prey to terrorism. Although the level of terrorist violence had abated since Sikh extremists had lost their charismatic leader, individual acts of terrorism still rocked the state. In March 1985 the vice-president of the BJP was shot in Chandigarh, and it was suggested that Bhindranwale's hit list of prominent Hindus had been revived. Subsequently in June the general secretary of the Congress (I), R.L. Bhatia, was injured in a gun attack carried out by the Sikh extremist Hindu group, the Babbar Khalsa. If such acts continue unabated they could merely play into the Congress (I)'s hands balancing the country's politics between extremism and fanaticism.

By mid-1985, to prevent events from taking such a turn, the government was under pressure, out of pure political self-interest, to bring an early political settlement to the Punjab. The Centre had already taken a number of welcome steps last March by releasing Akali leaders arrested the previous year under the National Security Act. But the government's underlying motives were interpreted by many as a ploy to undermine Longowal's leadership further as the subsequent rivalry for Akali party leadership between Longowal and released Akali leaders like the extremist, J.S. Talwandi, indicates.

Another welcome step last March was the government's agreement to hold a judicial inquiry into the November massacre, after refusing for almost six months demands from Opposition parties, civil liberties organizations, groups of eminent non-Sikhs and the entire Sikh community to investigate the killings. Once again, however, the government's goodwill remained in doubt because of the commission's limited terms of reference. A judge of the Supreme Court is to constitute a one-man commission of inquiry and its terms of reference have been diluted to avoid pinpointing the cause and the course of the disturbances, the adequacy of measures to control them and the identity of those responsible. Another government concession was the lifting of the ban on the Akali Dal's student wing, the All-India Sikh Students' Federation (AISSF) which had supported Bhindranwale and his demands for Khalistan throughout.

By June the internecine struggle for leadership among the various Akali factions which had been going on the previous month was resolved when moderate leader, H.S. Longowal, reasserted himself as president of the main Akali party, thus gaining a victory over the radicals now led by Bhindranwale's father, Joginder Singh. Most observers were pessimistic over any early settlement with the Centre because right up until the end of July Longowal was insisting, in his public declarations, that his party would only negotiate if the government conceded seven major demands. These included the release of all jailed Sikh political activists, the repeal of anti-terrorist laws that permitted the authorities to arrest and search without a warrant and hold trials in special courts, and the withdrawal of army troops from the Punjab. The government's goodwill was underscored by the leniency that is to be shown to the army deserters who had mutinied in the aftermath of 'Operation Bluestar' and who are to be rehabilitated rather than court-martialled.

By July a settlement was reached under which the government conceded a major demand of the Sikhs, the merger of Chandigarh with the Punjab, previously shared as a state capital with Haryana. Another Sikh demand regarding the sharing of the waters of interstate rivers is to be referred to a tribunal. The government also announced that it was withdrawing the Armed Forces Special Powers Act which gives the state authorities extraordinary powers to search and arrest without a warrant. Special courts that were set up in the Punjab in 1984 under an anti-terrorist law would now try only those people arrested on charges of hijacking and waging a war against the country. The main demand of the Akalis, that of decentralization, has been referred to the Sarkaria Commission, a commission set up by the government in June 1983 to review the existing arrangements between the Centre and the states with regard to the sharing of functions and which has yet to give its final report.

The Akali demands are based on a party programme drawn up in 1977 called the Anandpur Sahib resolution. The most serious issue raised was the question of devolution of powers to the states, a proposal consistently rejected by Mrs Gandhi. The document also contained various political, territorial and religious demands (see pp. 294–6). Despite the fact that the Akalis have never advocated a separate Sikh state of Khalistan or secession, the document had always been controversial in the eyes of many Hindus because some of its wording had been interpreted as a demand for a separate Sikh state.

As a rift had been created between the Sikhs and Hindus by recent events, the Anandpur Sahib resolution had acquired even more sinister implications in the eyes of the majority community. The resolution was considered to pave the way for the disintegration of the nation. References to the interests of the Sikh nation were regarded as implying a recognition of separate nationhood for the Sikhs. Moreover, the proposal that the Centre's power be limited to defence, foreign affairs and currency was seen by the Hindus as carrying the seeds of the country's disintegration.

Whatever mistrust had been created between the two communities, by early June, when secret negotiations began between Rajiv Gandhi and Longowal with Arjun Singh, the Governor of the Punjab, acting as intermediary, it was clear to the government that the situation was getting out of hand and that Longowal had to be strengthened against the extremists. In the immediate aftermath of the agreement, the Punjab was simmering down, terrorism had decreased; some detainees held under the various special laws were being released, although thousands were still being held; and the army had adopted a low profile in the state with its functions being taken over by the parliamentary Border Security Force (BSF).

Certainly it has been clear right along that the alienation in the Punjab could not be ignored as it had been in Mizoram and Nagaland in the remote North-East, for the Punjab is vital to India in many ways. It is a strategic border state; the centre for modern industry and military facilities: and constitutes India's breadbasket. Sikhs occupy top posts in the administration and the army. They represent 20 per cent of the Indian Army's officer corps and 11 per cent of its soldiers, despite constituting only 1.8 per cent of India's total population.

The prospect for a peaceful return to Sikh politics seemed a hopeful one as the settlement appeared to have enough support among the Sikhs and Hindus to curb the level of violence. Yet from the very outset of the agreement those political analyses pointing to an attenuation of the terrorist activities, now that the government had conceded most of Longowal's demands, should have paid more heed to reactions to the agreement from the Sikh extremists who categorically rejected it as a sellout. Even within Longowal's moderate Akali Dal party the settlement came under strident criticism. It should have been clear that the settlement itself implied an isolation of the extremists and that, given their own recent history of determined and ruthless politics of violence, and in their desperation at being delivered a near political death-blow, they were bound to react vehemently against the accord with their own brand of political self-expression. This was soon forthcoming.

On 20 August 1985 Longowal's assassination by Sikh extremists, less than a month after he signed a peace accord with Rajiv Gandhi, threatened to plunge the Punjab into renewed political turmoil. Longowal's martyrdom was a sobering reminder of how deep and wide the Punjab problem still runs. The ramifications of his murder were considerable. Firstly, it left a leadership void in the moderate section of the Akali Dal very difficult to fill, especially as the record of the leaders in the past months had been a dismal one smacking of opportunism. The party, in the best of times an unwieldy political vehicle, had been provided with sound leadership since Longowal had assumed the presidentship in 1980 as he had steered a midway course, avoiding confrontation both with the Centre and with the more radical Sikh elements. Indeed Longowal's ritual three-day period of mourning was hardly over when reports spread of renewed factional infighting as two of the Akali Dal's largest factions clashed over the naming of his interim successor. However, once again the issue was resolved through consultation and Surjit Singh Barnala emerged as the new leader while strategies were adopted to accommodate other political contenders like G.S. Tohra. Suspicion arises whether such reports of infighting are sometimes inspired exaggerations of genuine internal party debates on alternatives with a view to weakening the Akali Dal. This would be in line with earlier Congress (I) and Central government tactics.

Secondly, the assassination posed a serious challenge to Rajiv Gandhi and the future of his tenuous peace accord, notwithstanding his attempts to make conciliation the keynote of his leadership. Thirdly, Longowal's murder had also cast doubts on the wisdom of Rajiv Gandhi's decision to hold early polls despite the warning that it would trigger terrorism. Many prominent Hindu and Sikh public figures issued a statement in the immediate aftermath of Longowal's murder saying Rajiv Gandhi's Congress (I) wanted early elections to install itself in power in the Punjab regardless of the cost, a victory which analysts said stood a good chance of being realized. Their statement blamed the government's decision on early polls for Longowal's assassination. Longowal himself had urged the government to delay elections till the spring of 1986, pointing out that the state was still tense, urging that time was required to restore normalcy and broaden popular support for the peace agreement. Longowal had eventually agreed, however, to go ahead with early polling and his party was in the process of fielding candidates for 117 state assembly seats and 13 parliamentary seats when he was gunned down.

Despite the demands for the postponement of elections in the wake of Longowal's murder, the government decided to go ahead with polling on 25 September, three days later than originally planned, lest any prolonged postponement be interpreted as a sign of weakness and serve to encourage terrorism. For, whatever the date set, the extremists could be expected to create trouble. Certainly postponement of the elections beyond January 1986 would have made election issues of the forthcoming tribunal awards, as agreed upon in the July 24 settlement, whereas the new government will be in a position to implement them. For example, the territorial commission entrusted with the transfer of some of the Hindi-speaking areas of Punjab to Haryana was to give its award by 31 December and the transfer of Chandigarh to Punjab and these areas to Haryana is to take place by 26 January 1986.

The Punjab had been under direct federal administration, or President's rule, since late 1983 when the state government was dissolved on the plea that it failed to stop terrorism. President's rule expired on 5 October 1985 and a constitutional amendment was required to extend it. Should the government have wished to do so this would not have posed a problem, for the Congress (I) held an overhwelming majority in Parliament. However, any extension of President's rule was against the government's interest for it would create uncertainty and give an excuse to the Akali hardliners, notably Joginder Singh and other detractors of the accord, to create trouble.

With most of the extremists, including Joginder Singh's militant breakaway faction of the Akali Dal, announcing a boycott of the elections, a position supported by the All-India Sikh Students' Federation (AISSF), more violence and terror were expected in the terrorists' desperate attempt to disrupt the poll. But the consensus of opinion amongst the Sikhs, especially in the wake of Longowal's murder, had turned against the mindless and relentless campaign of extremist terror so that even if terrorism continued in the future, the terrorists' support base would be more marginalized. The extremists' refusal to participate in elections and to press for their demands for an independent Khalistan by constitutional means – with the exception of a faction belonging to Joginder Singh's group which broke away in early September to form a hardline faction of the Akali Dal to fight the elections – can be interpreted as an unspoken admission of the limited degree of their popular base. For despite the extremist rhetoric and terrorist violence, the majority of Sikhs in Punjab do not support the idea of an independent Khalistan. They have too much at stake, including economic prosperity in Punjab whose success is closely dependent on remaining with India. The miracle of the Green Revolution in agriculture in the state was made possible by the supply of fertilizers from India and an assured grain market for their produce, together with accessibility to Indian ports for imports and exports – all of which would no longer be available in a landlocked independent Khalistan. Furthermore, the few million Sikhs living in other Indian states as thriving businessmen, traders, administrators etc., have too much at stake to support Khalistan.

A Congress (I) victory in the forthcoming elections would not necessarily have been in the Punjab's interest. In the end the Akali Dal won a convincing majority. This is sometimes interpreted on the basis of population figures that part of the Hindu vote swung over to them, thus reversing the trend towards communal polarization. More plausible is the view that the Mazhabis, or Scheduled Caste Sikhs, which earlier constituted a Congress (I) vote bank, swung into solidarity with the Akalis and were joined by some of the immigrant Untouchable Hindu labour, while the urban and higher-caste Hindus polarized into the Congress (I) vote.

The next important battleground in the contest for power was the elections to the Shiromani Gurdwara Prabandhak Committee

(SGPC), or Central Gurdwara Management Committe. This is a kind of Sikh parliament wielding enormous influence in Sikh politics and which, among other things, controls the purse strings of the Sikh temples, whose revenues are estimated at Rs 160–240 million a year. The existing president, G.S. Tohra, a mercurial and wily figure in Sikh politics, now in the presidentship for 14 years, faced some opposition to his candidature which was opposed by extremists, but won handsomely. Such a development could provide the solution for bringing to heel the extremely dangerous nature of extremist Sikh nationalism. The precedents for such a dénouement are of some relevance. The popular force of Indian subnationalism should not be underestimated and it is of some pertinence to the Punjab problem to recall that similar upsurges and ideological movements in other regions were solved when state governments of similar, less extreme persuasion, came to power. It was only when the regional party, the Dravida Munnetra Kazhayam (DMK), came to power in Tamil Nadu in 1967 that Tamilian demands for a separate nation ceased. Similarly, it was only when the CPI(M) came to power in West Bengal that the tactics of selective murder and other forms of violent activities by the extremist Maoist group, the Naxalites, could be curbed.

The settlement with the Akalis attests to the fact that the government cannot ignore regional aspirations. Today the most important issue facing the government will be that of Centre-state relations and the need to concede demands for decentralization. The latter will not be yielded so easily, for unfortunately the pattern for a centralized state was firmly set by Mrs Gandhi. Throughout her tenure as prime minister she remained staunch in her conviction that only a highly centralized state could safeguard India's fragile unity because she believed the country's integrity to be under continuing threat.

It was a belief inherited from her father, Nehru's generation, nurtured by the trauma of Partition which cost half a million lives. It was reinforced in the fifties with the integration of hundreds of small princedoms of the old British Raj and in the sixties with the subsequent struggle to prevent India from disintegrating into independent linguistic states. Mrs Gandhi had to battle against national political leaders and in the seventies and eighties she was confronted with the growth of regionalism and the demand by non-Congress (I)-ruled states for decentralization. In her mind this was further proof of the dangerous trend of centrifugal forces to Indian unity.

What Mrs Gandhi and her son, Rajiv, have failed to understand is that the only way a firmly rooted pattern of unity can be forged, and the Punjab and Assam problems solved, is by building on a concept of unity centred on the concept of the plural nature of society. Indeed the basis of India's strength in the fifties and sixties arose primarily from her heterogeneity and the continuous dialogue between her different cultures. Today with the growing tide of violence and unrest of so many ethnic and religious groups the reversal of this trend, which took place from the seventies onwards, must be checked. Yet the Centre may be tempted to justify the preservation of its authority and powers by virtue of the fact that Rajiv Gandhi's main platform in the Congress (I)'s December 1984 general election victory stressed the need for a kind of unity based on a strong centralized state to combat the 'foreign hand' and 'secessionist trends'. But if Rajiv Gandhi chooses to forge a united India by further consolidating the authoritarian state and seeking to destroy political, religious and ethnic diversities, this will merely serve to exacerbate tensions. The danger that this trend may become a reality was given a further boost in the last elections with the total elimination of all the national Opposition parties, for it could strengthen Rajiv Gandhi's hand in any quest for further centralization of power and emphasis on homogenization of the country's pluralities. Today, given the new mood in the country, there is a real danger that the whole federal process may be undermined and the religious and ethnic minorities suppressed, although this could not be achieved so easily given a contradictory pull emerging in the continuing growth of regionalism.

The results of the December 1984 elections brought out this trend clearly with the results in the peripheral areas showing the consolidation of regional parties. In Andhra Pradesh the Telugu Desam won an overwhelming victory, polling all but one seat and receiving 42 per cent of the total vote. In Tamil Nadu the Congress (I) victory was achieved only thanks to its alliance with the regional party, the AIADMK. In Kerala, the local Congress(J), albeit an ally of the Congress (I), won 12 seats against 5 for its major opponent the CPI(M). In Kashmir Farouq Abdullah and the National Conference party was voted back. In West

Bengal and Tripura the CPI(M) retained their seats. In Sikkim the Congress (I) also lost. In Punjab and Assam elections could not be held because of the ongoing political disturbances in both states. In effect the Congress (I), despite its overwhelming victory, polling 49.2 per cent of the total vote and capturing 79 per cent of the seats in Parliament, is no longer a federal party but has been transformed into a party of the Hindi heartland.

The newly established basis of the Congress (I) in this belt was a development sought by Mrs Gandhi in the eighties as she attempted to draw the tide of Hindu fundamentalism towards her party away from Hindu revival groups. The latter had begun to declare that Hinduism was in danger in a Hindu majority state following the spate of several thousand conversions of Harijans to Islam in Meenakshipuram, Tamil Nadu, in 1981. Charges brought against her party for her appeasement of the minorities to the detriment of the Hindus also strongly influenced her new course of electoral politics.

It led Mrs Gandhi to the conviction that a Hindu backlash would arise from any further wooing of the minorities. Instead of challenging the emerging trend, she chose to exploit it for her party's benefit. Her stance sometimes became interpreted as anti-minority. Communal outbreaks between Hindus and Muslims were blamed on the 'foreign hand'. The same accusations were levelled against the Sikhs, especially the Akali party, which was described as potentially secessionist in both her and Rajiv Gandhi's speeches. Similarly, when a problem arose in Kashmir, Muslims were accused of treachery.

By thus seeking out the Hindu vote bank she transformed the Congress (I) into a major communalist force. This development was a deliberate creation of her electoral politics and was in no way inevitable. In 1947, despite the violence of the subcontinent's communalist Partition, India remained secular and as an ideological force Hindu fundamentalism was inconsiderable and confined to marginal groups.

Many would argue that India's commitment to secularism had not been total right from 1947 and point to the Congress' guilt about accepting Partition along religious lines. Certainly a sense of failure at not being able openly to declare India to be a Hindu country has plagued extreme Hindu organizations like the RSS and Jan Sangh. Moreover, recent years have seen the steady erosion of the country's secular dialogue. This is evident from the use of communal organizations at the local level, a case in point being the Shiv Shena in Bombay whose main platform is a Maharashtra for Maharashtrians; by the displacement of political organizations by cultural associations like the RSS and the fundamentalist Muslim party, the Jamaat-e-Islami; and, lastly, by the infiltration of lumpen elements into the Congress (I) party, a process started by Mrs Gandhi's younger son, Sanjay.

Apart from the move away from the secularism by the Congress (I) in recent years, the party has also shifted its ideological stance. From the end of the Nehru era to all but the last two years of Mrs Gandhi's term in office, the Congress party cultivated a progressive image for itself by coopting the Communist programme for social and economic transformation into its socialist rhetoric. It attracted the minorities into its fold by pledging to provide them with security and upliftment. Today the retreat from poverty as a political issue has led to an erosion of the traditional support base of the party among minorities, tribals and the poor, becoming instead the new social base of the Hindu upper and monied classes.

It is not only the Congress (I) that has cultivated a new image for itself. The contours of politics have been changing as more and more groups are being mobilized into the political arena. Today political parties have become instruments of change and it is perhaps precisely because more and more social groups are achieving social mobility that the Brahmins and Kshatriyas, who form the bulwark of the Congress (I), are shedding their traditional rivalry and seeking to end this dependence of the Muslims and Harijans. They are instead creating new linkages with the Vaishyas and Sudras by pandering to Hindu sentiment. This is the analysis of former Muslim MP Syed Shahabuddin, who believes that although, in the long-term, some sort of understanding will be established by the Brahmins and Kshatriyas with the Vaishyas, he discounts any rapprochement with the Sudras. For this would involve a drastic redistribution of power and wealth since the Sudras, or Backward Castes, constitute over 50 per cent of the country's population.

If the interests of the minorities are to be safeguarded Syed Shahabuddin advocates the creation of a national party of all the disadvantaged groups, the Backwards Castes, Scheduled Castes, Scheduled Tribes and Muslims to defend their interests and achieve their objectives. For as he points out: 'In a plural society like India the real struggle is for a new equilibrium, a new balance, a new pattern of sharing power, goods and services.'[14]

One of the causes of the unprecedented tide of violence sweeping Gujarat since March 1985 stems precisely from the fact that Gujarat has become a battleground in the fight for a new distribution of power and resources in an increasingly competitive society as all castes and communities in the state have become conscious of their rights. The unfolding of the drama – which has cost upwards of 200 lives at the time of writing, disrupted the state economy and led to a state of civil war involving all castes and communities, pitting the police against the administration and the Congress (I) state government against the Opposition, with the army called in for the longest time since 1947 to quell a civilian disorder – needs to be recounted in detail for it shows the kind of ferment taking place in society as political and economic forces in favour of non-privileged groups threaten to erode the power base of the traditional dominant castes.

The ongoing wave of communal and caste violence, which began as a student-led agitation in mid-March 1985, was launched in response to an election promise given by Chief Minister Madhavsingh Solanki's Congress (I) state government in early 1985 to increase reservations from 10 to 18 per cent for the Backward Castes bringing the total reservations in Gujarat to 49 per cent. It was essentially an election strategy to win the votes of the largest group in the state, the Backward Castes, who constitute 40 per cent of the total population. The agitationists, led by upper-caste students and parents' associations, began to stage strikes in protest after Solanki had been re-elected with a massive mandate. By mid-March, as the students and parents' associations began calling for a boycott of the state college and high school examinations, the Solanki government retreated and announced suspension of the implementation of the new quota for a year and rescheduled the exams for 25 March.

At this point the movement had served its purpose and it had no reason to survive. Yet Solanki's move was interpreted by the students as an act of weakness and they now began demanding an end to all reservations. The agitators were also encouraged by the equivocal statements being made at this time by Rajiv Gandhi who stressed the need for a revision of the reservation policy as a whole, a position which he subsequently changed in support of reservations, albeit only for Scheduled Castes and Tribes.

Although Solanki himself was to blame for starting the agitation, the violence soon engulfed both the ruling Congress (I) and Opposition parties. In many localities of the state capital, Ahmedabad, mob attacks on Harijans and Muslims were led by local leaders of all parties, including the Congress (I).

Within a few weeks the pattern of violence was beginning to defy analysis by the national media as the movement began turning into a battle between all castes and communities with upper-caste Patels attacking Muslims and other groups being drawn into the battleground of confrontation. In some instances Backward Castes, whose alignment should logically have been with other underprivileged groups, joined upper-caste Patels against Harijans. The movement became more violent and acquired communal overtones on March 18 when some Muslims were attacked for refusing to close their shops in response to a strike called by the upper-caste parents' and students' associations. The Muslims soon retaliated by throwing stones at the agitators who came out into the streets of Ahmedabad staging anti-reservation demonstrations.

The next day tensions were exacerbated when the State Reserve Police cracked down on the walled city of Khadia, a traditional BJP stronghold with a long history of opposition to government, which left 30 people injured. This coincided with another development which merely served to focus a more determined anger against the Solanki government. On the very day of the police action in Khadia, the press broke a major scandal in which Mrugesh Jaikrishna, an industrialist of Ahmedabad and close patron of the chief minister, was arrested while attempting to transfer Rs 4.6 million out of the country. The next day Rajiv Gandhi visited the state capital to apprise himself of developments, while the movement gathered ground and began to press for the overthrow of the government.

One violent outbreak of caste and communal violence was hardly over when other outbreaks followed in other localities of Ahmedabad. From March 21 to mid-April there were daily incidents of mob violence, including looting and arson in the old walled city; in other places knifings occurred; in others local clashes between upper castes and Harijans. During this time the scale of the violence was threatening to tear Gujarat's social fabric asunder: upper castes, determined to do away with reservations, vented their anger by attacking lower castes; Hindus were pitted against Muslims; the police began battling both the upper-caste Hindus and the press, which had backed the agitators from the outset; finally the state government was fighting the Opposition.

On 15 April communal riots once again took place in the Dariapur locality, while in Khadia the police failed to impose a curfew. On 17 and 18 April the police tried to enter the Khadia and Gomtipur areas, strongholds of the Patels, a powerful upper-caste group of Gujarat. As the forces of law and order sought to enter these localities in the old walled city of Ahmedabad, they were met by brickbats from the residents stationed on the terraces as they sought to prevent the police from entering the maze of narrow lanes. Any member of the police force who succeeded in penetrating these alleys was met by a phalanx of women demonstrators who heckled and harassed the police by mouthing obscenities and gesticulating lewdly. The major newspaper, *Gujarat Samachar*, featured such scenes as an inspector being slapped by a woman demonstrator which merely served to fuel police anger. It rose to a still higher pitch when the local press reported that the police force had staged a naked parade through Gomtipur, an allegation which national journalists despatched to the spot found to have been deliberately fabricated.

The agitators now resorted to the judiciary to intimidate the police force and to render the strongholds of the agitation invulnerable to the police. The agitators obtained an unprecedented court order banning particular police inspectors from stepping into the areas under their charge. It included a commandant of the State Reserve Police whose ban was issued by the Gujarat High Court. The ban orders were now followed up by appeals for an official commission of inquiry into police atrocities.

By 19 April the agitators seemed to be gaining ground on two fronts. On that day Solanki entered into negotiations with the anti-reservationists and gave in to all their demands, agreeing to order an inquiry into alleged police atrocities and promising to punish any policeman found guilty. At the same time the agitators' strongholds became impregnable as the prohibitory orders from the courts against the police were issued and the army had to be called in again in Khadia. The situation in the city now went out of control. Mob attacks on slums erupted into an all-out caste war. On 22 April the worst massacre of the agitation took place in which an entire Muslim slum was completely destroyed and a number of people killed by armed mobs.

By this time police anger over the court bans was brought to the point of no return when a head constable, who was accompanying the commission of inquiry's members into Khadia, was stabbed to death. The police force, in an unprecedented sequel, now revolted by going on a seven-hour rampage which left the *Gujarat Samachar*, the state's largest selling newspaper, gutted, several middle- and upper-middle-caste colonies were attacked and the streets were littered with burnt scooters and autorickshaws.

The trouble soon spread to other cities like Baroda, Surat and elsewhere. The army was now called in for a second time in five weeks to impose a curfew that the state government had been unable to enforce. This did not prevent fresh outbreaks of killings, bringing the death toll at this point to about a hundred. Indeed despite the agitation being suspended on 23 April in the wake of Solanki's concessions, it was again resumed on 1 May with the same pattern of violence being repeated and which, at the time of writing at the end of July 1985, had left a toll of over two hundred dead.

For a period Gujarat had not seen a normal day's life for months on end. Curfew remained in force most of the time, while schools and colleges were shut. Business and commerce had come to a standstill. In the first week of June 45 trade and business organizations of Gujarat went on strike to protest against the failure of the Solanki government to control the law-and-order situation. The protest soon spread as a hundred businesses all over the state came to a halt. In mid-June the circle of protest widened as municipal employees of Ahmedabad began a civic stir in protest against the policies of the Solanki government. Huge sections of the population now rose in revolt because of the ineffectiveness of the state government. For months after the worst spells of violence in March and April, the government failed to restore the confidence of the people affected by the riots, with 5,000 people in Ahmedabad still in relief camps.

While Solanki had become a general target of attack for his inept handling of the situation, he himself sought to blame the Opposition for the continuing agitation. Amidst the pressures for his resignation from the Centre, which he finally yielded to at the beginning of July, allegations were made by both the Congress (I) and Opposition accusing each other of inciting the communal riots which press investigations claimed were not spontaneous. This fact was given credence when the agitationists, in their negotiations with the government, demanded a judicial probe by a High Court judge into the communal and caste violence for which they disclaim responsibility. In fact there have been widespread allegations that pro-Congress (I) lumpen elements have been behind the bloodbath in an attempt to discredit the anti-reservationists, an allegation made by the political scientist, Rajni Kothari, from the agitation's outset. This confirms his assertion of the growing criminalization of politics all over the country, the current example of which has been truly horrifying and has led to the creation of an unprecedented sense of insecurity among people.

An analysis of the changing patterns of economic and political power in Gujarat shows that a social dynamic has been at work for the past few decades as a result of political movements and economic change which have created new avenues of mobility for all underprivileged groups in the state. The first social upsurge was that of the Patidars, a lower-caste group who migrated to the cities and bettered themselves. This was followed by the rise of the Kshatriyas, a heterogeneous conglomeration of subcastes which has now become the platform of the Backward Castes. Finally, more than three decades of reservations have benefited certain segments of the Scheduled Castes and Tribes. Over the past fifteen years the rise of these latter groups has upset the social balance and a backlash has been taking place. For Gujarat is a highly conservative society with an extremely narrow class base where traditional intolerance of the lower castes, Harijans and minorities is amongst the strongest in India. For example, Gujarat has the highest rate of untouchability according to official government-sponsored studies and the most brutal carnage of Muslims took place in Gujarat in 1969.

Traditionally the reins of economic and political power in Gujarat have been held by the Patels, a powerful commercial caste, comprising no more than 8 per cent of the state's population. However, the years since Independence have seen a steady erosion of their power base. They were first undermined as a landed class when land reforms and ceilings reduced the size of their properties. The creation of panchayats then cut away at their political power, although their political influence had declined considerably with the rise of the Kshatriyas, a group largely composed of small farmers. By the eighties the Congress (I) was winning elections in the state with the support of the Kshatriyas,

Scheduled Castes, Scheduled Tribes and Muslims. The latest concession to the Backward Castes, if implemented, appears all the more threatening to the upper castes because, unlike the other underprivileged groups, they possess a well-established political power base. Solanki's attempt to woo the Backward Castes by extending reservations to their group merely illustrates how the political process has led to the mobilization of different groups in society and contributed to India's ferment.

Certainly the caste factor continues to play a not inconsiderable role in political arithmetic as the Centre's calculations over Solanki's replacement shows. To avoid a 'Kshatriya backlash' from the pro-Solanki elements in the State Assembly, a report of the All India Congress Committee (I) (AICC (I)) recommended that Solanki be sworn in as a member of the union council of ministers. This would follow the same pattern as that of the former Bihar state chief minister Chandrashekhar Singh, who, after being replaced by Bindeshwari Dubey, was inducted into the Central government to pacify the Rajput lobby in Bihar. By August, with the replacement of Solanki and conceding of most of the demands of the upper-caste agitationists, the situation seemed to be simmering down. However, the problem remains far from final solution. There has been a growing together of local Muslim, tribal and Scheduled Caste communities, sometimes supported by sections of the Backward Castes who feel that the government has given in to the upper-caste lobby of agitationists who have the sympathy of the press and establishment. Reports of this backlash against the upper castes, including a huge rally in Ahmedabad, were played down in the media. The underprivileged now seem to be organizing and have been heartened by a High Court judgment directing that a 31-per-cent reservation for them in Class XI of schools which was announced recently, to the anger of the upper castes, should not be disturbed. The upper castes are again threatening agitation and a caste struggle seems again to be polarizing. A particularly disquieting earlier incident involved serious embarrassment for the army who had earlier been charged with stopping a defiant Hindu procession into a Muslim locality. When the mob surged forward the political orders were changed, so that the false impression was created that the army merely stood by in the face of a defiant crowd who later inflicted casualties on the Muslims in a communal killing.

The turbulent events in Gujarat in recent months serve as a testimony to the vital and fluid currents of change that are flowing through Indian society. As every region, with its own local histories and power group structures, is coming to terms with the forces of modernization and change according to its own momentum, old structures are breaking down and new avenues of mobility are being created, giving rise to new pressures and tensions. Certainly the political process has helped to bring this about for over the past ten years group after group has used politics to obtain, more and more, privileges it can secure as a member of a group rather than the rights and privileges that should be available to every citizen by virtue of citizenship. As more and more groups are co-opted into the power structure and competition for scarce resources intensifies, Indian society will be convulsed by outbreaks of violence similar to the current Gujarat experience if the state becomes increasingly repressive in its effort to maintain the hegemony of the traditional élite.

What is needed today is sound political leadership, combined with a strong vision, if India is to come to terms with the caste, ethnic, communal and religious tensions which at times appear to tear the social fabric apart by the frightening intensity of their outbreaks. Mrs Gandhi's legacy of exploiting the latter for short-term political gain must be put aside for a politics of consensus to reestablish a dialogue between the different groups in society. It is a tribute to Indian democracy that, amidst the violence and turbulence accompanying his mother's death, Rajiv Gandhi was able to effect a transition of interim rule, to call elections so soon after his mother's demise and establish a smooth changeover of leadership. This is proof that democracy has been firmly implanted on Indian soil. The challenge in the years ahead will be to mould a framework of democracy that will accommodate the interests of a multi-ethnic and multi-religious society and allow federalism to develop in favour of devolution of power to the states. Above all, attitudes of mind among the élite with their increasing proclivity to intolerance of underprivileged groups and minorities will have to be confronted if the stirrings of unrest and the rising tide of consciousness among the latter are to be contained and absorbed within the parameters of Indian democracy.

It seemed for a time that the new atmosphere created by Rajiv Gandhi had begun to assuage the earlier bitterness of such confrontations. There was widespread euphoria that his prag-atic forward-looking policies were rapidly 'solving' such seem-ingly intractable problems as those of Punjab and Assam; that Gujarat seemed to be simmering down and that the 20-year-old insurgency in Mizoram was also about to be ended with another imminent agreement. Obviously the defusing of tension by a belated recognition of realities by the Centre on these various issues was a great step forward, but it merely bought time to deal more calmly with the fundamentals of each of the problems which very much remain as they were. Suspicion is now reviving that the change of tactics was purely pragmatic with the aim less of solving the problems as of weakening opponents like the Akalis, the Assam agitationists and so forth by softer and more subtly divisive approaches when uncompromising confrontation had proved counterproductive. The territorial commission on the Punjab is already running into problems with suspicion of a lack of good faith on the part of the Centre in manipulating the terms of reference beyond the Rajiv Gandhi–Longowal agreement limit-ing territorial transfers to 'contiguous' areas. If the Akalis, who had responded to the atmosphere of compromise, become dis-illusioned and there is a renewed drift to confrontation, the Sikh–Hindu divide, which is far from healed, will again widen and community sympathy for the extremists will revive. The Assam settlement, although eminently reasonable and practical in the circumstances, is again being obfuscated in political debate with terms like 'foreigners' and 'minorities' again becoming con-fused; and no group among the many communities in Assam being really happy. There is a reluctance to face the issue of what happens to foreigners who entered Assam after 1971 and who under law should be deported, as also about practical steps to safeguard Assamese cultural identity which itself is fragmented with Assam tribal groups somewhat suspicious of the higher-caste 'Assam movement' leadership.

In the Mizo negotiations there is also obviously a deep-seated mutual suspicion of bona fides on each side.

This all brings one back again to Indian perceptions of the social ferment which continues to intensify. It will be a mistake to view this intensification as some sort of prelude to disintegration during the coming 'dangerous decades'. It is a process which has been continuing over millennia and the fermentation is itself a sign of vitality. Perhaps some of the impressions described in this book will assist in focusing a few insights into the current churning of India's social ocean.

New Delhi
December 1985

Notes

* Full details of these references will be found in the Bibliography.

Introduction

1 Malati Shengde, *The Civilized Demons of the Rig Veda.**
2 O.K. Ghosh, *The Changing Indian Civilization.**
3 Richard Lannoy, *The Speaking Tree*, p. 171.*
4 B.N. Dhoundiyal, *Rajasthan District Gazetteers, Ajmer*, Government Central Press, Jaipur, 1966, pp.740–41.
5 Pupul Jayakar, *The Earthen Drum: an Introduction to the Ritual Arts of Rural India.**
6 'This Mahmoud of Ghazni's second . . . expedition into . . . Guzerat, the carrying off of the idol of Somnat, and dividing it into four pieces, one of which he is reported to have placed on the threshold of the Imperial Palace, while he sent two others to Mecca and Medina respectively.' Elliott and Dowson, *History of India as told by its own historians*, Cosmopolitan Publishers, Aligarh, 1952 reprint, vol. II, p. 537.
7 Gaudefroy-Demonbynes, *Histoire du Monde*, vol. VII, *Le Monde musulman et byzantin*, 1931, p.61. See also Gordon T. Bowles, *The People of Asia*, Weidenfeld & Nicolson, London, 1977, p. 90: 'The initial basis of Islam seems to have been the polytheistic religion of the proto-Arabic Nabateans, which centred around the worship of the chief deity Allah and the Black Stone of the Ka'aba.'
8 Dr V.C. Channa, interview.*
9 Louis Dumont, *Homo Hierarchicus.**
10 V.S. Naipaul, *A Wounded Civilization*, 1977, p. 157.*
11 M.N. Srinivas, 'The Future of Indian Caste'.*
12 D.D. Kosambi, *The Culture and Civilization of Ancient India in Historical Outline*, p. 50.*
13 Dr Sudhir Kakar, interview.*
14 Richard Lannoy, interview.*
15 M.N. Srinivas, *Social Change in Modern India*, Orient Longman, New Delhi, 1980, p. 54.
16 N. Chaudhuri, *The Continent of Circe*, Chatto, London, 1965.
17 Supreme Court Justice D.A. Desai, interview.*

1   India on the threshold of the eighties

1 Lannoy, *The Speaking Tree*, p. 166.

2   André Béteille, interview, 28 March 1983.*
3   Kakar, interview.
4   Dumont, *Homo Hierarchicus*, p. 276.
5   André Béteille, *Studies in Agrarian Social Structure*, p. 196.*
6   Gunnar Myrdal, *Asian Drama*, p. 44.*
7   André Béteille, *Equality and Inequality: Theory and Practice*, p. 18.*
8   Dr Karan Singh, interview.*
9   Béteille, interview.
10   A.B. Vajpayee, interview.*
11   André Béteille, *Caste, Class and Power*, p. 187.*
12   Syed Shahabuddin, interview.
13   Lannoy, *The Speaking Tree*, p. xix.
14   Karan Singh, interview.
15   Shahabuddin, interview.
16   Karan Singh, interview.
17   Shahabuddin, interview.
18   Shahabuddin, interview.
19   M.S. Golwakar, *We or Our Nation Defined*, Bharat Prakashan, Nagpur, 1947, pp. 55–6, quoted in Mohan Ram, *Hindi against India*, Rachna Prakashan, New Delhi, 1968, p. 64.
20   Nari Rustomji, *Imperilled Frontiers – India's North-Eastern Borderlands*, excerpt published in *Sunday*, 27 March 1983.
21   Vajpayee, interview.
22   Vajpayee, interview.
23   Brian Mathieson, *The Masks of Power*, Eyre & Spottiswoode, London, 1969, p. 354.
24   P.K. Bose, 'Social Mobility and Caste Violence: a Study of the Gujarat Riots', *Economic and Political Weekly (EPW)*, 18 April 1981, p. 714.
25   Lannoy, *The Speaking Tree*, p. 252.
26   André Béteille, interview, 4 April 1983.*
27   Béteille, *Caste, Class and Power*, p. 184.
28   Lannoy, interview.
29   Shahabuddin, interview.
30   Shahabuddin, interview.
31   Shahabuddin, interview.
32   Shahabuddin, interview.
33   Shahabuddin, interview.
34   Quoted in *Commissioner's Report for Scheduled Castes and Scheduled Tribes, 1969–1970*, p. 192.
35   Vajpayee, interview.
36   *Statesman*, 21 September 1982.
37   *Statesman*, 21 September 1982.

38 *Indian Express*, 19 September 1982.
39 Joan P. Menscher, *Agriculture and Social Structure in Tamil Nadu*, p. 154.*
40 Marc Galanter, 'Abolition of Disabilities: Untouchables and the State' in J. Michael Mahar (ed.), *The Untouchables in Contemporary India*, p. 252.*
41 Gobinda Mukhoty, interview.*
42 Galanter in *The Untouchables*, p. 253.
43 *Gazetteer of the Bombay Presidency*, vol. XVIII, part II, 1885, pp. 116–17.
44 Desai, interview.
45 Desai, interview.
46 Desai, interview.
47 Desai, interview.
48 Supreme Court Justice (now Chief Justice of India) P.N. Bhagwati interview.*
49 Srinivas, 'The Future of Indian Caste'.
50 Shahabuddin, interview.
51 Béteille, interview, 28 March 1983.

2   The countryside

1 Inderjit Singh, *Small Farmers and the Landless in South Asia.*
2 Béteille, *Class, Caste and Power*, pp. 219–20.
3 Susan George, *How the Other Half Dies*, p. 125.*
4 Kripa Shankar, 'Poverty and Economic Growth', *Mainstream*, 28 November 1981, p. 13.
5 'Land Reform and Rural Poverty', book review, *Mainstream*, 19 December 1981.
6 *Economic Times*, 9 March 1981.
7 John Harriss, *Capitalism and Peasant Farming: Agrarian Structure and Ideology in Tamil Nadu*, p. 231.*
8 Francine Frankel, *India's Political Economy, 1947–1977*, p. 190.*
9 Frankel, *India's Political Economy*, p. 317.
10 T.J. Byres, 'The New Technology, Class Formation and Class Action in the Indian Countryside', *Journal of Peasant Studies*, part II, p. 425.
11 V.M. Dandekar and Nilakantha Rath, 'Poverty in India', *EPW*, 9 January 1971, p. 114.
12 Harriss, *Capitalism and Peasant Farming*, p. 178.
13 Sheilla Bhalla, 'New Relations of Production in Haryana Agriculture', *EPW*, Review of Agriculture, March 1976, p. A–29.

14   Bina Agarwal, *Mechanization in Indian Agriculture: an Analytical Study of the Punjab.**

15   Harriss, *Capitalism and Peasant Farming*, p. 124.

16   S.A. Barnett, 'The Process of Withdrawal in a South Indian Caste' in M. Singer (ed.), *Entrepreneurship and the Modernization of Occupations*, Duke University Press, 1973, p. 190, cited in Harriss, p. 147.

17   Joan P. Menscher, 'Agricultural Labourers and Poverty', *EPW*, 2–9 January 1982, p. 43.

18   *World Development Report 1982*, p. 80.**

19   Dandekar and Rath, 'Poverty in India', p. 115.

20   V.K. Garg, *Rural Economics*, Premier Book Co., New Delhi, 1983, p. 54.

21   Inderjit Singh, *Small Farmers*, p. I:34.**

22   Byres, *New Technology*, p. 439.

23   Harriss, *Capitalism and Peasant Farming*, p. 439.

24   B.N. Chinnapa, 'Impact of Cultivation of HYVs of Paddy on Employment and Incomes' in B.N. Farmer (ed.), *Green Revolution: Technology and Change in the Rice Growing Areas of Tamil Nadu and Sri Lanka*, p. 220.**

25   Menscher, 'Agricultural Labourers and Poverty', *EPW*, 2–9 January 1982, p. 39.

26   Bunker Roy, interview, 6 April 1982.**

27   Figures calculated from *Selected Plan Statistics of Bihar*, Planning Board, 1976.

28   Cited in monograph prepared as part of the Lokayan Project of the Centre for the Study of Developing Societies, New Delhi.

29   Menscher, *Agriculture and Social Structure*.

30   G. Parthasarathy and K. Adiseshu, 'Real Wages of Agricultural Labour in Andhra Pradesh: Two decades of Stagnation', *EPW*, 31 July 1982, p. 1246.

31   Abhijit Sankar Dasgupta, 'Rural Indebtedness: a Case Study', *Mainstream*, 31 October 1981, p. 21.

32   Sudha Pai, 'In a U.P. Village: Changing Agrarian Relations', *Mainstream*, 23 August 1980, p. 24.

33   Lannoy, *The Speaking Tree*, p. 261.

34   Jagjivan Ram, interview.**

35   Ram, interview.

36   A. Srivastava, 'Bihar: Landlord's Mafia in Bhojpur', *EPW*, 3–10 January 1981, p. 17.

37   D. Bandyopadhyaya, interview, 12 April 1983.**

38   Desai, interview.

39   *Census of India 1961*, vol. XIX, part VI, no. 12, Delhi, 'A Socio-economic Study of Village Shinghu', p. 55.

40 *Census of India 1961*, vol. XIV, Rajasthan, part VI, 'A Village Survey', Monograph no. 6, Bhangarh, 1965, p. 31.
41 *The Economist*, 'Survey of India', London, 28 March 1981, p. 43.
42 N.N. Vyas, *Bondage and Exploitation in Tribal India.**
43 Bhagwati, interview.
44 Christoph von Fürer Haimendorf, *Tribes of India: the Struggle for Survival*, p. 49.*
45 B.M. Desai (ed.), *Intervention for Rural Development: Experiences of the Small Farmer's Development Agency.**
46 Desai, *Intervention for Rural Development*, p. 200.
47 Desai, *Intervention for Rural Development*, p. 200.
48 J.C. Jetli, interview.*
49 Inderjit Singh, *Small Farmers*, VI, p. 8.
50 Inderjit Singh, *Small Farmers*, VI, p. 13.
51 Inderjit Singh, *Small Farmers*, IX, p. 9.
52 Quoted in Charan Singh, *India's Economic Policy: The Gandhian Blueprint*, p. 103.*
53 Kripa Shankar, 'Employment for Rural Areas', *Mainstream*, 21 February 1981, p. 20.
54 V. Sivalinga Prasad and V. Bhaskara Rao, 'Obstacles to Organizing the Rural Poor', *Mainstream*, 13 December 1980, p. 21.
55 People's Union for Democratic Rights (PUDR), *Agrarian Unrest in Patna: an Investigation into Recent Repression.**
56 Béteille, *Studies in Agrarian Social Structure*, pp. 166–7.
57 Special correspondent, 'Andhra Pradesh: Casteism through Elections'. *EPW*, 12 February 1983, p. 213.
58 Gail Omvedt, 'Maharashtra: Rasta Roko, Kulaks and the Left', *EPW*, 28 November 1981, pp. 1937–40.
59 S. Rajadurai, 'Tamil Nadu: Green Power on the March', *EPW*, 27 December 1980.
60 Gail Omvedt, 'Politico-economic Developments in Maharashtra', *EPW*, 4 October 1980, p. 1673.
61 *Indian Express*, 18 May 1983.
62 Editorial, 'The Caste of the Poor', *EPW*, 1 March 1980, p. 449.
63 *Indian Express*, 25 May 1983.
64 PUDR, *Agrarian Unrest.*

3   Land: radical laws and tardy reforms

1 *Gazetteer of the Bombay Presidency*, p. 112.
2 Frankel, *India's Political Economy*, p. 194.
3 Frankel, *India's Political Economy*, p. 190.
4 Mahar, *The Untouchables*, p. 46.
5 *Report of the Committee on Ceiling on Land Holdings*, New Delhi, 1961, pp. 5–8.

6   P.C. Joshi, 'Land Reform and Agrarian Change in India and Pakistan since 1947: II', *The Journal of Peasant Studies*, vol. I, no. 3, April 1974, p. 329.

7   Ashok K. Upadhyaya, 'Peasant Organizations in Thane District: a Critical Overview', *EPW*, 30 January 1982, p. 165.

8   Sailen Dasgupta, 'West Bengal: Evasion of Land Ceiling', *Mainstream*, 5 July 1980, p. 13.

9   Béteille, *Caste, Class and Power*.

10   Béteille, *Caste, Class and Power*, p. 121.

11   Béteille, *Caste, Class and Power*, p. 119.

12   P.C. Joshi, 'Problems of Land Reforms in the Second Stage', *Man and Development*, vol. III, no. 1, March 1981, p. 16.

13   Narendar Pani, *Reforms to Preempt Change: Land Legislation in Karnataka*, p. 62.*

14   These figures are cited in *Land Reforms in Andhra Pradesh*, Government of Andhra Pradesh, 1979, pp. 2–4.

15   P. Radhakrishnan, 'Land Reforms in Theory and Practice: the Kerala Experience', *EPW*, Review of Agriculture, 26 December 1981, p. A–130.

16   B.S. Rathore and P.N. Sharma, *Evaluation of the Implementation of Agricultural Ceiling Laws in Bhilwara District, Rajasthan*, p. 121.*

17   Rathore and Sharma, *Evaluation*, p. 122.

18   Pani, *Reforms to Preempt Change*, p. 83.

19   A.R. Bandyopadhyay, interview, 13 April 1983.*

20   A.R. Bandyopadhyay, interview, 13 April 1983.

21   D. Bandyopadhyaya, interview, 12 April 1983.

22   Pani, *Reforms to Preempt Change*.

23   A.R. Bandyopadhyay, 'Distribution of Land to the Landless: an Appraisal', *Kurukshetra*, special number, 1 January 1980.

24   Louis J. Walinsky (ed.), *The Selected Papers of Wolf Ladejinsky: Agrarian Reform as Unfinished Business*, p. 541.*

25   *Agricultural Census Bulletin No. 22*, Government of India, Ministry of Agriculture (Department of Agriculture and Cooperation), Agricultural Census Division, Annexure II.

26   Quoted in Joshi, 'Problems of Land Reforms in the Second Stage', p. 11.

27   *Task Force on Land Reforms*, Planning Commission, 1973, p. 22.

28   Walinsky (ed.), *Ladejinsky Papers*, p. 541.

29   Menscher, *Agriculture and Social Structure*, p. 117.

30   N.N. Vyas, interview.*

31   D. Bandyopadhyaya, interview, 12 April 1983.

32   G. Omvedt, 'Capitalist Agriculture and Rural Classes in India', *EPW*, Review of Agriculture, 26 December 1981, p. A–148.

33   D. Bandyopadhyaya, interview, 12 April 1983.

34 *Agricultural Census 22.*

35 *Agricultural Census 22.*

36 D. Bandyopadhyaya, interview, 12 April 1983.

37 A.R. Bandyopadhyay, 'Lessons from Consolidation Operations', *Papers Presented at the Commonwealth Workshop on the Consolidation of Landholdings*, Technical Paper no. 2, New Delhi, 4–11 April 1983.

38 A.R. Bandyopadhyay, interview, 13 April 1983.

39 Bunker Roy, interview.

40 David Selbourne, *An Eye to India*, p. 213.*

41 V.C. Pande, interview.*

42 Lalu Singh, interview.*

43 A.R. Bandyopadhyay, interview, 16 April 1983.*

44 'Grass Roots Experience: Land Distribution under Sarvodaya: Myth and Reality', extracts from detailed study by A.N. Sinha Institute of Social Sciences, Patna, *HOW*, New Delhi, June 1979, p. 24.

45 *Report of the Task Force on Agrarian Relations*, p. 10.

46 McKim Marriott, 'Social Structure in a U P Village' in M.N. Srinivas (ed.), *India's Villages.* *

47 Gunnar Myrdal, *Asian Drama: an Inquiry into the Poverty of Nations*, vol. II, The Twentieth Century Fund, New York, 1968, p. 1367.

48 Bikram Sarvar, 'Defects in Land Reform Administration', *Mainstream*, 4 February 1981, p. 21.

49 A.R. Bandyopadhyay, interview, 16 April 1983.

50 Kripa Shankar, *Concealed Tenancy and its Implications for Equity and Economic Growth: a Study of Eastern Uttar Pradesh.*

51 Béteille, interview, 28 March 1983.

52 Myrdal, *Asian Drama*, p. 203.

53 *Report of the Congress Agrarian Reforms Committee*, All India Congress, New Delhi, 1st edition 1949, 2nd edition 1951, p. 112.

54 A.R. Bandyopadhyay, interview, 13 April 1983.

55 Myrdal, *Asian Drama*, p. 203.

56 Sharat G. Lin, 'Theory of Dual Mode of Production in Post Colonial India', *EPW*, 8 March 1980, p. 519.

57 Rathore and Sharma, *Evaluation*, p. 49.

58 Khem Raj, interview, 6 April 1982.*

59 A.R. Bandyopadhyay, interview, 13 April 1983.

60 A.R. Bandyopadhyay, interview, 13 April 1983.

61 See Dandekar and Rath, 'Poverty in India', *EPW*, 9 January 1971.

62 A.M. Khusro, *Economics of Land Reforms and Farm Size in India.* *

63 Cited in Joshi, 'Problems of Land Reforms', p. 12.

64 Cited in Joshi, 'Problems of Land Reforms', p. 12.

65 Pande, interview.

66 *Area and Production of Principal Crops in India, 1980–1981,* Directorate of Economics and Statistics, Department of Agriculture and Cooperation, Ministry of Agriculture, Government of India, p. 192.

4 West Bengal: a Marxist alternative

1 Pande, interview.
2 D. Bandyopadhyaya, interview, 28 December 1981.*
3 D. Bandyopadhyaya, interview, 28 December 1981.*
4 D. Bandyopadhyaya, interview, 12 April 1983.
5 D. Bandyopadhyaya, interview, 12 April 1983.

5 Caste: a factor affecting social change

1 *The Cultural Heritage of India,* vol. 1, 'The Early Phases', Ramakrishna Mission Institute of Culture, Calcutta, reprint, 1970, p. 225.
2 Dumont, *Homo Hierarchicus,* pp. 78–9.
3 Christoph von Fürer-Haimendorf, *A Himalayan Tribe,* Vikas Publishing House, New Delhi, 1980, pp. 87–8.
4 von Fürer-Haimendorf, *Tribes of India,* p. 215.*
5 Sachidanand Sinha, *Caste System: Myth and Reality,* pp. 168–73.*
6 Béteille, *Studies in Agrarian Social Structure,* p. 39.
7 Dumont, *Homo Hierarchicus,* p. 143.
8 Benjamin Walker, *Hindu World: an Encyclopedic Survey of Hinduism,* vol. 2, Allen & Unwin, London, 1968, p. 75.
9 Harriss, *Capitalism and Peasant Farming,* p. 245.
10 Srinivas, *Social Change,* p. 117.
11 Srinivas, *Social Change,* p. 117.
12 Béteille, interview, 4 April 1983.
13 T.K. Oommen, interview, 2 June 1983.
14 J.H. Hutton, *Caste in India,* p. 125.*
15 Béteille, interview, 4 April 1983.
16 Quoted in Lannoy, *The Speaking Tree,* p. 307.
17 Béteille, interview, 4 April 1983.
18 Karan Singh, interview.
19 Lannoy, *The Speaking Tree,* p. 370.
20 Lannoy, *The Speaking Tree,* p. 166.
21 Béteille, interview, 4 April 1983.
22 Channa, interview.
23 Lannoy, *The Speaking Tree,* p. 166.
24 Satish Saberwal, 'Roots of Enervation', *Seminar,* April 1982, p. 17.

25 Satish Saberwal, interview, 31 May 1983.*
26 Oommen, interview.
27 Rajni Kothari (ed.), *Caste in Indian Politics*, p. 4.*
28 von Fürer-Haimendorf, *Tribes of India*, p. 195.
29 Dumont, *Homo Hierarchicus*, p. 244.
30 Béteille, interview, 4 April 1983.
31 Channa, interview.
32 Lannoy, *The Speaking Tree*, p. 338.
33 Myrdal, *Asian Drama*, p. 204.
34 'In a U.P. Village: Changing Agrarian Relations', *Mainstream*, 23 August 1980, p. 15.
35 Myrdal, *Asian Drama*, p. 321.
36 Myrdal, *Asian Drama*, p. 235.
37 Béteille, interview, 4 April 1983.
38 Srinivas, *Social Change*, p. 64.
39 Srinivas, *Social Change*, p. 63.
40 Béteille, 'Caste and Politics in Tamil Nadu', cited in Srinivas, *Social Change*, p. 102.
41 *Report of the Commissioner for Scheduled Castes and Scheduled Tribes, 1977–1978*, pp. 5–6.
42 Béteille, interview, 4 April 1983.
43 Ram, interview.
44 Chanderjit Yadav, interview, 28 April 1983.*
45 Channa, interview.
46 Ram Vilas Paswan, interview, 19 May 1983.*
47 *Patriot*, 8 June 1983.
48 Oommen, interview.
49 Resolution issued on 13–14 April 1983.
50 Saberwal, interview.
51 Naipaul, *A Wounded Civilization*, p. 159.
52 Lloyd Rudolph and Suzanne H. Rudolph, 'Transformation of the Congress Party: Why 1980 was not a Restoration', *EPW*, 2 May 1981, p. 813.
53 Rudolph and Rudolph, 'Transformation of the Congress', p. 817.
54 Sinha, *Caste System*, p. 217.
55 Hutton, *Caste in India*, p. 354.
56 Srinivas, *Social Change*, p. 73.
57 Béteille, *Studies in Agrarian Social Structure*, p. 51.
58 Hein Streefkerk, 'Employment in Small Scale Industries in Rural South Gujarat, *EPW*, 18 April 1981, p. 725.
59 Harriss, *Capitalism and Peasant Farming*, p. 270.
60 Béteille, *Studies in Agrarian Social Structure*, p. 166.
61 E. Miller, 'Village Structure in North Kerala', in Srinivas, *India's Villages*, pp. 44–5.

62   Béteille, *Studies in Agrarian Social Structure*, p. 5.
63   *Patriot*, 18 April 1982.
64   Nagindas Sanghini, 'Gujarat: Vidhan Sabha Profile', *EPW*, 10 May 1980, p. 843.
65   Lannoy, *The Speaking Tree*, pp. 136–7.
66   *Commissioner's Report for the Scheduled Castes and Scheduled Tribes, 1977–1978*, p. 141.
67   Saberwal, interview.
68   J. Sarkar, *Shivaji and his Times*, S.C. Sarkar & Sons Ltd, Calcutta, 1929, 3rd edn, pp. 209–10.
69   Oommen, interview.
70   Karan Singh, interview.

6   Corruption: a factor affecting social change

1   *Report of the Committee on Prevention of Corruption*, Government of India, Ministry of Home Affairs, 1964, p. 105.
2   Myrdal, *Asian Drama*, p. 171.
3   Frankel, *India's Political Economy*, p. 321.
4   V.S. Mahajan and V.K. Mahajan, 'Eradicating the Evil of Black Money', *Yojna*, 1–15 April, 1983, p. 26.
5   Shankar Acharya, 'The Unaccounted Economy in India: a Critical Survey of Some Recent Estimates', National Institute of Public Finance and Policy, New Delhi, June 1983.

7   The Scheduled Castes

1   *Sixth Plan Document 1980–1985*, Government of India, Planning Commission, p. 417.
2   Nagindas Sanghani, 'Gujarat: Vidhan Sabha Profile', *EPW*, 10 May 1980, p. 843.
3   *Report of the Commissioner for Scheduled Castes and Scheduled Tribes, 1978–1979*, p. 250.
4   *Commissioner's Report, 1977–1978*, p. 119.
5   *Commissioner's Report, 1978–1979*, p. 231.
6   *Commissioner's Report, 1977–1978*, p. 3.
7   *Commissioner's Report, 1979–1981*, p. 345.
8   *Commissioner's Report, 1979–1981*, p. 345.
9   *Commissioner's Report, 1978–1979*, p. 2.
10   *Commissioner's Report, 1978–1979*, pp. 139–40.
11   *Commissioner's Report, 1975–1976 and 1976–1977*, Part 1, p. 112.
12   For a fairly good compilation of crimes against Scheduled Castes the reader is referred to *Torture on Untouchables*.* Serious cases are

also discussed in the annual reports of the Commissioner for Scheduled Castes and Scheduled Tribes.

13 *Statesman*, 4 January 1980.
14 *Times of India*, 5 January 1980.
15 *Commissioner's Report 1978–1979*, p. 256.
16 *Times of India*, 14 March 1980.
17 M. Karlekar, 'Education and Inequality', in Béteille (ed.), *Equality and Inequality*, p. 216.
18 Central Institute of Research and Training in Public Cooperation, 'School Drop Outs Amongst Harijan Children', New Delhi, 1975, in Béteille (ed.), *Equality and Inequality*, p. 217.
19 Geo W. Briggs, *The Religions of India: the Chamars*, Association Press (YMCA), Calcutta, Oxford University Press, Oxford, 1920, pp. 230–31.
20 I.P. Desai, 'Anti-reservation Agitation and Structure of Gujarat Society', *EPW*, 2 May 1981, p. 819.
21 Desai, 'Anti-reservation Agitation'. One study states that many Scheduled Castes are ill treated by teachers and points out that: 'The high handed, arrogant and aggressive attitude of school mates mostly belonging to upper castes' caused 23 per cent of them to drop out. 'School Drop Outs Among Harijan Children', pp. 52–9, in Béteille (ed.), *Equality and Inequality*, p. 216.
22 Cited in Barbara Joshi, *Democracy in Search of Equality: Untouchable Politics and Indian Social Change*, Hindustan Publishing Corporation, New Delhi, 1982, p. 14.
23 Yogendra Singh, interview, 8 June 1983.*
24 Ram, interview.
25 B.P. Maurya, interview, 14 June 1983.*
26 *Times of India*, 28 July 1981.
27 *Hindustan Times*, 23 August 1981.
28 *Indian Express*, 12 September 1981.
29 Asghar Ali Engineer, 'Gujarat: Communal Violence in Ahmedabad', *EPW*, 23 January 1982, p. 100.
30 *Times of India*, 26 July, 1982.
31 *Indian Express*, 13 September, 1982.

8 Reservations

1 Pradip Kumar Bose, 'Mobility and Caste Violence: a Study of the Gujarat Riots', *EPW*, 18 April 1983, p. 714.
2 *Commissioner's Report 1978–1979*, part II, p. 23.
3 *High Power Committee to Review the Performance Regarding Recruitment of Scheduled Castes and Scheduled Tribes in the Services*, 20

October 1978, Agenda and Notes, Government of India, Ministry of Home Affairs, Department of Personnel and Administrative Reform, New Delhi, p. 114.

4 *Commissioner's Report 1977–1978*, p. 59.

5 This was confirmed by a member of the faculty of Jawaharlal Nehru University with regard to this institution.

6 A survey of sample Scheduled Caste school and college students found that, though the Mangs, a subcaste of Scheduled Castes, formed a third of Maharashtra's Scheduled Caste population, they constituted only 5 per cent of the college sample and 10 per cent of the school sample. The Mahars who constitute 36 per cent of the state's Scheduled Caste population constituted 73 per cent of the school sample and 65 per cent of the college sample. S. Chitnis, 'A Long Way to Go . . .', Centre for Social Studies, Surat, 1977, pp. 24–7, in Béteille (ed.), *Equality and Inequality*, p. 219.

7 Following figures are from a study by Suma Chitnis, 'Education and the Scheduled Castes', *Journal of Higher Education*, autumn 1975, vol. 1, no. 2, p. 171, in Béteille (ed.), *Equality and Inequality*, pp. 220–21.

9   The tribes of India

1 Kosambi, *Culture and Civilization*, p. 95.
2 Lannoy, *The Speaking Tree*, p. 171.
3 Kosambi, *Culture and Civilization*, p. 49.
4 Jayakar, *The Earthen Drum*, p. 208.
5 Lannoy, *The Speaking Tree*, p. 162.
6 Kosambi, *Culture and Civilization*, p. 23.
7 Sinha, *Caste System*, p. 120.
8 Kosambi, *Culture and Civilization*, p. 44.
9 Lannoy, *The Speaking Tree*, p. 179.
10 S.C. Varma, *The Bhil Kills*, Kunj Publishing House, Delhi, 1978, p. 1.
11 Kosambi, *Culture and Civilization*, p. 87.
12 Pupul Jayakar, interview, 5 May 1983.*
13 Kosambi, *Culture and Civilization*, p. 116.
14 Sinha, *Caste System*, p. 153.
15 Sinha, *Caste System*, p. 155.
16 Jayakar, *The Earthen Drum*, p. 12.
17 Jayakar, interview.
18 Jayakar, *The Earthen Drum*, p. 217.
19 Jayakar, *The Earthen Drum*, p. 36.
20 Jayakar, *The Earthen Drum*, p. 76.

21 Lannoy, *The Speaking Tree*, p. 169.
22 Jayakar, *The Earthen Drum*, p. x.
23 Lannoy, *The Speaking Tree*, p. 169.
24 Lannoy, *The Speaking Tree*, p. 169.
25 *Report of the Backward Classes Commission*, Government of India, 2nd part, vols. III–VII, 1980, p. 241. The Report also lists the Bhujan as a Backward Caste of Orissa (see page 257). The etymology of this word seems to be related to 'Bhuiyan' and both may have constituted part of the original tribe.
26 Sinha, *Caste System*, p. 50.
27 Hutton, *Caste in India*, p. 19.
28 Hutton, *Caste in India*, p. 114.
29 Hutton, *Caste in India*, p. 116.
30 Kosambi, *Culture and Civilization*, p. 34.
31 Kosambi, *Culture and Civilization*, p. 85.
32 Kosambi, *Culture and Civilization*, p. 101.
33 Hutton, *Caste in India*, p. 39.
34 Hutton, *Caste in India*, p. 35.
35 R.V. Russell, *Tribes and Castes of the Central Provinces*, vols. 1–4, first published by Macmillan, London, 1916, reprinted Cosmo Publications, New Delhi, 1975, p. 53.
36 Sinha, *Caste System*.
37 Russell, *Tribes and Castes*, p. 65. With regard to their hierarchical ranking he states (p. 31): 'In the fourth group are the non-Aryan or indigenous tribes. Most of these cannot properly be said to form part of the Hindu social system at all, but for practical purposes they are admitted and are considered to rank below all castes except those who cannot be touched. The lower group consists of the impure castes whose touch is considered to defile the higher castes.'
38 Hutton, *Caste in India*, pp. 188–9.
39 Hutton, *Caste in India*, pp. 183–4.
40 Hutton, *Caste in India*, p. 188.
41 Kosambi, *Culture and Civilization*, p. 171.
42 Hutton, *Caste in India*, p. 56.
43 Kosambi, *Culture and Civilization*, p. 82.
44 Lannoy, *The Speaking Tree*, p. 169.
45 A cult of personal devotion and surrender to the deity. One of the earliest expositions of its influence may be found in the Gita. Later it became associated with the submergence of all caste and class affiliations in this devotional spirit.
46 Lannoy, *The Speaking Tree*, p. 189.
47 Lannoy, *The Speaking Tree*, p. 187.

48   Briggs, *The Chamars*, p. 32; he also gives further proof of the tribal origins of this caste: 'The caste is divided into a number of endogamous divisions with exogamous septs, some of which seem to be totemistic.', p.32.
49   Lannoy, *The Speaking Tree*, p. 48.
50   Sinha, *Caste System*, p. 201.
51   Jayakar, *The Earthen Drum*, p. 6.
52   See A. Eschmann, Hermann Kulke and G.C. Tripathi (eds.), *The Cult of Jagannath and the Regional Tradition in Orissa*, Manohar Publications, New Delhi, 1978.
53   Sinha, *Caste System*, pp. 146–7. See also Eschmann *et al.*, *The Cult of Jagannath*, p. 264.
54   Kosambi, *Culture and Civilization*, p. 145.
55   Quoted in Romila Thapar, *Ashoka and the Decline of the Mauryas*, Oxford University Press, 1961, p. 256.
56   *Report of the Scheduled Areas and Scheduled Tribes Commission*, vol. 1, 1960–1961, Government of India, p. 490.
57   von Fürer-Haimendorf, *Tribes of India*, p. 317.
58   Bhupinder Singh, 'Dynamics of Tribal Development in India', contributed to the Symposium on Rural Development in South Asia, 1981, International Union of Anthropological and Ethnological Sciences Inter-Congress, Amsterdam, April 1981, p. 14.

*10   Losers in the development process:
Bhil tribals of South Rajasthan*

1   Srilata Swaminathan, interview 23 April 1982.*
2   Vyas, interview.
3   K.L. Kothari, interview, 20 April 1982.*

*11   Losers in the assimilation process:
the tribals of Chotanagpur*

1   From a study by a senior officer who must remain nameless.
2   Same confidential documentary source as note 1.

Conclusion

1   Balakrishna Nair, *The Dynamic Brahmin*, Popular Book Depot, Bombay, 1959, p. 88.

2   Russell, *Tribes and Castes*, pp. 196–7.

3   See Srinivas, 'The Future of Indian Caste'.

4   Béteille, *Studies in Agrarian Social Structure*, p. 178.

Postscript

1   In the initial days Mrs Gandhi promoted Bhindranwale to counter the Akalis. The Sikh, Giani Zail Singh (now President of India), when he was still a Congress (I) leader in the Punjab in 1979, tried to embarrass the Akalis by financing and propping up the extremists who had their own grievances against the Akalis. For an account of Mrs Gandhi's and the Congress (I)'s politics of support for Bhindranwale to weaken the Akalis see M.J. Akbar, *India: The Siege Within: Challenges to a Nation's Unity*, Penguin, Harmondsworth, 1985, pp. 175–209.

2   It was not until the Punjab accord was signed on 24 July 1985 that the facts regarding 'Operation Bluestar' and its aftermath began to emerge as the government somewhat relaxed the rigid press censorship it had introduced from 4 June 1984 at the onset of the storming of the Golden Temple. Till that time the Indian public heard only one side of the story, notably the version published in the government White Paper released in July 1984. For example, the number of casualties had been grossly underestimated in the White Paper which gave a figure of 493 dead and 86 injured. This 'left 1,600 people unaccounted for' (Mark Tully and Satish Jacob, *Amritsar: Mrs Gandhi's Last Battle* (Rupa, by arrangement with Pan Books, 1985), p. 185). The Citizens for Democracy report, *Oppression in Punjab*, which was banned by the government, claims 'not hundreds but thousands could well have died during the operations, and thousands maimed or injured,' p. 75. It quotes many witnesses, one of whom, for example, saw 'hundreds of people, including women and children, being shot down by Army commandos as they came out to surrender on the afternoon of 6 June outside the Golden Temple', p. 75.

3   PUDR, *Black Laws and the People; see also PUCL, Black Laws, 1984 – 85.**

4   Rajni Kothari, interview.

5   PUDR, *Black Laws and the People.* p.2.

6   For accounts of the November riots see the following: *Report to the Nation: Oppression in Punjab*, foreword by Justice V.M. Tarkunde, Citizens for Democracy, Bombay, a Hind Mazdoor Kisan Panchayat Publication, 1985; Kuldip Nayar and Khushwant Singh, *Tragedy of Punjab*, Vision Books, New Delhi, 1984, pp. 180–87; Rahul K. Bedi, 'Politics of a Pogrom – the Carnage' and Arun Shourie, 'Them and Us' in Arun Shourie, Prannoy Roy, Rahul

Bedi and Shekhar Gupta, *The Assassination and After*, Roli Books International, New Delhi, 1985; PUDR and PUCL, *Who are the Guilty?, Report of the Joint Enquiry into the Causes and Impact of the Riots in Delhi from October 31 to November 4, 1984*, New Delhi, 1984; *Report of the Citizens' Commission, Delhi, 31 October to 4 November 1985*, Citizens' Commission, New Delhi, 1985; Amiya Rao, A. Ghose and N.D. Pancholi, *Report to the Nation: Truth about Delhi Violence*, Citizens for Democracy, New Delhi, January 1985; 'The Violent Aftermath', *India Today*, 30 November 1984.

7 This is brought out in three independent commissions of inquiry: *Truth about Delhi Violence*, p. 18, *Report to the Nation*, p. 32 and the joint PUDR-PUCL report, *Who are the Guilty?*, p. 2.

8 *Truth about Delhi Violence, Report to the Nation* and PUDR-PUCL, *Who are the Guilty?*

9 PUDR-PUCL, *Who are the Guilty?*, pp. 2–3.

10 PUDR-PUCL, *Who are the Guilty?*, pp. 2–3.

11 Lt.-Gen. J.S. Aurora, interview, 28 May 1985.*

12 *Report of the Citizens' Commission, Delhi, 31 October to 4 November 1985.*

13 S.K. Sinha, 'Outlook on Punjab I – Bluestar Hurt, Riots Alienated', *Statesman*, 21 May 1985.

14 Editorial, *Muslim India*, New Delhi, March 1985.

Bibliography

Books

Agarwal, Bina, *Mechanization in Indian Agriculture: an analytical Study of the Punjab*, Allied Pubs., Ltd, New Delhi, 1983.

Akbar, M.J., *India: the Siege Within: Challenges to a Nation's Unity*, Penguin, Harmondsworth, 1985.

Béteille, André, *Caste, Class and Power*, University of California Press, Berkeley, 1972.

——, *Studies in Agrarian Social Structure*, Oxford University Press, Delhi, 1974.

——, *Equality and Inequality: Theory and Practice*, Oxford University Press, Delhi, 1983.

Desai, B.M. (ed.), *Intervention for Rural Development. Experiences of the Small Farmer's Development Agency*, Indian Institute of Management, Ahmedabad, Gujarat, 1979.

Dumont, Louis, *Homo Hierarchicus*, first published in Great Britain by Weidenfeld & Nicolson, 1970; Paladin, Granada Publishing, 1972.

Farmer, B.N., *Green Revolution, Technology and Change in the Rice Growing Areas of Tamil Nadu and Sri Lanka*, Macmillan, London, 1977.

Frankel, Francine, *India's Political Economy, 1947–1977*, Oxford University Press, Delhi, 1978.

von Fürer-Haimendorf, Christoph, *Tribes of India: The Struggle for Survival*, Oxford University Press, Delhi, 1982.

George, Susan, *How the Other Half Dies: the Real Reasons for World Hunger*, Penguin, Harmondsworth, 1976.

Ghosh, O.K., *The Changing Indian Civilization*, Minerva Assocs. Publications Private Ltd., Calcutta, 1976.

Government of India, *Agricultural Census Bulletin, No. 22*, Ministry of Agriculture, New Delhi: Agricultural Census Division, Annexure II.

——, *Area and Production of Principal Crops in India 1980–1981*. Ministry of Agriculture, New Delhi, Department of Economics and Statistics, June, 1982.

——, 'Delhi: A Socio-Economic Study of Village Shinghu', *Census of India, 1961*, vol. IV, Part VI, No. 12.

————, 'A Village Survey: Bhangarh', *Census of India, 1965,* vol. xiv on Rajasthan, Part VI, Monograph no. 6.

————, *Report of the Commissioner for Scheduled Castes and Scheduled Tribes, 1969–1970* (hereinafter called *Commissioner's Report*).

————, *Commissioner's Report, 1975–1976 and 1976–1977* (24th report) (Amalgamated)

————, *Commissioner's Report, 1977–1978* (25th report).

————, *Commissioner's Report, 1978–1979* (26th report).

————, *Commissioner's Report, 1979–1980 and 1980–1981* (27th report) (Amalgamated).

————, *Report of the Backward Classes Commission,* New Delhi, 1980.

————, *Report of the Congress Agrarian Reform Committee,* All India Congress, New Delhi, first edition, 1949. Second edition, 1951.

————, *Report of the Committee on Ceiling on Land Holdings,* New Delhi, 1961.

————, *Task Force on Land Reforms,* Planning Commission, 1973.

————, *Report of the Committee on Prevention of Corruption,* Ministry of Home Affairs, New Delhi, 1964.

————, *Sixth Plan Document, 1980–1985,* Planning Commission, March, 1981.

Harriss, John, *Capitalism and Peasant Farming: Agrarian Structure and Ideology in Tamil Nadu,* Oxford University Press, Delhi, 1982.

Hutton, J.H., *Caste in India,* first published by Cambridge University Press, 1946. Fourth edition, Oxford University Press, 1963. Fifth impression, 1980.

Jayakar, Pupul, *The Earthen Drum: an Introduction to the Ritual Arts of Rural India,* National Museum, New Delhi, 1980.

Khusro, A.M., *Economics of Land Reforms and Farm Size in India,* Institute for Economic Growth, New Delhi, 1971.

Kosambi, D.D., *The Culture and Civilization of Ancient India in Historical Outline,* Vikas Publishing House Private Ltd, New Delhi, 1977.

Kothari, Rajni (ed.), *Caste in Indian Politics,* Orient Longman Ltd, New Delhi, 1970.

Lannoy, Richard, *The Speaking Tree,* Oxford University Press, New York, 1975.

Mahar, J. Michael (ed.), *The Untouchables of Contemporary India,* University of Arizona Press, Tucson, Arizona, 1972.

Menscher, Joan, *Agriculture and Social Structure in Tamil Nadu: Past Origins, Present Transformations and Future Prospects,* Allied Publishers Private Ltd., Bombay, 1978.

The Minority Rights Group, Report No. 65, *The Sikhs* by Christopher Shackle, Amrit Publishing House, New Delhi, 1985.

Myrdal, Gunnar, *Asian Drama,* Pelican, Harmondsworth, 1977.

Naipaul, V.S., *A Wounded Civilization,* Penguin, Harmondsworth, 1977.

Nayar, Kuldip and Singh, Khushwant, *Tragedy of Punjab: Operation Bluestar and After*, Vision Books, New Delhi, 1984.

Pani, Narendar, *Reforms to Preempt Change: Land Legislation in Karnataka*, Concept Publications, New Delhi, 1983.

People's Union for Civil Liberties (PUCL), *Black Laws 1984–85*, New Delhi, June, 1985.

People's Union for Democratic Rights (PUDR), *Agrarian Unrest in Patna: an Investigation into Recent Repression*, Document, New Delhi, December, 1981.

———, *Black Laws and the People: an Enquiry into the Function of Black Laws in the Punjab*, New Delhi, April, 1985.

——— and People's Union for Civil Liberties (PUCL), *Who Are the Guilty? Report of a Joint Enquiry into the Causes and Impact of the Riots in Delhi from October 31 to November 10*, New Delhi, 1984.

Rao, Amiya, Aurobindo Ghose and N.D. Pancholi, *Report to the Nation: Truth About Delhi Violence*, Citizens for Democracy, New Delhi, January, 1985.

Rathore, B.S. and Sharma, P.N., *Evaluation of the Implementation of Agricultural Ceiling Laws in Bhilwara District, Rajasthan*, University of Udaipur, Rajasthan, Department of Agricultural Economics, 1978.

Report of the Citizens' Commission, Delhi, 31 October to 4 November 1985, Citizens' Commission, New Delhi, 1985.

Report to the Nation: Oppression in Punjab, foreword by Justice V.M. Tarkunde, Citizens for Democracy, preface by George Fernandez, a Hind Mazdoor Kisan Panchayat Publication, Bombay, 1985.

Selbourne, David, *An Eye to India*, Penguin, Harmondsworth, 1977.

Shankar, Kripa, *Concealed Tenancy and its Implications for Equity and Economic Growth: a Study of Eastern Uttar Pradesh*, Concept Publications, New Delhi, 1980.

Shengde, Malati, *The Civilized Demons of the Rig Veda*, Abhivan Publications, New Delhi, 1977.

Shourie, Arun, Prannoy Roy, Rahul Bedi and Shekhar Gupta, *The Assassination and After*, Roli Books International, New Delhi, 1985.

Singh, Charan, *India's Economic Policy: the Gandhian Blueprint*, Vikas, New Delhi, 1978.

Singh, Inderjit, *Small Farmers and the Landless in South Asia*, World Bank, Developmental Economics Department. Summary of monograph submitted to the World Bank, July 1981.

———, *Small Farmers and the Landless in South Asia*, World Bank, Washington, DC, October, 1981.

Singh, Jagmohan, Dogra, Bharat and Gurucharan, *The Agony of Punjab*, Shaheed Bhagat Singh Reseach Committee, Ludhiana, March 1985.

Sinha, Sachchidanand, J. Singh, Sunil and G.K.C. Reddy, *Army Action in Punjab: Prelude and Aftermath*, a Samata Era Publication, New Delhi, 1984.

Sinha, Sachchidanand, *Caste System: Myth and Reality,* Intellectual Publishing House, New Delhi, 1981.

Srinivas, M.N., *India's Villages*, Asia Publishing House, Bombay, 1960.

——, 'The Future of Indian Caste', Valedictory Address to the Tenth International Congress of the Anthropological and Ethnological Sciences at Delhi on 16 December 1978, Institute for Social and Economic Change, Bangalore (xeroxed copy).

Tortures on Untouchables: a Document, Victory Recreations, Bangalore, Karnataka, December, 1978.

Vyas, N.N., *Bondage and Exploitation in Tribal India*, Rawat Publications, Jaipur, Delhi, 1980.

Walinsky, Louis J. (ed.), *The Selected Papers of Wolf Ladejinsky: Agrarian Reform as Unfinished Business*, Oxford University Press, New York, 1977.

World Development Report, 1982, Oxford University Press, 1983.

Articles

Acharya, Shankar, 'The Unaccounted Economy in India: a Critical Survey of Some Recent Estimates', National Institute of Public Finance and Policy, New Delhi, 1983.

Bandyopadhyay, A.R., 'Distribution of Land to the Landless: an Appraisal', *Kurukshetra* (India's Journal of Rural Development), New Delhi, special number, January 1980.

Bhalla, Sheilla, 'New Relations of Production in Haryana Agriculture', *Economic and Political Weekly (EPW)*, Bombay, Review of Agriculture, March 1976.

Bose, Pradip Kumar, 'Mobility and Caste Violence: a Study of the Gujarat Riots', *EPW*, 18 April 1981.

Byres, T.J., 'The New Technology, Class Formation and Class Action in the Indian Countryside', *Journal of Peasant Studies*, University of Sussex, England, Part II (no date).

Dandekar, V.M. and Rath, Nilakantha, 'Poverty in India', *EPW*, 9 January 1971.

Dasgupta, Abhajit Sankar, 'Rural Indebtedness: a Caste Study', *Mainstream*, New Delhi, 31 October 1981.

Das Gupta, Sailen, 'West Bengal: Evasion of Land Ceiling', *Mainstream*, 5 July 1980.

Desai, I.P., 'Anti-Reservation Agitation and Structure of Gujarat Society', *EPW*, 2 May 1981.

'Dialogues on the Changing Character of Communal Tension in India', *Lokayan*, New Delhi, Bulletin No.2, November 1984.

Editorial, 'The Caste of the Poor', *EPW*, 1 March 1980.

Fera, Ivan, 'On the Rampage', *Illustrated Weekly of India*, Bombay, 19 May 1985.

'Grass Roots Experience: Land Distribution Under Sarvodaya: Myth and Reality', *HOW*, New Delhi, June 1979.

Gupta, Shekhar, 'Crackdown in Punjab: Operation Bluestar', *India Today*, New Delhi, 30 June 1984.

——, 'The Violent Aftermath', *India Today*, 30 November 1984.

——, 'The Caste Crunch', *India Today*, 15 April 1985.

—— and Menon, R., 'Gujarat: State of Siege', *India Today*, 15 May 1985.

Joshi, P.C., 'Land Reforms and Agrarian Change in India and Pakistan since 1947', *The Journal of Peasant Studies*, Vol. 1, No. 3, April 1974.

——, 'Problems of Land Reforms in the Second Stage', *Man and Development*, Vol. III, No. 1, March 1981.

Kapoor, C., Gupta, S. and Santhanan, R., 'The Lethal Lapses', *India Today*, 30 November 1984.

'Land Reforms and Rural Poverty', book review, *Mainstream*, 19 December 1981.

Lin, Sharat G., 'Theory of a Dual Mode of Production in Post-Colonial India', *EPW*, 8 March 1980.

Mahajan, V.S. and Mahajan, V.K., 'Eradicating the Evil of Black Money', *Yojna*, New Delhi 1–15 April 1983.

Mehta, M. and Dev, Atul, 'Punjab: The Critical Phase', *Gentleman* magazine, New Delhi, May 1985.

Menscher, Joan, 'Agricultural Labourers and Poverty', *EPW*, 1–9 January 1982.

Omvedt, Gail, 'Politico-Economic Development in Maharashtra', *EPW*, 4 October 1980.

——, 'Maharashtra: Rasta Roko, Kulaks and the Left', *EPW*, 28 December 1981.

——, 'Capitalist Agriculture and Rural Classes in Tamil Nadu', *EPW*, Review of Agriculture, 26 December 1981.

Pai, Sudha, 'In a U.P. Village, Changing Agrarian Relations', *Mainstream*, 23 August 1980.

Parthasorathy, G. and Adiseshu, K., 'Real Wages of Agricultural Labourers in Andhra Pradesh: Two Decades of Stagnation', *EPW*, 31 July 1982.

Prasad, V.S. and Rao, V.B., 'Obstacles to Organizing the Rural Poor', *Mainstream*, 13 December 1980.

Radhakrishnan, P., 'Land Reforms in Theory and Practice: the Kerala Experience', *EPW*, Review of Agriculture, 26 December 1981.

Rajadurai, S.V., 'Tamil Nadu: Green Power on the March', *EPW*, 27 December 1980.

Rudolph, Lloyd and Rudolph, Suzanne H., 'Transformation of Congress Party: Why 1980 Was Not a Restoration', *EPW*, 2 May 1981.

Rustomji, Nari, 'Imperilled Frontiers: India's North-Eastern Borderlands', *Sunday*, Calcutta, 27 March 1983.

Saberwal, Satish, 'Roots of Enervation', *Seminar*, New Delhi, April 1982.

Sanghani, Nagindar, 'Gujarat: Vidhan Sabha Profile', *EPW*, 10 May 1980.

Sarkar, Vikram, 'Defects in Land Reform Administration', *Mainstream*, 4 February 1981.

Shankar, Kripa, 'Employment Policy for Rural Areas', *Mainstream*, 21 February 1981.

————, 'Poverty and Economic Growth', *Mainstream*, 8 November 1981.

Sinha, S.K., 'Outlook on Punjab I – Bluestar Hurt, Riots Alienated', *Statesman*, New Delhi, 20 May 1985.

————, 'Outlook on Punjab II – Issues seen in Communal Colours', *Statesman*, 21 May 1985.

————, 'Outlook on Punjab III – Political Response to Terrorism Needed', *Statesman*, 22 May 1985.

Special correspondent, 'Andhra Pradesh: Casteism Through Elections', *EPW*, 12 February 1983.

Special issue, 'Views from a Scarred City: the November Carnage and After', *Lokayan*, Bulletin No. 3, January 1985.

Srivastava, Arun, 'Bihar: Landlord's Mafia in Bhojpur', *EPW*, 3–10 January 1981.

Striefkerk, H., 'Employment in Small-Scale Industries in Rural South Gujarat', *EPW*, 18 April 1981.

Survey of India, *The Economist*, London, 28 March 1981.

Upadhyaya, Ashok K., 'Peasant Organizations in Thane District: a Critical Overview', *EPW*, 30 January 1982.

'What the Punjab Accord Means', *Samata Era*, New Delhi, August–September 1985.

Interviews

Lt.-Gen. J. Singh Aurora, New Delhi, 28 May 1985.

A.R. Bandyopadhyay, Central Land Reforms Commissioner, New Delhi, 13 and 16 April 1983.

D. Bandyopadhyaya, former West Bengal Land Reforms Commissioner, Calcutta, West Bengal, 28 December 1981, and New Delhi, 12 April 1983.

Professor André Béteille, Delhi School of Economics, New Delhi, 28 March and 4 April 1983.

Supreme Court Justice (now Chief Justice of India) P.N. Bhagwati, New Delhi, 9 February 1983.

Professor V.C. Channa, Delhi University, New Delhi, 4 April 1983.

Supreme Court Justice D.A. Desai, New Delhi, 12 March 1983.

Pupul Jayakar, author, *The Earthen Drum*, New Delhi, 5 May 1983.

J.C. Jetli, Joint Secretary, National Rural Employment Programme (NREP), New Delhi, 1 June 1983.

Sudhir Kakar, New Delhi, 21 March 1983.

K.L. Kothari, Dungarpur, 20 April 1982.

Rajni Kothari, Centre for Developing Societies, New Delhi, 28 May 1985.

Richard Lannoy, author, *The Speaking Tree*, New Delhi, 19 March 1983.

Harji Malik, journalist, New Delhi, 25 May 1985.

B.P. Maurya, MP, New Delhi, 14 June 1983.*

Gobinda Mukhoty, President, People's Union for Democratic Rights, New Delhi, 6 February 1983 and 26 May 1985.

Professor T.K. Oommen, Jawaharlal Nehru University, New Delhi, 2 June 1983.

V.C. Pande, Planning Commission, New Delhi, 8 April 1983.

Ram Vilas Paswan, former MP, New Delhi, 19 May 1983.

Khem Raj, Social Work Research Centre, Tilonia, Rajasthan, 6 April 1982.

Jagjivan Ram, MP, New Delhi, 13 May 1983.

Bunker Roy, Director, Social Work Research Centre, Tilonia, Rajasthan, 6 April 1982.

Professor Satish Saberwal, Jawaharlal Nehru University, New Delhi, 31 May 1983.

Syed Shahabuddin, former MP, New Delhi, 15 March 1983.**

Dr Karan Singh, President, Virat Hindu Samaj, New Delhi, 16 March 1983.

Khushwant Singh, former editor *Hindustan Times*, New Delhi, 28 May 1985.

Lalu Singh, Jamuna Ravines, Etawah District, Uttar Pradesh, 9 March 1983.

Professor Yogendra Singh, Jawaharlal Nehru University, 8 June 1983.

Srilata Swaminathan, Head, Social Work Research Centre, Ghantali, Banswara, Rajasthan, 23 April 1982.

Chanderjit Yadav, former MP, New Delhi, 28 April 1983.**

A.B. Vajpayee, Leader, Bharatiya Janata Party (BJP), New Delhi, 15 March 1983.**

N.N. Vyas, Principal, Tribal Research Institute, Udaipur, Rajasthan, 10 April 1982.

* By 1985 term as Rajya Sabha member had expired.
** These MPs lost their seats in the December 1984 general elections.

Index